The FCC Rule Book

Edited by Richard K. Palm, K1CE

Contributors

W. Dale Clift, NA1L
Bruce S. Hale, KB1MW
Robert J. Halprin, K1XA
John C. Hennessee, KJ4KB
Joel P. Kleinman, N1BKE
Edward Mitchell, KF7VY
Paul L. Rinaldo, W4RI
Mark J. Wilson, AA2Z

Published by
The American Radio Relay League
Newington, CT USA 06111

Editor's Note: Special thanks to John Johnston, W3BE, of the FCC staff, for his assistance with the editorial production of this book and *QST*'s "Washington Mailbox" column.

This work is Publication No. 47 of the Radio Amateur's Library, published by the League.

Printed in USA

Library of Congress Catalog Card Number: 82-074262
ISBN: 0-87259-245-6

$9.00 in USA

Eighth Edition
Fifth Printing, 1991

Foreword

As communications technology has grown more complicated, the FCC Rules governing Amateur Radio have grown accordingly. Unfortunately, by the end of the '70s, trying to figure them all out was not a trivial pursuit. In 1980, the FCC tried to improve the situation with a "Plain Language" rewrite of the rules, but for various reasons, it didn't fly. Throughout the '80s, the rules kept getting longer and longer. Finally, the FCC proposed a pretty good rewrite of the rules. There were some problems, however. The League, not wanting to lose an opportunity to gain a significant improvement in the rules, addressed those problems in its comments, and proposed its own complete version. On May 31, 1989 the FCC took into account many of the League's and other's suggestions, and adopted a completely reorganized and updated Part 97.

The new Part 97 includes the clarification of certain rules and the codification of certain existing policies that have grown in importance as modern amateur communications practices have evolved. The result is a set of rules that encourages the experimental nature and uses of Amateur Radio.

Every US amateur, and anyone actively pursuing a ham ticket, should have handy a copy of the new set of rules. This ARRL publication is designed to meet that need in a compact, inexpensive volume. But, *The FCC Rule Book* does even more. Taking its cue from the popular "Washington Mailbox" column in *QST*, it presents the new rules in a style that is easy to read and understand.

You'll also learn how FCC rules are made, and how you can have a voice in the process. You'll learn about the Communications Act of 1934, which still governs all telecommunications in the country more than five decades after its original enactment. You'll discover the international agreements which affect our daily Amateur Radio operation, and why decisions made in far-off places like Geneva, Switzerland, are so important to hams.

Like the old Part 97, earlier editions of the *Rule Book* had become a patchwork. This new 8th edition was completely rewritten from scratch to address the new Part 97 and upgrade the presentation of rule explanations. We hope you will be pleased with the result.

David Sumner, K1ZZ
Executive Vice President, ARRL
Newington, Connecticut

Table of Contents

At Press Time . . .

As this book goes to press, a number of important activities are going on in the regulatory arena. Here is a summary of recent, ongoing and possible future rule-making matters before the FCC and the amateur community:

DOCKET 91-36: FCC SEEKS INPUT ON LOCAL "SCANNER LAWS"

The FCC has issued a Notice of Inquiry, numbered 91-36, in reply to an ARRL request for a declaratory ruling preempting state statutes and local ordinances which prohibit the mere possession of an amateur mobile transceiver capable of receiving police and other public safety communication. Some amateur transceivers are capable of receiving public safety frequencies, but transmit only within the amateur bands. The ARRL stated numerous instances in which amateurs, operating their transceivers lawfully, were fined or had their equipment confiscated because the equipment can incidentally receive police frequencies.

In its NOI, the FCC asked for input on a number of questions concerning this issue. Amateurs can help by encouraging their own local public safety departments to respond to the NOI by noting the value of radio amateurs in assisting them in time of emergency by being able to receive public safety frequencies. The Comment deadline is June 7, 1991 and the Reply Comment deadline is July 8, 1991. See May 1991 *QST,* page 59 for details.

DOCKET 89-552: FCC SETS DATE FOR AMATEURS TO VACATE 220-222 MHz

The FCC issued its final Report and Order in PR Docket 89-552, adopting rules for the use of 220-222 MHz by the Private Land Mobile Service. This order ends a several-year-long battle to retain this segment. Amateurs now have 222-225 MHz on a primary basis (we were secondary users before). Amateurs are required to discontinue all operations in the 220-222 MHz segment effective 0000 UTC August 28, 1991.

H. R. 73: BILL IN CONGRESS WOULD PROTECT AMATEUR FREQUENCIES

A new bill, H.R. 73, before the US House of Representatives offers the amateur community a marvelous opportunity to prevent the FCC from reducing amateur frequency allocations. On January 3, 1991, the first day of the 102nd Congress, Tennessee Congressman Jim Cooper, with the active support of ARRL, introduced the Amateur Radio Spectrum Protection Act of 1991.

If passed, the proposed legislation would ensure that "the Federal Communications Commission shall not diminish existing allocations of spectrum to the Amateur Radio Service after January 1, 1991. The Federal Communications Commission shall provide equivalent replacement spectrum to the Amateur Radio Service for any frequency reallocation after January 1, 1991."

At press time, H.R. 73 has 81 cosponsors. Have you asked your Congressman to cosponsor this bill? If not, see March 1991 *QST,* page 41 for details. *QST, The ARRL Letter* and W1AW bulletins will carry the latest on this important bill.

DOCKET 90-561: FCC ADDRESSES PART 97 "CLEANUP" PETITIONS

The FCC has addressed proposals from ARRL and others seeking clarifications and minor changes which were not dealt with when the FCC completely revised and renumbered Part 97 on September 1, 1989. Here are the highlights to the FCC Notice of Proposed Rulemaking:

The FCC agreed with the ARRL request to define the terms "telecommand," "telemetry" and "space telemetry," but decided not to define "tactical call sign" and "digipeater." The ARRL asked that the minimum number of people necessary to apply for a club station license be changed from two to four, but the FCC declined stating that club calls haven't been issued in more than a decade and it was unnecessary. The FCC declined a request that an amateur station must be independent of all other radio apparatus installed on a ship or aircraft.

In the matter of automatic control of amateur stations when third party traffic is being handled, the League sought a rules revision to put responsibility of such traffic on the originating station. The FCC said that traffic content is the responsibility of every station, including those who retransmit the communications, and proposed no change. The ARRL had sought a clarification of Section 97.109(d), to emphasize that a Commission representative may order an automatically controlled station to shut down because of improper operation or harmful interference only after the alleged offending station has been given the opportunity for a hearing. The FCC declined saying that the licensee is not entitled to a hearing. The FCC also declined to permit retransmission of NOAA weather broadcasts and the FCC also asked for comments concerning identification at the beginning of communications through repeaters. The FCC declined a proposed change to incorporate due process procedures in cases involving "quiet hours" saying it was unnecessary.

In the area of Special Operations, the FCC proposed to: 1) Delete the condition that an auxiliary station can be automatically controlled only when it is part of a repeater, so that amateurs can experiment with new system configurations; 2) Expand the permissible types of space telemetry transmissions; 3) Change "remote control" to "telecommand." The FCC again refused to change its rules banning 10-meter amplifiers. The comment deadline ended in January and the Reply Comment deadline ended March 4, 1991.

Chapter One

Introduction

Amateur Radio means different things to different people. That's one of its beauties—diversity. Like a fine cut gem, it shines in many directions.

To old-timers Amateur Radio means the memory of a past era of racks of black, wrinkle-finished, meter-spattered radio chassis replete with glowing tubes and humming transformers. To many newer amateurs today, it equates to high tech and the concomitant opportunity to pioneer and develop the latest experimental digital code, data network or satellite technique. To others, it means things perhaps less heady—simply an opportunity to make friends around the world on the long-haul high-frequency bands or across town through the local repeater. Or, it means community service—the chance to use radio to help fellow human beings in times of need whether it be assisting safety services in dealing with a tornado watch, or organizing a local walkathon. To students, it means a head start on a career path. To most, it's a little of all of the above.

A common thread through Amateur Radio's history has been a dynamic regulatory environment that has encouraged both technological growth, and the diversity described above. This thread continues today to sew together the elements of contemporary Amateur Radio, preparing it for tomorrow's challenges.

In this chapter, we'll look at the basics of the present regulatory structure as a launching pad for discussions in the rest of the book. What better place to start than with a basic definition of Amateur Radio.

"From Spark to Space" is the history of Amateur Radio, and its national organization, the ARRL.

TOWARDS A DEFINITION

The Amateur Radio Service is for all individuals who are interested in the technical side of radio and are able to provide emergency communications in disasters, all for the general benefit of the public. It is called "amateur" because it is strictly non-commercial: No business may be conducted using amateur frequencies. Amateur Radio is a voluntary, disciplined service guided by five traditional objectives that have withstood the test of time:

1) to provide emergency and public service communications;
2) to advance the state of the art;
3) to improve individual skills in radio operation;
4) to provide a reserve pool of qualified radio operators and technicians; and
5) to promote international goodwill.

Amateur Radio began with a few experimenters in the early 1900s, and has since grown to over 450,000 licensed operators in the US alone. Amateur Radio represents principles of radio communications that have endured and advanced since the days of the earliest radio pioneers.

Today, the service flourishes domestically and internationally. For hard evidence of this fact, one need not look any further than the 1979 World Administrative Radio Conference (WARC) in Geneva, where Amateur Radio was granted a number of new frequency bands by international spectrum allocators. Domestically, the Federal Communications Commission (FCC) attaches the same importance to Amateur Radio, granting large chunks of spectrum to amateurs, knowing that it is spectrum well spent.

What is the Federal Communications Commission? The FCC is the federal agency charged by Congress with regulating interstate and foreign communication involving US radio, television, wire, cable and satellite. This includes Amateur Radio. The overall objective of the FCC is to provide for orderly development and operation of radio and wire services.

A major goal of the FCC is to promote the use of radio for protecting the safety of life and property, a goal that is manifested in the foundation of Amateur Radio. The FCC issues licenses, makes and enforces rules and defines the scope of the various radio services under its wing. For a closer look at international regulation, Congress and the FCC, refer to Chapter 13.

FCC'S DEFINITION IS A GOOD DEFINITION

You might imagine that the FCC has a good definition for Amateur Radio. You're right, it does, and it's found at the beginning of its set of Amateur Radio rules—Part 97. No one yet has been able to come up with a better definition, so let's expend some ink reviewing it, and its embodiment, the basis and purpose of Amateur Radio.

Although the FCC's basic definition of the Amateur Service at Section 97.3 is quite simple—"A radiocommunication service for the purpose of self-training, intercommunication and technical investigations carried out by amateurs, that is, duly authorized persons interested in radio technique solely with a personal aim and without pecuniary interest"—it is fleshed out quite nicely by the presentation of the "Basis and Purpose" at Section 97.1. A review of each of the five principles, introduced above, will show why:

Recognition and enhancement of the value of the amateur service to the public as a voluntary noncommercial communication service, particularly with respect to providing emergency communications.

Probably the best-known aspect of Amateur Radio in the public eye is its ability to provide life-saving emergency communications when normal means of contact are down.

N6ELP provides communications support for firefighting efforts in California recently.

EMBASSY OF JAMAICA
1850 K STREET, N.W.
SUITE 355
WASHINGTON, D.C. 20006

TELEPHONE: (202) 452-0660

REF. NO.

December 2, 1988

The President
American Radio Relay League
Newington, CONN 06111

Dear President:

I write to express sincere appreciation and thanks to the many members of your organization who gave much needed assistance in our effort to send and receive information to and from Jamaica, during the recent disaster created by Hurricane Gilbert.

It is my understanding that all across the United States, amateur radio operators sought to use their facilities to assist communities and individuals desirous of obtaining information on the situation in Jamaica.

Please convey our gratitude and very best wishes to your membership through the appropriate media, on behalf of the Government and People of Jamaica.

Sincerely

Keith Johnson
Ambassador

Thanks: The Jamaican Ambassador to the US sent this letter expressing thanks on behalf of his country for the assistance rendered by US amateurs after Hurricane Gilbert hit Jamaica hard in 1988.

In hurricanes, earthquakes, tornadoes, airplane crashes, missing person cases, and other accidents and disasters affecting civil population, Amateur Radio is often the first contact with the outside world available to an affected area. Red Cross and civil preparedness agencies often rely heavily on the services of volunteer radio amateurs.

One of the most important aspects of the service is its noncommercial nature. In fact, amateurs are prohibited from receiving any form of payment for operating their stations. This means that hams, whether they are assisting a search-and-rescue operation in the high Sierras, relaying health-and-welfare messages from a disaster-stricken Caribbean island or providing communications assistance at the New York City Marathon, make their services available free of charge. Amateurs operate their stations for the benefit of the public and for their own personal enjoyment only.

Hams have contributed greatly in recent years to the development of computer communications techniques, another example of the amateur's ability to advance the state of the radio art.

Continuation and extension of the amateur's proven ability to contribute to the advancement of the radio art.

For more than 80 years, hams have carried on a tradition of learning by doing, and since the beginning have remained at the very forefront of technology. Through experimenting and building, hams have pioneered advances such as the techniques for single sideband, and are currently engaged in state-of-the-art designs in packet-radio and spread-spectrum techniques. Amateurs were among the first to bounce signals off the moon to extend signal range. And hams' practical experience has led to numerous technical refinements and cost reductions beneficial to the commercial radio industry.

Continuation and extension of the amateur's unique ability to enhance international goodwill.

Hams are unique—they can travel to the far reaches of the earth and talk with other amateurs in foreign countries simply by walking down a flight of stairs to their radio "shacks." H. G. Wells had his time machine—hams have their space machines!

In this time when global community initiatives are so important, amateurs can make substantial contributions in support by representing their respective countries as ambassadors of goodwill. Amateur-to-amateur communications often transcend the cultural boundaries between societies. Amateur Radio is a teacher in Lincoln, Nebraska, trading stories with a London boarding-school headmaster or a tropical fish enthusiast learning about different species in the Amazon River from a missionary stationed in Brazil; it is a means of making friends everywhere.

Encouragement and improvement of the amateur service through rules which provide for advancing skills in both the communication and technical phases of the art.

It is the Commission's obligation to see that the rules allow room for amateurs to move in new directions so they can live up to their potential for advancing technical

The United Nations' station 4U1UN, at UN Headquarters in New York. Mister United Nations Radio, Max DeHenseler, HB9RS, at the helm. Amateur Radio is an excellent means of promoting international goodwill.

and communications skills. The amateur service is constantly changing to meet new challenges, and dynamic rules are needed to provide for this. For more on the purpose of the rules, see the next section.

As we will see in Chapter 13, amateurs themselves may play an important role in the rule-making process.

Expansion of the existing reservoir within the amateur radio service of trained operators, technicians and electronic experts.

Self-training, intercommunication and technical investigation are the names of the game for the Amateur Radio Service—the more amateurs proficient in communications techniques, the greater the national resource to the public. During World War II, hams were a significant resource to the military—many were called upon to be radio operators and to fight for the interests of our country.

PURPOSE OF THE RULES

These objectives place a large responsibility on the shoulders of the amateur community. It is the Commission's responsibility to ensure that amateurs are able to operate

"It's endless the good you can do" with ham radio, says Henny Picaud, KA7LYO, a member of the Rogue Valley (Medford, OR) ARC. Henny is 82 years young. The club helped Henny receive her Novice license in 1982. Henny is a trained operator, and a potential community and national resource.

their stations in a manner consistent with these objectives. Also, the FCC, like its counterparts in other countries, must ensure that amateurs have the ability to operate powerful and potentially dangerous equipment safely without causing a lot of interference to other radio services. To these ends, the FCC requires examination of all amateurs: An applicant must pass exams in theory, regulations and if HF privileges are sought, Morse code, before a license will be issued authorizing operation in the Amateur Radio Service. The FCC also makes rules and regulations that every amateur must abide by.

The FCC seeks to achieve other goals in its rule making: The rules must be responsive to the current nature and operating practices of a growing, rapidly advancing and changing radio service. The rules must create a flexible regulatory environment which encourages, rather than limits, the further development of Amateur Radio and its use of modern technology. The FCC reviews its rules from time to time to remove uncertainty, incorporate existing, interpretive policy where necessary, and delete unnecessary or obsolete rules.

Amateur Radio is akin to the public parks in that both require protection from exploitation or conversion to commercial use so that the public can both use them and benefit from their use. If commercial interests use us to provide communications services as alternatives to the more appropriate land mobile services, and we let them, it looks as though we have frequency space we're willing to give away, and land mobile services don't have enough. The FCC then has some basis for taking away from the perceived spectrum-rich amateurs, and giving to the poor land mobile service. The rules help protect us from encroachment by other spectrum-hungry services.

BASIS FOR THE RULES

The basis for the FCC's regulations is found in treaties, international agreements and statutes that provide for the allocation of frequencies and that place conditions on how the frequencies are to be used. For example, Article 32 of the international Radio Regulations limits the types of international communications amateur stations may transmit, and mandates that the technical qualifications of amateur operators be verified.

The Commission's statutory authority to make operational and technical rules, authorize frequencies and license amateurs and stations comes from the Communications Act of 1934. For a comprehensive discussion of the international regulations, and Communications Act of 1934, refer to Chapter 14.

Three other acts of Congress affect FCC rule making. First, and most importantly, the Administrative Procedures Act allows the public to participate in the rule making process. You may petition the FCC for rule changes, comment on current proposals, and ask FCC to reconsider decisions. The FCC must take into consideration your input when making rules. More on the Administrative Procedures Act in Chapter 14.

Under the Regulatory Flexibility Act, the Commission certifies that new rules will not have a significant economic impact on a substantial number of small entities, such as businesses.

Finally, the FCC analyzes its rules under the Paperwork Reduction Act to make sure they tend to decrease the information collection burden imposed on the public.

A JOURNEY THROUGH PART 97

The Amateur Radio rules are designed with the five basic principles described earlier in mind, and are organized in six major subparts: General Provisions, Station Operation Standards, Special Operations, Technical Standards, Providing Emergency Communications and Qualifying Examination Systems. Here's a brief description of the purpose and contents of each, highlighting new rules:

General Provisions

This first subpart, Subpart A, covers, as its name suggests, some basics that apply to all facets of Amateur Radio. The Basis and Purpose of Amateur Radio, discussed above, is found at the very beginning of this subpart. First established in 1951, it has withstood the test of time.

A large section contains specific FCC definitions of key terms used throughout the rules. Although some may appear obvious and unnecessary, the definitions form the very foundation of Part 97, and are keys to unlocking its mysteries. As such, they are all placed in one centralized location for convenient reference.

The more esoteric definitions will be explained as their subjects come up in the rest of this book, but a few of the more basic definitions, germane to this introductory chapter, are presented and discussed here:

Amateur operator. *A person holding a written authorization to be the control operator of an amateur station.* This is simply a person who holds a valid amateur license authorizing him or her to be the control operator of an Amateur Radio station. He or she could also be a non-resident who holds a US reciprocal operating permit.

Amateur station. *A station in an Amateur Radio Service consisting of the apparatus necessary to carry on radiocommunications.*

Amateur radio services. *The amateur service, amateur-satellite service and Radio Amateur Civil Emergency Service (RACES).* This simply means that included in the overall category of Amateur Radio, there is the main Amateur Service, and two major subservices—the Amateur-satellite service and RACES.

Amateur-satellite service. *A radiocommunication service using stations on Earth satellites for the same purposes as those of the amateur service.*

RACES. *A radio service using amateur stations for civil defense communications during periods of local, regional or national civil emergencies.*

Other definitions cover everything else from automatic control to Volunteer Examiners. Most are consistent with the definitions specified in the international rules promulgated by the UN's International Telecommunication Union (ITU), the recognized authority on global communications regulation. More on the ITU later.

Many of the definitions are simpler and clearer than past versions. The operating modes, and other technical terms, are defined in the most basic, nontechnical manner. For example, the FCC's new definitions for emission types consolidates some 1300 designators under nine terms already familiar to most amateurs. They are designed to offer you the ability to experiment with practically every conceivable kind of emission, providing flexibility needed in order to achieve the objectives of our service.

Although the definitions are simplified, they are also as precise as possible. The definition of "earth station," and "space station," for example, are premised on a commonly accepted dividing line of 31 miles (50 kilometers) above the surface of the earth, to provide a precise point at which an amateur station can be determined to be one or the other.

Included in a section on antennas is a useful incorporation of commission policy on limited pre-emption of state and local restrictions on antenna installations. That policy has encouraged open cooperation and dialogue between the communities seeking to regulate ham towers and antennas, and the amateur community itself. It has promoted the relationship between amateurs and the public they serve. Almost without exception, those communities which have sought to regulate amateur stations unreasonably have done so without advance knowledge of the commission's policy. The inclusion of the policies in the rules should help bring them to their attention. A complete discussion of the problems associated with local and state regulation of Amateur Radio is presented in Chapter 3.

The remainder of Subpart A is devoted to other basic issues involving licensing and station location such as authorization, antenna location and restrictions, control operators, license classes, and stations on boats and airplanes.

Station Operation Standards

Subpart B, "Station Operation Standards," sets the table for basic operating practices that apply to all types of operation. Amateurs must operate their stations in accordance with good engineering practice, and must share the frequencies with others. No one ham or group has any special claim to any frequency.

You must not deliberately interfere with, or "jam," other radio signals and communications. The entire subject of amateur-to-amateur interference is addressed in Chapter 7. We will discuss the basic philosophies of band sharing, and attempt to define "malicious interference" the most serious aspect of the subject.

The basic question of who is responsible for the operation of a station is covered. The station licensee is always responsible, except where the control operator of his station is someone else in which case both share responsibility equally. The FCC assumes you are always the control operator of your station unless there is some written record to the contrary.

Although there is no requirement that you keep a log, you must make your station and any records you have available to an FCC inspector upon request. On a case-by-case basis, a local FCC official can require you to maintain a log of your operations.

The fundamental requirements of control operators and station control are covered in this subpart. Each station must have a control point where operation of the transmitter is effected. A control operator must always be at the control point except in a few cases where the transmitter is being controlled automatically. Repeaters and packet radio stations are often controlled by automatic means. More on control aspects in Chapters 4 and 10.

"Authorized transmissions" covers permissible one- and two-way communications. You can talk with foreign amateurs except where a country has given notice that it does not allow its amateurs to communicate with us. At present, there are no "banned countries;" FCC lets us know by public notice if the situation changes.

You can communicate with stations in other services in an emergency situation. You can also communicate with government stations in connection with RACES activities.

You can send one-way communications to make adjustments to your equipment (tuning up, for example), call CQ, remotely control devices, communicate information in emergencies, send code practice, and transmit information bulletins of interest to amateurs. Broadcasting to the public is strictly prohibited.

"International communications" is essentially a restatement of the important international requirement that hams in different countries limit their on-the-air remarks to those of a technical or personal nature that are not important enough to warrant use of the international public communications systems.

Station identification, a critical aspect of any amateur communication, is addressed in Subpart B. The purpose of station identification is to make the source of its transmissions known to those receiving them. The rules cover ID requirements for the various operating modes. The FCC tries to keep the station ID requirements as simple as possible, and towards this end has recently eliminated the suffix identifiers for repeaters, auxiliary and beacon stations.

A major portion of this subpart, "Prohibited transmissions," covers many no-no's such as getting paid for operating your station, business communications, music, obscenity, newsgathering, false signals, and ciphers. Because of the serious nature of these prohibitions, and the fact that some are open to a considerable amount of interpretation, they are discussed in detail in Chapter 7. In that chapter, we will look at recent FCC decisions that help the amateur define actionable obscenity violations.

Regarding public event communications, two preeminent principles apply, and are discussed in Chapter 12: 1) Amateur Radio should not be used as an alternative to the land mobile service (commercial, business radio), to the extent that the latter could be used to perform the necessary services; and 2) logistical services, communications necessary to facilitate the public's safe observation of the event, or safe participation in the event, are permissible where the benefit to the event's sponsor is incidental, and the main beneficiary is the public. The rules incorporate and expand on these two principles that have been long-standing commission policy.

New rules covering what an amateur can and cannot do when approached by the media for news information in various situations are contained in this subpart. We will discuss these, and the new set of ARRL Amateur Radio/Media guidelines, in Chapter 7.

In the recent past, Amateur Radio has been exploited by the broadcast media in their efforts to cover major disasters. Amateurs have been called upon, for example, to transmit broadcast network personnel manifests, and equipment and supply requisitions from disaster sites. Though amateurs have been willing to assist in any way possible in such a situation, the new rules define the specific legal limits on the extent to which amateurs can participate in the newsgathering process. Basically, this amounts to amateurs being permitted to convey news information which "involves" the immediate safety of life and protection of property directly related to the event where normal communications systems, including telephone and radio, are unavailable.

It's interesting to note, however, a subtle distinction between the word "involves," which appears in the FCC's new rules, and the words "critical to," that appeared in early FCC proposals. The Radio-Television News Directors Association (RTNDA)

Amateurs are not just emergency communicators—we often are called on to provide communications for public events. We help observers and participants enjoy a public event such as a marathon, walkathon, parade or boat race safely.

persuaded the FCC to relax its limitations by changing the terms. Now, the news information only needs to be about the event's dangers to life and property to assist journalists in filing their reports, and not limited to the narrower purpose of actually relieving the threat to life and property. The transmission of reports for journalists, however, must not detract from the efforts of other stations that are actually engaged in providing direct emergency communications. The FCC felt that the relaxation did not compromise either service—Amateur or Broadcast. The FCC still feels the new rules sufficiently protect Amateur Radio from overzealous news journalists who would use us as alternatives to more appropriate (and expensive) communications services, despite the distinction described above.

"Swap nets" and the related question of sale and purchase of amateur equipment on-the-air are addressed in new rules in this subpart. The rules prohibit such communications by those seeking to derive a profit by buying or selling amateur gear on a regular basis. These rules provide the necessary protection against commercialization of the service.

You can't retransmit signals from any other radio service. The sole exception is for space shuttle communications. Some hams have asked the FCC to specifically allow the retransmission of NOAA weather bulletin broadcasts. The League went a step further to suggest that hams be allowed to retransmit weather, propagation and time bulletins transmitted by the Government. The FCC, however, said that these broadcasts can be widely received by very affordable receivers, and saw no reason to allow the use of amateur frequencies for such retransmissions. The FCC apparently feels that Amateur Radio would be used as an inapproriate alternative to the government services in these cases.

Third party traffic rules are covered in this subpart, specifying the restrictions on stations sending messages to foreign countries for other people. "Third party traffic" is defined in the definitions part of Subpart A. The rules here have been clarified to permit third party traffic between the US and other countries in cases where the third party is an amateur licensee. This is consistent with the policies of virtually all national telecommunications administrations.

A final section addresses restricted operation and sets forth the conditions that must exist in an interference case before the Commission can impose "quiet hours," hours of the day and week when an amateur may not operate his transmitter. Time-tested rules here take into account "due process" considerations protecting amateurs from unilateral sanctions imposed by the FCC without an investigation first being made. The Commission may require an amateur to assist in the resolution of a local RFI problem. Because of its complexity and importance, this entire issue is discussed extensively in Chapters 6 and 9.

Special Operations

Subpart C, "Special Operations," addresses some of the esoterica of Amateur Radio: Auxiliary links, beacon operation, repeater operation, data and RTTY communications, telecommand functions and satellite operations.

Repeater operation, of course, is part and parcel of most every amateur's daily activity. The rules for repeaters and auxiliary links should be understood by every trustee and user. These topics are the subjects of Chapter 9.

An important regulatory approach to solving interference problems between repeaters is addressed here: The two repeater station licensees are equally responsible for resolving the interference problem unless one of the repeaters is approved for operation by the recognized repeater coordinator for the area, and the other is not. In this case, the uncoordinated repeater has primary responsibility to resolve the problem. The station might even have to stop operation. Refer to Chapter 10 for more discussion on repeater coordination.

Technical Standards

The word *standard* means consistency and order—and this is what the technical standards, Subpart D, is all about. The Commission has made these standards a basic framework so all the different kinds of amateur operation can live together peacefully in the same house, and so the Amateur Radio household as a whole can live peacefully with other radio occupants in the spectrum neighborhood.

Amateurs may operate their stations in certain segments of the radio spectrum specified in this subpart. In addition to restrictions on the use of the various operating modes on each band, there are limits associated with license class, power and bandwidth.

In many cases, amateurs share operating privileges on a primary or secondary basis with other radio services. Depending on the status of the amateur occupancy of a particular band, amateurs may have to avoid causing interference to, and tolerate interference from, the other occupant(s).

Amateurs must use the minimum amount of power necessary to carry out the desired communications effectively and reliably. An amateur doesn't need a planet-crushing amplifier to reach his friend across town on 2 meters! Some amateurs often forget this rule in their zeal to have the biggest signal on the band, a condition once described by Doctor Freud. The entire subject of power limitations is addressed in Subpart D.

The amplifier type acceptance rules are found in the technical standards. These rules have their origin in the days of the CB craze when CBers were purchasing amateur amplifiers for illegal use at 27 MHz, just below the amateur 10-meter band. Under the rules, FCC does not permit manufacturers to market amplifiers capable of operation between 24 and 35 MHz. Amateurs are, however, allowed to modify their purchases for 10-meter capability.

Providing Emergency Communications

Subpart E, "Providing Emergency Communications," is brief, but important. It enjoys a prominent place of its own in the rules, and addresses disaster communications, stations in distress, communications for the safety of life and protection of property and the Radio Amateur Civil Emergency Service (RACES).

When it comes to supplying emergency communications, that is, communications related to the *immediate* safety of life, and/or the *immediate* protection of property, in the absence of other communications facilities, the rules permit amateurs wide latitude. The rules permit the FCC to specify conditions and rules for amateur operation during an emergency situation. The Commission can set aside specific frequencies for emergency use only.

The Radio Amateur Civil Emergency Service (RACES) uses amateurs for civil defense communications during local, regional or national civil emergencies. To participate, you must be enrolled as a member of a local civil defense agency.

New RACES rules permit more flexibility in connection with drills. They support, for example, the assistance of RACES operators in evacuation drills in the proximity of nuclear facilities, which often require many hours of participation.

Bexar County, Texas Emergency Coordinator Ken Harwood, WA5QZI, sending message traffic from the San Antonio Red Cross Chapter of the American Red Cross, where the San Antonio station, W5SC, is located, during the Hurricane Gilbert emergency.

Qualifying Examination Systems

As mentioned earlier, bound by international law, and common sense, the FCC is required to ensure that people who want to operate a transmitter in the amateur service are able to do so without (1) hurting themselves or others and (2) causing interference to other users of the radio spectrum.

The FCC also wants to promote the development of individual amateurs' abilities in technical, and operating facets of radio communications. This is consistent with its desire to extend the amateur's "proven ability to contribute to the advancement of the radio art," and expand the "existing reservoir within the amateur radio service of trained operators, technicians and electronics experts."

The Commission attempts to accomplish all this through its licensing program. Amateurs must pass tests in technical theory, rules and regulations, operating practice and safety before a license to operate a station will be granted. Five different levels of licensing—Novice, Technician, General, Advanced and Amateur Extra—each with a carrot of additional privileges, promotes personal development of the abilities of the individual amateur.

The final subpart of the rules, Subpart F, deals with the examination system. It covers such things as qualifying for a license, exam requirements, elements and standards. Test procedures are specified, and exam preparation is covered.

In 1982, the Commission delegated much of the exam administration program to the amateurs themselves. The rules provide for checks and balances on "volunteer examiners" who administer exams at the local and regional levels. These checks and balances protect against fraud and provide integrity for the exam process.

The examining process is covered in Chapter 3.

RULE INTERPRETATIONS

The purpose of this book is to provide the reader first and foremost with a complete set of the rules, and secondly, a companion text which describes the rules in a comprehensive manner to help an amateur apply them in specific situations. The following chapters provide time-tested and FCC-approved interpretations, and copies of FCC letters and news releases, all describing the application of the rules. Graphic depictions of rules are provided where possible to lend clarity—portrayals of antenna structures near airports and glide slope rules are examples.

There are other parts of the Commission's rules that affect Amateur Radio. In many cases, they are referenced in Part 97. This book discusses these rules and provides the text for reference.

A FINAL NOTE

Generally speaking, the rules are meant to be inclusive, rather than exclusive. Some hams stay up all night thinking of ways that a certain interpretation will prevent them from doing something with their radio. *Operating flexibility* is the name of the game—the rules provide a framework within which amateurs have a wide latitude to do all kinds of constructive things in accordance with the basis and purpose of the service. The rules should be viewed as positive vehicles for promoting healthy activity and growth, not as negative constrainers leading to stagnation.

Chapter Two

Meeting the Test

Three forces drive the FCC's licensing machine. First is its obligation under international agreement to ensure that you have a license before you operate on amateur frequencies, that you can operate your station safely, and limit interference to others. Second, it must make sure you can copy Morse code if you want to operate on the HF bands. Again, this is an international requirement. And finally, FCC must do what it can to develop your individual operating and technical skills.

To meet these ends, the Commission manages a time-tested licensing program consisting of five different grades of license: two entry-level grades and three others, each carrying a bigger carrot of increased operating privileges. To win additional privileges, you must pass a test demonstrating increased proficiency in Morse code, as well as additional knowledge of the rules, operating procedures and technical theory. Licensing and the exam process are the subjects of this chapter.

GET A LICENSE FIRST

If you are controlling a transmitter on any frequency where Amateur Radio is regulated by FCC, you must have written authorization to do so from the Commission. If you don't, you will be in serious trouble, fast. Every operator must have this authorization; FCC makes no exceptions. In most cases, authorization will be in the form of an amateur license, FCC Form 660. Anyone is eligible to hold a US amateur license except a representative of a foreign government.

An amateur license actually has two parts: The operator license conveys your license class and privileges, and lists your mailing address. The station part authorizes operation and provides the call sign of your station at the geographic location specified on the ticket. You are responsible for all FCC mail sent to your mailing address—make sure your address is always current!

Additional types of station licenses and permits issued by FCC exist for clubs, military recreation facilities, civil defense centers and foreign amateurs visiting the US. FCC no longer issues *new* club, military recreation or RACES station licenses, but it will renew and modify existing ones.

The original written authorization, or a photocopy, must be present when you are operating. You can post it on the wall above your rig or keep it in your wallet, just as long as you have it available when you operate.

Examination is always required for a new amateur license and for each change in license class. FCC makes no exceptions.

CLASSES OF LICENSE

Becoming a ham is easy. With a little studying, just about anyone can do it. There are two entry level licenses.

Like a driver's learner permit, the *Novice* license affords enough basic privileges to give the operator a little experience and understanding before he enters the mainstream later. This entry level license allows you to use voice, Morse code and other modes, depending on the band, and gives ample opportunity for local, regional and worldwide contacts. See Table 1 for a complete description of Novice privileges.

A candidate must pass a 5 word-per-minute (WPM) Morse code test [Element 1(A)], and a written exam in elementary theory and regulations (Element 2). The exam has 30 questions concerning the privileges of the Novice license; 22 must be answered correctly to pass.

The second type of entry level amateur license is the Technician. This license requires that the applicant pass a 55 question test composed of Elements 2 and 3(A). It gives the applicant all privileges above 30 MHz. There is no Morse code requirement for Technician as of February 14, 1991. Successful candidates for the codeless Technician must answer correctly a minimum of 22 of the 30 questions on Element 2 and at least 19 of the 25 questions in Element 3(A). Technicians have a wider door

Table 1
Amateur Operator Licenses

Class	*Code Test*	*Written Examination*	*Privileges*
Novice	5 WPM (Element 1A)	Elementary theory and regulations (Element 2)	CW on 3675-3725, 7100-7150* and 21,100-21,200 kHz with 200 W PEP output maximum; CW and RTTY on 28,100-28,300 kHz and CW and SSB voice on 28,300-28,500 kHz with 200 W PEP max; all amateur modes authorized on 222.1-223.91 MHz, 25 W PEP max; all amateur modes authorized on 1270-1295 MHz, 5 W PEP max.
Technician	no code test	Elementary theory and regulations; Technician-level theory and regulations. (Elements 2 and 3A)	All amateur privileges above 30.0 MHz. (Technicians who pass Element 1(A), the 5 WPM code test, will be granted Novice HF privileges.)
General	13 WPM (Element 1B)	Elementary theory and regulations; Technician and General theory and regulations. (Elements 2, 3A and 3B)	All amateur privileges except those reserved for Advanced and Amateur Extra class.
Advanced	13 WPM (Element 1B)	All lower exam elements, plus intermediate theory. (Elements 2, 3A, 3B and 4A)	All amateur privileges except those reserved for Extra class.
Amateur Extra	20 WPM (Element 1C)	All lower exam elements plus special exam on advanced techniques (Elements 2, 3A, 3B, 4A and 4B)	All amateur privileges.

*Varies according to region; see Chapter 5.

open for VHF, UHF and microwave experimentation as well as computer-to-computer communications.

Technicians who pass the 5 WPM code examination (Element 1(A)) will be given a Certificate of Successful Completion of Examination (CSCE). In addition to all privileges above 30 MHz which they gained as Technicians, the Technician Plus CSCE class operators will be granted the current Novice HF privileges.

Next is the *General* class license, considered to be the ticket to mainstream Amateur Radio. The license conveys a large number of high-frequency privileges where numerous mainstream activities such as DXing, net operation, RTTY and contesting occur. Because of the extensive amount of privileges on the "low bands," the exam [Element 3(B)] focuses on the regulatory, operating and technical aspects of HF. The exam has 25 questions concerning these additional privileges; 19 must be answered correctly to pass. Additionally, the applicant must pass a more difficult code test—13 WPM [Element 1(B)].

If you can demonstrate technical knowledge at the intermediate level [Element 4(A)], the *Advanced* class license offers additional, prime choice, HF phone privileges. The exam contains 50 questions dealing with the special privileges of the Advanced class; 37 must be answered correctly to pass. The code test is the same as for General—13 WPM [Element 1(B)].

At the top is the *Amateur Extra* class license, conveying all amateur privileges, and accordingly, rights to operate on segments reserved exclusively for Extras, away from the crowds on the rest of the band. As expected, the written examination [Element 4(B)] is difficult; it contains 40 questions on advanced techniques; 30 must be answered correctly to pass. Also, the applicant must demonstrate expert proficiency in Morse code at 20 WPM [Element 1(C)].

For a list of the number of questions required for each specific topic on each exam, see the table in §97.503(c).

COMMON QUESTIONS AND ANSWERS—CODELESS TECHNICIAN

Until February 14, 1991, Morse code had always been part of the requirements for obtaining an Amateur Radio license. It was on that date that the FCC created the first codeless Amateur Radio license in its history by eliminating the code requirement from the Technician class and, upon the applicant's passing a 55 question exam, giving these new amateurs all privileges above 30 MHz. Technicians licensed after February 14, 1991 who would like the HF privileges below 30 MHz which are presently enjoyed by Novices will be required to pass a 5 WPM Morse code exam before three accredited Volunteer Examiners.

The FCC stated that this new codeless license creates a tremendous opportunity for Amateur Radio by opening the door to many people who are enthusiastic about Amateur Radio and technically competent. These people have a great deal to contribute to the hobby, but have been discouraged by the code requirement.

Q. What does the creation of the codeless Technician do to the Novice license?

A. The Novice license is retained without modification as an alternate point of entry for persons willing to pass a 5 WPM code test and simpler examination in lieu of the more difficult Technician written exam.

Q. What happens to Technicians licensed prior to February 14, 1991?

A. All Technicians licensed prior to February 14, 1991 will be grandfathered so as not to lose any privileges. "New" Technicians licensed after February 14, 1991 will be given privileges on all frequencies above 30 MHz and, upon passing a 5 WPM code test, will be given the "old" Novice and Technician HF privileges.

Q. How much power can codeless Technicians use?

A. Technician power levels have not been changed. New Technicians may use the legal limit in their authorized bands.

Q. What kind of call signs will new Technicians receive?

A. Technicians will receive Group C call signs in call areas where they are still available. There is no call sign designator to indicate which Technicians have or have not passed the code test. The FCC will, however, have records of Technicians who have passed the code test.

Q. Why didn't the FCC give codeless Technicians HF privileges?

A. International regulations specify that an amateur must demonstrate Morse code proficiency before gaining access to HF.

Q. What options are available to codeless Technicians who later decide to learn the code?

A. Codeless Technicians, upon passing a 5 WPM code test, will be given a Certificate of Successful Completion of Examination (CSCE). In addition to their already acquired frequencies above 30 MHz, Technicians who pass the 5 WPM code examination will also be given current Novice HF privileges.

Q. How will the FCC know which Technicians have and haven't passed the code?

A. Volunteer examiners will be required to notify the FCC of the 5 WPM Morse CSCE issued to codeless Technicians so the FCC will have the information for enforcement purposes.

Q. How is this codeless license different from earlier attempts by the FCC to create a codeless license, especially the one in 1983 which was rejected overwhelmingly by the amateur community?

A. Many countries have had codeless VHF/UHF licenses for decades, especially European and Pacific Rim countries. Reflecting the view of the amateur community, the ARRL had long opposed any form of codeless license. In 1988, amateurs began discussing a codeless license in an altogether different light. Opinions varied as to what caused the change, but one thing was for sure: amateurs opposition, while still significant, had diminished considerably. The support for such a license was undeniable. This led to the League's filing a petition for a codeless license with the FCC.

EXAM CREDIT

When you upgrade, you will be required to pass only those test elements for the new license that are not included in the exam for the amateur license you currently hold. For example, when you change from Novice to Technician you will be required to pass Element 3(A). You won't be asked to pass Element 2 again. Note that your license must be unexpired (or within the grace period for reinstatement of expired licenses—see "License Terms" in Chapter 4).

Credit for any element will be given to applicants who produce a valid Certificate of Successful Completion of Examination (CSCE). For example, if you take the Amateur Extra class exam, pass the code, but fail the written test, you will receive a CSCE for the code element. Then, you've got 365 days to use the certificate for credit at another sitting for the Amateur Extra exam.

If you're trying for Technician or higher, and have just passed the Novice but don't have the ticket in hand yet, you can get credit for the Novice written element by showing the examiners a photocopy of your FCC Form 610 indicating you qualified within the previous 365 days.

Anyone holding a current (or expired within the past five years) commercial radiotelegraph operator license or permit may receive credit for Element 1(C), the expert code test (20-WPM).

Any applicant holding a Technician license issued before March 21, 1987 (the date when new rules provided for separate General and Technician written elements) will receive credit for the General written exam (Element 3(B)). Any applicant holding a Technician license issued on or after March 21, 1987, and before February 14, 1991, will receive credit for Elements 1(A) 2 and 3(A).

Credit for code elements 1(B) and 1(C) may be granted to physically handicapped applicants. More on this special provision later in this chapter.

No other exam credit will be allowed on the basis of holding or having held any other license.

NOVICE EXAMS

Exam procedures for Novice applicants are a little different from those used for Technician and above. Novice exams are given by volunteer examiners at any location convenient to candidates and examiners.

With increased privileges accorded Novices in 1987 (as part of the "Novice Enhancement" action) came increased responsibility and accountability. To provide more integrity in the Novice exam procedures, FCC now requires two volunteer examiners, where before it required only one. To be an examiner, you must: 1) hold a current General, Advanced or Amateur Extra class license; 2) be at least 18 years of age; 3) not derive income from Amateur Radio-related commerce (see questions and answers that follow for discussion on this requirement); and 4) never have had your license revoked or suspended.

You are not allowed to give exams to your spouse, children, grandchildren, stepchildren, parents, grandparents, stepparents, brothers, sisters, stepbrothers, stepsisters, aunts, uncles, nieces, nephews and in-laws.

Volunteer examiners need not be accredited by Volunteer Examiner Coordinators (VECs—the organizations that coordinate higher-class exams); you need only meet the requirements above before administering a Novice exam.

Novice Exam Session

An exam session begins when both examiners receive from the examinee a properly completed application form (FCC Form 610), and any document for which the examinee is claiming examination credit (see the previous section, "Exam Credit").

The examiners should screen the application to verify that the examinee is actually the person applying for the license.

They make sure the FCC Form 610 is completed correctly:

Item 2C (new license) should be checked.

Item 5 (examinee's name) should match any identifying documents.

Item 6 (date of birth) must not be the current year!

Item 7 (mail address) must be a mailing address in the US, its territories or possessions.

Item 8 (station location) must be an actual location, not a PO Box number, RFD number or General Delivery.

Item 9 (environmental effect) must be checked. See Chapters 3 and 4 for discussion of this item.

Item 10 (other application) should be checked "no." If "yes" is checked, the examiners must not give the test.

Item 13 (signature) must match name in Item 5. It must match the signature shown on the identifying documents. If the examinee does not sign Item 13 in their presence, examiners should have the examinee sign another paper for comparison with the application, and identifying document signatures.

Item 14 (date signed) must be filled in.

In the *Administering VEs' Report*, examiners must check the box for each element for which the examinee is eligible to receive credit.

For more information on completing the FCC Form 610, see discussion in Chapter 4.

The exam is given at a location and a time specified by the examiners. Both examiners must be present and observe examinees throughout the entire examination. They are responsible for the proper conduct and necessary supervision of each exam, and must immediately stop the test if the examinee doesn't follow instructions. It is up to the examinee to follow directions! The examiners must never give an exam if there is a possibility that the exact contents of any portion might be known in advance by the examinee.

Novice Code Test

Examiners giving Novice code tests use a variety of methods to test their candidates. The most reliable way is to load a five- to six-minute message into a

Table 2
Characters Required for Morse Code Tests

Letters

a	•—	j	•———	s	•••
b	—•••	k	—•—	t	—
c	—•—•	l	•—••	u	••—
d	—••	m	——	v	•••—
e	•	n	—•	w	•——
f	••—•	o	———	x	—••—
g	——•	p	•——•	y	—•——
h	••••	q	——•—	z	——••
i	••	r	•—•		

Figures

1	•————	6	—••••
2	••———	7	——•••
3	•••——	8	———••
4	••••—	9	————•
5	•••••	0	—————

Punctuation marks and miscellaneous signs

Full stop (period)	[.]	•—•—•—
Comma	[,]	——••——
Question mark (note of interrogation or request for repetition of a transmission not understood).	[?]	••——••
Fraction bar or division sign $\overline{\text{DN}}$	[/]	—••—•
Double hyphen $\overline{\text{BT}}$	[=]	—•••—
Cross or addition sign $\overline{\text{AR}}$	[+]	•—•—•
End of work $\overline{\text{SK}}$		•••—•—

COMMON QUESTIONS AND ANSWERS —NOVICE EXAMS

Q. As volunteer Novice examiners, do we have to publicize exam sessions in advance?

A. No. Only volunteer examiner teams for higher-class license exams are required to announce exam sessions in advance.

Q. Can we be reimbursed for our out-of-pocket expenses incurred in administering the exam?

A. No reimbursement may be accepted for preparing, processing or administering Novice class examinations.

Q. Is there a minimum or maximum number of Novice applicants that we must test at one time?

A. There is no minimum or maximum number.

Q. Is there a specific order in which the exam elements must be administered?

A. No. Traditionally, the code test comes first, but there is no legal requirement that it be done in any specific order.

Q. Is it necessary to administer the code test and written test to an applicant on the same day?

A. There's no rule that says you must give both elements on the same day. If you do not, however, you should certify any successful completion of an element on the Form 610 and return it to the applicant. He then should bring it back to you when he sits for the other element. Element credit is valid for 365 days following successful completion.

Q. Who is responsible for constructing the exam?

A. Both volunteer examiners.

Q. Can I use Farnsworth spacing in the code test?

A. Normal spacing or Farnsworth spacing (code sent at 13 to 18 words-per-minute but with added space between characters to bring the overall speed down to 5 words-per-minute) may be used.

Q. Must I give a sending test too?

A. That's up to you. The FCC has found that the receiving test alone is adequate proof of both sending and receiving ability.

Q. May I use a "cute" Novice QSO as a test?

A. This is generally permissible, but you should not use any language that would be improper over the air.

Q. Is the candidate allowed to use a slide rule or calculator during the test?

A. Yes, but it should not be necessary for a Novice test. If the candidate uses a calculator, be sure that it is nonprogrammable or that any programs have been erased from the calculator before the test begins.

Q. What if we catch a candidate cheating?

A. Simply terminate the exam.

Q. What should we do if the candidate fails the code test?

A. You may elect to administer the written portion. If he passes, you may certify his successful completion of that element on the Form 610. He then will retain credit for the written element for a period of 365 days. Next time, within 365 days, you need only give him the code test.

Q. Although I don't yet have my General class ticket back from the FCC, I do hold a Certificate of Successful Completion of Examination (CSCE) for the General. Can I still qualify as a volunteer Novice examiner?

A. No. You must hold the actual document for a General, Advanced or Amateur Extra license, the FCC Form 660, in order to qualify as a volunteer Novice examiner.

Q. Can I give a Novice exam if I work for a local retail ham radio store?

A. You may not be a volunteer Novice examiner if you own a significant interest in, or are an employee of, any company or other entity that is engaged in the manufacture or distribution of equipment used in connection with Amateur Radio, unless you do not normally communicate with these parts of the company.

Q. I work for a company that publishes books for amateurs. Can I give Novice exams?

A. If your company prepares or distributes any publication used in preparation for obtaining amateur licenses, you are not eligible to be a volunteer Novice examiner unless you don't normally communicate with that part of your company that is engaged in the manufacture or distribution of those books.

Q. We've given a Novice exam to the same individual 15 times. He's flunked the written element every time. He wants his license so badly, but he just can't do the written part. Can we, or the FCC, waive the written test just this one time?

A. The knowledge and skills needed to qualify for a license are exactly the same for everyone. The FCC does not grant requests to dispense with (or lower) any operator qualification requirement. No volunteer examiner has the authority to waive license requirements.

Q. Where can I get FCC forms, or inquire about the status of an application?

A. Contact Consumer Assistance Branch, FCC, Gettysburg, PA 17326. Their office telephone is 717-337-1212. ARRL HQ also has forms available: Write or telephone ARRL HQ, 225 Main St, Newington, CT 06111, telephone 203-666-1541. Please include an SASE.

Q. Where can we ask about the preparation or administration of an exam?

A. You may contact ARRL HQ for information.

Q. Is there a minimum waiting period before an applicant can be retested?

A. No. There is no waiting period for retesting.

Q. Can we use a good photocopy of a Form 610 in lieu of the actual form?

A. The FCC has stated that Form 610s may be reproduced privately "as long as your copies are exact duplicates of the FCC form, including paper size, weight, color, etc." If you use a photocopy, you'll be running the risk of having it returned to you without action.

Q. Is the question pool revised periodically?

A. Yes. The pool is updated from time to time. Watch the Amateur Radio media for news of question pool updates. ARRL HQ maintains a stock of the current question pool at all times.

memory keyer or computer and play it back to the candidate. Another method is to tape record the test message. The least reliable (but still acceptable) method is to hand-send the code using a keyer or straight key.

The message should be typical of those usually encountered while operating an amateur station on the Novice HF bands. It must be unknown to the applicant, and not be a well known phrase from a poem, song or book. The message must be at least five minutes long. It must never be readministered to the same person! The examinee is responsible for knowing all the characters—letters, numerals, punctuation marks and other signs—shown in Table 2. Examiners must ensure that the applicant is tested on *all* these characters.

To pass, the examinee must prove to the examiners the ability to send and receive the code at 5 WPM. Each five letters of the alphabet count as one word. Grading the code test is left to the judgment of the examiners. Traditionally, a passing mark is earned if the candidate can copy one minute (25 characters) solid with no errors. Letters of the alphabet count as 1 character. Numerals, punctuation marks, and prosigns each count as 2 characters.

In recent years, examiners have used a 10-question comprehension quiz, with a requirement that at least seven out of the ten questions be answered correctly, letter-for-letter as sent in the message. Examiners can use fill-in-the-blank or multiple-choice methods.

If the applicant passes the code test, the examiners will check the Element 1(A) box in Item D of the *Administering VEs' Report* on the Form 610.

Novice Written Test

Again, it is up to the examiners to devise the test, using a pool of more than 300 questions. The examiners devise an exam of at least 30 questions by pulling the required number of questions on the following topics from the pool: FCC rules (10), operating procedures (2), propagation (1), practices (4), electrical principles (4), circuit components (2), practical circuits (2), signals and emissions (2), and antennas and feed lines (3). It is up to the examiners to choose a testing style—essay, fill-in-the-blank, true-false or multiple-choice format may be used.

It's also up to the examiners to determine the correctness of the candidate's answers. There is no published answer key. (ARRL, however, produces a "Novice Exam Kit," with instructions, exam papers, and answer keys—available from ARRL HQ). The passing grade is 22 correct answers out of 30 questions.

Following completion of each exam element, the examiners grade the examinee's answers. When the examinee is credited for all exam elements required for the Novice license [Elements 1(A) and (2)], the examiners check Item E1 (Novice) of the *Administering VEs' Report* on the Form 610. If the examinee does not pass either or both elements, Item E (none) is checked, indicating that the applicant is not eligible for a license at this time.

The examiners must return the Form 610 to the applicant and inform him of his grade.

If the applicant passes one element, but fails the other, the examiners certify successful completion of the passed element on the Form 610, and return it to the applicant for credit at a later session. The credit is valid for 365 days.

Following the test session, the examiners must attest to the fact that the exam was administered in accordance with the rules and test procedures by signing and dating the application at Items 1A, B, and C, 2A, B and C. If the examiners certify an exam result fraudulently or for compensation, they are subject to having their licenses revoked or suspended.

If the examinee qualifies for the Novice license, the properly completed and certified Form 610 must be sent *within 10 calendar days of the exam date* to FCC, Gettysburg, PA 17326. If the application is forwarded late, an explanation must be included. If the examinee does not qualify for a Novice license, the application must be returned to the examinee, not to the FCC. Normal processing time of an application for a new Novice license is four to six weeks.

Handicapped Applicants

Examiners must take into account the physical disabilities of examinees by permitting them to demonstrate their qualifications in ways that accommodate their disabilities. For instance, a hearing-impaired examinee should be allowed to use a vibrating surface or a flashing light for the code test. If writing is difficult, the examinee may dictate the answers to the examiners. The examiners may read the written exam questions to a blind examinee or allow the use of Braille. Examiners should avoid using questions involving diagrams with a blind examinee.

Examiners should use such special procedures only where it is appropriate. The examiners are permitted to request a physician's certification indicating the nature of the disability before determining which, if any, special procedures must be used.

TECHNICIAN AND HIGHER CLASS LICENSE EXAMS

Teams of three accredited amateur *Volunteer Examiners (VEs)*, under the supervision of umbrella organizations known as *Volunteer Examiner Coordinators (VECs)*, administer exams for Technician, General, Advanced and Amateur Extra license applicants at thousands of locations across the country and throughout the world, on convenient schedules, following advance public notice. Examples of locations are public halls, schools, conventions and hamfests, club meetings and flea markets. VEs are present and observe candidates throughout the entire exam process, and are responsible for its proper conduct and supervision under instructions from the VEC. They grade test papers, report results, and handle all paperwork with their VEC. The VEC, in turn, serves as the interface between the Volunteer Examiners and FCC.

Application

Each candidate must present the examiners with a properly completed Form 610 on or before the registration deadline if preregistration is required. Otherwise, applicants present the completed Form 610 to the examiners at the session prior to the beginning of the exam. If registration deadlines are imposed, they will be determined by the Volunteer Examiner Coordinator issuing the exam papers to the VEs. Candidates should bring thorough identification documents, including their original (not a photocopy) license documents and Certificates of Successful Completion of Examinations (CSCE).

Following Instructions

Candidates must follow the instructions given by the examiners to the "T." The examiners will immediately terminate the exam if the candidate doesn't follow directions. At the end of the exam, the candidate must turn the test papers over to the examiner.

VEs must accommodate an examinee whose physical disabilities require a special exam procedure—see the section, "Handicapped Applicants," earlier in this chapter.

Code Test

The 13 WPM code test [Element 1(B)] and the 20 WPM code test [Element 1(C)] can be prepared by the examiners or obtained from the VEC. The person preparing these tests must hold an Amateur Extra class license. The test must prove the applicant's ability to receive the code at the prescribed speeds. The sending test is no longer required, because the FCC has found that those who can receive the code can send it as well.

The applicant is responsible for knowing, and will be tested on, the characters—letters, numerals, punctuation marks and other signals—shown in Table 2. In cases where "straight copy" testing is used, letters of the alphabet count as 1 character; numerals, punctuation and procedural signals count as 2 characters. The style of test—fill-in-the-blank, multiple-choice, straight-copy—is chosen by the VEC or, in some cases, the VEs themselves.

Elements 1(B) and 1(C) may be waived in cases where a physician has certified an applicant's inability to pass the exam because of a physical handicap. The FCC will permit those examinees to obtain a *Doctor's Certification* which indicates that, due to a severe handicap, the examinee is unable to pass a 13 or 20 WPM Morse code examination. This certification, if completed correctly, must then be accepted by VEC-accredited volunteer examiner teams for credit for Element 1(C). If this credit is used in conjunction with additional written element credit(s) held, volunteer examiners will issue a CSCE based upon the credit(s) held which permits temporary operation with the operating privileges of that higher class license while the FCC is processing the Form 610 application for the license upgrade.

Written Test

The formula for creating written tests [Elements 3(A), 3(B), 4(A) and 4(B)] is determined by the FCC, see §97.503(c). The VEC, or in some cases the VEs themselves, select questions for each test from the appropriate pool of questions approved by the majority of VECs (see the section, "Question Pools" later in this chapter). The VEC keeps the exact exam designs secret, but the general question pools are available to the public. (Copies of each element's pool are available from ARRL HQ.)

VEs receive test papers from their VEC, or in some cases create their own, and administer them to the candidates in accordance with the VEC's instructions.

Amateur Extra class VEs can administer exams for any element. Advanced class VEs can give exams for Technician candidates only.

CSCE

When an applicant passes an exam element, the examiners issue a Certificate of Successful Completion of Examination (CSCE). This certificate is required for already licensed applicants operating with newly acquired privileges of a class higher than that of their permanent license. It serves the same purpose as the FCC's former interim permit under which the applicant could operate with new privileges prior to receiving the permanent ticket from Gettysburg. The certificate also carries with it a one-year credit for those elements passed when taking subsequent exams.

The CSCE is evidence of a new Technician's successful completion of the 5 WPM code exam, granting Novice HF privileges, and must be retained by the licensee.

When the candidate passes all of the exam elements for a higher-class license, the examiners must certify the following information on the candidate's application form: (1) examiners' names and call signs; (2) examiners' qualifications to give the test; and (3) examiners' signed statements that the applicant has passed the required exam elements. Within 10 days following the exam, the examiners must send the application of a successful candidate to the VEC. The VEC processes the data before sending it on to the FCC Licensing Division in Gettysburg.

Retesting Waiting Period

There is no waiting period before reexamination after failing an exam element. FCC requires, however, that VECs not use the same set of exam questions in successive exam sessions to ensure that "retest" doesn't mean "remembering." Most VEs will retest candidates immediately if more than one version of the failed elements(s) is available at the session.

Special FCC Exams

At any time, the FCC may readminister any exam given by a VEC, either itself, or under the supervision of VEs it designates. FCC can cancel the new license of a licensee who doesn't show up for, or flunks, an FCC-directed reexam. This allows the FCC to spot check and maintain integrity in the exam process.

Volunteer Examiners

To be accredited by a VEC as a Volunteer Examiner, you must meet the standards described earlier in this chapter. VEs may not accept compensation for their services, but may recover out-of-pocket expenses. See the section "Examination Expense Reimbursement" later in this chapter. If your license has ever been suspended or revoked, the FCC will not accept your services as a VE.

Finding an Exam Opportunity

To determine when and where an exam will be given, contact your VEC, local club or repeater group. The ARRL/VEC offers information on test activity throughout

AMERICAN RADIO RELAY LEAGUE
VOLUNTEER EXAMINER COORDINATOR

STATEMENT OF PURPOSE

PURPOSE:

The Purpose of the **ARRL/VEC** is to provide initial licensing examination for prospective new hams and upgrade examination opportunities for those already licensed.

OBJECTIVES:

- The **ARRL/VEC** will provide a sufficient number of examination opportunities to meet the above purpose, on a schedule that is convenient to the applicants.
- The **ARRL/VEC** will provide the examination candidate with tests that meet all applicable requirements of current FEDERAL COMMUNICATIONS COMMISSION Rules and Regulations and are administered in accordance with those requirements and generally accepted educational testing principles and practices.
- The **ARRL/VEC** will provide a service level of the highest order to our **CUSTOMERS, THE VOLUNTEER EXAMINERS.**

Resolution of the ARRL Board of Directors
at the 1989 Annual Board Meeting

Fig 1—ARRL/VEC statement of purpose.

VOLUNTEER EXAMINER
accredited by the
AMERICAN RADIO RELAY LEAGUE

This certifies that ______________________ has been trained and is accredited to serve as a Volunteer Examiner for Amateur Radio license examinations. This certificate of accreditation is issued by the Volunteer Examiner Coordinator Office of the American Radio Relay League, Inc., in Newington, Connecticut. This certificate of accreditation is valid, subject to the eligibility requirements contained in the current rules and regulations of the Federal Communications Commission (Parts 0, 1 and 97), the Volunteer Examiner's current Amateur Radio License class, and the expiration date stated on the latest renewal endorsement affixed below.

Larry E. Price

Larry E. Price, W4RA
President, ARRL

Bart J. Jahnke

Bart J. Jahnke, KB9NM
VEC Manager, ARRL

VALID THROUGH THE DATE SHOWN ON MOST RECENT ENDORSEMENT

Fig 2—Sample Volunteer Examiner Certificate

all VEC regions. One of the major benefits of the Volunteer Examiner Program is enhanced exam opportunity, an answer to the very limited exam sessions given in the past by FCC.

Volunteer Examiner Coordinators

VECs are umbrella organizations that serve as interfaces between the Commission and the field Volunteer Examiners. They coordinate the efforts of VEs, print and distribute exam papers to VEs and forward successful applicants' Form 610s to the FCC's licensing division.

Volunteer Examiner Coordinators have entered into special agreements with the FCC after having met certain qualifications: A VEC must be organized for the purpose of furthering the interests of Amateur Radio, and be at least regional in scope. It must be able to serve at least one of the FCC's VEC regions, and agree to coordinate test sessions for all classes of license exams (except, of course, Novice).

VECs must not have conflict of interest. An entity (organization or company) that manufactures or distributes ham gear or prepares ham radio license study materials may be a VEC only if it can show the Commission that preventive measures have been taken to eliminate any possible conflict of interest. For example, the ARRL is certainly involved in publishing licensing study guides, but the League has proven to the FCC that it maintains a separation between the publishing aspects and the VEC functions.

VECs coordinate the scheduling of dates and times for exams set by the local VE teams. A VEC may coordinate scheduling of testing opportunities even in other countries. For example, the ARRL/VEC has VE teams in Saudi Arabia, Japan, West Germany and New Zealand. A VE team is free to administer exams anywhere in the world.

It's the VEC's job to accredit a broad range of hams to be Volunteer Examiners, regardless of race, sex, religion or national origin. A VEC may not refuse to accredit a volunteer on the basis of membership (or lack thereof) in an Amateur Radio organization, nor on the basis of the person accepting or declining to accept reimbursement. However, a VEC must not accredit a volunteer to be an examiner if (1) he or she does not meet the VE qualifications outlined previously; (2) the FCC refuses to accept the services of the volunteer; (3) the VEC determines that the volunteer is not competent to perform the function of a VE; or (4) the VEC determines that questions of the volunteer's integrity or honesty could compromise the exams.

At the completion of each exam, the VEs collect the candidates' application forms, answer sheets and test results and forwards them to the VEC. Then, the VEC records the date and place of the test, the names of the VEs and their qualifications, the names of the candidates, test results and any related information. It screens applications for completeness and authenticity, and forwards them within 10 days to the FCC's Gettysburg licensing unit. The VEC must have exam records available upon FCC request.

Interim Identification

If you qualify for a new license, you may use your new privileges immediately. The FCC has established temporary identifier codes for each class of license. This code is a slant (/) followed by a two-letter group: KT for Technician class, AG for General class, AA for Advanced class, and AE for Amateur Extra class. The ID code must be shown on the certificate issued to you when you successfully complete your exam. It must be added as a suffix to your call sign when you operate with newly won privileges, until your permanent license arrives.

Question Pools

Question pools are large numbers of questions arranged by topic from which specific question sets for tests are extracted. Pools exist for each written test element; they are developed by all VECs cooperating together. Amateur Extra class VEs are allowed to prepare questions for the pool, and question sets for specific exams, for any element. Advanced class VEs may prepare questions for Technician [Element 3(A)] and General class [Element 3(B)] written exams only. General class VEs may prepare questions for written Element 3(A) (Technician class) test only.

To keep question pools current, they are changed in accordance with a published schedule. The pools must contain at least 10 times the number of questions required for a single exam. For example, the Advanced class test consists of 50 questions, so the pool must have at least 500 questions available. Thus, while a candidate can see the exact questions that might appear on his exam, he won't know which 50 will show up.

The question pools must be published and made available to the public prior to their use in making a question set. No question may appear on an exam unless it appears in the appropriate, current question pool!

Examination Expense Reimbursement

FCC allows VEs and VECs to charge exam fees to recover their out-of-pocket expenses incurred in preparing, processing and administering exams of Technician class and higher. However, there is a ceiling on fees, announced annually by FCC. The basis for the maximum fee allowable is $4.00 for 1984 adjusted annually each January 1 thereafter for changes in the Consumer Price Index. The 1991 lid is $5.27 per exam.

VEs and VECs are required to keep records of out-of-pocket expenses and reimbursements collected for each exam session. Written certifications must be filed with the FCC each year that all expenses for the past year were necessarily and prudently incurred. All records concerning expenses and reimbursements must be kept by VEs and VECs for three years, and must be available to FCC upon request. VEs must forward their certifications to their VEC by January 15; VECs forward the VEs' and their own certification to the FCC by January 31 of each year. VECs must disaccredit any VE who does not file a certification.

VE Conduct

No VE may administer or certify any exam by fraudulent means or for monetary or other gift including reimbursement in excess of the permitted amount. Violations may result in the revocation or suspension of the VE's license.

Here's what can happen:

News Item: FCC REVOKES LICENSES—The FCC on February 3 issued an Order of Revocation and Affirmation in the case of a group of 11 amateurs from Puerto Rico who, according to the FCC, committed fraud in obtaining amateur licenses or upgrades, or who fraudulently certified that others had passed examinations for amateur licenses.

The Order stated that the violations arose in connection with three VEC sessions held in Guaynabo, Puerto Rico, on August 16, August 30 and October 4, 1986. The FCC found that the examiners for those sessions had assisted others in obtaining amateur licenses by fraudulent means, and had misrepresented material facts to the FCC. The candidates were found to have obtained amateur licenses by fraudulent means.

Two of the 11 amateurs had earlier surrendered their licenses for cancellation, rendering their cases moot. Three of the examiners, due to what the Commission described as their exemplary cooperation, had their operator licenses suspended for six months, and their station licenses were not revoked. The remaining six amateurs had their operator licenses suspended for the remainder of the license term and their station licenses revoked.

These investigations were carried out by the FCC field office in San Juan, Puerto Rico. (from *The ARRL Letter*)

News Item: FCC INVALIDATES LICENSES—The ARRL/VEC has received notification that the FCC has voided the upgrades of 23 amateurs in the New York City area.

The session in question was administered by a VEC in January 1986, and has been under investigation by both the FCC and the VEC for irregularities. The VE Team Liaison was disaccredited in November of 1986 for irregularities detected in several sessions that year. (Liaisons are responsible for test material security while in the possession of the VE team.)

Each individual's license class (if any) reverts to the class that he or she held prior to the test. The individuals *are* still eligible to apply for upgrades. (from *The ARRL Letter*)

POSTSCRIPT: 75 YEARS OF LICENSING

Prior to 1912, there was no licensing, no regulations, no governing body to oversee "wireless" activities on the airways. Before long, however, it became evident to federal authorities that some regulation was needed to maintain order: Conflicts between amateur stations and those used by the Navy and commercial services were on the increase. The first regulation came in the form of licensing.

The era of mandatory licensing began when the Department of Commerce and Labor, under the authority of the Radio Act of 1912, created the Amateur First Grade and Amateur Second Grade operator licenses. The two classes bestowed identical privileges and, at least theoretically, required identical qualifications.

Amateur First Grade applicants took written tests on radio laws, regulations, and the proper adjustment and operation of equipment. The code sending and receiving tests, originally 5 WPM, increased to 10 WPM by 1919. Candidates for Amateur Second Grade, in contrast, certified to Radio Inspectors by mail that they could meet these requirements but were unable to attend an examination.

Until 1933, station and operator licenses were issued as separate, diploma-sized-certificates. The type of station license held (originally General, Special or Restricted) determined permissible operating wavelengths and power.

In 1923, the Department of Commerce created the Amateur Extra First Grade, a license so special it was printed on pink paper! Only Amateur Extra First Grade licensees thereafter qualified for "Special" station licenses, which had distinctive call signs and conveyed CW privileges on wavelengths longer than 200 meters.

Qualifications for the new class included two years' experience as a licensed operator and a written examination that, among other items, required the applicant to diagram a transmitter and receiver and then explain their principles of operation. The code tests were given at 20 WPM, the speed required of Commercial First Class operators.

As amateur interests shifted to short waves, the Amateur Extra First Grade's popularity declined. Only six such licenses were issued in 1926, and the class was discontinued the following year. Reinstated in 1928 with new privileges (described later) added in 1929, the class attracted several hundred licensees most years until its permanent deletion in 1933.

The Radio Act of 1927 transferred the power to issue station licenses to the Federal Radio Commission while preserving the authority of the Commerce Department's Radio Division to issue operator licenses. Months later, the Radio Division redesignated the Amateur First and Second Grade classes as Amateur Class and Temporary Amateur, respectively. To First Grade licensees, the change meant little more than a new name. Temporary Amateur differed from the previous Second Grade, however, in that the former expired in one year and (after 1932) could not be renewed. Hams could no longer indefinitely avoid taking an examination.

In late 1929, the Radio Division began endorsing Amateur Extra First Grade licenses for "unlimited radiotelephone privileges." Initially, the endorsement authorized voice privileges on the 20-meter band. In 1932, the endorsement became available to other amateurs having at least one year of experience, upon passing a special test on radiotelephone subjects. At the same time, phone use of 75 meters was also reserved to holders of endorsed licenses.

The Radio Division merged with the Federal Radio Commission in 1932. A year

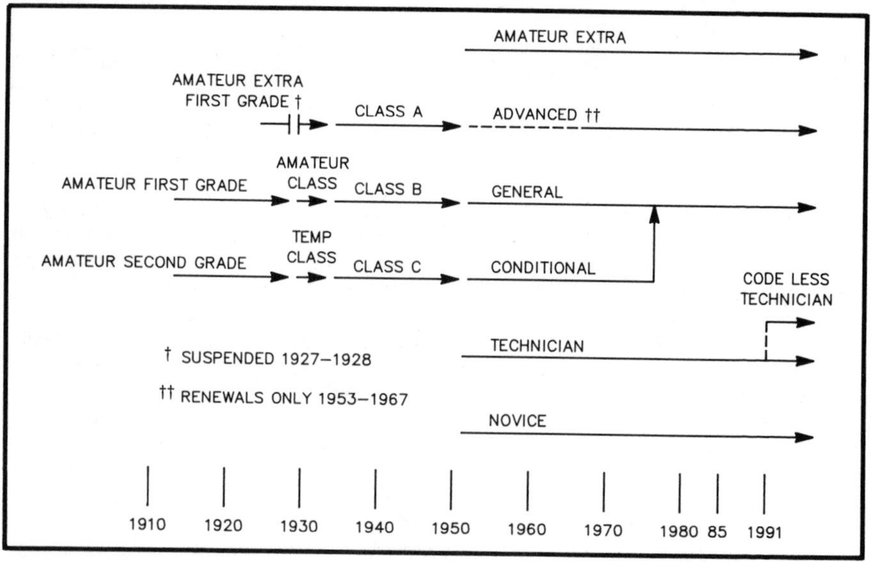

Fig 3—The evolution of Amateur Radio licensing over the past eight decades.

later, the FRC completely revised the amateur regulations. Station and operator licenses were thereafter combined on a single, wallet-sized card.

The Amateur's basic license was endorsed as Class A, B or C. All three classes required code tests at 10 WPM (13 WPM after 1936). Class A conveyed exclusive phone use on 20 and 75 meters. It required one year of prior experience and a written examination on radiotelephone and radiotelegraph theory and amateur regulations.

Classes B and C conveyed all privileges other than those reserved to Class A. The written test for those classes was less comprehensive than that for Class A with regard to radiotelephone theory. The two classes differed in that Class C written examinations were furnished by mail to applicants residing at least 125 miles from the nearest FRC quarterly examining point. Class C code tests were administered by Class A and B licensees acting as volunteer examiners.

Amateur Extra First Grade licensees qualified for Class A privileges upon renewal. Amateur Class licensees were grandfathered into Class B. Temporary Amateur licenses could not be renewed, however, so holders of this class had to qualify anew in Class B or C upon expiration of their licenses.

The Federal Communications Commission succeeded the FRC in 1934. It revised the regulations in 1951 to create the license class names that are familiar today. Advanced, General and Conditional licenses replaced Classes A, B and C, respectively. The Advanced class was closed to new applicants in January 1953, although renewal of existing licenses continued. A month later, the 20- and 75-meter "Class A Phone Bands" were opened to General and Conditional licensees.

The same rule-making action also created the Amateur Extra, Novice and Technician classes. The Amateur Extra class originally required two years' experience as a Conditional (or Class C) licensee or higher, code tests at 20 WPM and a theory examination more comprehensive than that previously given for Class A. No exclusive privileges were reserved for the new class.

The Technician ticket originally conveyed all amateur privileges above 220 MHz. Novices were initially restricted to CW operation on portions of the 11- and 80-meter bands, and voice at 145-147 MHz, at 75-W input, crystal-controlled. The first Novice licenses expired after one year and could not be renewed. After 1954, Novice and Technician exams were obtained from the FCC by mail and administered through volunteer examiners. In 1976, the system changed again: Potential Technician class licensees were required to appear before an FCC examiner, although existing Technician licensees were grandfathered in.

A glimpse at our current regulations reveals that the licensing system has undergone many changes since 1951. While it is beyond the scope of this book to examine them all, some of the most important have been the establishment of license upgrading incentives in 1967; the reopening of the Advanced class to new licensees in 1967; elimination of activity and code speed requirements for renewal; the expansion and realignment of Novice and Technician frequency privileges, notably in 1976; the increase of the Novice power level, the removal of the crystal-control requirement and the merger of Conditional licenses into the General class in 1976; the extension of license terms to 10 years, in 1983; and Novice Enhancement in 1987.

On February 14, 1991, the FCC removed the code requirement from the Technician class license, creating the first codeless license class in the US. Ever since the early days, the Amateur Service has been in a constant state of evolution, and there is every reason to believe that the Amateur Radio of another decade from now will look quite different. Stay tuned!

Chapter Three

Antennas

We radio amateurs consider an antenna a thing of beauty, the essential conduit to the exciting world of Amateur Radio communication. Amateurs have been erecting antennas and support structures (such as towers, poles and the like) for nearly a century. During this same time, local municipalities have adopted zoning ordinances and regulations as part of their duty to preserve what the law calls the public health, safety, convenience, welfare and property values. Beauty is in the eye of the beholder, of course, whether it be in terms of a five-element monobander atop a 65-foot tower or a large billboard sign advertising a local bistro, groundbreaking for another shopping mall or an addition on your home. All these matters are affected by zoning. You shouldn't get the impression that hams have been singled out for attention by local politicians. However, the role of local regulators has often proved incompatible with the legitimate desire of radio amateurs to put up the most effective antennas possible within their individual circumstances.

Restrictions imposed on amateur antennas come in more than one flavor. Besides public zoning ordinances, nongovernmental private deed restrictions and covenants specific to a particular parcel of land are quite common. So, don't buy the beer and pizza for your antenna-raising party until you've done your homework. Before we delve into the critically important world of local zoning and covenants, however, a word about the few antenna restrictions imposed by Uncle Sam is in order.

FEDERAL RESTRICTIONS

Fortunately, Part 97 is silent as to any antenna limitations, except in unusual isolated cases, as follows:

- You are obliged to protect FCC monitoring stations from harmful interference if you're operating within one mile of one. The location of each monitoring facility and further discussion is found in Chapter 4.
- You must notify the Interference Office of the National Radio Astronomy Observatory if you intend to put up a repeater or beacon antenna in what is called the National Radio Quiet Zone, a small area in Maryland, Virginia and West Virginia, the coordinates of which are defined in Chapter 4.
- You must notify the FCC on Form 854 and the FAA (Federal Aviation Administration) on Form 7460-1 if you are planning to put up a tower more than 200 feet high. The rules also require FCC and FAA notification for some towers 200 feet or lower adjacent to airports.
- If you have filled out a Form 610 lately to renew/modify your license or to sit for an exam, you've noticed that Question 9 asks if your application would have a significant environmental effect or will be located near a site of historical significance, according to §1.307 of the FCC rules. Virtually everyone answers no. See §§1.305-1.319 of the FCC rules, as well as Part 17, "Construction, Marking and Lighting of Antenna Structures," for further details. These rules are available from ARRL HQ.

Federal Communications Commission

Request for Approval of Proposed Amateur Radio Antenna and Notification of Action

Approved by OMB
3060-0139
Expires 3/31/89

Instructions:

- Complete this form only if the height of the antenna will exceed -
  60.96 meters (200 feet) or -
  1/100 of the minimum distance between the antenna site and any aircraft landing area.
- Mail this application to the FCC, Antenna Survey Branch, Washington, D.C. 20554.
- See Statements on back.

FCC USE ONLY

Approved by:

Date:

☐ No obstruction marking required.

☐ Obstruction marking required.

☐ Form 715 par. ________

☐ Form 715A par. ________

1. First Name　　M.I.　　Last Name

2. Mailing Address: Number & Street　　Telephone No. (　　)

City　　State　　ZIP Code　　3. Amateur Call Sign

4. Antenna Location

NOTE: To find the north latitude, west longitude, and site elevation of the antenna location, use a 7.5 minute topographic quadrangle map. This may be purchased from the U.S. Geological Survey, Washington, D.C. 20242 or U.S. Geological Survey, Denver, Colorado 80225. You must determine your north latitude and west longitude to the nearest second.

	Degrees	Minutes	Seconds
North Latitude			

	Degrees	Minutes	Seconds
West Longitude			

5. Check the type of support structure proposed for the antenna. ☐ Tower ☐ Pole ☐ Bldg. ☐ Other (specify) ________

6 (a) Give the elevation of the ground above mean sea level at antenna site . . . ________ feet
(b) Give the overall height of the antenna structure above ground level . . . . . ________ feet
(c) The overall height above mean sea level is (add 6(a) and 6(b)) . . . . ________ feet

7. Will this antenna require notification of proposed construction to the FAA? ☐ Yes ☐ No (See FCC Rules & Regulations Section 17.7 & 17.14) If "Yes" give the following information:

Location of FAA Office Notified	Date of Notification	FAA Study Number

8. Will the antenna share an existing structure? ☐ Yes ☐ No If "Yes" give the following information:

Name of Licensee	FCC Call Sign	Radio Service

I certify that I am the above-named applicant and that all statements made on this application and any attachments hereto are true and complete to the best of my knowledge.

Signature　　Date　　**A willfully false statement is a criminal offense; U.S. Code, Title 18, Section 1001**

FCC USE ONLY

When validated by the FCC Seal, this form and any attachment(s) become part of your amateur radio station license. Keep it with your station files.
NOTE: THIS IS NOT AN AUTHORIZATION TO TRANSMIT.

Licensee's Name	Amateur Call Sign	Location of Antenna City	State

Antenna Coordinates

North Latitude	West Longitude
Degrees - Minutes - Seconds	Degrees - Minutes - Seconds

Remarks:

NOT VALID WITHOUT FCC SEAL

☐ Antenna height approved at ________ feet (AGL)

☐ No obstruction marking or lighting

☐ Marked & Lighted per FCC Form(s):

☐ 715 Par: ________

☐ 715A Par: ________

FCC 854
May 1986

Fig 1—FCC Form 854

STATEMENT REQUIRED BY THE PRIVACY ACT AND THE PAPERWORK REDUCTION ACT

The Communications Act of 1934 authorizes solicitation of personal information requested in this application. The information is to be used principally to determine if the benefits requested are consistent with the public interest, convenience and necessity.

Commission staff will routinely use the information to evaluate and render a judgment as to whether to grant or deny this application.

If all of the requested information is not provided, the application may be returned without action or processing may be delayed while a request is made to provide the missing information. Therefore, extreme care should be exercised in making certain that all the information requested is provided. Your response is required to obtain this approval.

Limited file material may be included in the Commission Computer Facility. Where a possible violation of law is indicated, the records may, as a matter of routine use, be referred to the Commission's General Counsel and forwarded to other appropriate agencies charged with responsibilities of investigating or prosecuting such violations.

THE FOREGOING NOTICE IS REQUIRED BY THE PRIVACY ACT OF 1974, P.L. 93-579, DECEMBER 31, 1974, 5 U.S.C. 552a (e) (3) AND THE PAPERWORK REDUCTION ACT OF 1980, P.L. 96-511, DECEMBER 11, 1980, 44 U.S.C. 3507.

HOW AND WHERE TO NOTIFY FAA

Forward one completed set of FAA Form 7460-1 to the Chief, Air Traffic Division, Federal Aviation Administration, (Name of office - see below), for the office having jurisdiction over the area within which the proposed construction or alteration will be located. The geographic area of jurisdiction for each FAA office is indicated below:

ADDRESSES OF THE FAA REGIONAL AREA OFFICES

AAL - Alaskan Region

Alaskan Regional Office
Air Traffic Division
701 "C" Street
Anchorage, AK 99513
Mail Address
701 "C" Street Box 14
Anchorage, AK 99513
Tel. (907) 271-5892

ANM - Northwest Mountain Region

Northwest Mountain Regional Office
Air Traffic Division
17900 Pacific Hwy South
C-68966
Seattle, WA 98168
Tel. (206) 431-2530

AGL - Great Lakes Region

Great Lakes Regional Office
Air Traffic Division
2300 East Devon Avenue
Des Plaines, IL 60018
Tel. (312) 694-7458

ACE - Central Region

Central Regional Office
Air Traffic Division
601 East 12th Street
Kansas City, MO 64106
Tel. (816) 374-3408

AEA - Eastern Region

Eastern Regional Office
Air Traffic Division
JFK International Airport
Federal Building
Jamaica, NY 11430
Tel. (718) 917-1228

ANE - New England Region

New England Regional Office
Air Traffic Division
12 New England Executive Park
Burlington, MA 01803
Tel. (617) 273-7150

AWP - Western-Pacific Region

Western-Pacific Regional Office
Air Traffic Division
15000 Aviation Boulevard
Hawthorne, CA 90260
Mail Address
P.O. Box 92007
Worldway Postal Center
Los Angeles, CA 90009
Tel. (213) 297-1182

ASW - Southwest Region

Southwest Regional Office
Air Traffic Division
4400 Blue Mound Road
Fort Worth, TX 76101
Mail Address
P.O. Box 1689
Fort Worth, TX 76101
Tel. (817) 624-4911 Ext. 306

ASO - Southern Region

Southern Regional Office
Air Traffic Division
3400 Whipple Street
East Point, GA 30344
Mail Address
P.O. Box 20636
Atlanta, GA 30320
Tel. (404) 763-7646

FCC 854
May 1986

U. S. GOVERNMENT PRINTING OFFICE: 1985—494-355

DO NOT REMOVE CARBONS

Form Approved OMB No. 2120-0001

US Department of Transportation
Federal Aviation Administration

NOTICE OF PROPOSED CONSTRUCTION OR ALTERATION

Aeronautical Study Number

1. Nature of Proposal

A. Type	B. Class	C. Work Schedule Dates
☐ New Construction	☐ Permanent	Beginning ________
☐ Alteration	☐ Temporary (Duration ______ months)	End ________

3A. Name and address of individual, company, corporation, etc. proposing the construction or alteration. *(Number, Street, City, State and Zip Code)*

( ) ________
area code Telephone Number

B. Name, address and telephone number of proponent's representative if different than 3 above.

2. Complete Description of Structure

A. Include effective radiated power and assigned frequency of all existing, proposed or modified AM, FM, or TV broadcast stations utilizing this structure

B. Include size and configuration of power transmission lines and their supporting towers in the vicinity of FAA facilities and public airports

C. Include information showing site orientation, dimensions, and construction materials of the proposed structure

(if more space is required, continue on a separate sheet.)

4. Location of Structure

A. Coordinates *(To nearest second)*	B. Nearest City or Town, and State	C. Name of nearest airport, heliport, flightpark, or seaplane base
° ' " Latitude	(1) Distance to 4B Miles	(1) Distance from structure to nearest point of nearest runway
° ' " Longitude	(2) Direction to 4B	(2) Direction from structure to airport

5. Height and Elevation *(Complete to the nearest foot)*

A. Elevation of site above mean sea level	
B. Height of Structure including all appurtenances and lighting *(if any)* above ground, or water if so situated	
C. Overall height above mean sea level *(A + B)*	

D. Description of location of site with respect to highways, streets, airports, prominent terrain features, existing structures, etc. Attach a U.S. Geological Survey quadrangle map or equivalent showing the relationship of construction site to nearest airport(s). *(if more space is required, continue on a separate sheet of paper and attach to this notice.)*

Notice is required by Part 77 of the Federal Aviation Regulations (14 C.F.R. Part 77) pursuant to Section 1101 of the Federal Aviation Act of 1958, as amended (49 U.S.C. 1101). Persons who knowingly and willingly violate the Notice requirements of Part 77 are subject to a fine (criminal penalty) of not more than $500 for the first offense and not more than $2,000 for subsequent offenses, pursuant to Section 902(a) of the Federal Aviation Act of 1958, as amended (49 U.S.C. 1472(a)).

I HEREBY CERTIFY that all of the above statements made by me are true, complete, and correct to the best of my knowledge. In addition, I agree to obstruction mark and/or light the structure in accordance with established marking & lighting standards if necessary.

Date	Typed Name/Title of Person Filing Notice	Signature

FOR FAA USE ONLY *FAA will either return this form or issue a separate acknowledgement.*

The Proposal:

☐ Does not require a notice to FAA.

☐ Is not identified as an obstruction under any standard of FAR, Part 77, Subpart C and would not be a hazard to air navigation.

☐ Is identified as an obstruction under the standards of FAR, Part 77, Subpart C, but would not be a hazard to air navigation.

☐ Should be obstruction ☐ marked, ☐ lighted per FAA Advisory Circular 70/7460-1, Chapter(s) ________

☐ Obstruction marking and lighting are not necessary.

Remarks:

Supplemental Notice of Construction FAA Form 7460-2 is required any time the project is abandoned, or

☐ At least 48 hours before the start of construction.

☐ Within five days after the construction reaches its greatest height.

This determination expires on ________________ unless:

(a) extended, revised or terminated by the issuing office;
(b) the construction is subject to the licensing authority of the Federal Communications Commission and an application for a construction permit is made to the FCC on or before the above expiration date. In such case the determination expires on the date prescribed by the FCC for completion of construction, or on the date the FCC denies the application.

NOTE: Request for extension of the effective period of this determination must be postmarked or delivered to the issuing office at least 15 days prior to the expiration date.

If the structure is subject to the licensing authority of the FCC, a copy of this determination will be sent to that Agency.

Issued In	Signature	Date

FAA Form 7460-1 (8-85)

DO NOT REMOVE CARBONS

Fig 2—FAA Form 7460-1

Don't worry: 99% of all amateurs will be unaffected by these special cases. Most of the time you don't need to be concerned with these restrictions. That is, you will not come up against these few antenna restrictions specified or alluded to in Part 97 unless you plan to put up a monster 201-foot tower or live near an airport runway. However, most amateurs need to be aware (and beware) of the ordinances and covenants that serve to limit the location and height of even modest antennas.

QUESTIONS-AND-ANSWERS— ANTENNAS NEAR AIRPORTS

Q. I live near an airport. What regulation must I keep in mind when putting up my tower?

A. First, ask yourself the following questions. Is the airport available for public use and listed in the *Airport Directory* of the current *Airman's Information Manual* or in either the *Alaska* or *Pacific Airman's Guide and Chart Supplement*? Is it an airport or heliport under construction that is the subject of a notice or proposal on file with the FAA, and except for military airports, is it clearly indicated that the airport will be available for public use? Is it an airport or heliport that is operated by the US armed forces?

If the answer to any of these questions is "yes," then you must file FAA Form 7460-1 with FAA and FCC Form 854 with FCC, and await approval for your antenna structure, if it is to be higher than 61 meters (200 feet) above ground, or:

1) more than 1 meter (3.25 feet) higher than the airport elevation for each 100 meters (325 feet) from the nearest runway longer than 1 kilometer (3250 feet), a slope of 100 to 1, within 6.1 kilometers (3¾ miles) (refer to Figure 3);

2) more than 2 meters (6.5 feet) higher than the airport elevation for each 100 meters (325 feet) from the nearest runway shorter than 1 kilometer (3250 feet), a slope of 50 to 1, within 3.1 kilometers (2 miles) (refer to Figure 4); or

3) more than 4 meters (13 feet) higher than the airport elevation for each 100 meters (325 feet) from the nearest helicopter landing pad within 1.5 kilometers (4875 feet), a slope of 25 to 1 (refer to Figure 5).

For example, your antenna tower, a mile away from a runway longer than 3250 feet, must be within the glide slope of 100 to 1 if you want to avoid the hassle of notifying FCC/FAA on all those forms. A convenient equation for determining this height is *distance from nearest runway in feet* divided by the *slope*. In your case, that's 5280 feet/100 = 52.8 feet of tower height.

Note that you can always put up an antenna up to 20 feet high above the ground and other natural features, or on top of your house (or other manmade objects except antenna towers)—these antennas are exempt from the rules described above.

Also note that because of recent legislation, the FAA now has certain new authority over air-to-ground communications; there have been cases where FAA has objected to amateur antenna installations based on RFI concerns. If you should experience a problem of this sort, please contact ARRL HQ for assistance.

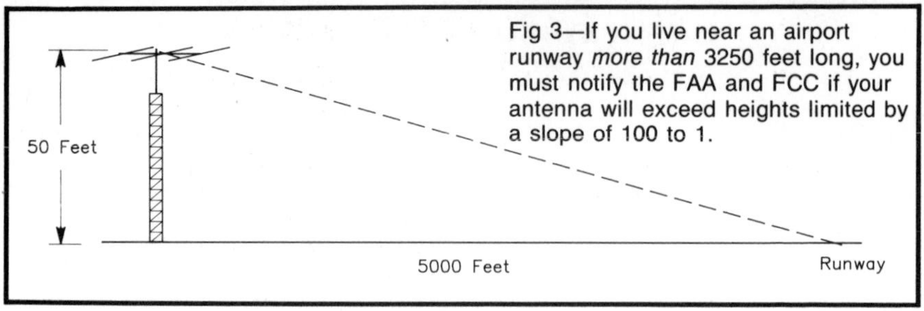

Fig 3—If you live near an airport runway *more than* 3250 feet long, you must notify the FAA and FCC if your antenna will exceed heights limited by a slope of 100 to 1.

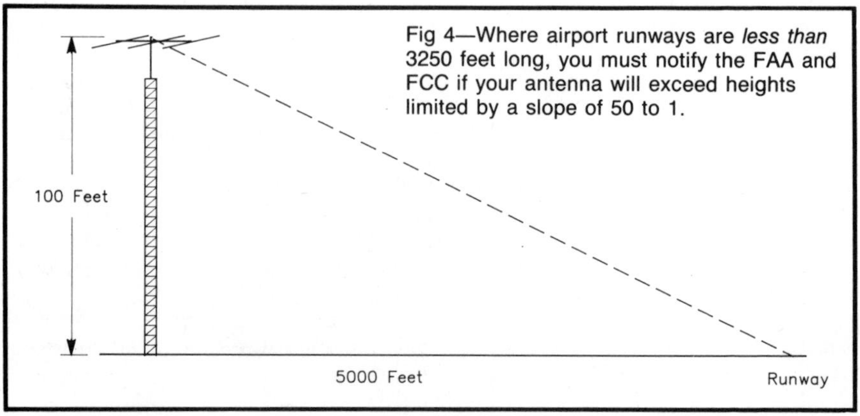

Fig 4—Where airport runways are *less than* 3250 feet long, you must notify the FAA and FCC if your antenna will exceed heights limited by a slope of 50 to 1.

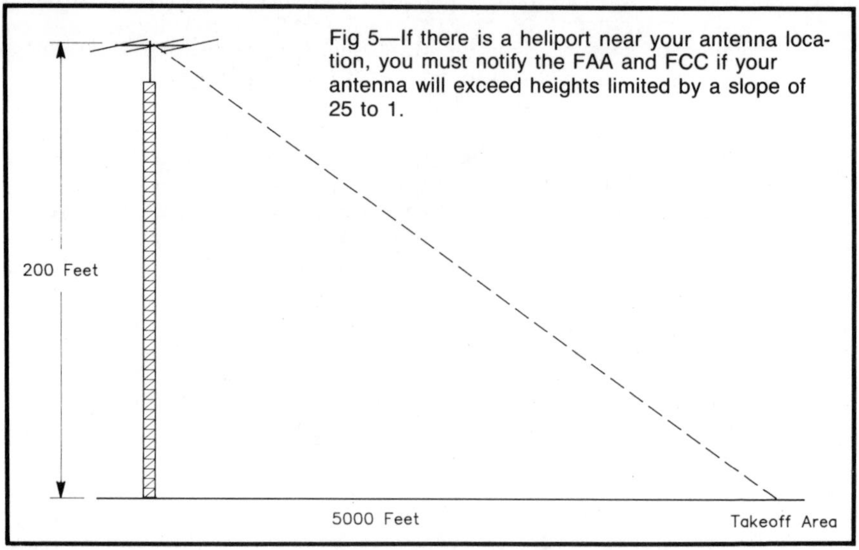

Fig 5—If there is a heliport near your antenna location, you must notify the FAA and FCC if your antenna will exceed heights limited by a slope of 25 to 1.

LOCAL ZONING ORDINANCES

In the past, amateurs relied on their powers of persuasion when dealing with local officials. Conflicts between amateurs and local authorities over the antenna height, placement in the yard, number of antennas on a particular support structure (a tower, for example), and the like, had become quite common. In the absence of detailed federal regulations governing amateur antennas (except for those aspects discussed previously), municipal leaders often fill in the void and used their broad discretion in public health and safety matters to enact regulations that limit antennas and supporting structures. The people who write these regulations have a lot of other things on their minds, so these regulations seldom take into account your need for an antenna of certain dimensions and height to be effective (for working DXpeditions, running phone patches to the South Pole and so on), so conflicts arise.

The situation reached epidemic proportions in the early 1980s, and amateurs who invested family savings in fighting local zoning, building code and covenant restrictions in courts around the country were losing. This happened because there was no clear statement of any federal interest in the matter by the FCC. The courts held that the FCC certainly regulates radio, but since the FCC had issued no statement restraining the zoning power of cities and counties, the traditionally local interest in zoning regulations which protects the public generally superseded the interests of the individual amateur.

By October of 1983, the ARRL Board of Directors reviewed the adverse court decisions and realized that antenna restrictions would continue to be a major stumbling block unless a statement of federal preemption emerged from the FCC. On July 16, 1984, the League filed a formal request asking the FCC to issue just such a declaratory ruling that would declare void all local ordinances that preclude or significantly inhibit effective, reliable amateur communications. Many hundreds of comments were filed when FCC established a pleading cycle, labeled PRB-1. ("PRB" is the designation for the FCC's Private Radio Bureau, the Bureau in the FCC's internal organization that handles Amateur Radio matters). Comments were filed by amateurs, zoning authorities and city planners.

September 19, 1985 was a red-letter day in the history of Amateur Radio, as the FCC issued its now famous PRB-1 declaratory *Memorandum Opinion and Order*, which says, in pertinent part, that "state and local regulations that operate to preclude amateur communications in their communities are in direct conflict with federal objectives and must be preempted." See Appendix for the complete text of PRB-1.

May 31, 1989 marked another milestone in the history of Amateur Radio, when the Commission adopted the revised and reorganized Part 97. §97.15(e) of the new rules codifies the essence of the PRB-1 ruling: ". . . State and local regulation of a station antenna structure must not preclude amateur service communications. Rather, it must reasonably accommodate such communications, and must constitute the minimum practicable regulation to accomplish the state or local authority's legitimate purpose."

The specific holding of PRB-1 has been of extreme benefit to amateurs and, with only a few exceptions, has encouraged open cooperation and dialogue between the communities seeking to regulate amateur antennas and we amateurs ourselves. Now that important language of PRB-1 has been incorporated into the FCC rules themselves, the federal interest and official FCC policy with respect to amateur communications can be even more easily demonstrated to municipal officials, who need to be educated by you and your fellow hams.

COMMON QUESTIONS-AND-ANSWERS—PRB-1

Q. My city has an ordinance that clearly prohibits ham radio antenna installations. What does PRB-1 and its inclusion in §97.15(e) mean for me?

A. PRB-1, cited as "Amateur Radio Preemption, 101 FCC2d 952 (1985)," is a limited preemption of local zoning ordinances. It delineates three rules for local municipalities to follow in regulating antenna structures: (1) state and local regulations which operate to preclude amateur communications are in direct conflict with federal objectives and must be preempted; (2) local regulations which involve placement, screening or height of antennas based on health, safety or aesthetic considerations must be crafted to reasonably accommodate amateur communications; and (3) such local regulations must represent the minimum practicable regulation to accomplish the local authority's legitimate purpose. PRB-1 is codified in the FCC rules in a more concise manner at §97.15(e). Of course, what is "reasonable" depends on all the circumstances, which may mean whose ox is being gored! For further suggestions about what to do when you are faced with a restrictive ordinance, see "Interacting with Municipal Officials," later in this chapter.

Q. How can the federal government limit the local zoning power of the mayor, city council or zoning board, who are much closer to the local land use conditions and the local community?

A. PRB-1 recognizes that local leaders can regulate amateur installations to ensure the safety and health of persons in the community. This general function has been termed part of a state and local government's "police powers" by legal authorities. But PRB-1, in striking a balance between the proper exercise by the city of its police powers *and* the federal interest in promoting the Amateur Radio Service, also holds that such regulations cannot be so restrictive that amateur communications are impossible. Nor can the regulations be more restrictive than that necessary to accomplish the purpose of protecting the community.

The theory of PRB-1 and its incorporation into the rules at §97.15(e) is that there is a reasonable accommodation to be made between the amateur's communications needs and the obligation of the zoning authorities to protect the community's health, safety and general welfare. Just as it is the zoning official's legitimate concern, for example, that your tower doesn't come crashing down on your neighbor's house, it is the FCC's legitimate concern (as delegated to it by Congress) that you be allowed to legally put up a tower of some reasonable size so that you can successfully conduct interstate and international radio communications on the ham bands.

Q. Why doesn't PRB-1 or §97.15(e) specify a "reasonable" height?

A. Whole legal textbooks have been devoted to trying to define what's "reasonable." As discussed before, the line between legitimate amateur communication goals and the local authority's interests must be determined on a case-by-case basis on a local level. It's true that the FCC declined to indicate what it considered a reasonable height below which a city cannot regulate antennas. What might be reasonable in one area might not be reasonable in others. For example, erecting a full-size 80-meter Yagi atop a 150-foot tower behind a townhouse in a densely populated suburb would probably not be considered reasonable. Yet the same antenna might be entirely acceptable in a more rural environment. As a general principle, however, a municipality that establishes a blanket height limitation of any type, especially one which does not permit at least 65 feet of antenna height, will have a difficult time justifying that limitation as a technical matter in light of PRB-1.

Q. Now that PRB-1 and §97.15(e) have put the brakes on local zoning authorities, can I just put my antennas up to what I consider a reasonable height and assume that the ordinance in my city is in violation of the FCC's official policy?

A. *Absolutely not!* The PRB-1 Order and its codification in §97.15(e) is not a panacea; it's not an overnight cure by any means. If you believe your city's ordinance is not valid in light of PRB-1, it's up to *you* to establish that and get the ordinance changed by the city council or have the existing ordinance declared invalid by the courts. To violate the ordinance, or to put up an antenna without a permit, can subject you to serious fines and even criminal penalties. In encouraging local municipalities to pay appropriate attention to the federal interest in amateur communications, the FCC said that if you believe the local zoning authorities have been overreaching in terms of interfering with your ability to operate Amateur Radio, you can use the PRB-1 document and the FCC rule to bring FCC policies to their attention. The bottom line is that it's still up to you to *prove* that the existing ordinance is not in accord with PRB-1.

Q. What do I need to do to prove that the ordinance in my city is in violation of PRB-1?

A. Essentially, the issue is one of engineering evidence. You should be able to establish that you need an antenna of a certain height to reliably communicate on HF, VHF and/or UHF as the case may be. Your city is usually concerned, moreover, with issues of aesthetics, safety, property values and RFI. As to the interrelated issues of aesthetics and property values, the city's interests must, of course, be balanced against yours. You probably can't convince your busybody neighbor that a three-element tribander looks "good" if he or she feels otherwise by inclination. It can, however, be established one way or another what effect, if any, an antenna of a certain height will have on property values. Studies conducted by ARRL have shown that nearby antennas have *no effect whatsoever* on property values (contact ARRL HQ for details). The written opinion of a local professional appraiser can be a crucial piece of evidence for your side. The safety factor can best be addressed through exhibition of tower manufacturer's specifications for proper installation. Be sure to explain that there is no relationship between antenna height and safety. The safety issue is best dealt with by ensuring the integrity of your installation, especially relative to the size of the base section and proper guying. Finally, as to RFI, you might assert (although remember that interference is a sensitive subject to your neighbors) that RFI is an FCC matter and not appropriate for local zoning regulation. (See Chapter 9 of this *Rule Book* for more information on RFI.) But hasten to add that your modern equipment has less chance of causing interference to television sets than a neighbor's blowdryer.

Various materials are available from ARRL HQ to assist you in this regard. Send a large SASE with $2.40 postage to the Regulatory Information Branch, at HQ for details on how to obtain a "PRB-1 Kit." HQ can also refer you to ARRL Volunteer Counsels in your area. These are ham-attorneys who will be willing to provide an initial consultation about your zoning matter free of charge. For further suggestions about resolving your zoning matter in a friendly fashion, see "Interaction with Municipal Officials," later in this chapter.

Q. What if I can't get any satisfaction from the Building Inspector and/or the Zoning Board of Appeals, and I decide to take the city to court. Has PRB-1 been used in any court cases successfully?

A. Yes. John Thernes, WM4T, successfully sued the city of Lakeside Park,

Kentucky, after he initially received an adverse determination by a Federal District Court Judge. WM4T had applied in 1982 for a building permit for a 78-foot tower and antennas. The city denied his application, claiming that the zoning ordinance did not permit antennas and support structures. Thernes sued the city, but a US District Court dismissed his complaint, noting that there was no statement from the FCC preempting local zoning ordinances. WM4T appealed to the US Court of Appeals for the Sixth Federal Circuit (which covers Kentucky), and on the eve of oral argument in that case, the FCC came out with PRB-1. That was enough for the Appeals Court to send the case back to the District Court for reconsideration.

The same District Judge who had ruled against WM4T previously indicated this time around that because of PRB-1, he was inclined to rule *in favor of* Thernes. By agreement of the parties, judgment was entered against the city and in favor of WM4T, and Thernes was finally able to put up a 73-foot tower. He received an award of attorney's fees as well. The judge, in the consent decree, noted that PRB-1 obligates municipalities to cooperatively arrive at an accommodation for amateur antennas in local zoning ordinances. (The final disposition of this case is cited at 62 Pike and Fisher Radio Regulations 2d, 284 (1987).)

Another US District Court Judge used PRB-1 to void an antenna ordinance in Sands Point, New York, which limited antennas to no more than 25 feet. The case had been brought by noted contester Andrew Bodony, K2LE, to overturn the denial by Sands Point officials of his application for a building permit and later a variance (which was also denied) for an 86-foot crank-up tower. The Court found PRB-1 to be a proper exercise of FCC authority and that the town's blanket 25-foot height limitation seriously interfered with the ability of K2LE to operate his Amateur Radio station. The Court also noted that there was no showing that K2LE's tower would endanger the health, safety or general welfare of neighborhood residents or was detrimental to the character of the neighborhood. The judge's decision is cited at 61 Federal Supplement 2d, 307 (1987).

Keep in mind that you should only consider taking your matter to court if you've exhausted all your options and appeals with your town government. You must observe all the legal technicalities, including deadlines, on your way to your final administrative appeal. Only then do you have grounds to take your matter to the court system. Make sure the record at the zoning-board level is as complete as possible (include every bit of evidence you can muster) because it is generally that record, that paper trail, that a court will rely on most heavily. If you then take your case to court, you must be prepared for the long haul; you must have the time, money and patience to see it through.

Q. What if I avoid all the hassle and just put up my antenna, hoping no one will notice?

A. This question is often asked because we all know of cases where one ham simply put up an antenna and didn't have any trouble, while another one in the same town, following the rules like a good citizen, applied for a building permit for his tower and had all kinds of grief from zoning authorities and/or his immediate neighbors. Remember, all it takes is *one* complaint to cause problems not only for you but, possibly *all* the other radio amateurs in town, if you haven't secured the proper permit when one is required. A ham who has no permit is in a difficult spot if he or she is found to be in violation of the building code or zoning ordinance.

INTERACTION WITH MUNICIPAL OFFICIALS

Don't be intimidated by the thought of going to city hall for a permit. Virtually all ham radio operators who own the physical area necessary for the safe installation of a tower should be able to legally erect a tower of *some* size. Here are the steps to take to enhance your chances of getting as much tower as you wish.[1]

Information Gathering

Because regulations pertaining to antennas and the way building and zoning departments (or the equivalent) process permits vary from city to city, the first and most important step is information gathering. This means either a visit or a phone call to your local building/zoning department, or the equivalent, to obtain a copy of the zoning ordinances. Don't settle for anything less than the *whole booklet* of regulations! If the clerk or secretary offers to photocopy for you only the pages that pertain to antennas, keep in mind the sections mentioned, and politely thank him or her. But then make sure to get the entire booklet (which normally costs between $5 and $15).

You should get the whole booklet because you need to know a lot more than just the sections under which the town regulates antenna heights. You need to know what procedures to follow when you apply for a permit. You will also need to know how to appeal an adverse decision if you don't get a favorable ruling from the building inspector (or the zoning enforcement officer, or the equivalent) on the first try. Furthermore, if you ever need to seek the advice of a lawyer, the first thing the attorney will need to see is the entire body of regulatory law affecting land use regulations for the town. Therefore, obtain the entire book and study the regulations carefully.

Zoning Regs Defined

But what are zoning regulations exactly? Zoning regulations are rules that establish the permitted uses and the minimum and maximum dimensional requirements of structures in established areas or "zones." Ninety-nine percent of the time, a ham will want to put up an antenna/tower at his home, which will be located in a residential zone. Since the overwhelming number of jurisdictions hold Amateur Radio to be a normal, accessory (as opposed to primary) use of residential property, it is proper in a residential zone. Similarly, such edifices as swimming pools, tennis courts and tool sheds are considered accessory structures on residential property.

But in addition to use rules, zoning regulations also establish rules as to how *high* structures are permitted to be. You may find your proposed tower being held to the same height standards as other "buildings" or "structures" permitted in a residential zone. Read the definitions section near the beginning of the zoning rules. Sometimes the definition of "building" is broad enough to include a tower, or antennas may be defined specifically. If the regulations do *not* define antennas specifically, see if they mention "accessory structures." Read the definition to see if antennas are included in that definition. You may find a section that defines flagpoles, church steeples and similar structures in language that could easily apply to towers as well.

Your town may also be concerned with building codes, which are standards relating to safety that have been agreed upon by engineers from the architectural, structural, civil and other engineering disciplines. Once the building inspector determines that your tower is proper and would not violate zoning regulations pertaining to use and dimensions, your construction must still be carried out in

[1]This section is © 1989 by Wyland Dale Clift, NA1L. Reprinted with permission, from an article that first appeared in *CQ 1989 Antenna Buyers Guide*.

accordance with building codes. Fortunately, this is rarely a problem. Tower manufacturers provide detailed specifications and plans for proper installation in accordance with all building codes.

Meeting the Building Inspector

After you have had a chance to study the regulations, you probably can tell which of the rules apply to your particular installation. If the clerk or secretary pointed out certain sections, you should look at those sections first to see if you agree. The regulations, when read in the context of your proposed antenna installation, should be understandable.

If the regulations are full of legal mumbo jumbo, however, now is the time to consult a lawyer, such as an ARRL Volunteer Counsel. But if you feel confident about your level of understanding and have familiarized yourself enough to be able to carry on an intelligent conversation about the regulations, you should make an appointment with the building inspector (or the appropriate city official). You should be prepared to discuss the proposed location, height and purpose of your structure, and you should take along the basic engineering data provided by the tower manufacturer to satisfy any building code concerns. Also, take along a rough drawing of your property that shows the location of your boundary lines, the house and other buildings nearby, and the proposed location of the tower.

The building inspector, much like a police officer walking a beat, is the first interpreter of the law—in this case the zoning law. What he or she says will be the first indication of the steps you will have to take in order to get a permit for your installation. After you present your proposal, be sure to listen carefully to what the building inspector says. Building inspectors are often willing to be helpful and grant your permit, provided you follow the correct application procedures. For example, you may need to file a map of your property drawn to scale.

If the building inspector appears negative, pay attention nevertheless to what he has to say, even if his reasoning may be wrong. It is important to thoroughly understand the basis for his opinion. Do not go into the confrontation mode with the building inspector; keep your "grid current" low! Don't ever wave a copy of PRB-1 or Part 97 in his face and "command" him to give you the permit because of federal law. He's not going to know what you're talking about, nor is he likely to make a snap decision in your favor that might get him into hot water later. If you are going to talk legal issues, moreover, he's going to want his lawyer (the town attorney) in on it.

In many situations, the building inspector will have the authority to grant a building permit or other approvals without the involvement of any of the higher-ups. This is why it's important to maintain a good relationship with him if at all possible.

Sometimes (especially if you're lucky), zoning ordinances specifically exempt antennas from the height restrictions of other structures. However, depending on how your town's ordinances are written, it may be necessary for you to seek the permission of a zoning commissioner or other land-use board. Usually this means that the zoning regulations are set up to allow antennas to a certain height limit without the need of a hearing, but if you want to exceed the "usual" height threshold, you need to apply for a special permit. This simply means that the drafters of the zoning ordinances decided that certain uses of structures could only be permitted after a public hearing and demonstration of special need.

While this undoubtedly means more red tape and delay for you if you find yourself in this situation, such a requirement in and of itself is not illegal in the eyes of the law (including PRB-1). It does provide a forum for potential opposition from neighbors, however, and preparation for the hearing is all-important.

If there is a problem, it will be one of two varieties. It may be a matter of interpretation of the ordinance by the building inspector. Or the ordinance may be written in such a way that he is unable to reasonably come up with any other interpretation. If their ordinance is prohibitive under any reasonable interpretation, you should immediately seek the advice of a lawyer.

If the problem is that you disagree with the building inspector's interpretation of the zoning regulations, that is not as serious. While you ultimately may need a lawyer to resolve the issue, you can still carry the issue yourself a little further. Tell the building inspector in a *nonconfrontational* manner that you have a different interpretation and ask him for his comments. See if you can narrow it down as to where the problem lies. If it is a problem with the way the ordinance is written, ie, under no possible interpretation can you get your permit, that is a more serious problem. It may mean that the ordinance is illegal, and therefore invalid. The town officials won't like that, and they are more apt to fight vigorously against having their ordinance invalidated. They would much rather change an interpretation for a particular situation rather than throw out their entire ordinance and have to start from scratch.

If you run into an unresolvable problem with the building inspector, you should then, as a last resort, calmly tell him about PRB-1 and §97.15(e). As mentioned previously, more often than not you will find that it does not help at the building-inspector level. At most, all you may be able to get across is that the federal government, through the FCC, has acted under a preemption order called PRB-1. You can say that local governments cannot prohibit antenna towers, nor can they unreasonably restrict them in terms of size and height. However, you really can't expect the building inspector to be equipped to engage in a lengthy discussion of the nuances of the legalities of federal preemption.

The Appeal

If there is a reasonable interpretation or even a loophole in the regulations under which you should be allowed to put up the antenna/tower, you can usually appeal that decision to your town's Zoning Board of Appeals (ZBA) or the equivalent body. If you have absolutely no alternative, you can ask the ZBA for a variance. This means you are asking the ZBA to relax the zoning rules in your case, to give you a special exemption because of some exceptional difficulty or unreasonable hardship. Variances are generally granted sparingly because it is often difficult to establish the severe hardship. Remember, too, that if you apply for a variance, you are admitting in the eyes of the law that the ordinance applies to your antenna. This means that you can't contest or challenge the applicability or the jurisdiction of the ordinance in a later proceeding.

The procedure for appealing the building inspector's ruling will be outlined in the regulations. Basically, you are given a chance to explain what Amateur Radio is and to present your alternative interpretation that would permit you to legally erect your tower or to explain that your hardship is severe enough that you ought to be allowed to put up your tower despite the zoning rules.

PRB-1 should be used to persuade the ZBA that they should adopt your more reasonable interpretation because federal law requires them to adopt as reasonable an interpretation as possible. If there is no possible interpretation of the zoning regulations that will allow your tower to go up, then tell the ZBA that PRB-1 and §97.15(e) are binding federal regulations that supersede their own law if there is a conflict. That is, their interpretation of their own zoning ordinance should be guided by the binding order that was rendered by the FCC in PRB-1. In other words, the local regulations cannot regulate in the "overkill mode." But make no mistake about it; state and local governments can, under the specific language of PRB-1, still regulate antennas for reasons of health, safety and welfare, as long as the regulations are reasonable.

Additional Guidelines for the Presentation

Here are a few other things to keep in mind when you make your presentation before the ZBA: Make sure you can establish the safety factors of your tower. On matters of safety, there can and should be *no compromise* by the municipality. If your installation does not meet building-code requirements, no board (or court, if it comes to that) will allow it. The manufacturer's specifications must be followed.

On the other hand, aesthetics and welfare, particularly the effect on the surrounding property values, are more likely to be areas of compromise by the ZBA. Your task here is basically three-fold. You have to demonstrate your *need* for the proposed tower and the *safety* of the structure, and you have to show that you have taken reasonable steps to *lessen the impact on the surrounding property.*

As mentioned previously, ARRL HQ has helpful materials to assist you in preparing for the hearing in the form of the "PRB-1 Kit." The League can also refer you to one or more ARRL Volunteer Counsels near you. Contact the Regulatory Information Branch at ARRL HQ for details.

If you haven't done so, try to gauge the opposition, if any, of your neighbors prior to the hearing. Those neighbors who show up at the hearing can either be friendly or adversarial; touching base with your neighbors in advance is a good way to transform some adversaries into persons who will actually speak in support of your position. Be prepared to answer all questions that you can anticipate. While the touchy area of radio-frequency interference (RFI) does not fall under the jurisdiction of the ZBA, your reaction to questions about RFI might be used by the ZBA members to judge your character (which could form the unwritten/unstated basis for approval or denial). A ZBA member is more likely to give the benefit of the doubt to someone who sounds like a responsible good neighbor.

If certain neighbors or ZBA members raise concerns about RFI, one of the most effective statements you can make is to explain that, while years ago the home-brew nature of ham stations may have resulted in hams being responsible for RFI, today that is hardly the case. With the present level of Amateur Radio sophistication, RFI is rarely a problem, and when it is, it is usually the fault of the stereo, TV or other home-entertainment device. But make sure to explain to the ZBA members that you will work with your neighbors to resolve any RFI problems in the rare event that RFI problems occur.

When you're making your presentation, keep it clear, concise and above all else, simple. Use a written outline so you don't forget key points, but speak directly and respectfully to the ZBA members in your own words. Avoid technical language or ham radio jargon which will be incomprehensible to nonhams. Remember, the ZBA does not, and has no reason to, care about dB, SWR, wavelengths, DX or anything else "sacred" to Amateur Radio operators. They do care about how high or how big your aerial is going to be, as well as what kind of damage it could do to a neighbor's home if it does fall. (You might point out that towers rarely fall or break, and if they do, it is generally not from the bottom.) Don't forget to emphasize the public-service nature of Amateur Radio even if all you plan to do with your antenna is to run Europeans and JAs in the DX contest on 20-meter SSB!

Make sure your demeanor is professional, and dress in a conservative businesslike manner (leave your ARES jumpsuit or your painter's pants at home). Make sure, also, not to operate in a vacuum; enlist the support of the entire Amateur Radio community and ask as many of your fellow hams as possible to show up for the hearing. A unified show of support will make a profound impression on ZBA members who are, after all, ordinary folks yet politicians at heart.

Private Restrictions

There are some circumstances under which it is legally *impossible* to erect a tower. Condominium owners are a prime example. A condo owner "owns" only that which exists *within* the confines of the four walls that forms his unit. The rest of the building and the land are either owned by someone else, or they are owned in common by all the unit owners. Unless you can persuade the condominium association to allow you to put up an antenna in a common area, you had better either concentrate on operating mobile from your car or bone up on so-called invisible or limited-space antennas in attics or crawl spaces in the ceiling. (This is most likely a violation of the condominium bylaws as well.) You cannot expect to be able to put up a tower on land or a building that you do not own outright.

Private restrictions, commonly called *CC&Rs* (covenants, conditions and restrictions) are another aspect of antenna/tower regulation that exist outside of the zoning regulatory body. CC&Rs are the "fine print" that may be referenced in the deed to your property, *especially* if you are in a planned subdivision that has underground utilities. Your best bet before proceeding with your tower plans is to take a copy of your deed to an attorney to have a limited title search done for the specific purpose of determining whether any private restrictions will affect your rights. If you're thinking about buying a new home, make sure you have a title search done *before* you sign on the dotted line. When you agree to purchase the property, you also agree to accept any and all covenants and deed restrictions on the land records, which may preclude you from being able to put up a tower at your new dream home. See "Deed Restrictions" later in this chapter.

Summary

With respect to governmental, as opposed to private, restrictions, it all boils down to one simple fact. Any licensed ham radio operator, holding title to private property of a sufficiently sized parcel of land, has the right under federal law to erect a tower and antenna subject to the reasonable regulation of local and state government.

A substantial amount of money has been spent in legal costs by several amateurs in attempts to have courts tell local governments that their idea of reasonable is *not* reasonable under PRB-1. Sometimes a clash cannot be avoided. But if you're like most of us, you want to know how best to go about putting up the highest tower you can without getting into a big legal struggle and alienating your otherwise friendly neighbors.

Emphasis from the start should be on the more practical aspects of planning a successful campaign for getting the necessary approvals:

- Be realistic about the physical limitations of your backyard.
- Go on an information-gathering mission at the local town hall to determine which officials and regulations are applicable to your proposed antenna installation.
- Then discuss your plans with the local building inspector.
- Determine whether the building inspector's interpretation of how the zoning rules apply to your plans is fair or should be respectfully challenged.
- Then, if you are dissatisfied with the inspector's interpretation, obtain information from ARRL HQ and seek legal advice from a competent attorney as to whether there is any reasonable interpretation of the regulations that would allow you to put up the tower.
- If no such interpretation presents itself, you need to seek either a variance or make a frontal assault on the ordinance as being in violation of PRB-1. Once you get into this area of the law, legal advice is often a necessity.

Most amateurs who have followed these steps have come out of it with a positive result. However, if a final decision by your local zoning board is unsatisfactory, you have the option of taking the matter to court.

DEED RESTRICTIONS

Long before zoning regulation of land existed, private restrictions in deeds controlled how land could be used. The English system of common law, which we have inherited, permitted a seller of land to impose certain restrictions on the use of that land, which the seller, even after the sale was long past, could enforce in the courts. These restrictions or covenants were included in the deed from seller to buyer. Today, as noted before, deed restrictions are typically referred to as covenants, conditions and restrictions, *CC&Rs*.

These days, covenants are commonly used, especially in new housing developments, by builders or developers as a means of controlling land use after individual parcels are sold off. Suppose that a builder has a tract of 100 homes, and is selling them one at a time. The builder, until he is able to sell all of the lots, wants to maintain uniformity so that, for example, one of the buyers cannot paint his house 20 different Day-Glo™ colors, making the remaining unsold lots less marketable.

There Goes the Neighborhood

Since the CB boom of the mid-70s, builders and developers have included antennas in the standard list of things they don't want homeowners to install while the builder is attempting to sell the remainder of the houses in the development. They are concerned that some people will find antennas or towers unattractive. So when the subdivision plan is filed in a town's land records, a list of covenants is filed as well. Every deed from the builder makes reference to the list, subjecting every buyer down the line to the restrictions.

Typically, the declaration of covenants provide that enforcement authority passes from the developer to the homeowner's association after the developer sells all the houses in the development and goes on his merry way. The homeowner's association is, among other things, charged with maintaining the aesthetics of the neighborhood, and often can determine whether any additional structures, such as a tool shed, swing set or antenna can be built at all. If a homeowner installs an antenna in violation of a covenant, the homeowner's association can bring that owner to court to enforce the covenant.

COMMON QUESTIONS-AND-ANSWERS—DEED RESTRICTIONS

Q. How can I find out if there are any deed restrictions on my land?

A. Deed restrictions and/or covenants are filed with the town clerk (or the equivalent) in your town (or county, depending on your state). These records are completely open to the public; you don't have to be a lawyer or a real-estate broker to examine land records. Some deed restrictions are mentioned in the deed you received at your closing, so check your paperwork. Such restrictions need not be mentioned in your individual deed, however. A master list of covenants, usually termed "Declaration of Covenants" or something similar, is a list of things that cannot be done on a particular tract of land. The master list may be referred to in subsequent deeds from the seller to the buyer. The land is sold to a buyer "subject to" the covenants on file.

Even if you do not buy your land from the original builder who filed them, covenants are considered to "run with the land;" they are referenced in the deed to any particular buyer. Even though you may never have seen the list of covenants on file and even though they are not fully explained in your particular deed, and yes, even though you did not buy your home directly from the builder who established them, you are nevertheless bound by them. Why? Because you voluntarily bought land which is itself subject to those restrictions, and as such, in the eyes of the law (remember, justice is blind!), you have submitted yourself to those covenants and have agreed to them. This is why attorneys and others spend hours looking through boring, old land records; they're trying to find the "land mines" before it's too late. Before you sign a contract to buy a new home, always have your attorney or other competent title searcher check the land records for covenants.

Q. How can I avoid antenna covenants when I buy my new house?

A. You can't, but you may be able to avoid surprises. Make sure that your contract for the purchase of land specifies that the sale is contingent on the absence of any deed restrictions, covenants or conditions which would prevent or restrict your ability to install an amateur antenna at least (fill in the blank) feet in height. Require that within two weeks of the signing of the sales contact, the seller must give you a notarized statement to that effect. If it turns out that there are covenants, you could attempt to obtain approval for your proposed antenna from the homeowner's association, architectural control committee or the builder, in accordance with the covenants, before signing a contract to buy the house.

Don't rely on oral representations of anyone involved. Unless you have written, unconditional authorization from whoever has the enforcement authority, you should not assume that you will be able to put your tower after you move in. Your attorney should be consulted before signing anything.

Q. Some amateurs have successfully asserted their rights to put up a tower despite of deed restrictions prohibiting them. How can this be done?

A. There are some standard defenses to covenants. The best one is to show that the restriction has not been enforced against others in the neighborhood. If there are CB antennas or other amateur antennas, it may not be possible to enforce the restriction against you. Even in this case, however, there are limitations. One court has held that the existence of TV antennas in a development where covenants prohibited all antennas did not constitute "abandonment or waiver" of the covenant. An amateur could not put up a beam because that was held to be significantly different from small TV antennas. Also, don't assume that abandonment of one covenant will extend to others. If, for example, your neighbor keeps a boat in his driveway in violation of a covenant, this would not waive an anti-antenna covenant.

There are other defenses, however. The longer a covenant goes unenforced, the more difficult it is to enforce, as courts require prompt objections to covenant violations. Further, if actions of the homeowner's association have led the amateur to believe that approval was given or that the covenants would not be enforced, you can argue that you should be allowed to keep your antenna in the air, even in the violation of a covenant.

Q. The covenants in my development do not prohibit antennas or towers, but do require the approval of the homeowner's association. How do I convince them to approve my antenna?

A. Tactics differ, but generally the best strategy is to prepare in advance for the questions you are likely to encounter: (1) how you have planned the installation to minimize visual impact; (2) how it will be safe; (3) how it will enable you to conduct emergency and public service communications for the neighborhood; (4) how it will *not* affect property values; (5) how RFI is minimized by higher antennas; and (6) that you need it to communicate effectively and reliably. Also, follow the general guidelines for the ZBA presentation as discussed previously, as applicable.

The best thing to do is sit down with your immediate neighbors on all sides, explain in a friendly way what you'd like to do, and assure them that the Voice of America is not being constructed next door to them! If you can obtain the approval of your immediate neighbors, the homeowner's association is much less likely to object. If you are anticipating much opposition, you might consider the advantages of a crank-up tower, and as a compromise, offer to keep it cranked down when you're not using it.

Q. It sounds as though the FCC, in PRB-1, has protected us from some antenna restrictions imposed by my town, but not from my neighbors. What gives?

A. The ARRL Board of Directors considers covenants the most serious cumulative problem that faces amateurs at present. The League's Legal Strategy Committee is preparing factual data as to the pervasiveness of covenants to show that nowadays deed restrictions are not simply a matter of contractual agreement between the buyer and seller. As it is the FCC's stated policy to protect its licensees against unreasonable local restrictions, the FCC should also officially announce that antenna covenants are not in accordance with public policy. The League continues to work on this problem; stay tuned.

SUMMARY

Some hams are blessed with living in communities where there are neither zoning nor covenant restrictions on their antenna farms. However, you can't assume that this is the case in your own particular situation. The time to start looking into whether its okay to put up a tower is *before* and not *after* you start pouring the concrete for your base section. If you exercise both common sense (ie, you resist the temptation to put up a Big Bertha on a city lot) and good-faith compliance with the legal procedures, you will undoubtedly be successful in securing permission for an appropriately sized tower for your antenna system. But please keep in mind that what you do, and how you go about doing it, not only affects you, it also affects all the other radio amateurs in your town, and perhaps—through precedent-setting court cases—amateurs throughout the entire United States of America.

Chapter Four

Forms, Forms, Forms —And The Gettysburg Address

LICENSE RENEWALS, MODIFICATIONS, AND APPLICATIONS: MEET THE FAMOUS FORM 610

The FCC Form 610 is the Commission's multipurpose amateur licensing form. It's the only official contact most amateurs have with FCC. Amateurs use it to apply for a new license, an upgraded license, license renewal, modification and reinstatement.

Three versions of the 610 exist for different purposes. For most, the standard FCC Form 610 is used. Foreign amateurs applying for permission to operate in the US use FCC Form 610-A. Club, military recreation and RACES station trustees use Form 610-B for station license renewal and modification purposes.

Be sure to use a current edition of the Form 610. Forms showing a revision date earlier than June 1984 are no longer valid, and will be returned if you attempt to use one. If you have any old forms, throw them away. (At the time of this writing, there are six versions of the FCC Form 610 that are valid. Only four show release dates, which are located in the lower right corner of the form: June 1984, July 1985, March 1986, September 1987 and February 1990. The other version, virtually identical to the September 1987 form, was released in February 1987, but it does not show a release date. This form has an expiration date of 12/31/89 printed in the upper right corner, however, as does the September 1987 one.) All but the latest three versions will require some modifications to the form when it is filled out, so it's best to obtain a copy of the 610 form that has an expiration date of 12/31/89 or later.

To obtain a new Form 610, 610-A or 610-B, send a business-sized, self-addressed, stamped envelope to: Federal Communications Commission, Form 610, Gettysburg, PA 17326 or: Form 610, ARRL, 225 Main St, Newington, CT 06111.

Filling Out FCC Form 610

Fig 1 shows a current FCC Form 610. Complete **Section I** if you're applying either for a new or upgraded license, or for renewal, reinstatement or modification of your present license.

Item 1—First, attach a photocopy (or the original) of your license. If you've lost the license (or it was destroyed), simply explain the circumstances in a note attached to the form.

Item 2—This item specifies the purpose of the application: new license, renewal, reinstatement, call-sign change (see Chapter 2), name change, mailing address change or station location change. Simply check the appropriate box and any corresponding blanks provided to the right of the item. For example, if you're applying for a reinstatement of your license which expired less than five years ago, you would check box 2B, despite the new 2-year statement on the form, and follow the corresponding

FEDERAL COMMUNICATIONS COMMISSION
GETTYSBURG, PA 17326

Approved OMB
3060-0003
Expires 12/31/92
See instructions for information regarding public burden estimate

APPLICATION FOR AMATEUR RADIO STATION AND/OR OPERATOR LICENSE

ADMINISTERING VEs' REPORT		EXAMINATION ELEMENTS							
Applicant is credited for:		1(A)	1(B)	1(C)	2	3(A)	3(B)	4(A)	4(B)
A. CIRCLE CLASS OF FCC AMATEUR LICENSE HELD: N T G A	Class →	(NT)	(GA)		(NTGA)	(TGA)	(GA)	(A)	
B. CERTIFICATE(S) OF SUCCESSFUL COMPLETION OF AN EXAMINATION HELD:	→	Date Issued	Date Issued	Date Issued	Date Issued	Date Issued	Date Issued	Date Issued	Date Issued
C. FCC COMMERCIAL RADIOTELEGRAPH OPERATOR LICENSE HELD:	Number: Exp. Date:								
D. EXAMINATION ELEMENTS PASSED THAT WERE ADMINISTERED AT THIS SESSION:	→								

E. APPLICANT IS QUALIFIED FOR OPERATOR LICENSE CLASS: ☐ NONE:

E1. ☐ NOVICE (Elements 1(A), 1(B), or 1(C) and 2)

E2. ☐ TECHNICIAN (Elements 1(A), 1(B), or 1(C), 2 and 3(A))
☐ GENERAL (Elements 1(B) or 1(C), 2, 3(A), and 3(B))
☐ ADVANCED (Elements 1(B) or 1(C), 2, 3(A), 3(B) and 4(A))
☐ AMATEUR EXTRA (Elements 1(C), 2, 3(A), 3(B), 4(A), and 4(B))

F. NAME OF VOLUNTEER-EXAMINER COORDINATOR: (VEC coordinated sessions only)

G. EXAMINATION SESSION LOCATION: (VEC coordinated sessions only)

H. Date of VEC coordinated examination session:

I. VEC Receipt Date:

SECTION I

1. **IF YOU HOLD A VALID LICENSE ATTACH THE ORIGINAL LICENSE OR PHOTOCOPY ON BACK OF APPLICATION. IF THE VALID LICENSE OR CERTIFICATE OF SUCCESSFUL COMPLETION OF AN EXAMINATION WAS LOST OR DESTROYED, PLEASE EXPLAIN.**

2. **CHECK ONE OR MORE ITEMS, NORMALLY ALL LICENSES ARE ISSUED FOR A 10 YEAR TERM.**

2A. ☐RENEW LICENSE—NO OTHER CHANGES → EXPIRATION DATE (Month, Day, Year)
2B. ☐REINSTATE LICENSE EXPIRED LESS THAN 2 YEARS →
2C. ☐EXAMINATION FOR NEW LICENSE
2D. ☐EXAMINATION TO UPGRADE OPERATOR CLASS — FORMER LAST NAME — SUFFIX (Jr., Sr., etc.)
2E. ☐CHANGE CALL SIGN (Be sure you are eligible—See Inst. 2E)
2F. ☐CHANGE NAME (Give former name) → FORMER FIRST NAME — MIDDLE INITIAL
2G. ☐CHANGE MAILING ADDRESS
2H. ☐CHANGE STATION LOCATION

3. CALL SIGN (If you checked 2C above, skip items 3 and 4)

4. OPERATOR CLASS OF THE ATTACHED LICENSE:

5. CURRENT FIRST NAME — M.I. — LAST NAME — SUFFIX (Jr., Sr., etc.)

6. DATE OF BIRTH __/__/__ MONTH DAY YEAR

7. CURRENT MAILING ADDRESS (Number and Street) — CITY — STATE — ZIP CODE

8. CURRENT STATION LOCATION (Do not use a P.O. Box No., RFD No., or General Delivery. See Instruction 8) — CITY — STATE

9. Would a Commission grant of your application be an action which may have a significant environmental effect as defined by Section 1.1307 of the Commission's Rules? See instruction 9. If you answer yes, submit the statement as required by Sections 1.1308 and 1.1311. ☐ YES ☐ NO

10. Do you have any other amateur radio application on file with the Commission that has not been acted upon? If yes, answer items 11 and 12. ☐ YES ☐ NO

11. PURPOSE OF OTHER APPLICATION

12. DATE SUBMITTED (Month, Day, Year)

CERTIFICATION

I CERTIFY THAT all statements herein and attachments herewith are true, complete, and correct to the best of my knowledge and belief and are made in good faith; that I am not a representative of a foreign government; that I waive any claim to the use of any particular frequency regardless of prior use by license or otherwise; and that the station to be licensed will be inaccessible to unauthorized persons.

WILLFUL FALSE STATEMENTS MADE ON THIS FORM OR ATTACHMENTS ARE PUNISHABLE BY FINE AND IMPRISONMENT U.S. CODE TITLE 18, SECTION 1001

13. SIGNATURE OF APPLICANT: (Must match Item 5)

14. DATE SIGNED:

(OVER) FCC Form 610, February 1990

Fig 1—FCC Form 610.

arrows to fill in the applicable boxes, EXPIRATION DATE in this case. See "License Terms" later in this chapter.

Important note concerning call signs: Licensees who do not already hold a call sign reflecting their license class or call sign district may request a call-sign change. All call signs are issued in sequence by the Commission, and requests by amateurs for specific call signs will *not* be honored. An amateur may swap a current call sign for another one issued in the regular sequence. According to an FCC Public Notice dated April 9, 1990, by filing a Form 610 with the FCC and requesting a change in

ATTACH THE ORIGINAL LICENSE OR PHOTOCOPY HERE

SECTION II—EXAMINATION INFORMATION

SECTION II-A FOR NOVICE OPERATOR EXAMINATION ONLY. To be completed by the Administering VEs after completing the Administering VE's Report on the other side of this form.

CERTIFICATION

I CERTIFY THAT I have complied with the Administering VE requirements stated in Part 97 of the Commission's Rules; THAT I have administered to the applicant and graded an amateur radio operator examination in accordance with Part 97 of the Commission's Rules; THAT I have indicated in the Administering VE's Report the examination element(s) the applicant passed; THAT I have examined documents held by the applicant and I have indicated in the Administering VE's Report the examination element for which the applicant is given examination credit in accordance with Part 97 of the Commission's Rules.

1A. VOLUNTEER EXAMINER'S NAME: (First, MI, Last, Suffix) *(Print or Type)*

1B. VE'S MAILING ADDRESS: (Number, Street, City, State, ZIP Code)

1C. VE'S OPERATOR CLASS: ☐ GENERAL ☐ ADVANCED ☐ AMATEUR EXTRA | **1D.** VE'S STATION CALL SIGN

1E. LICENSE EXPIRATION DATE: | **1F.** IF YOU HAVE AN APPLICATION PENDING FOR YOUR LICENSE, GIVE FILING DATE:

1G. SIGNATURE: (Must match Item 1A) | DATE SIGNED

2A. VOLUNTEER EXAMINER'S NAME: (First, MI, Last, Suffix) *(Print or Type)*

2B. VE'S MAILING ADDRESS: (Number, Street, City, State, ZIP Code)

2C. VE'S OPERATOR CLASS: ☐ GENERAL ☐ ADVANCED ☐ AMATEUR EXTRA | **2D.** VE'S STATION CALL SIGN

2E. LICENSE EXPIRATION DATE: | **2F.** IF YOU HAVE AN APPLICATION PENDING FOR YOUR LICENSE, GIVE FILING DATE:

2G. SIGNATURE: (Must match Item 2A) | DATE SIGNED

SECTION II-B FOR TECHNICIAN, GENERAL, ADVANCED, OR AMATEUR EXTRA OPERATOR EXAMINATION ONLY. To be completed by the Administering VEs after completing the Administering VE's Report on the other side of this form.

CERTIFICATION

I CERTIFY THAT I have complied with the Administering VE requirements stated in Part 97 of the Commission's Rules; THAT I have administered to the applicant and graded an amateur radio operator examination in accordance with Part 97 of the Commission's Rules; THAT I have indicated in the Administering VE's Report the examination element(s) the applicant passed; THAT I have examined documents held by the applicant and I have indicated in the Administering VE's Report the examination element(s) for which the applicant is given examination credit in accordance with Part 97 of the Commission's Rules.

1A. VOLUNTEER EXAMINER'S NAME: (First, MI, Last, Suffix) *(Print or Type)*	**1B.** VE'S STATION CALL SIGN:
1C. SIGNATURE: (Must match Item 1A)	DATE SIGNED:
2A. VOLUNTEER EXAMINER'S NAME: (First, MI, Last, Suffix) *(Print or Type)*	**2B.** VE'S STATION CALL SIGN:
2C. SIGNATURE: (Must match Item 2A)	DATE SIGNED:
3A. VOLUNTEER EXAMINER'S NAME: (First, MI, Last, Suffix) *(Print or Type)*	**3B.** VE'S STATION CALL SIGN:
3C. SIGNATURE: (Must match Item 3A)	DATE SIGNED:

FCC Form 610
February 1990

call sign (Item 2E), the applicant will be issued a call sign appropriate for his license class from the standard rotation of new call signs. All amateurs have the option of keeping their present call signs under all circumstances, even when moving to another call-sign district or upgrading to a higher-class license. The Commission will not change your call sign unless you request it and are eligible for a change. Once the change is made, however, your previous call sign cannot be reinstated. Details of the call-sign assignment system can be found later in this chapter.

Item 3—List your call sign if you hold one.

Item 4—Give your operator class and, if applicable, your operator class listed on your CSCE.

Item 5—Enter your name and any suffix such as Jr. or III. Remember that your name must agree with your signature in Item 13.

Item 6—Give your birthdate in the form of month, date and year, such as 12-25-53.

Item 7—Give your current mailing address. Remember that the address must be in the US or its territories. A postal box, RFD number or General Delivery is sufficient. Keep in mind that you will be responsible for all FCC mail sent to that address.

Item 8—Give your current station location (it may be different than that of your mailing address in Item 7). The station location address must be a specific geographical location, not a box number. This address must also be within the US or its territories. Any other location is not within FCC jurisdiction.

Item 9—Virtually all amateurs will check "no" to this major action question. A "major action" is defined by FCC as (a) a new antenna or structure, or an increase in height of an existing structure by more than 10%, which results in a final height of over 300 feet, (b) facilities which are to be located in an officially designated wilderness area, wildlife preserve area or a nationally recognized scenic and recreational area, or facilities which will affect sites significant in American history and (c) construction which involves extensive changes in surface features. If the answer to Item 9 is "yes," you must submit the required Environmental Impact Narrative Statement (EINS) along with your application. For more information, contact ARRL HQ.

Items 10, 11 and 12—If you have any other Amateur Radio application on file with the Commission that has not been acted upon (a renewal, for example), answer "yes." Enter the purpose of the other application in Item 11 and the date it was filed in Item 12.

Item 13—Sign the application certifying that your statements are true, complete and correct to the best of your knowledge.

Item 14—Date the application.

Section II-A is completed by the administering volunteer Novice examiners who passed a Novice applicant. See Novice testing discussion in Chapter 2.

Section II-B deals with Technician, General, Advanced and Extra class exams. This section is filled out by all three Volunteer Examiners (VEs) who will be administering the upgrade test to the applicant.

An exam applicant should fill out Section I prior to the examination date. If advance registration is required, the applicant should make sure the form is in the hands of the VE team before the registration cutoff date. If advance registration is not required, the applicant can simply bring the completed form to the test site. The VE Team (VET) will take it from there.

Before the test, the VET fills out the VET report for each applicant, checking the appropriate boxes, giving exam credit wherever it's due. The team usually gives the code exams first—20, 13 and 5 WPM in descending order. The tests are graded as they are completed. Then, the written tests are given and graded, and the VET fills in the appropriate boxes on the Form 610. If the applicant fails to upgrade, the application is returned. If he or she passes, the VET enters the name of the VEC in item F of the VET report. The place and date of the examination must be entered as well.

License Renewals

If you file for renewal of your unexpired license in a timely fashion (between 60 and 90 days prior to expiration is recommended), you may continue to operate until your new license arrives, even if that occurs after the expiration of your license term. If you let your license lapse before applying for renewal, you may request that it be reinstated under a grace period—see "License Terms" below.Use Form 610 for your license renewal or reinstatement application.

The Gettysburg Address

All applications except registrations for VEC-sponsored exams should be sent to FCC, Gettysburg, PA 17326. While there are no fees for filing applications for license renewal and modification, you may have to pay up to $5.27 to take a VEC-sponsored examination. The 1991 fee is $5.25 for the ARRL/VEC. If you have not received a response from the FCC concerning your application within 90 days, write to the Gettysburg FCC office. Include with your letter a photocopy of your application, or the following information: name and address, birth date, present call sign

1 The end of the line for your 610 is the FCC Licensing Division in Gettysburg, Pennsylvania.

2 Your Form 610 arrives at the FCC. It is immediately date-stamped and forwarded to the Amateur Processors. Here, *every* Form 610 that is submitted to the FCC is checked for validity by a professional staff equivalent to only 2½ people!

3 Once your Form 610 passes muster, it's forwarded to the Support Services Branch where your record is updated on the FCC computer. Then, usually one day per week, licenses are printed and mailed to those radio amateurs whose transactions have been entered since the previous processing date. The time between your exam and the day you receive your license in the mail typically runs six to eight weeks.

4 Problems or questions concerning a license? The Consumer Assistance Branch is the public's contact point with the FCC Licensing Division. People seated at terminals along the wall are not FCC staff but visitors who are researching questions.

5 Your Form 610 has done its job. Its final resting place is FCC storage. It's kept on file in case the need arises to review the original document on which the decision to issue your license was based.

and class of license, purpose and date of application, volunteer examiners' names (if Novice exam) or VEC (if VEC-supervised exam).

License Terms

Licenses are normally good for ten years. If you have a license good for the old five-year term, a grace period of five years is allowed should you forget to renew. After two years of the grace period has passed, you will lose your call sign and will be assigned a new one.

If you have a new 10-year-term license, issued since January 1984, the grace period for reinstatement is two years.

If you apply for reinstatement of your license under the grace period, you may not operate your station until your reinstated ticket arrives.

Lost or Destroyed Licenses

To get a replacement for a lost or destroyed license, simply mail a letter explaining the situation to FCC in Gettysburg. They'll provide you with a duplicate license with the same expiration date as the lost/destroyed license. If the original license is later found, it or the duplicate should be returned to the Commission's Gettysburg office with a brief note of explanation.

FCC PRINTS LICENSES ON LASER PRINTER

In response to complaints that licenses were hard to read, the FCC, effective in mid-April 1991, began printing Amateur Radio licenses on a laser printer. Amateurs will receive two official licenses: one credit-card-sized license suitable for use in wallets and a 5 by 7-inch document suitable for framing.

CALL SIGNS

If ever there was a subject whose significance is more apparent to radio amateurs than to nonhams, it is call signs. There's an emotional dimension to that set of letters and numerals by which we're identified that is fully understood by very few of our unlicensed brethren.

Back in 1978, the FCC closed a call-assignment program where eligible hams could request and be granted special consideration in call sign selection. FCC went to the present system of computer-assigned call signs, where you become eligible (at your option) for progressively more desirable (ie, shorter) call signs as you progress up the licensing ladder. The elimination of any human element from the selection process was quite deliberate on the Commission's part. Unfortunately, back in the '70s one of its Gettysburg staffers was convicted for dispensing, in exchange for cash, call signs and licenses to people who weren't eligible for them. Understandably, that stain on an otherwise proud record of service compiled by the Gettysburg office colors the Commission's thinking to this day.

At about the same time, as an economy measure, FCC also proposed to eliminate the licensing of club stations. They didn't simply want to stop issuing new club licenses, but renewals as well! This set off a storm of protest from clubs, many of whom had held the same call since long before the FCC itself was created. The idea of not renewing existing licenses was dropped, but no new club licenses have since been issued. Military recreation stations, RACES stations and short-term special-events stations fell victim to the same budget-cutting ax. Present club, military recreation and RACES station records aren't even in the Commission's computer data base, but instead are maintained manually on file cards.

COMMON QUESTIONS-AND-ANSWERS—CALL SIGNS

Q. How does the present FCC call sign system work?

A. See Figs 2 and 3. Call signs are issued sequentially by the FCC computer

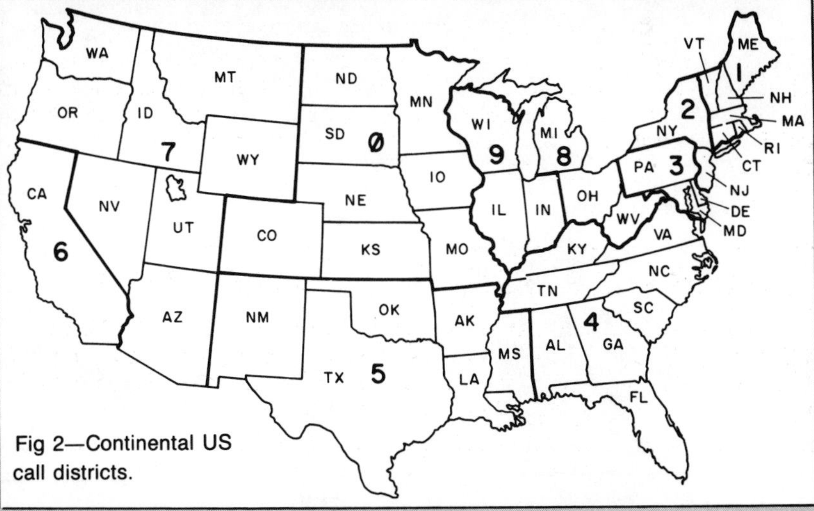

Fig 2—Continental US call districts.

Group A Call Signs

Block no.	Contiguous USA
*1	K#$$
*2	N#$$
*3	W#$$
4-13	AA#$-AK#$
14-36	KA#$-KZ#$
37-59	NA#$-NZ#$
60-82	WA#$-WZ#$
83-92	AA#$$-AK#$$
93	Group B

The following prefixes will *not* be assigned to stations in the contiguous 48 states: AH KH NH NL AQL KL WL KP NP WP AP WH. Pacific-area stations will be assigned AH#$ KH#$ WH#$, then Group B. Alaska-area stations will get WL7$ KL7$ NL7$, then Group B. Atlantic-area stations will be assigned KP#$ NP#$ WP#$, then Group B.

Group B

Block no.	Contiguous USA
1[1]	KA1$$
2-23	KB#$$-KS#$$
24-46	NA#$$-NZ#$$
47-69	WA#$$-WZ#$$
70	Group C

[1]KA prefixes will be assigned only to persons living in the first call district. Other KAs are assigned to US personnel living in Japan. The following prefixes will *not* be assigned to stations in the contiguous 48 states. KH KL KP NH NP WH WL WP. Pacific-area stations will be assigned calls in the format, AH#$$, Alaska-area stations, AL7$$, and Atlantic-area stations, KP#$$. Once these blocks are used up, assignments will be made from Group C call signs.

Group C Call Signs

Block no.	Contiguous USA
*1	K#$$$
2	N#$$$
*3	W#$$$
4	W#$$$

Pacific-area stations will be assigned KH#$$ NH#$$ WH#$$, in that order, Alaska-area stations KL7$$ NL7$$ WL7$$; Atlantic-area stations NP#$$ WP#$$. After these are depleted, Group D will be used.

*Call signs using these prefixes are not currently being issued.

Group D Call Signs

Block no.	Contiguous USA
1-23[1]	KA#$$$-KZ#$$$
24-41	WA#$$$-WZ#$$$

[1]Except KC4AAA-AAF and KC4USA-USZ.

The following call sign formats will *not* be assigned to stations in the contiguous 48 states: KH#$$$ KL#$$$ KP#$$$ WC#$$$ WH#$$$ WK#$$$ WL#$$$ WM#$$$ WP#$$$ WR#$$$ WT#$$$. Pacific-area stations will be assigned KH#$$$ WH#$$$; Alaska-area stations will be assigned KL7$$$ WL7$$$; Atlantic-area stations KP#$$$ WP#$$$.

Fig 3—Call sign groups.

in Gettysburg. *FCC will not honor requests for specific call signs!*

The computer selects call signs from "blocks" or "groups" of calls which reflect the licensee's operator class, mailing address and call-sign region. Only a small fraction of the nearly 10.3 million possible call signs available under the current system have been issued.

The FCC issues calls from four groups. Refer to the chart on this page. **Group A** calls of the 2 × 1 format, such as KR1R, are currently being issued only to Amateur Extra class operators. With the exception of the First and Third (as well as some US territorial areas) call sign districts, all 2028 2 × 1 calls have been issued. Extra class operators in other districts are receiving 2 × 2 calls issued from Group A, such as AA4AT. In time, this will happen in the remaining call districts.

All **Group B** calls use the 2 × 2 format, and they are assigned to amateurs holding Advanced licenses, such as KF4NJ. **Group C** calls are issued to General and Technician class operators. These are 1 × 3 calls with N, K or W prefixes, such as N4LOM.

Group D calls go to Novice class operators, and they all use the 2 × 3 format with prefixes beginning with K or W, such as KA1SIP.

Q. How many calls are available for distribution?

A. There are approximately 5,000 unissued calls in Group A, 500,000 in Group B, 350,000 in Group C and over 8.8 million in Group D!

The present FCC call-sign assignment system selects only calls which have never previously been issued. The present system does not have the ability to recover call signs from those who become Silent Keys or who drop out. The system assigns calls from the next lower group after all call signs from one group have been depleted.

Q. I would like to know what the most recent call issued in my district is. Can this information be obtained?

A. Yes. At the beginning of each month, the FCC releases a public notice which lists the latest calls issued in each group. The FCC's Gettysburg consumer assistance office maintains a "call sign hotline" for obtaining this information, 717-337-1212. General inquiries regarding licensing may also be directed to this number. The same information is available from the ARRL's Regulatory Information Branch for an SASE. This information is frequently printed in *The ARRL Letter* and monthly in the Happenings column of *QST*.

Q. When am I eligible for a new call sign?

A. You are eligible for a new call sign when you upgrade your operator license or when you change your mailing address to a different call-sign area. A new call sign may also be obtained when your present call does not reflect your license class, or call sign district. The FCC does not grant requests for specific call signs, although an amateur may swap a current call sign for another one issued in the regular sequence. According to an FCC Public Notice dated April 19, 1990, by filing a Form 610 with the FCC and requesting a change in call sign (Item 2E), the applicant will be issued a call sign appropriate for his license class from the standard rotation of new call signs.

Q. When I upgrade, can I keep my present call?

A. Yes, you can keep your present call sign if you want to. Calls are changed only when you specifically request it.

Q. A local ham recently became a Silent Key. Will his call automatically be deleted from FCC records?

A. The FCC no longer deletes the calls of Silent Keys unless cancellation is specifically requested. Since the term of an amateur license is now 10 years, the family of the deceased amateur could continue to receive unwanted correspondence for quite some time. To avoid this, the family of the deceased amateur should return the license to the FCC, or, in the event that the license cannot be found, a letter should be sent to the FCC stating that the amateur is deceased, and requesting cancellation of the license.

Q. Fifteen years ago I held the call W4AAA, but I let my license lapse. Recently I passed my Technician examination, and I received the call N4XXX. Is there any chance that I may regain my old call of W4AAA?

A. It is impossible to regain lost call signs, and it looks like this will be the case for some time to come.

NATIONAL RADIO QUIET ZONE

If you're thinking about putting up a repeater or automatically controlled beacon in the National Radio Quiet Zone (in Maryland, West Virginia and Virginia—see coordinates below), you must give written notification of your plan to the Interference Office, National Radio Astronomy Observatory, PO Box 2, Green Bank, WV 24944.

If you're planning to modify an existing repeater there, you must notify the Interference Office, too. Station modification is any change in frequency, power, antenna height or directivity, or the location of the station. The notification must include the geographical coordinates of the antenna, antenna height (above mean sea level, and above ground level), antenna directivity (if any), proposed frequency, emission type and power.

If the FCC receives an objection to your proposal from the National Radio Astronomy Observatory at Green Bank, for itself, or on behalf of the Naval Research Laboratory at Sugar Grove, within 20 days from the date of notification, the Commission will consider all aspects of the problem and take appropriate action.

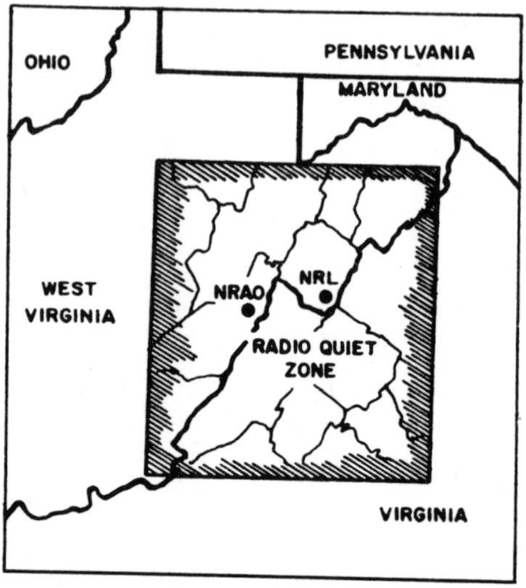

Fig 4—Boundaries of the National Radio Quiet Zone.

The National Radio Quiet Zone is the area in Maryland, West Virginia, and Virginia bounded by 39°15′ N on the north, 78°30′ W on the east, 37°30′ N on the south, and 80°30′ W on the west. See Fig 4.

FCC MODIFICATIONS TO YOUR LICENSE

The FCC reserves the right to modify your license at any time if it determines that such action is in the public interest, convenience and necessity. At the same time, however, the FCC must give you the opportunity to show why your license should not be modified. If you don't respond adequately, or don't take an active interest in the issue, your license may be changed temporarily or permanently.

The FCC can inspect your station and records. An FCC EIC can also require you to keep a log of your operations to ensure compliance with the rules—see Appendix.

CLUB STATIONS

Several years ago, the Commission decided that certain special station licenses were luxuries it could not afford. Provisions for issuance of new RACES, repeater, auxiliary, military-recreation, special event, secondary and club station tickets were felled under the FCC's deregulatory blade. These various types of special operation are still permitted, of course, but under the auspices of your primary license. FCC will, however, continue to modify and renew existing club, RACES and military recreation station licenses. Club station license trustees must be designated by an officer of the club, and hold at least a Technician class license. Clubs must be composed of at least two persons, and have a name, a document of organization, management, and devoted primarily to Amateur Radio.

COMMON QUESTIONS-AND-ANSWERS —CLUB STATIONS

Q. Our club holds a club station license. How do we go about changing our mailing address on record with the FCC?

A. You'll need a Form 610-B—entitled "Application For Amateur Club Or Military Recreation Station License." See Fig 5. This is one of three in the series of 610 forms. To change your mailing address for the club, or to make any other modification, the station trustee sends the completed Form 610-B to

Federal Communications Commission
P. O. Box 1020
Gettysburg, PA 17326

Approved by OMB
3060-0079
Expires 8/31/88

APPLICATION TO RENEW OR MODIFY AN AMATEUR CLUB, RACES OR MILITARY RECREATION STATION LICENSE

BE SURE TO READ INSTRUCTIONS ON REVERSE SIDE. ***PLEASE PRINT OR TYPE***

ATTACH PRESENT CLUB, RACES OR MILITARY RECREATION LICENSE OR PHOTOCOPY THEREOF TO THE BACK OF APPLICATION. IF THE LICENSE HAS BEEN LOST OR DESTROYED, ATTACH EXPLANATION.

1. CLUB, RACES OR MILITARY RECREATION STATION CALL SIGN: EXPIRATION DATE:

2. NAME OF CLUB STATION TRUSTEE OR LICENSE CUSTODIAN: (First, MI, Last, Suffix)

3. DATE OF BIRTH: (Month,Day,Year)

4. CURRENT MAILING ADDRESS: (Number and Street, City, State, ZIP Code)

5. CURRENT STATION LOCATION: (Number and Street, City, State)

6. NAME OF CLUB, RACES ORGANIZATION OR MILITARY RECREATION ENTITY:

7. TRUSTEE'S PRIMARY STATION CALL SIGN: TRUSTEE'S OPERATOR CLASS: EXPIRATION DATE:

8. If trustee has any other amateur radio application on file with the Commission that has not been acted upon, state its purpose and date submitted.

CERTIFICATIONS

RESPONSIBLE OFFICIAL: I CERTIFY that the above-named person is the station trustee or license custodian authorized to apply for and hold an amateur radio station license for this organization, society or entity.

WILLFUL FALSE STATEMENTS MADE ON THIS FORM ARE PUNISHABLE BY FINE AND IMPRISONMENT. U.S. CODE, TITLE 18, SECTION 1001.

9. Signature: (Must not agree with Item 2) (Title or authority to approve) Date Signed:

APPLICANT: I CERTIFY that all statements herein and attachments herewith are true, complete and correct to the best of my knowledge and belief and are made in good faith; that I am not the representative of a foreign government; that I waive any claim to the use of any particular frequency regardless of prior use by license or otherwise; that the station to be licensed will be inaccessible to unauthorized persons.

WILLFUL FALSE STATEMENTS MADE ON THIS FORM ARE PUNISHABLE BY FINE AND IMPRISONMENT. U.S. CODE, TITLE 18, SECTION 1001.

10. Applicant's Signature: (Must agree with Item 2) Date Signed:

FCC Form 610B
March 1986

Fig 5—FCC Form 610B.

FCC, Gettysburg, PA 17326. FCC will, in turn, modify the license and send it back to the trustee in about a month. The modified club-station ticket will bear the same expiration date as the trustee's primary station license. In all cases, the club call sign is retained.

Q. How do we go about renewing the club license?

A. Simply have the station trustee complete the Form 610-B, and send it to Gettysburg along with his or her own Form 610 for renewal of the primary station license (remember, the two tickets run for the same duration).

Q. Who is responsible for the proper operation of our club station?

A. The station trustee, together with the control operator, is responsible for the station's operation. The control operator may operate the station up to the privileges of his or her own operator license only. If the privileges in use exceed those of the station trustee's, however, then the station ID must consist of the club station's call sign followed by the home station call of the control op: WA1JUY/K1CE, for example.

Q. Why did I get my renewed primary license back three weeks before the renewed club ticket?

A. The trustee will always receive his or her renewed primary license two to three weeks before the renewed club ticket is returned. The FCC's primary licensing system is automated; club tickets are processed by hand.

Q. Our new club, the Rochester Radio Ruminators, wants to set up a station at our club headquarters. Since no club station licenses are being issued, what are we supposed to do for station authorization?

A. Designate a responsible member of your group as a station caretaker. Since no club station license is involved, there is no need to inform FCC of your actions. The club station uses the caretaker's own primary station license for authorization and call sign for ID purposes. The caretaker is operating his or her own station in portable operation (at a fixed location, the club HQ, away from the station location shown on the caretaker's home ticket). As always, the station licensee (the caretaker) and the duty control operator are responsible for the proper operation of the station.

QUESTIONS-AND-ANSWERS: FOREIGN VISITORS OPERATING

Q. I am a foreign national. May I operate in the US?

A. Aliens who hold a valid amateur license issued by *their* government may apply to the Federal Communications Commission for a permit to operate in the US only if a reciprocal operating agreement exists between the US and the above mentioned government. Reciprocal agreements are currently held with these 74 countries: Antigua, Argentina, Australia, Austria, Bahamas, Barbados, Belgium, Belize, Bolivia, Botswana, Brazil, Canada, Chile, Colombia, Costa Rica, Cyprus, Denmark, (Commonwealth of) Dominica, Dominican Republic, Ecuador, El Salvador, Federated States of Micronesia, Fiji, Finland, France, Germany, Greece, Grenada, Guatemala, Guyana, Haiti, Honduras, Hong Kong, Iceland, India, Indonesia, Ireland, Israel, Italy, Jamaica, Japan, Jordan, Kiribati, Kuwait, Liberia, Luxembourg, Monaco, Netherlands, Netherlands Antilles, New Zealand, Nicaragua, Norway, Panama, Paraguay, Peru, Phillippines, Portugal, Seychelles, St. Lucia, St. Vincent, Sierra Leone, Solomon Islands, South Africa,

Spain, Surinam, Sweden, Switzerland, Thailand, Trinidad, Tuvalu, United Kingdom (including VP2M, VP2V, VP5, VP8, VS6, VP9, ZB2, ZD7, and ZF), Uruguay, Venezuela, and Yugoslavia.

Q. How do I apply?

A. Send a completed FCC Form 610-A (after June 1, 1991, versions dated August 1986 or later must be used) to the *FCC, PO Box 1020, Gettysburg, Pennsylvania 17326, USA*. You should apply at least 60 days in advance of your need, to allow for ample processing time. Be sure to include a photocopy of your current Amateur Radio operator and station license. Canadians may take advantage of automatic reciprocity between the US and Canada, and do not need to file any form.

FCC Form 610-A
August 1986

UNITED STATES OF AMERICA
FEDERAL COMMUNICATIONS COMMISSION
Gettysburg, PA 17326

Approved by OMB
3060-0022
Expires 6/30/89

APPLICATION OF ALIEN AMATEUR RADIO LICENSEE FOR PERMIT TO OPERATE IN THE UNITED STATES

ARE YOU USING THE CORRECT FORM? Use this form to request a RECIPROCAL PERMIT to operate your amateur radio station in areas where communications are regulated by the FCC. You must possess a valid amateur radio license issued by the country of which you are a citizen. If you are a citizen of the United States, you are ineligible for a reciprocal permit—even if you are also a citizen of another country. If you will be in the United States for an extended period, you are encouraged to obtain an FCC amateur radio license.

1. NAME OF APPLICANT (Last) (First) (M.I.)

2. DATE OF BIRTH (Month,Day,Year)

3. COUNTRY ISSUING YOUR AMATEUR LICENSE

4. AMATEUR CALL SIGN

5. EXPIRATION DATE OF STATION LICENSE (Month,Day,Year)

6. YOU ARE A CITIZEN OF WHAT COUNTRY?

7. UNITED STATES MAILING ADDRESS

8. ADDRESS WHERE YOU WANT PERMIT MAILED, if issued

9. NATIVE COUNTRY MAILING ADDRESS

10. LIST ALL STATION LOCATIONS FROM WHICH YOU WILL OPERATE FOR A PERIOD OF 30 DAYS OR MORE WHILE IN THE UNITED STATES. IF YOU WILL NOT BE OPERATING AT ANY LOCATION FOR 30 DAYS OR MORE WRITE "NONE".

11. APPROXIMATE DATES OF STAY IN THE UNITED STATES (Beginning) (Ending)

READ CAREFULLY BEFORE SIGNING

I, the above-named alien amateur licensee, request a reciprocal permit for operation of my amateur radio station in the United States. I understand that, if a permit is granted, my operation of a station in the United States must be in accord with: (1) the terms and conditions of the bilateral agreement on this subject between my Government and the Government of the United States; (2) Subparts A through E, G and H of Part 97 (Amateur Radio Service) of the Rules and Regulations of the Federal Communications Commission; (3) the terms and conditions of the amateur license(s) issued to me by my Government, but not to exceed the FCC Amateur Extra class privileges; and (4) any further conditions attached to the permit by the Federal Communications Commission. I also understand that any permit issued to me may be modified, suspended or cancelled by the Commission without advance notice. I am familiar with Part 97 of the United States Federal Communications Commission's Rules and Regulations and I certify that all of the information I have submitted on the application is true, complete and correct to the best of my knowledge; that I am not a foreign Government or a representative thereof.

WILLFUL FALSE STATEMENTS MADE ON THIS FORM OR ATTACHMENTS ARE PUNISHABLE BY FINE AND IMPRISONMENT, U.S. CODE TITLE 18, SECTION 1001.

12. SIGNATURE OF APPLICANT

13. DATE SIGNED

FOR AGENCY USE ONLY EFF. DATE: EXP. DATE:

GENERAL INSTRUCTIONS

A. Please print or type. All items must be completed, except areas indicated for agency use only.

B. You should obtain a current copy of Part 97 of the FCC Rules and Regulations from a commercial supplier or from the Government Printing Office. Prices are subject to change without notice. It is suggested that you contact the United States Government Printing Office, Washington, D.C. 20402, or telephone (202) 783-3238 for the correct price.

C. Mail your completed application together with a photocopy of your amateur radio operator and station license, to the Federal Communications Commission, P.O. Box 1020, Gettysburg, PA., 17326, U.S.A. Allow at least 60 days for processing.

D. An alien who becomes a citizen of the United States is no longer eligible to hold an alien amateur operator permit, even if the license from his former country is still valid. He/she must obtain an FCC amateur radio license to operate an amateur station. No examination credit is allowed toward an FCC amateur radio license on the basis of holding an amateur license issued by another country. You may obtain further information on how to apply for an FCC amateur operator license by contacting the FCC Field Office nearest you.

INSTRUCTIONS FOR SPECIFIC ITEMS

6. Show the name of the country of which you are a citizen. If different than Item 3, do not submit this application. You must be a citizen of the country that issued your amateur license to be eligible for this permit.

7. You must provide a complete United States mailing address at which you can be reached during your stay in the United States. The Embassy or Consulate of your country may be able to serve this purpose for you during short visits to the United States.

8. You are required by law to provide the FCC with a United States mailing address at which you may be reached or through which your mail will be forwarded to you.

9. State your mailing address in your own country. If you are an alien resident in the United States, and do not have a mailing address in your own country, please state this in Item 9.

BE SURE TO READ THE ENTIRE STATEMENT FOLLOWING ITEMS 10 AND 11, AND THEN SIGN AND DATE THE APPLICATION.

NOTICE TO INDIVIDUALS REQUIRED BY PRIVACY ACT OF 1974 AND THE PAPERWORK REDUCTION ACT OF 1980

Sections 301, 303, and 308 of the Communications Act of 1934, as amended, (licensing powers) authorize the FCC to request the information on this application. The purpose of the information is to determine your eligibility for a license. The information will be used by FCC staff to evaluate the application, to determine station location, to provide information for enforcement and rulemaking proceedings and to maintain a current inventory of licensees. No license can be granted unless all information requested is provided. This information is available to the public on request. Your response is required to obtain this authorization.

Fig 6—FCC Form 610A.

Copies of FCC Form 610-A (see Fig 6) are available from the Regulatory Information Branch of the ARRL Headquarters at 225 Main Street, Newington, Connecticut 06111, USA. Please enclose an SAE and two IRC with your request.

Q. I am a US citizen living overseas, but have only an alien license. Can I obtain a reciprocal permit for operating in the US?

A. No. Only noncitizens may obtain permits. If an alien becomes a US citizen, the reciprocal permit becomes invalid, and the amateur must then take a US amateur exam and apply for a regular US license and call sign.

Q. How will I identify on the air?

A. You will sign the representative prefix of the call area where you are located, plus the Morse "/" or phone "stroke," followed by your home (native) call, (for example, W1/LU1AAA and KP4/YU7ZZZ). At least once during each contact with another amateur station, you must give your geographical location in English as nearly as possible by city and state, commonwealth or possession.

Q. On what frequencies will I be able to operate, and with how much power?

A. You will have all the privileges that you have in your home country as long as they do not exceed the privileges of the Amateur Extra class license of the USA. However, code-free class licensees must not operate below 30 MHz even if they have HF privileges in their home countries. You are also bound by the provisions of the reciprocal agreement.

Q. How long will my permit be valid? May I renew it?

A. The permit is valid for one year, unless your native license expires sooner. It is not renewable. You may apply again for a new permit.

Q. My home country has not yet entered into a reciprocal operating agreement with the US. I would like to have US privileges, signing a regular US callsign.

A. The FCC says that any alien who can provide the FCC with a US mailing address can take a US amateur examination. For detailed information, please contact the Volunteer Examiner Department of the ARRL Headquarters.

Q. What if this hasn't answered all my questions?

A. The Regulatory Information Branch of the ARRL Headquarters will be pleased to answer any further questions you might have regarding operation in the USA.

Chapter Five

The Bands

Amateur Radio enjoys a wealth of operating space up and down the whole radio spectrum. In fact, it has enjoyed its "own space" since the earliest days of radio, but not before a few hurdles were jumped.

A NAVAL BATTLE

In 1909, hundreds of amateur stations outnumbered Navy and commercial stations. Interference and bedlam reigned. The Roberts Bill of 1909, a trust measure sponsored by the US Navy, was one of the first attempts to alleviate the situation. The measure was killed by the Marconi Company, which argued that the interference existed because of commercial operators' antiquated, obsolete equipment not incorporating the most modern tuners. The Marconi Company, along with amateurs, were the only operators using such tuners.

Amateur Radio grew to be a major issue of the day. There were numerous other attempts to snuff out Amateur Radio, some rather devious, and all unsuccessful. In 1912, the government, smarting from its losses, had a new ploy. In new regulations, amateur stations were limited to wavelengths of less than 200 meters. The body of scientific thought at the time held that radio waves became more effective and useful as a direct ratio to their length. The feeling was that amateurs would be dissolved by relegating them to the "useless" spectrum 200 meters and below. And, the rest is history! Thanks to this "banishment," amateurs were able to become the greatest pioneers of communications science and technology.

SHARING THE BANDS

Today, there are numerous other radio services vying for pieces of the spectrum pie, all with legitimate purposes. To accommodate them all, the international and domestic regulatory agencies often put some together, taking into consideration priority of importance of each service, and compatibility factors. The result is that, in many instances, we amateurs share our bands with others.

While some of our allocations are *exclusive*, we share with others on the basis of priority. In some cases, we are the *primary* occupant, but share the band with other *primary* occupants on a *coprimary* basis. We operate on a basis of equality: We must not cause harmful interference to the other *primary* occupants, and they must not interfere with us.

In other cases, Amateur Radio is designated a *secondary* service: We must not cause harmful interference to, and must tolerate interference from, stations in the primary service.

Who Do We Share Our Bands With?

In the discussions of each of the amateur bands in this chapter, descriptions of the sharing arrangements will be provided. To help you understand the nature of these arrangements, and to help you tell what you're hearing, here is a basic set of definitions of some of the other services with which we share our bands:

Fixed Service: A radiocommunication service between specified fixed points.

Fixed-Satellite Service: A radiocommunication service between earth stations at specified fixed points when one or more satellites are used.

Mobile Service: A radiocommunication service between mobile and land stations, or between mobile stations.

Land Mobile Service: A mobile service between base stations and land mobile stations, or between land mobile stations. An example is the communications system for a taxi cab company. The base station at company headquarters dispatches its taxis via radio.

Maritime Mobile Service: A mobile service between coast stations and ship stations, or between ship stations.

Aeronautical Mobile Service: A mobile service between aeronautical stations and aircraft stations, or between aircraft stations.

Broadcasting Service: A radiocommunication service in which the transmissions are intended for direct reception by the general public.

Radionavigation Service: A radiodetermination service for the purpose of navigating a course. LORAN systems, for example, guide ships on their chosen courses.

Radiolocation Service: A radiodetermination service for the purpose of locating objects. Radar, for example, is used for tracking movement of ships and planes.

BANDS DIFFER FROM REGION TO REGION

For convenience in organizing frequency allocations for the various services, the International Telecommunication Union has divided the world into three regions: 1, 2 and 3. See the map on this page. North and South America comprise Region 2.

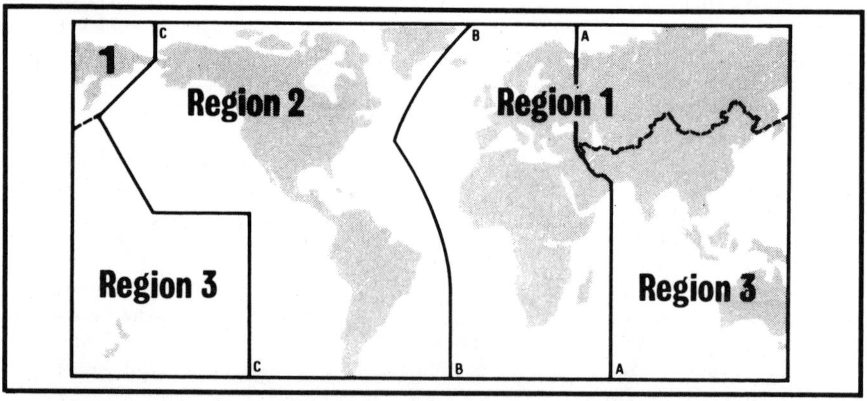

Fig 3-1—The three ITU regions. Region 1 includes the area limited on the east by line A (lines A, B and C are defined below) and on the west by line B, excluding any of the territory of Iran which lies between these limits. It also includes that part of the territory of Turkey and the USSR lying outside of these limits, the territory of the Mongolian People's Republic, and the area to the north of the USSR which lies between lines A and C.

Region 2 includes the area limited on the east by line B and on the west by line C.

Region 3 includes the area limited on the east by line C and on the west by line A, except the territories of the Mongolian People's Republic, Turkey, USSR, and the area to the north of the USSR. It also includes that part of the territory of Iran lying outside of those limits. Lines A, B and C are defined as follows:
Line A extends from the North Pole along meridian 40°E to parallel 40°N, thence by great-circle arc to the intersection of meridian 60°E and the Tropic of Cancer; thence along the meridian 60°E to the South Pole.
Line B extends from the North Pole along meridian 10°W to its intersection with parallel 72°N, thence by great-circle arc to the intersection of meridian 20°W and parallel 10°S; thence along meridian 20°W to the South Pole.
Line C extends from the North Pole by great-circle arc to the intersection of parallel 65° 30′N with the international boundary in Bering Strait; thence by great-circle arc to the intersection of meridian 165°E and parallel 50°N; thence by great-circle arc to the intersection of meridian 170°W and parallel 10°N, thence along parallel 10°N to its intersection with meridian 120°W; thence along meridian 120°W to the South Pole.
(Tnx RSGB *Operating Manual)*

Frequency allocations for Amateur Radio and other services can differ among ITU Regions. The same sharing rules as outlined previously apply. Where, in adjacent regions, a band is allocated to different services of the same category, the basic principle is the equality of right to operate. Stations in a *secondary* service must not cause harmful interference to, and are not protected from interference from, stations in the *primary* service.

VOLUNTARY BAND PLANS

There's another aspect to sharing the bands: voluntary band plans. Although the FCC rules set aside portions of some bands for specific modes, there's still a need to further organize our space among user groups by "gentlemen's agreements." These agreements usually emerge by consensus of the band occupants, and are sanctioned by a national body like ARRL. They help groups avoid getting in the way of each other. For example, a "DX Window" is a portion of a band that is set aside for DX work. Domestic QSOs are avoided so stations can hear and work weak-signal DX stations. There are others, and we will review them on a band-by-band basis in the following discussion. For a good review of why band plans are so important, see Chapter 10.

CW

CW is permitted throughout all the bands allocated to amateurs by the FCC. Please be sure to check the gentlemen's agreements as discussed below to find out where CW should and shouldn't be used.

160 Meters: 1800-2000 kHz

Sharing arrangements: In the US, Amateur Radio has secondary status to the primary radiolocation service from 1900 to 2000 kHz. US amateurs enjoy exclusive use of 1800-1900 kHz.

A possible dark cloud looms over the horizon with respect to 1900-2000 kHz: A future rule making proceeding in conjunction with expansion of broadcasting into the 1625-1705 kHz band may require some shifting of assignments in this portion of the spectrum.

In the rest of Region 2, 1800-1850 kHz is exclusively amateur, while 1850-2000 kHz is shared on a coprimary basis among amateur, fixed, mobile, radiolocation and radionavigation stations.

Other regions: In ITU Region 1, Radiolocation is the sole primary service at 1800-1810. Amateur is primary from 1810-1850. 1850-2000 is allocated to the fixed and mobile services, with no amateur presence at this segment.

In ITU Region 3, Amateur Radio shares the entire segment 1800-2000 kHz on a coprimary basis with fixed, mobile and radionavigation services; radiolocation is secondary here.

License privileges: General, Advanced and Extra class amateurs have access to the entire segment, 1800-2000 kHz.

Mode privileges: CW, phone, image, RTTY and data modes are permitted across the entire segment.

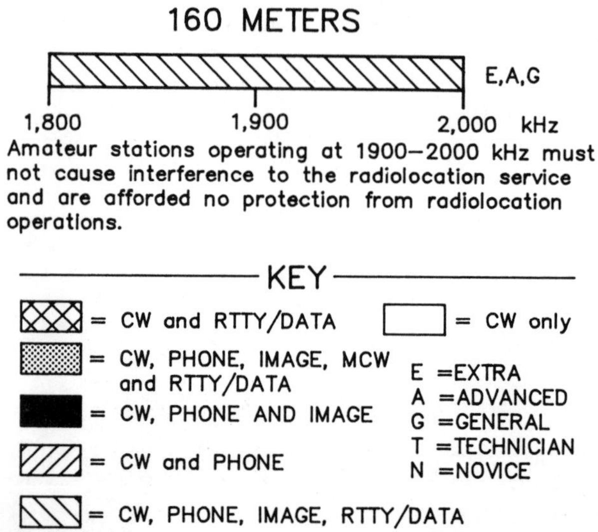

Band planning: The 160-meter band has traditionally been known as the "gentleman's band" or "top band." Our lowest-frequency amateur allocation, its history can be traced to the earliest experiments at "200 meters and down." Like all amateur bands, it is used for many things: local and regional ragchewing, DXing and some net operation. Accordingly, a voluntary band plan has developed over time to provide coordination of the various operating activities: ARRL recommends use of 1800-1840 for CW, RTTY and other narrow-band modes. 1840-2000 should be reserved for phone, CW, slow-scan television and other wideband modes.

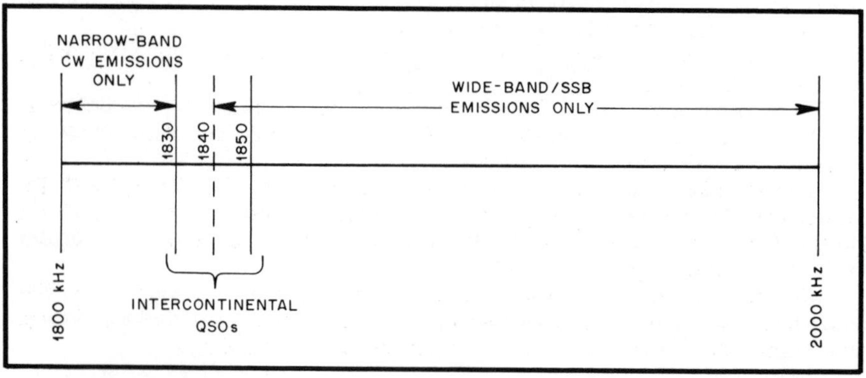

Fig 2—160-meter band plan

The "DX Window," where only intercontinental QSOs should occur, is 1830-1850. This allows your neighbor to hear DX stations without local interference. Were it not for the voluntary cooperation of all operators on the band in keeping this segment clear, DXing would be difficult and frustrating at best. The band plan for the rest of Region 2, and other regions, are outlined in *The ARRL Operating Manual*.

1802.3 kHz is the suggested center frequency for packet radio automatic message forwarding when propagation is favorable.

80 Meters: 3500-4000 kHz

Sharing arrangements: In Region 2, Amateur Radio enjoys exclusive status from 3500-3750 kHz, and shares the rest of the band with foreign fixed and mobile services on a coprimary basis. In the US, amateurs enjoy exclusive operation in the entire segment; the FCC has declined to put any other service here even though it would be permitted to do so under the international regulations.

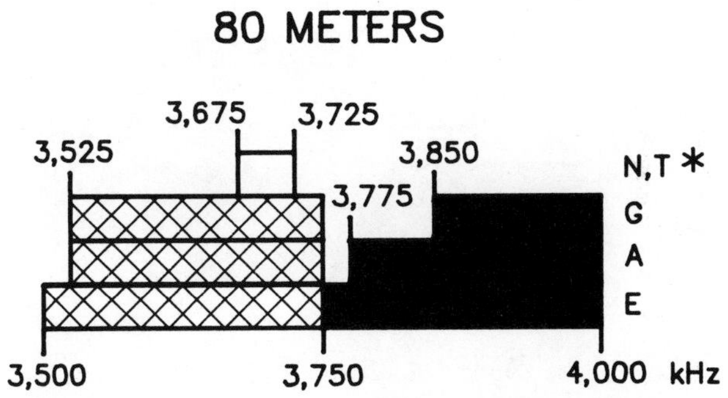

Other regions: In Region 1, Amateur, Fixed and Mobile stations share 3500-3800 kHz on a coprimary basis. The rest of the band excludes amateur operation; fixed and mobile are the occupants. Broadcasting can be found at 3950-4000 kHz.

In Region 3, amateurs share the 3500-3900 kHz segment on a coprimary basis with fixed and mobile stations. Amateurs are excluded from 3900-4000 kHz; fixed and broadcast stations are here.

License privileges: Novices (and Technicians who have passed Element 1(A), the 5 WPM code test) can operate at 3675-3725 kHz, international Morse code only. Generals may operate on 3525-3750 and 3850-4000 kHz. Advanced class licensees have access to 3525-3750 kHz, and 3775-4000 kHz.

Mode privileges: RTTY and data modes are authorized on the non-phone portion only, 3500-3750 kHz.

Phone and image emissions are authorized on the voice segment at 3750-4000 kHz.

All licensees must observe a 200 watt PEP power-output limit when operating in the Novice subband.

Band planning: The considerate operator recognizes 3605- 3645 kHz as the RTTY activity area. 3590 kHz is the RTTY DX frequency. The phone band extends from 3750-4000 kHz with recognition of 3790-3800 as the phone DX window, and 3845 kHz for slow-scan television (SSTV).

The use of the RTTY subbands is encouraged for packet radio operation. The center frequency 3594.3 kHz is suggested for intercontinental packet radio message forwarding; 3607.3 kHz for North American message forwarding.

*Technician operators must pass the 5 WPM code test, Element 1(A), in order to operate on the Novice HF subbands.

FCC moves Novice band: The 80-meter Novice band is moving. On January 10, 1991, the FCC announced a change in its rules to move the band from 3700-3750 kHz to 3675-3725. The change is intended to "reduce the amount of mutual interference between United States amateur stations and Canadian amateur stations," according to the FCC.

At the time the change (PR Docket 90-100) was proposed, Canadian amateurs operated radiotelephone down to 3725 kHz. The Commission proposed the change in the Novice allocation to prevent intermode interference with Canadian phone operators.

Last October, Canada's amateur service was "deregulated," and all mode subbands on 80 meters were removed. Canadian amateurs generally are observing their old subbands voluntarily.

The new Novice allocation is effective March 16, 1991.

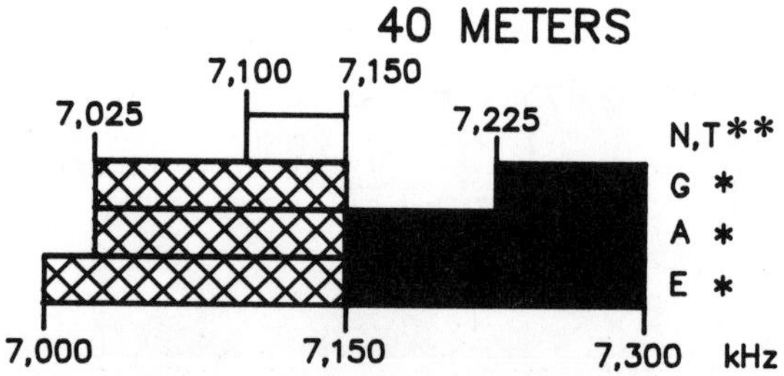

* Phone operation is allowed on 7075–7100 kHz in Puerto Rico. US Virgin Islands and areas of the Caribbean south of 20 degrees north latitude: and in Hawaii and areas near ITU Region 3, including Alaska.

40 Meters: 7000-7300 kHz

Sharing arrangements: The 40-meter band has a big problem: International broadcasting occupies the 7100-7300 kHz band in many parts of the world. During the daytime when sunspots are high, broadcasting does not cause much interference to US amateurs. However, at night, especially when sunspots are low, the broadcast interference is heavy. Some countries allocate only the 7000-7100 kHz band to amateurs. Others, particularly in our Region 2, allocate 7100-7300 as well, which at times is subject to interference. The result is that there is a great demand for frequencies in the 7000-7100 kHz slot. The effect is that there are two band plans overlaid on each other, ours that spreads out over 7000-7300 kHz and the foreign one that compresses everything into 7000-7100 kHz. Foreign stations typically use this segment for phone and the 7035-7045 kHz subband for RTTY. The two basic band plans coexist nicely until propagation permits stations in different regions to hear each other. The consolation is that 7000-7035 kHz is fine hunting ground for domestic and DX CW contacts.

License privileges: The Novice subband on 40 meters occurs at 7100-7150 kHz—international Morse code only (ditto for Technicians who have passed the 5 WPM

**Technician operators must pass the 5 WPM code test, Element 1(A) in order to operate on the Novice HF subbands.

code test). General class licensees are allowed operation on 7025-7150 kHz and 7225-7300 kHz. Advanced class operators have privileges at 7025-7300 kHz. All licensees must limit power output to 200 watts PEP output in the Novice subband.

Mode privileges: RTTY, and data modes are allowed on the nonvoice frequencies, 7000-7150 kHz.

The phone segment is 7150-7300 kHz. Image modes are also permitted here. Stations in Hawaii, Alaska and other areas in Region 2 west of 130° West longitude, Caribbean insular regions (Puerto Rico, US Virgin Islands and other areas south of 20° North latitude) and in Regions 1 and 3 may operate phone on 7075-7100 kHz. (Note: US stations in the Pacific outside of Region 2—Guam, Northern Marianas, American Samoa, Baker, Howland, Jarvis Island, Kingman Reef, Palmyra and Wake Islands—do not have access to 7100 to 7300 kHz.)

Band planning: The range 7080-7100 kHz is generally recognized as the RTTY zone, with 7040 kHz being the RTTY DX window. Slow-scan TV centers around 7171 kHz. The use of the RTTY subbands is encouraged for packet operation. The center frequency 7038.3 kHz is suggested for intercontinental packet radio automatic message forwarding; 7091.3 kHz for North American autoforwarding.

30 Meters: 10,100-10,150 kHz

Sharing arrangements: The Amateur Service is secondary in this band to stations in the Fixed Service outside of the US. You must avoid causing harmful interference to these foreign fixed stations. If you do, you must be prepared to stop transmitting, if necessary, to eliminate the interference.

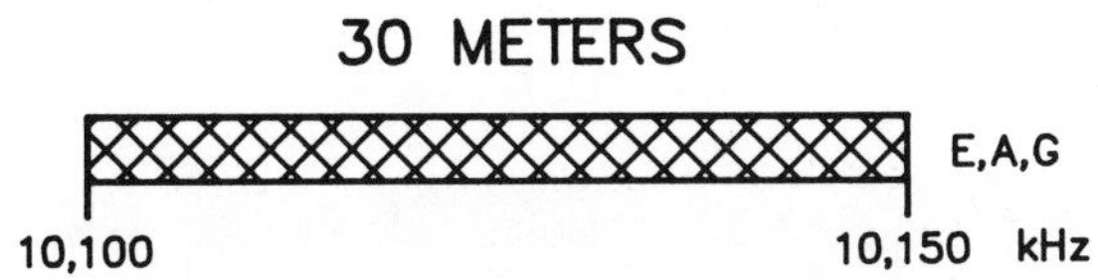

Maximum power on 30 meters is 200 watts PEP output. Amateurs must avoid interference to the fixed service outside the US.

License privileges: General, Advanced and Extra class licensees have access to the entire segment, but are limited to 200 watts PEP output, CW, RTTY and data emissions only.

The 200-watt PEP power limit applies to all operations on this band.

According to the band plan, RTTY emissions should be restricted to 10,140-10,150 kHz. Packet operation is encouraged on the RTTY subband. The center frequency 10,145.3 kHz is suggested for intercontinental packet automatic message forwarding; 10,147.3 kHz for North American autoforwarding.

20 Meters: 14.000-14.350 MHz

A premier DX band, 20 meters is allocated to amateurs exclusively throughout the world.

License privileges: No Novice or Technician privileges are afforded at 20 meters. The General class segments of the band occur at 14.025-14.150 and 14.225-14.350 MHz. Advanced class licensees have access to 14.025-14.150 MHz, and 14.175-14.350 MHz.

Mode privileges: The voice segment is 14.150-14.350 MHz. Image emissions are permitted on this voice segment also. RTTY and data modes are permitted on the nonvoice segment 14.000-14.150 MHz.

20 METERS

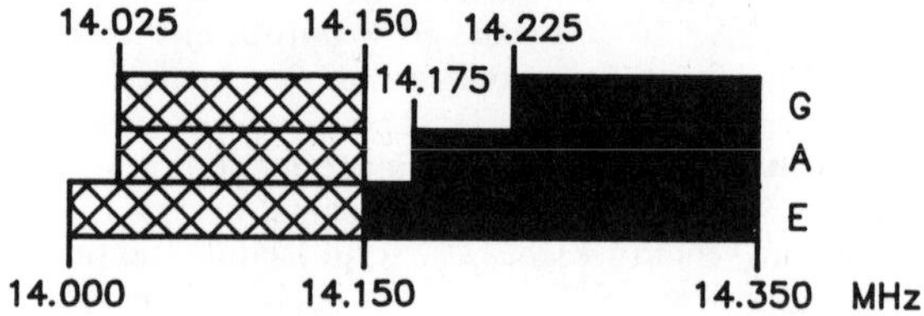

Band planning: RTTY activity is found between 14.070 and 14.0995 MHz. Beacons can be found at 14.0995-14.1005 MHz. The SSTV channel centers on 14.230 MHz. Packet operation is encouraged on the RTTY subband. The center frequency 14.1023 MHz is suggested for intercontinental packet automatic message forwarding; 14.1083 MHz for intracontinental message forwarding.

17 Meters: 18.068-18.168 MHz

The new 17-meter band was awarded to amateurs on an exclusive basis, worldwide, at WARC-79. It was made available for amateur use in the US in January 1989. The entire segment is available to General, Advanced and Extra class amateurs. RTTY and data modes are allowed on 18.068-18.110 MHz. Phone and image modes are allowed on the rest of the band—18.110-18.168 MHz.

17 METERS

The US band plan calls for CW operation at 18.068-18.100 MHz; RTTY at 18.100-18.110 MHz; and phone/CW at 18.110-18.168 MHz. The center frequencies 18.1063 MHz and 18.1083 MHz are suggested for packet automatic message forwarding.

15 Meters: 21.000-21.450 MHz

Another popular DX band, 15 meters is also worldwide amateur exclusive.

License privileges: The Novice/Technician* subband is 21.100-21.200 MHz, international Morse code only. General class operators are allowed to use the 21.025-21.200 MHz, and 21.300-21.450 MHz segments. Advanced class licensees have 21.025-21.200 MHz and 21.225-21.450 MHz. All licensees must keep their power down to 200 watts PEP output when operating in the Novice band.

Mode privileges: The phone band is 21.200-21.450 MHz. Image modes are permitted on this voice segment only. RTTY and data modes are permitted on the nonvoice segment only: 21.000-21.200 MHz.

Band planning: The low CW band is 21.000-21.070 MHz. RTTY activity occurs at 21.070-21.100 kHz. The middle CW band is 21.100-21.1495 MHz. Beacons are

*Technician operators must pass the 5 WPM code test, Element 1(A), in order to operate on the Novice HF subbands.

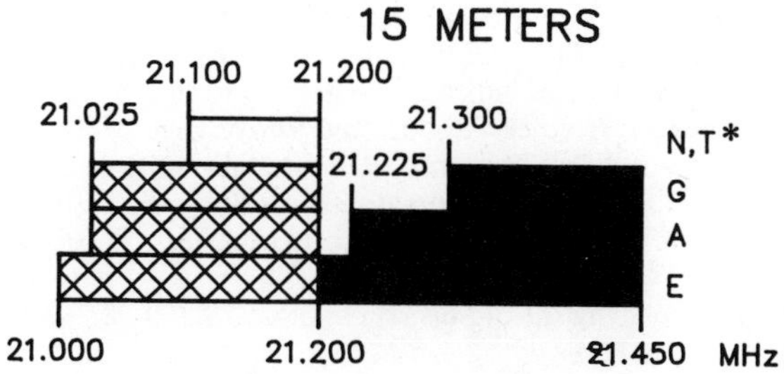

found at 21.1495-21.1505. The upper CW band is 21.1505-21.200 MHz. The phone band is 21.200-21.450 MHz with an SSTV channel at 21.340 MHz. The center frequencies 21.0963 MHz and 21.0983 MHz are suggested for packet message autoforwarding.

12 Meters: 24.890-24.990 MHz

The 12-meter band was made available for use by US amateurs in 1985. It is an amateur exclusive band worldwide.

License privileges: General, Advanced and Extra class licensees have access to the entire segment.

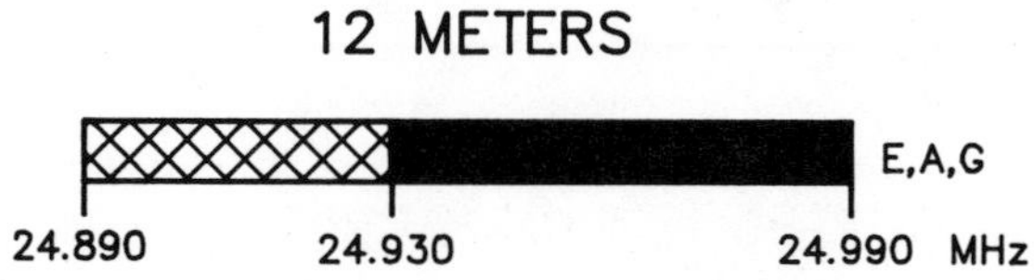

Mode privileges: RTTY and data modes are authorized from 24.890-24.930 MHz. The phone and image band is 24.930-24.990 MHz.

The band plan calls for CW only at 24.890-24.920 MHz; CW and data modes at 24.920-24.930 MHz; and phone, SSTV and CW at 24.930-24.990 MHz. The center frequencies 24.9263 MHz and 24.9283 MHz are suggested for packet message automatic forwarding.

10 Meters: 28.0-29.7 MHz

The entire 10-meter band is amateur exclusive worldwide. The Novice/Technician* band is 28.1-28.5 MHz. All other licensees have access to the entire band.

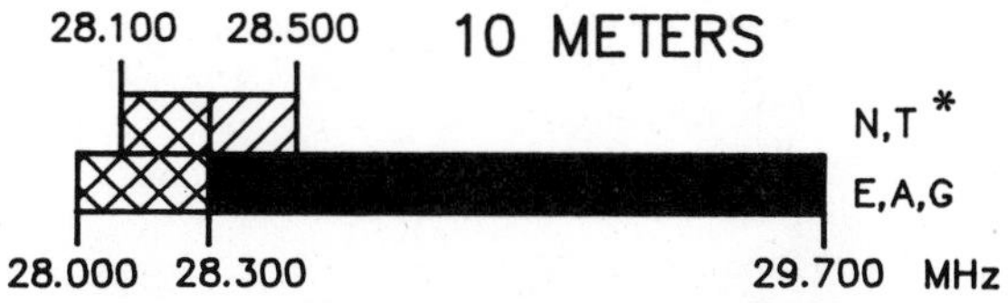

Novices and Technicians are limited to 200 watts PEP output on 10 meters.

*Technician operators must pass the 5 WPM code test, Element 1(A), in order to operate on the Novice HF subbands.

Mode privileges: RTTY and data modes are permitted at 28.0-28.3 MHz.

The phone band is 28.3-29.7 MHz. Image emissions are allowed here, too. While below 29.0 MHz, FM voice bandwidths are restricted to that of double-sideband AM voice; wider-bandwidth FM voice is permitted above 29.0 MHz.

SSB (double-sideband full-carrier AM is not allowed) may be used at 28.3-28.5 MHz by Novice and Technician* operators with 200 watts PEP output maximum.

Band planning: RTTY activity generally occurs between 28.070 and 28.150 MHz. SSTV activity centers around 28.680 MHz. There is a new beacon band at 28.100-28.200 MHz, replacing the old beacon band at 28.200-28.300 MHz. The phone band is 28.300-29.300 MHz.

Satellite downlinks exist between 29.300 and 29.510 MHz. Repeater operation exists from 29.510 to 29.700 MHz. The FM simplex call frequency is 29.600 MHz.

The center frequencies 28.1023 MHz and 28.1043 MHz are suggested for packet automatic message forwarding. These frequencies may also be considered for network entry points for Novices and Technicians.

6 Meters: 50-54 MHz

In Regions 2 and 3, the 6-meter band is amateur exclusive. It is exclusively allocated for broadcasting in Region 1. The entire band is available for use by Technician, General, Advanced and Extra class licensees. No Novice privileges exist on this band.

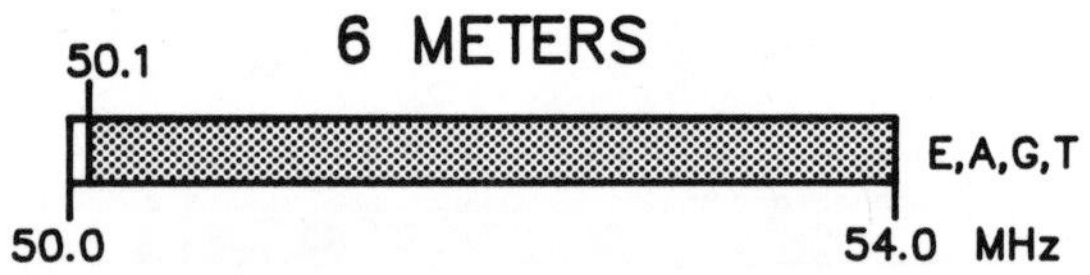

There is a CW exclusive subband from 50.0 to 50.1 MHz. MCW, phone, image, RTTY and data modes are permitted throughout the rest of the band, 50.1-54.0 MHz.

Test emissions including unmodulated carriers are allowed from 51 to 54 MHz.

Band planning: Activities in the 6-meter band are depicted in the following band plan.

50.000-50.100	CW and beacons as follows:
50.060-50.080	Automatically controlled beacons
50.100-50.600	SSB and AM as follows:
50.110	SSB DX calling frequency
50.200	SSB domestic calling frequency (Note: Suggest QSY up for local and down for long-distance QSOs)
50.400	AM calling frequency
50.600-51.000	Experimental and Special Modes as follows:
50.700	RTTY Calling Frequency
50.800-50.980	Radio Control (R/C), 10 channels with 20-kHz spacing
51.000-51.100	Pacific DX window
51.700	National packet simplex frequency
51.100-52.000	FM Simplex
52.000-52.050	Pacific DX window
51.000-54.000	FM repeater and simplex—see below.

*Technician operators must pass the 5 WPM code test, Element 1(A), in order to operate on the Novice HF subbands.

FCC Widens 6-Meter Repeater Subband

The FCC has expanded the 6-meter repeater subband from 52-54 MHz to 51-54 MHz effective April 9, 1990. The FCC stated that this expansion will permit operation of additional repeaters to meet increased demand.

The Commission said a majority of the commenters supported the expansion. In its comments, the ARRL stated that it was in favor, even though the proposal does not conform to the present ARRL 6-meter band plan. The ARRL reported that the band plan would be revised so operations now conducted in the 51-52 MHz expansion segement would be adequately protected from repeater operations.

The FCC went on to say that some operations in some areas of the 51-52 MHz segment can continue undisturbed, and that in other areas, relocation to the 50-51 MHz segment may be necessary.

2 Meters: 144-148 MHz

Throughout Region 2, amateurs enjoy exclusive use of the entire two-meter band: 144-148 MHz.

In Region 1, amateurs are limited to 144-146 MHz, but it is an exclusive allocation. Fixed and mobile stations occupy 146-148 MHz in this region.

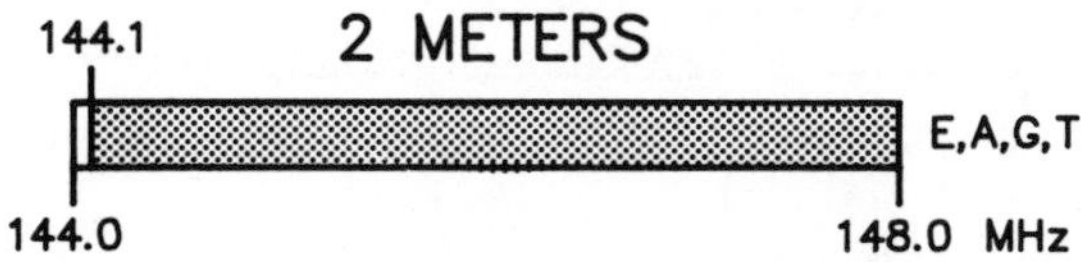

In Region 3, amateurs enjoy 144-146 exclusively, and share 146-148 MHz with fixed and mobile stations on a coprimary basis.

There is a CW-only segment from 144.00 to 144.10 MHz. All of the remaining emissions except pulse and spread-spectrum are permitted above 144.100 MHz.

Licensees holding Technician class licenses and above are permitted to use the entire segment.

Band planning: The following band plan explains typical operation on the 2-meter band:

144.00-144.05	EME (CW)
144.05-144.10	General CW and weak signals
144.10-144.20	EME and weak-signal SSB
144.20	National calling frequency
144.20-144.275	General SSB operation
144.275-144.300	Propagation beacons
144.30-144.50	New OSCAR subband
144.50-144.60	Linear translator inputs
144.60-144.90	FM repeater inputs
144.90-145.10	Weak signal and FM simplex (145.01,03,05,07,09 are widely used for packet radio)
145.10-145.20	Linear translator outputs
145.20-145.50	FM repeater outputs
145.50-145.80	Miscellaneous and experimental modes
145.80-146.00	OSCAR subband

146.01-147.37	Repeater inputs
146.40-146.58	Simplex
146.61-146.97	Repeater outputs
147.00-147.39	Repeater outputs
147.42-147.57	Simplex
147.60-147.99	Repeater inputs

1.25 Meters: 220-225 MHz

Sharing arrangements: In the US, amateurs have historically shared the band with radiolocation (government radar systems). Although the international tables have shown amateur, fixed and mobile services as coprimary occupants, FCC declined, until recently, to place fixed and mobile stations here. In a Report and Order released September 6, 1988, FCC allocated 220 to 222 MHz on an exclusive basis to the Land Mobile Service and allocated 222 to 225 MHz exclusively to the Amateur Radio Service. Amateurs are required to discontinue operation in the 220-222 MHz segment by 0000 UTC August 28, 1991.

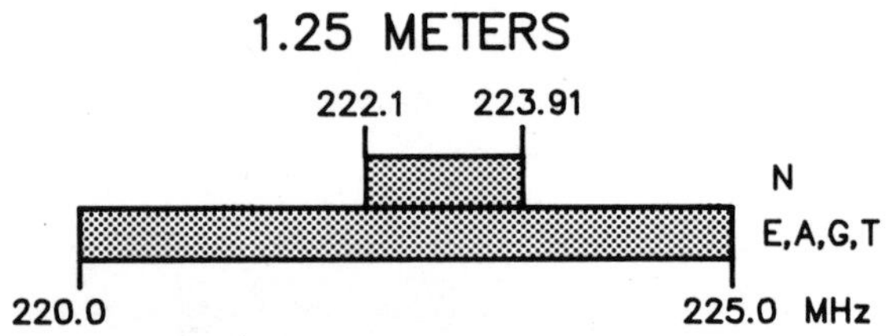

In Region 1, broadcasting, fixed and mobile services occupy the segment 223-230 MHz. In Region 3, fixed, mobile, broadcasting, radionavigation, and radiolocation are the 223-230 MHz occupants. There are no amateur allocations outside Region 2.

All licensees, except Novices, have access to the entire band 220-225 MHz. Novices may operate at 222.10-223.91 MHz, but are limited to 25 watts PEP output.

All modes except pulse and spread spectrum are permitted.

Band planning: (Note: A new band plan is under development by ARRL which will address the FCC's reallocation of the band.)

220.00-220.05	EME (Earth-Moon-Earth)
220.05-220.06	Propagation beacons
220.06-220.10	Weak signal CW
220.10	Calling frequency
220.10-220.50	General weak signal, rag chewing and experimental communications
220.50-221.90	Experimental and control links (221.01,03,05,07,09 are packet channels)
221.90-222.00	Weak-signal guard band
222.00-222.05	EME
222.05-222.06	Propagation beacons
222.06-222.10	Weak-signal CW
222.10	Calling frequency
222.10-222.30	General operation CW or SSB, etc
222.34-223.38	Repeater inputs
223.34-223.90	Simplex and repeater outputs (local option)

223.40	National packet simplex (223.40,42,44,46,48 are packet channels shared with FM voice. Check with local coordinator prior to use)
223.94-224.98	Repeater outputs

70 Centimeters: 420-450 MHz

In the US, we share the band with Government radiolocation (radar). We are the secondary service, and therefore must not interfere with the priority Government stations. We are also secondary to fixed and mobile stations in other countries at 420-430 MHz, and to Region 2 and 3 radiolocation stations at 430-440 MHz. We share the 430-440 MHz segment with Region 1 radiolocation stations on an equal basis.

As part of WARC-79 implementation proceedings, the 420-430 MHz portion of the band was removed from the Amateur Radio Service north of Line A [see Fig 3; also see §97.3(a)(26)]. In a later action, FCC allocated portions of the band 421-430 MHz to the Land Mobile Service within 50-mile radii centered on Buffalo, Detroit and Cleveland. Amateur stations south of Line A in the vicinities of these cities may continue to operate in the 421-430 MHz spectrum as long as they do not cause interference to land mobile or government radiolocation users.

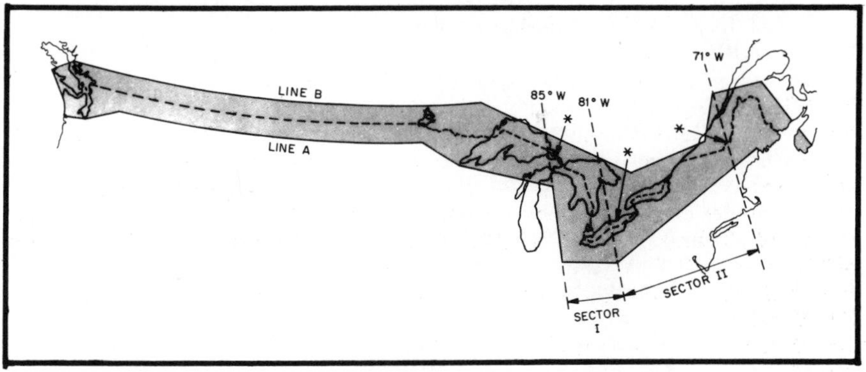

Additionally, 50-watt PEP output power limitations apply to amateurs operating within circles centered on designated military installations in the US. Exceptions may be granted when expressly authorized by FCC after mutual agreement, on a case-by-case basis, with the FCC Engineer-In-Charge and the area's military area frequency coordinator. An Earth station or telecommand station may, however, transmit on the 435-438 MHz segment without authorization; see §97.313(f). The affected areas are:

1) Portions of New Mexico and Texas bounded on the south by latitude 31° 45′ North, on the east by 104° 00′ West, on the north by latitude 34° 30′ North, and on the west by longitude 107° 30′ West.

2) The entire state of Florida including the Key West area and the areas enclosed within a 200-mile radius of Patrick Air Force Base, Florida (latitude 28° 21′ North,

longitude 80° 43′ West), and within a 200-mile radius of Eglin AFB, Florida (latitude 30° 30′ North, longitude 86° 30′ West).

3) The entire state of Arizona.

4) Those portions of California and Nevada south of latitude 37° 10′ north, and the areas enclosed within a 200-mile radius of the Pacific Missile Test Center, Point Mugu, California (latitude 34° 09′ North, longitude 119° 11′ West).

5) In the state of Massachusetts within a 160-kilometer (100-mile) radius around locations at Otis AFB, Massachusetts (latitude 41° 45′ North, longitude 72° 32′ West).

6) In the state of California, within a 240-kilometer (150-mile) radius around locations at Beale AFB, California (latitude 39° 08′ North, longitude 121° 26′ West).

7) In the state of Alaska, within a 160-kilometer (100-mile) radius of Clear, Alaska (latitude 64° 17′ North, longitude 149° 10′ West). (The military area frequency coordinator for this area is located at Elmendorf AFB, Alaska.)

8) In the state of North Dakota, within a 100-kilometer (100-mile) radius of Concrete, North Dakota (latitude 48° 43′ North, longitude 97° 54′ West). (The military area frequency coordinator for this area can be contacted at: HQSAC/SXOE, Offutt AFB, Nebraska 68113.)

When operating at 449.75-450 MHz, amateurs must not cause interference to, and must accept interference from space operation service and space research service stations or government or nongovernment space telecommand stations.

License privileges: Amateurs holding Technician class licenses and above have access to the entire band, 420-450 MHz.

Mode privileges: All mode privileges except pulse are authorized across the entire band.

Band planning:

420.00-426.00	ATV repeater or simplex with 421.25 MHz video carrier control links and experimental
426.00-432.00	ATV simplex with 427.250-MHz video carrier frequency
432.00-432.070	EME (Earth-Moon-Earth)
432.07-432.10	Weak-signal CW
432.100	70-cm calling frequency
432.10-432.30	Mixed-mode and weak-signal work
432.300-432.400	Propagation beacons
432.400-433.00	Mixed-mode and weak-signal work
433.00-435.00	Auxiliary/repeater links
435.00-438.00	Satellite only (internationally)
438.00-444.00	ATV repeater input with 439.250-MHz video carrier frequency and repeater links
442.00-445.00	Repeater inputs and outputs (local option)
445.00-447.00	Shared by auxiliary and control links, repeaters and simplex (local option); (446.0: national simplex frequency)
447.00-450.00	Repeater inputs and outputs

33 Centimeters: 902-928 MHz

Sharing arrangements: In the US, amateurs must not cause interference to, and must accept interference from, the government radiolocation (radar) stations. In other parts of Region 2, amateurs share secondary status with radiolocation and mobile services; the fixed service is the primary occupant. There are no 902-928 MHz amateur allocations outside Region 2.

Amateurs may encounter emissions from Industrial, Scientific and Medical (ISM) equipment. Examples are dialysis machines and manufacturing equipment. We must accept interference from, and not cause interference to, these applications.

We must also accept interference from microwave ovens operating at 915 MHz, manufactured before January 1, 1980. Intentional radiators (garage door openers, wireless stereo speakers, wireless remote controls, for example) and unintentional radiators (computers, for example) are permitted to operate in this region of the spectrum; we may encounter interference from these sources.

Additionally, amateurs located in the following areas may not transmit on this band except as noted:

1) in the states of Colorado and Wyoming, bounded on the south by latitude 39° North, on the north by latitude 42° North, on the east by longitude 105° West, and on the west by longitude 108° West. Note: 97.303(g)(1) waived by FCC, July 2, 1990, to permit amateurs in the restricted area to transmit in the following segments: 902.0-902.4, 902.6-904.3, 904.7-925.3, 925.7-927.3 and 927.7-928.0 MHz.

2) in the states of Texas and New Mexico bounded on the south by 31° 41′ North, on the north by latitude 34° 30′ North, on the east by longitude 104° 11′ West, and on the west by longitude 107° 30′W.

License privileges: All licensees except Novices have full access to the segment.

33 CENTIMETERS

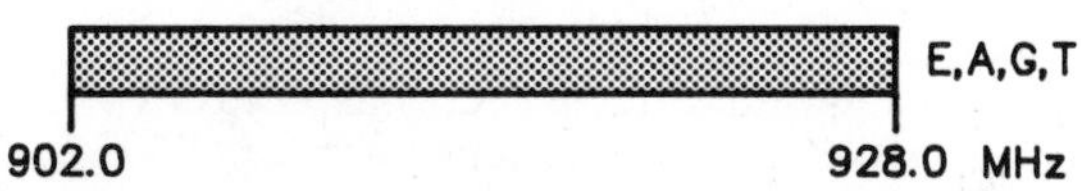

Mode privileges: All modes may be used on the entire band.

Band planning:

The following band plan was adopted by the ARRL Board of Directors in July 1989:

Frequency	*Activity*
902.0 - 903.0	Weak signal [902.1 calling frequency]
903.0 - 906.0	Digital [903.1 alternate calling frequency]
906.0 - 909.0	FM repeater outputs
909.0 - 915.0	Amateur TV
915.0 - 918.0	Digital
918.0 - 921.0	FM repeater inputs
921.0 - 927.0	Amateur TV
927.0 - 928.0	FM simplex and links

23 Centimeters: 1240-1300 MHz

All emission privileges except pulse are allowed on this band. The entire band is available to all licensees except Novices. Novice operators may use the 1270-1295 MHz band and are limited to 5 watts PEP output. This band, as are virtually all amateur bands between 220 MHz and 24.250 GHz (24.00-24.05 GHz is an exception), is allocated to amateurs on a secondary, noninterference basis, to the primary

23 CENTIMETERS

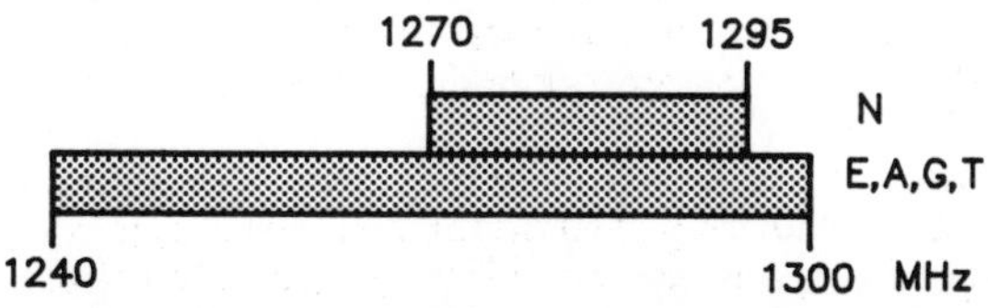

Novices are limited to 5 watts PEP output from 1270 to 1295 MHz.

Government Radiolocation services. We may encounter interference from unintentional and intentional radiators (Part 15 devices).

Band planning: The following band plan was adopted by the ARRL Board of Directors meeting in January 1985.

Segment	*Use*
1240-1246	ATV #1
1246-1248	Narrow-bandwidth FM point-to-point links and digital, duplex with 1258-1260.
1248-1252	Digital Communications
1252-1258	ATV #2
1258-1260	Narrow-bandwidth FM point-to-point links and digital, duplexed with 1246-1252
1260-1270	Satellite uplinks, reference WARC '79
1260-1270	Wide-bandwidth experimental, simplex ATV
1270-1276	Repeater inputs, FM and linear, paired with 1282-1288, 239 pairs every 25 kHz, eg 1270.025, .050, etc. 1271.0-1283.0 uncoordinated test pair
1276-1282	ATV #3
1282-1288	Repeater outputs, paired with 1270-1276
1288-1294	Wide-bandwidth experimental, simplex ATV
1294-1295	Narrow-bandwidth FM simplex services, 25-kHz channels
1294.5	National FM simplex calling frequency
1295-1297	Narrow bandwidth weak-signal communications (no FM)
1295.0-1295.8	SSTV, FAX, ACSSB, experimental
1295.8-1296.0	Reserved for EME, CW expansion
1296.0-1296.05	EME-exclusive
1296.07-1296.08	CW beacons
1296.1	CW, SSB calling frequency
1296.4-1296.6	Crossband linear translator input
1296.6-1296.8	Crossband linear translator output
1296.8-1297.0	Experimental beacons (exclusive)
1297-1300	Digital Communications

Above and Beyond

All modes and licensees (except Novices) are authorized on the following bands:

2300-2310 MHz	10.0-10.5 GHz	119.98-120.02
2390-2450	24.0-24.25	142.0-149.0
3300-3500	47.0-47.2	241.0-250.0
5650-5925	75.5-81.0	All above 300

For sharing arrangements, see §97.303. For band plans, see *The ARRL Operating Manual*.

Chapter Six

Standard Operating Procedures: The Basics

Operating a station goes to the heart of Amateur Radio. An Amateur Radio license is your passport to virtually every country in the world—without leaving your easy chair. Operating your radio on the ham bands is the goal that you set out to achieve during the process of studying for exams, assembling your station and putting up your antenna.

Accordingly, under Subpart B (Station Operation Standards), which is the subject of this chapter, you'll find one of the most significant, yet shortest, rules in all of Part 97. It's called "Good amateur practice," §97.101(a), which reads "In all respects not specifically covered by FCC rules each amateur station must be operated in accordance with good engineering and good amateur practice."

This rule, and, in fact, the entire body of FCC Part 97, recognizes that there exists a deeply rooted philosophy in the amateur fraternity that is as strong now as it was in the days of the radio pioneers: the philosophy of self-regulation. Both good amateur practice *and* strict rules compliance have always characterized the operations of the vast majority of US radio amateurs. Over the years, we amateurs have become known for our ability to maintain high standards of operating and technical skill without excessive regulation by the FCC. The Commission has continually praised the Amateur Service for this tradition of self-policing. Amateurs adhere not only to FCC rules, but to these "unwritten ethics" (unwritten only in terms of the FCC, but addressed constantly in ARRL literature) dictated by high standards of conduct through good amateur practice.

Perhaps the underlying reason for this is the amateur's sense of pride, accomplishment, fellowship, loyalty and concern for what is *more than* just a hobby to most amateurs.

Good engineering practice (that is, the electronics of your station) will be addressed in Chapter 8. For now, we're only concerned with good amateur practice in terms of *operating*. How do you know if your operations are above board and in compliance with the good-amateur practice standard? Good question. This chapter will discuss the specific rules and how to properly apply them to your on-the-air conduct. But again, good amateur practice also means working within the general parameters of "conventions" (a convention in this context is *not* the place where you find a big flea market and manufacturer displays, but a generally accepted on-the-air custom or mode of behavior). Amateur Radio has its share of such customs that have evolved over the years to make communicating with each other easier and more efficient.

The FCC, through the somewhat general §97.101(a), implicitly encourages us to operate in accordance with such standards and customs. (These customs are similar to social customs that have developed in society; we rise when meeting new people, we offer a cold one to guests in our home and we wave in acknowledgment to other drivers when they let us in their traffic lane.) This is why it is crucial to your operating success that you know *both* the black-letter law of operating and the conventions that have voluntarily evolved within the amateur community. Both comprise good amateur practice.

PEACEFUL COEXISTENCE

The amateur frequencies, especially at MF and HF (160-10 meters), tend to be congested; interference (QRM) is just a fact of Amateur Radio life. Indeed it is a positive result of Amateur Radio growth and vitality. As such, a cardinal rule of good amateur practice is to always *listen* before you transmit on any frequency. At best, transmitting without listening is a rude interruption of someone else's conversation. At worst, it could interfere with emergency communications in progress. See Chapter 7 for a more comprehensive discussion of amateur-to-amateur interference.

Before you transmit, listen first; if it appears the particular frequency is unoccupied, ask "Is this frequency in use?" (QRL? on CW). If the response is a simple "Yes," or C on CW, keep moving up the band. Once you've determined that a given frequency is clear, you're ready to make QSOs.

The FCC rules mandate that all amateur frequencies are shared and that cooperation is the key to making the most effective use of our bands. As one example, you don't want to ragchew with your local friend on the choicest DX portion of 20- or 75-meter phone. In that case, VHF, or the high end of 20 or 75, would be a more intelligent frequency choice and consistent with good amateur practice.

What about nets? Well, no one *owns* any particular amateur frequency, even a net that has been meeting on the same spot on the dial for the past 40 years. Except in an FCC-declared emergency, no one has any legal right to kick anyone else off of a particular frequency, and no one's particular use of the spectrum is any more valid than anyone else's. Note that the FCC considers emergency communications as Amateur Radio communications "directly relating to the immediate safety of human life and the immediate protection of property." Of course, there will be emergency situations where the FCC has not made any such declaration; you must steer clear of *any* net or frequency where emergency traffic is being handled. See Chapters 7 and 13 for more details on public service, traffic nets and related subjects.

WHO'S IN CHARGE HERE?

The control operator concept is fundamental in Amateur Radio. Some *person* must be responsible for the proper operation of an amateur transmitter. That's the control operator, defined in the rules as "an amateur operator designated by the licensee of a station to be responsible for the transmissions from that station to assure compliance with the FCC rules." What that mouthful means is that the radio amateur sitting at the mike or key (the *control point*, that is, the location where the control operator function is performed), the person who is running the immediate operation of the station, is the one who is legally in control. This is the case *regardless* if it's his home station or a station at the home of another amateur.

COMMON QUESTIONS AND ANSWERS —CONTROL OPERATORS

Q. Who is responsible for the proper operation of an amateur station?

A. You, as the licensee of your station, are *always* responsible for any transmission that originates there. When someone else is operating your station as its control operator, you are *both* equally responsible for the transmissions and compliance with the rules. The FCC, and everyone else for that matter, usually assumes you are the control operator of your own station. Keep a note of when someone else was your station's control op in case you later need to clarify who was operating.

Usually, the station licensee and the control operator are one and the same —you normally operate your own station. But occasionally you will invite a ham friend over to your shack to, say, help share operating duties in a contest. Or, you might operate the radio station at your ham friend's QTH. In such cases, you both share responsibility equally for the proper operation of the station.

The FCC Engineer in Charge and/or his staff can inspect your station records in those admittedly rare situations where compliance with FCC rules is at issue.

Q. Whose call sign is used when a friend operates my station?

A. The FCC has clarified the new rules concerning station identification when operating at a station other than your own. The wording in the new rules is to thwart bootlegging. It is not intended to prevent visiting operators from using their call signs at other stations—a practice that was okay under the old rules, and is still okay under the new rules.

There are a couple of acceptable procedures: (1) A visiting operator can be designated control operator of your station. In this case, the visitor signs your station call sign and operates within the privileges of your license to the extent his license permits; if he has greater privileges than you, he can use them by signing your call sign followed by his. (2) You may simply "lend" your equipment to your visitor, and the equipment in your shack then becomes your visitor's temporary station. Your visitor signs his own call and operates within the privileges of his license.

Q. Which stations need control operators?

A. *Every* station must have a control operator when transmitting. The control operator must be present at the control point. Most stations are under *local control*; the control operator is sitting right in front of the rig to directly twiddle and diddle with the knobs and watch the lights blink to make sure the station is operating properly!

There are exceptions to the rule that the operator must be at the control point, these being *automatic control* and *space stations*. Automatic control is used most often in repeaters and VHF packet stations, while space stations are amateur satellites and other operations more than 50-km from the earth's surface. For more details on these specialized communications techniques, see Chapters 10, 11 and 12.

A BREAK FOR STATION IDENTIFICATION

There is a very simple reason for station identification: You must clearly make known the source of your transmissions to anyone receiving them. No station may transmit unidentified communications or signals, or transmit as the station call any call not authorized to the station.

The basics are that you must identify your call at the end of each contact, and every ten minutes during the contact. This may be done using any of the modes presently legal in the Amateur Service, as long as it is by an authorized emission for the frequency in use.

When you identify by phone, you must use English, and you are encouraged to use phonetics (see the following section). If you use an automatic CW ID'er, you must keep its speed to no greater than 20 WPM. You can identify in Baudot, AMTOR or ASCII when all or part of your communications are transmitted in the same digital code as the station ID, or when sending data on 50 MHz and above. And, you can identify image (ATV and facsimile modes) using accepted color or monochrome transmission standards. Lastly, spread-spectrum transmissions must be identified by CW or phone.

COMMON QUESTIONS AND ANSWERS —STATION IDENTIFICATION

Q. Why do I have to bother to identify at all?

A. The FCC rules prohibit any unidentified transmissions or the use of bootleg calls. Proper identification is required so that the source of a transmission can be made known to those on the receiving end. Or, to put it another way, your ID is required so that other stations know where you're coming from!

Q. Do I have to give my call sign at the beginning of the contact?

A. Legally, you have to ID only at the *end* of the QSO and at least once every 10 minutes during the course of a QSO. There is no requirement to transmit your call sign at the beginning of a contact. As a practical matter, however, you're going to sign your call when you are calling another station for the first time. If you didn't, that station wouldn't have a clue as to who's calling him! It's also good amateur practice to identify your station during your first transmission on an FM repeater, for example.

During a contact, such as a ragchew when there is a lot of back and forth, you *do not* have to identify with every transmission, just at the required 10-minute intervals. If, for example, you have a conversation with someone that lasts eight minutes, then you would have to identify only once, at the conclusion of the QSO. If, however, you had a 35-minute contact, you would have to identify at least every 10 minutes and again at minute 35 as you were signing clear with that station.

Q. How often do I have to sign the call sign of the station I'm talking to?

A. You are not legally required to sign the other person's call *at any time*, which really helps in contest and DX situations, where brevity and swiftness of communication are essential. Also, simpler ID requirements mean smoother-flowing communications in emergencies and in emergency-preparedness exercises. The only exception is when handling traffic with foreign stations—you must then give the other station's call at the end of the exchange of third-party traffic.

Can you imagine being in a roundtable discussion with 10 or more stations on 2-meter FM or 10-meter SSB and having to sign the call of each one? Mind boggling! Of course, you are free to sign the other station's call any time you want, particularly if a band is congested and you want to verify who is calling whom. In those circumstances, it is good practice to keep your calls short. (Transmit the call sign of the station you're calling once or twice only, followed by your call once or twice, using phonetics when necessary.) Otherwise, good amateur practice is to keep your IDing to the minimum and only sign the other station's call when absolutely necessary.

Q. When my ham friends from the local radio club come to visit my home and operate my rig, or vice versa, whose call sign is used? What frequency privileges may they (I) use?

A. As discussed in the section on control operators, you may "lend" your station to your friend; he then uses his own call sign to identify his temporary station.

Or, you may designate him to be the control operator of your station. He signs your call sign and operates within the privileges of your license to the extent his license permits; if he has greater privileges than you, he can use them by signing your call followed by his. For example, if Rosalie, WA1STO, an Advanced, visits the shack of Kirk, NTØZ, an Extra, Rosalie signs Kirk's call, but must stay within her Advanced privileges. On the other side of the coin, if Kirk visits Rosalie's shack, and is using his Extra class privileges, Kirk must add his own call to the end of the station ID: WA1STO/NTØZ.

Q. I regularly conduct my QSOs in Esperanto. Is it okay to identify in Esperanto?

A. When operating phone, you must identify your station in the *English* language; Esperanto doesn't make it, sorry.

Q. What is this "Temporary AG" I keep hearing on the bands?

A. If you pass an amateur exam, accredited Volunteer Examiners are empowered to issue a Certificate of Successful Completion of an Examination (CSCE), a temporary permit that allows the use of your new privileges immediately. In the interim period after passing the exam and before your new ticket arrives from Gettysburg, you must add a special designator to your call sign when you are using your new privileges. For example, if you just upgraded from Novice to General and you are operating in the General subband with your new General-class temporary permit, you must sign your call followed by the words "Temporary AG," or the fraction bar (/) followed by the letters AG on CW and digital modes. The AG is the FCC indicator for General class (the other indicators are KT for Technician, AA for Advanced and AE for Extra).

Q. I'm a popular kind of guy; I like to make friends and influence people. This summer, G5BFU from England and VE3GRO from Ontario are coming to visit me and my family. How should G5BFU and VE3GRO identify while they're here in the states?

A. Well, first of all, make sure that G5BFU applies and obtains a reciprocal operating permit. (The US and Canada have instant reciprocity, so VE3GRO doesn't have any red tape to worry about.)

Let's say G5BFU gets his permit and is on the air from sunny California; his station ID consists of the US letter prefix and number followed by his home call sign: "W6/G5BFU." This is the European style of portable identification that the FCC adopted back in June of 1988. Because of treaty constraints, proper identification for VE3GRO is in the traditional manner—Canadian call sign *followed by* US prefix. VE3GRO in six-land would ID as "VE3GRO/W6." The "W6" portion of the identification is considered the "indicator" by the FCC. The call sign and the indicator are separated by the fraction bar (/) on CW or RTTY, or a pause (that refreshes) or the words "stroke," "slant," "slash" or "portable."

The rules also require that at least once during the QSO, the city and state must be mentioned, in English. G5BFU, who we wouldn't expect to have much trouble with the English language(!) might ID thusly: "This is W6 stroke G5BFU in beautiful downtown Burbank, California."

Q. Is it okay to give my call sign in phonetics when identifying?

A. Yes. The FCC has encouraged the use of a nationally or internationally recognized standard phonetic alphabet *when necessary* as good amateur practice. The International Telecommunication Union (ITU), an agency of the United Nations, has developed such a list, and the League encourages its use when phonetics are necessary to make the *initial* identification (such as when signals are weak or in the middle of a DX pileup when there is a lot of QRM). The ITU list is shown in Fig 1.

A—Alfa	J—Juliette	R—Romeo
B—Bravo	K—Kilo	S—Sierra
C—Charlie	L—Lima	T—Tango
D—Delta	M—Mike	U—Uniform
E—Echo	N—November	V—Victor
F—Foxtrot	O—Oscar	W—Whiskey
G—Golf	P—Papa	X—X-Ray
H—Hotel	Q—Quebec	Y—Yankee
I—India		Z—Zulu

Figure 1—The International Telecommunication Union (ITU) list.

For example, Shelly, WB1ENT, may identify her call sign by transmitting "Whiskey Bravo One Echo November Tango."

AUTHORIZED COMMUNICATIONS

As alluded to throughout this *Rule Book*, Amateur Radio is unique for its diversity and flexibility. As long as you don't violate the rules of Part 97, you're free to choose the quality, quantity and content of your Amateur Radio operating. Within this broad context, the FCC outlines what it considers "authorized transmissions," as follows.

Obviously, you can communicate with other amateur stations. You can also communicate with stations in other FCC-licensed radio services during emergencies and disasters. (For example, from time to time, both MARS and Coast Guard stations have come into the amateur bands to work directly with amateurs to save lives in emergency situations.) You can also communicate with RACES-affiliated stations. See Chapter 13 for more information on RACES. You may communicate with non-FCC-regulated stations, but authorized by FCC to communicate with amateurs. (You can exchange messages with a US military station during an Armed Forces Day Communications Test.)

To avoid any semblance of broadcasting in the Amateur Service, only *certain* "one-way" transmissions are permitted on the ham bands. Permissible one-way transmissions include when you're peaking your finals (for the "minimum time necessary;" good amateur practice would be to use a dummy load or to avoid tuning up on a pileup on a DX station) or when you're calling CQ; when you are in the beacon mode, remote control operation and other specialized modes (see Chapter 12); bulletins of interest to amateurs only and code practice such as that transmitted by W1AW (see "one-way transmissions" below); retransmission of space communications (play-by-play space-shuttle communications retransmissions is a regular amateur activity during almost every launch); and communications for emergencies.

Another aspect of Amateur Radio operating that is explicitly permitted by the rules is "international communications." The rules indicate that working foreign hams is fine, as long as the messages are of a "technical nature relating to tests" and unimportant "remarks of a personal character," and their governments permit ham communication with us (at present, there are no "banned countries").

ONE WAY BULLETINS

The most well-known one-way bulletins come from W1AW, the ARRL Headquarters station. For decades, W1AW has transmitted brief information bulletins. It is common practice for other amateur stations to conduct similar operations, usually on a localized basis, and usually as a part of a scheduled net or on some other limited, scheduled basis. Such bulletins are very important to the dissemination of timely and accurate information to radio amateurs.

W1AW and other stations providing this service generally have been careful to make such bulletins brief and factual. On rare occasions, such as during the launch of an Amateur Radio satellite or the Space Shuttle, amateur stations using phone have been put into a quasi-broadcast operation in order to provide real-time information about a developing situation of special interest to radio amateurs; such events are rare and amateurs have exercised restraint.

According to the rules, the content of bulletins must be limited to matters of direct interest to radio amateurs only, and never intended for the ears of the general public. As with business communications, the potential for abuse of the one-way transmissions rules has long existed. There is no room in the crowded amateur high-frequency bands for lengthy one-way transmissions on a regular, quasi-broadcast basis. Information bulletins by definition must be confined to factual matters, not matters of opinion. They must be intended to inform rather than to entertain. Solicitations of funds are particularly inappropriate and constitute business communications. Such transmissions in the context of bulletins should not be made.

RESTRICTED OPERATION

The rules give the FCC the latitude to impose so-called "quiet hours" on your operations. These quiet hours, when you would not be permitted to operate, are 8 PM to 10:30 PM local daily (roughly equivalent to network TV primetime) and additionally on Sunday from 10:30 AM to 1 PM. The quiet hours are applicable only to situations where there is interference with reception of transmissions from stations operating in the domestic broadcast service when receivers of good engineering design, including adequate selectivity characteristics, are employed. So quiet hours are not applicable to cases of telephone, stereo, or other home electronic interference, but rather only to broadcast receiver interference. Even then, there are no quiet hours applicable except when there has been a factual finding that the broadcast receiver is of good engineering design and of adequate selectivity characteristics.

After investigation by the FCC, however, the Commission may impose restrictions on operation, if there is interference to *stations operating in other services.* This does not include Part 15 devices, or home electronic equipment. In fact, Part 15 devices are subject to whatever interference is received.

Finally, if the FCC intends to put amateurs on quiet hours, or to other operating restrictions, it is obliged to afford the amateur an opportunity for a hearing before the restrictions are effective, pursuant to Sections 303(f) and 316 of the Communications Act.

ON THE ROAD AGAIN

While most of your ham radio activity will take place at your home shack, you will from time to time operate from other locations—your car, your vacation spot, at Field Day or even outside the country. Amateurs are *automatically* permitted to operate their stations portable or mobile anywhere in the United States, its territories and possessions. There is no need to notify the FCC, or make a log notation if you don't want to, of your portable operation in these areas. (Note that when there is a *permanent* change in your mailing address or station location, you must notify the FCC on Form 610). You do not have to sign "mobile" or "portable" if you don't feel like it, either. If you are operating your station away from home for a long period of time, arrange to have your mail forwarded to your temporary location in the unlikely event that the FCC sends you a Notice of Violation or other official correspondence to your permanent mailing address.

Drawing a distinction between mobile and portable operation is sometimes helpful. *Mobile* refers to talking on your 2-meter FM rig while driving your pick-up truck, or while jogging or backpacking. *Portable* means operation for an extended period of time at a specific, definable location, such as your cabin in the mountains or condo in Florida.

OPERATING AT SEA OR IN THE AIR

Gray areas sometimes occur in maritime mobile operation in and around foreign ports. Well-intentioned US hams often have trouble in determining just whose rules they're supposed to follow when sailing the seven seas.

Sometimes, regrettably, certain persons are not so well intentioned. Unscrupulous yachters and smugglers who do not, of course, hold ham tickets invade our amateur frequencies for such purposes as ordering parts and supplies for their vessels, conducting stateside business affairs or worse. They cling to the ill-conceived notion that because they're on the high seas, somehow the rules should not apply to them. Still others forego the standard marine mobile emergency communications gear, relying instead solely on an unlicensed ham transceiver—a dangerous proposition for an untrained, nonamateur in a maritime emergency.

Further, sometimes even licensed hams disregard the rules, complicating US and foreign efforts to reach important third-party and reciprocal operating agreements. Administrations unfriendly to international Amateur Radio are the first to cite these instances in attempting to remove privileges and frequencies at worldwide allocation conferences such as WARC-79. With WARC-92 on the horizon, all amateurs must be sensitive to this issue.

COMMON QUESTIONS AND ANSWERS —OPERATION AWAY FROM HOME

Q. My wife and I are setting sail on a luxury liner for a cruise among the Caribbean islands. I'd like to bring my ham rig with me. When I operate, whose rules do I follow?

A. The first determinant is the country of registry for the vessel. When you operate on the high seas (ie, international waters) on a US-registered vessel, you must follow the FCC rules. US and Canadian licensees need no special permit or authorization other than their own amateur licenses for operation aboard a US-registered vessel; these two countries share an automatic reciprocal-operating agreement.

If you are an alien (other than a Canadian citizen) licensee, you must obtain either a US amateur license or a reciprocal operating permit from the FCC *prior* to your operation aboard the US ship. A reciprocal permit may be issued by the FCC to licensed amateurs of a foreign country which has signed an agreement with the US to issue such permits on a reciprocal basis. (See Chapter 4 for details on reciprocal operating.) The amateur applying for such a reciprocal permit must be a citizen of that country (his home country). Note: US citizens who are licensed in another country (not the US) are *not* eligible for an FCC-issued reciprocal permit. If you are an alien operating on a non-US registered vessel, you must follow the licensing procedures of that particular country.

Q. Whose rules do I follow when my US ship sails into the territorial waters of another country?

A. When sailing or anchored in the territorial waters of another country, you must check the radio rules of that country before you operate your station. You must comply with those rules and obtain any required license or permit from that country's government. It is recommended that you study the country's requirements well in advance of your departure date (contact the Regulatory Information Branch at HQ for information—SASE please). Some administrations can take as long as six months or so to issue the necessary operating paperwork, so plan ahead! Never operate in a foreign country or in its territorial waters without proper authorization.

Q. What if the ship is of non-US origin even though I'm an FCC-licensed amateur?

A. If you are sailing in international waters aboard a non-US vessel, check the amateur rules of the country of the ship's registry. Contact the Regulatory Information Branch at HQ for information on a particular country. Since a ship is considered a part of the country in which it is registered, you must obey those rules and obtain any necessary license or permit from that country's government prior to your operation. If you are sailing in the waters of a foreign government's territory, you must observe the rules of that country and must obtain any necessary license or permit from that government prior to your operation in its territory. So you have a twofold responsibility: to obey the rules of the country of the ship's registry *and* the rules of the country(ies) whose territorial waters you're operating from.

Q. What do foreign Amateur Radio rules involve and how are they different from Part 97?

A. Generally, they are the same subjects as covered by our Part 97, although they tend to be more concise. Frequency privileges, power limitations, ID requirements, third-party traffic restrictions and other regulations can vary widely from country to country. We in the US often assume that Amateur Radio operators in other countries have been allocated the same frequencies that we have been. This is often not the case. Moreover, each of the three International Telecommunication Union (ITU) Regions has its own allocations for the various services, and they do not necessarily conform to our frequencies in the US (Region 2). When operating in a foreign country, always observe *all* of their rules.

Q. What other precautions must I take when I'm flying or sailing over/in US territory?

A. Concerning your equipment aboard a ship or plane, the rules require that the installation and operation of your station must be approved by the master of the vessel or the pilot. You must keep your radio gear separate from and independent of all other radio equipment installed on the ship or plane, except a common antenna may be shared with a voluntary ship radio installation.

Your transmissions must not cause interference to any other equipment installed on the ship or plane, for obvious reasons! Your station must not pose a hazard to the safety of life and property.

Additionally, you must not operate your rig on a plane when it is flying under Instrument Flight Rules (IFR), unless your station complies with all applicable FAA Rules. If you don't comply with these requirements, be prepared to walk the plank, or skydive (without your golden parachute!).

When you operate in ITU Region 2, frequencies used must be consistent with US frequency bands, and if you are a US licensee, you must operate within the privileges of your license. Outside Region 2 and subject to the limitations of your license class, the frequency segments listed in §97.301 may be used. For example, on 40 meters in Region 2, 7.0-7.3 MHz is allocated to the Amateur Radio Service, but in Regions 1 and 3, the amateur allocation is only 7.0-7.1 MHz.

Q. What ITU Region am I in?

A. If you're operating from Europe or Africa or the adjoining waters, you are in ITU Region 1. North and South America and the adjoining waters comprise Region 2. The rest of the world (the countries of Southern Asia as well as the islands of the Pacific and Indian Oceans) make up Region 3. See the map in Chapter 5.

Q. What type of station ID procedure should I use when I operate maritime mobile in international waters?

A. FCC rules place no special identification requirements on a station in maritime (or aeronautical) mobile operation. It is helpful to listeners, however, to follow your call with the words "Maritime Mobile" followed by the ITU Region in which you are operating. On CW, RTTY or some digital mode, you can send your call followed by the fraction bar, then the indicator MM (for maritime mobile) and the number of your ITU Region, such as KB1MW/MM2. Your ITU Region will always be 1, 2 or 3 (don't confuse ITU regions with domestic US call areas).

Q. Can I pass third-party message traffic?

A. In US territory, you may handle third-party message traffic, including phone patches, to countries with which the US holds third-party-traffic agreements. Most countries, however, *prohibit* third-party-traffic handling, or in some cases, prohibit phone patches while permitting other forms of message handling. You can't pass message traffic with countries which have *not* signed a third-party-traffic agreement with the US. The only exceptions are where the third party is a licensed amateur, and/or in a bona fide emergency. See Chapter 13 for a complete discussion of third-party-traffic handling, including the ARRL phone patch guidelines.

Q. How far do the territorial waters of a particular country extend?

A. The territorial limits extend to wherever that particular country says they do. The US claims only 3 nautical miles. Canada and Mexico claim 12 nautical miles. Most Caribbean island nations claim 3 to 12 miles, although there are exceptions. The territorial limits of certain Caribbean nations and other island nations whose area consists of many small islands often overlap, creating a larger territorial area than one would assume.

Q. A ham friend of mine recently told me that FCC-licensed amateurs who are within international waters could operate on all frequencies, regardless of their license class. Is this true?

A. No way. If an FCC-licensed station operates outsides the privileges of his/her license class, this is a violation of FCC rules. The FCC is aware of this problem, particularly with yachtsmen who choose to disobey the rules. The FCC continues to take enforcement action on these illegal operators. While most maritime-mobile operators are law-abiding citizens, as are most radio amateurs, the few who do exhibit improper behavior cast a bad light on all amateurs.

SUMMARY

The four cornerstones of successful ham radio operating are: knowledge, skill, dedication and courtesy. This chapter, along with the information in the other books from the ARRL bookshelf mentioned earlier, is intended to give the basic rules and knowledge needed for operating an amateur station. Skill is a product of operating ability and repeated practice so that the mechanics become almost second nature. Dedication involves spending the time to learn, then applying that to your enjoyment of this rich hobby. Courtesy in Amateur Radio goes beyond just being considerate and extends to being helpful to others.

Good amateur practice in on-the-air operating means all of the above, that is, being guided by the intent *and* the spirit of the rules. The FCC and the amateur community (collectively as the ARRL and individually) have worked together to forge a consensus represented in the new Part 97 that makes Amateur Radio operating more dynamic and creative than ever before.

SUMMARY

The four cornerstones of successful ham radio operating are: knowledge, skill, dedication and courtesy. This chapter, along with the information in the other books from the ARRL bookshelf mentioned earlier, is intended to give the basic rules and knowledge needed for operating an amateur station. Skill is a product of operating ability and repeated practice so that the mechanics become almost second nature. Dedication involves spending the time to learn, then applying that to your enjoyment of this rich hobby. Courtesy in Amateur Radio goes beyond just being considerate and extends to being helpful to others.

Good amateur practice in on-the-air operating means all of the above, that is, being guided by the intent *and* the spirit of the rules. The FCC and the amateur community (collectively as the ARRL and individually) have worked together to forge a consensus represented in the new Part 97 that makes Amateur Radio operating more dynamic and creative than ever before.

Chapter Seven

Thou Shalt Not. . .

At the outset of this book, we explained how the rules are set up to allow flexibility and breathing room. You can experiment with new ideas, help the public enjoy and participate safely in events such as parades and walkathons by providing support communications and promote goodwill between us and the peoples of other nations. And, of course, the rules allow room to move for providing emergency communications in support of disaster relief efforts, a major reason for the existence of Amateur Radio in the first place.

In other chapters, we've seen specifically just what Amateur Radio operators can do—how stations may be operated, and what frequencies and emissions can be used to get the most out of our service.

However, there are a few specific things you must *not* do—FCC calls them "prohibited transmissions." Many of these are common sense, black-and-white, needing little explanation or interpretation. But others, as we will see, lie in the gray area between black and white. These require interpretation and clarification for specific situations.

Because it is usually dangerous for the lay ham to ask FCC officials for interpretations (see Chapter 14), we will present comprehensive discussions of FCC letters, news releases, public notices, approved interpretations and so forth that will help you understand the gray area rules and apply them to your own activity. It is hoped you will not need to consult FCC after you read these interpretations.

These prohibited practices are important; some are required to preserve the very core of Amateur Radio. Examples include the prohibition against operating your station for compensation, public broadcasting, business purposes, and music.

DIRECT AND INDIRECT PAYMENT

You must never accept any money, or other consideration, for operating your station. This is consistent with one of the prime directives of our service:

"Recognition and enhancement of the value of the amateur service to the public as a *voluntary, noncommercial* communication service, particularly with respect to providing emergency communications." [emphasis added].

If your club is providing communications support to the town of Needham for a parade, you cannot accept their offer of payment for your work. You are volunteers, providing a community service on a noncommercial basis, period.

You should never accept anything for your Amateur Radio operating. FCC prohibits operation of an amateur station "for hire, nor for material compensation, direct or indirect, paid or promised." This includes direct payment (money, goods, food, and so forth) and indirect payment (publicity, advertising, and so on).

Back to our example. The Needham town officials may, however, provide you with items to verify the identity of participating amateurs—badges, caps, T-shirts, signs. These are not considered to be material compensation.

Well, then, how is it that W1AW (the ARRL HQ station) operators are allowed to be paid? The rules provide for just such an activity.

Organized groups of amateurs often provide communications support to civil preparedness agencies and others on a voluntary basis. Amateurs are strictly prohibited from accepting any form of compensation for their Amateur Radio operations! The noncommercial nature of Amateur Radio is one of the cornerstones of its foundation. The Mountain Amateur Radio Club, Cumberland, MD, serves the Allegany County Civil Defense.

Control operators of a club station may be compensated when the club station is operated primarily for code-practice transmissions or for transmitting bulletins consisting of Amateur Radio news having direct interest to hams. To qualify under this provision, however, the station must conduct code-practice sessions for at least 40 hours per week, schedule operations on six medium- and high-frequency amateur bands and publish the schedule of operating times and frequencies at least 30 days in advance of the actual transmissions. Control operators may accept compensation only when the station is transmitting code practice and bulletins.

BROADCASTING

Broadcasting refers to transmissions that are intended to be received by the general public. As such, broadcasting must be left to those services that are directly authorized to do so by the FCC—commercial television and radio, for example. Broadcasting is specifically prohibited in the Amateur Radio Service.

You must not transmit anything intended to be received by the public either directly or by intermediary relay stations. It's important to note the difference, however, between broadcasting and the permitted one-way transmissions of bulletins. As we've seen, bulletins dealing directly with Amateur Radio matters may be transmitted one-way to amateurs only; they may not be transmitted for the benefit of the general public. For example, an amateur may recite the latest ARRL bulletin over his local repeater, but may not give a rundown on the Middle East situation that is intended for the ears of the general public who have home scanners. You may not retransmit FM broadcast programs, or television audio. You may not retransmit NOAA weather broadcasts.

Occasionally, at a Field Day or other operating activity, a local broadcast station may ask you to let them record your station's transmissions and receptions for the local evening news. This is fine. You may consent to the retransmission, either live or delayed, of your amateur station transmissions by a radio or television broadcast station.

NEWS GATHERING AND THE MEDIA

You must not allow your amateur station to be used for any activity directly related to program production or news gathering for broadcast purposes. There is only one exception: You can transmit news information about an event if the following requirements are met: (1) the news information involves the immediate safety of life of individuals or the immediate protection of property; (2) the news information is directly related to the event; (3) the information can't be transmitted by any other means because normal communications systems have been disrupted or because there are no other communications systems available at the place where the information is originated; and (4) other means of communication could not be reasonably provided before or during the event.

FCC completed a sweeping review of the relationship between broadcasting and Amateur Radio in June 1985. A number of rules in both the Broadcast and Amateur services were modified or overturned altogether. One change was the elimination of the requirement that broadcasters obtain permission from amateurs to rebroadcast amateur signals: Such permission is no longer required, and broadcasters are no longer obligated to advise FCC that any such retransmission has occurred. This arises from Amateur Radio's exemption from the secrecy of communications provisions of Section 705 of the Communications Act of 1934, as amended. The FCC felt there was still sufficient protection against Amateur Radio stations being used for broadcast program production and news gathering.

Working With the Media

Face it, chances are that sooner or later your amateur activity may come to the attention of the media. For example, a local TV station may want to interview you at your station concerning the latest ham transmissions from a hurricane-devastated Caribbean island.

News reporters can be pushy, to say the least. To help you cope with one breathing heavily down your back, asking you to sell your soul (and license) for his evening edition, ARRL has come up with a set of guidelines to keep in the back of your mind when under the hot, bright camera lights:

- Amateur Radio operators may assist news media representatives in their efforts to gather information for relay to the public from areas where normal communications have been disrupted.
- Amateurs may ask questions of, or relay media questions to, amateurs in the emergency area. The responses may be electronically recorded by media representatives.
- Amateur Radio must not be used to assist the news media in gathering information when telephones or other commercial means of communication are available.
- Amateur Radio must not be used to facilitate the operation of any business.
- Amateur Radio operators should depend on their own judgment when dealing with the news media and when operating their station in the public interest, convenience and necessity.

MUSIC

The transmission of music is strictly prohibited in the amateur bands. For example, expect some mail from the FCC if you transmit Rossini's *The Barber Of Seville* on your favorite 75-meter phone net. Note that the FCC mail will not be a critical review of the performance; it will, however, be a notice of violation.

COMMON QUESTIONS-AND-ANSWERS—MUSIC

Q. At last night's club meeting, a fellow member told me that he could hear my car radio playing in the background during our repeater QSO. I didn't even think about it at the time—but, was I in violation of the rules?

A. What the FCC is really concerned about is the deliberate playing of music on Amateur Radio for purposes of providing entertainment. FCC doesn't want the general public tuning in to your amateur station to listen to music!

As a practical matter, you won't go to jail for an isolated incident involving a little background noise and music while you're talking on 2 meters. But, if the background radio music was loud enough to cause your friend to mention it to you, it was too loud. It might have disturbed others, too. Just keep it down next time!

Q. My friend and I are music composers. Can we trade compositions in ASCII code across town on 2 meters?

A. Sure. The music prohibition concerns the playing of music itself, not information about music. As long as no musical notes can be detected on-the-air, you're okay.

Q. What if we send commands to each other's MIDI synthesizers over the air?

A. Again, no problem, as long as no actual music is played on-the-air and the transmission took place on 50 MHz or higher.

Q. Can we sing "Happy Birthday" to our friend on the local 2-meter repeater?

A. No. Singing is actual music, and is prohibited, no matter how badly you sing.

CRIMINAL ACTIVITIES

Amateur Radio may not be used for any purpose, or in connection with any activity, that is contrary to Federal, state or local law. This means that if you use your 2-meter hand-held to communicate back to your get-away car during a bank heist, you'll not only be in trouble with the cops, but with the FCC as well. On top of getting 15 to 20, you could lose your license!

CODES AND CIPHERS

You may not hide the meaning of your communications by putting them into codes or ciphers. In this context, codes and ciphers refer to text that has been transformed to conceal its meaning. This restriction is consistent with the FCC's obligations under the international regulations that amateur communications be made in plain language. Universally accepted abbreviations may be used, however, when the intention is not to hide the meaning of the transmission; common Q signals are an example.

The rules do not apply to the legitimate use of secret telecommand codes used to protect the security of a space station.

Also, repeater trustees can use authentication codes to secure access to the control functions of their hilltop repeater. (Authentication codes are sent by control operators to the repeater control functions—the repeater checks, or authenticates, the code to ensure that the commands are coming from an authorized control operator.) Universally accepted Touchtone® pad tones are not considered to be codes and ciphers; their use in traditional repeater and other applications is fine.

OBSCENITY, PROFANITY AND INDECENCY

The rules say, quite simply, you cannot transmit obscene, indecent or profane words, language or meaning.

The FCC made the national news in a big way in April 1987. In a dramatic departure from a lengthy near-silence on the subject of indecent transmissions by its licensees, on April 16 the Commission put broadcasters and amateurs on notice that (1) standards for decency in radio transmissions exist in both services, and (2) henceforth, the standards will be enforced.

Two of the cases dealt with by the FCC involved broadcast stations in Los Angeles (KPFK-FM) and Philadelphia (WYSP-FM). KPFK, licensed to the Pacifica Foundation, Inc, was found to have broadcast material deemed indecent and possibly obscene at an hour, 10 PM, when there was a reasonable risk that children may have been in the listening audience. WYSP was found to have broadcast episodes of the Howard Stern weekday morning radio program that "dwelt on sexual and excretory matters in a pandering and titillating fashion that was patently offensive as measured by contemporary community standards for the broadcast medium." No sanctions were imposed on the licensees because prior rulings might have led them to believe that such conduct was not actionable; however, they were given stiff warnings that similar broadcasts in the future would render them liable to more severe sanctions, and the obscenity question was referred to the Justice Department for possible criminal prosecution.

A third case involved an amateur, David Hildebrand, N6BHU. Hildebrand had made transmissions on 2 meters in 1981, in the early evening and via a repeater with wide coverage, that were deemed indecent and therefore in violation of what was §97.119 of the FCC's rules. This prohibited the transmission of "communications containing obscene, indecent, or profane words, language, or meaning." The following year an Administrative Law Judge suspended Hildebrand's amateur station license and revoked his operator's license following a hearing. However, the FCC Review Board reversed that determination, holding that a 1978 Supreme Court ruling (also involving the Pacifica Foundation) did not explicitly apply to the Amateur Radio Service and that the FCC therefore could not regulate indecent transmissions in our service. The FCC Private Radio Bureau filed an Application for Review with the full Commission, and ARRL sought to support the Private Radio Bureau's position.

Almost five years later, the Commissioners acted to reverse the finding of the Review Board. When they did this, they noted that §97.119 [now §97.113(d)] specifically governs indecent transmissions in our service and that licensees should assume that Commission rules will be enforced. The Commission found that the principles applicable to complaints in the broadcasting service are equally applicable to the Amateur Service because (1) our frequencies are shared by many amateurs; (2) children are actively encouraged to become amateur licensees; and (3) it is not possible to separate adults from children in advance of specific transmissions. In the Commissioners' view, Hildebrand's violations "in this initial instance" did not warrant revocation or suspension of his licenses, but "further violations may lead to suspension or revocation of his license, in addition to forfeitures."

With release of a Public Notice on April 29, FCC notified its amateur licensees that "violations of the Commission's new standards. . . will subject them to the full range of sanctions available to the Commission." Here are the standards as they will be applied:

Obscenity: (1) an average person, applying contemporary community standards, must find that the material, as a whole, appeals to the prurient interest; (2) the material must depict or describe, in a patently offensive way, sexual conduct specifically defined by the applicable state law; and (3) the material, taken as a whole, must lack serious literary, artistic, political, or scientific value.

Indecency: language or material that depicts or describes, in terms patently offensive as measured by contemporary community standards for the broadcast medium, sexual or excretory activities or organs.

As to timing, obscenity and indecency are actionable whenever they are transmitted. The FCC had originally hoped to avoid a First Amendment confrontation, and provided a "safe harbor" for indecency by stating that "the regulation of indecency by channeling it to hours when there is not a reasonable risk that children may be in the audience is consistent with the First Amendment rights afforded newspapers and magazines." When indecent broadcasts are to be made, the FCC said advance warnings would be required. No specific time limits were established, but 10 PM is not late enough to avoid sanctions. However, in Public Law 100-459, signed by President Reagan on October 1, 1988, the FCC was given an explicit mandate to enforce the prohibitions against obscenity and indecency on a 24-hour-per-day basis. Congress told the Commission, in effect, to abandon caution and enforce its standards across the board.

Is the use of an expletive in itself indecent? According to the Commission, "deliberate and repetitive use of such expletives in a patently offensive manner would be a requisite to a finding of indecency." The context is also important.

FALSE SIGNALS

False signals are clearly prohibited in the amateur bands. You may not use someone else's call sign without authorization, or transmit a communication that is intended to deceive listeners. Sending a false $\overline{\text{SOS}}$ or MAYDAY will not win you any friends either.

RETRANSMITTING RADIO SIGNALS

Radio amateurs may retransmit only signals originating in the Amateur Radio Service, except for emergency communications. Often, amateurs find that retransmitting a friend's 20-meter signal over the local repeater adds some variety to their day-to-day activities. No problem, as long as this is done manually (with a control operator present). You must never record someone else's transmissions and play them back over the air without permission. That's poor amateur practice, and transmission of false signals.

You may retransmit space shuttle communications for the exclusive use of other amateurs, provided you get NASA's okay first.

Automatic retransmission of amateur signals may be done only by repeater, auxiliary and space stations.

MALICIOUS INTERFERENCE

Seventy years ago, it no doubt seemed to many amateurs that growth in numbers was surpassing our ability to absorb it. In those days it was hardly possible to put a station on the air without interfering with everyone else for miles around, and there was an uncountable horde of unlicensed, low-power spark-coil operators who were at best poorly informed about operating procedures and the capabilities of better-equipped stations. The number of amateurs who can remember those days is dwindling, someday to vanish altogether; the rest of us can only imagine what it must have been like.

Things today are simultaneously easier and far more complex. A combination of FCC-mandated and voluntary restrictions intended to keep us out of one another's way help, but these cannot completely eliminate QRM (interference) between amateur stations—nor should we expect them to.

Indeed, zero QRM is an utterly unrealistic expectation in Amateur Radio. Except when it concerns emergency communications, amateur-to-amateur interference is not, in and of itself, illegal. Each amateur station has an equal right to operate; just because you've used the same frequency since 1947 doesn't mean you have any more legal right to it than the guy who got his license in the mail five minutes ago. The rules specifically prohibit willful or malicious interference.

What's malicious interference? Here's an example. If two hams, or groups of hams, find themselves on the same frequency pursuing mutually exclusive objectives, that's happenstance, not malicious interference. On the other hand, if one moves to another frequency and the other follows, for the purpose of continuing to cause QRM to the first, the second has crossed the line. If he does it enough, he'll put his license in jeopardy. Of course, what sometimes happens is that they'll all sit on the one frequency and argue about who has more right to be there. All it accomplishes is to keep the frequency from being used by anyone for anything worthwhile.

Several other FCC rules are intended to minimize (but not to eliminate) interference. One says, "...an amateur station must use the minimum transmitter power necessary to carry out the desired communications." There's also a requirement that "...each amateur station must be operated in accordance with good engineering and good amateur practice." But our obligations to each other don't end with the rules; even more important is the need for common sense, and common courtesy, when we share our common spectrum resources.

We all have the right to pursue our legitimate objectives within the privileges conveyed by our licenses; but we also have the obligation to minimize the inconvenience and loss of enjoyment that we cause to others. If there's a tiny segment of a band that's used for international communication, surely it's not too much to ask that local ragchews take place elsewhere. If establishing a beacon in the middle of a densely populated segment is going to QRM nearby weak-signal enthusiasts, surely we can find another place to put it. (Insert your own favorite example here.) And surely, in such cases we don't need the FCC to tell us what growing up in a civilized society should already have taught us to do.

There are more amateur stations on the air today than there were yesterday. Tomorrow, there will be even more. The resulting interference will cause some of us to learn how to use less-populated bands—one of the desirable side effects of congestion. With that, and with a bit more common sense and courtesy, there will be room for even more newcomers—adding to our ability to deliver public service, and to earn public support.

COMMON QUESTIONS-AND-ANSWERS —MALICIOUS INTERFERENCE

Q. How can I fight malicious interference on a personal level?

When you experience malicious interference, use the most effective means of combating it at your disposal—ignore it on-the-air. Telephone your Section Manager and alert him or her to the situation. (A list of ARRL Section Managers appears on page 8 of every issue of *QST*.) Your Section Manager will relay your report to a representative of the Amateur Auxiliary to the FCC Field Operations Bureau. Simply give the facts—frequency and stations involved. Follow through with a brief written letter to your SM, or his or her designee, noting dates, times, frequencies and call signs. Encourage others to do the same. The Amateur Auxiliary is discussed in Chapter 15.

Above all, keep your on-the-air operation strictly above reproach. Don't make the Auxiliary's job more difficult by engaging interfering stations in their own game. By ignoring the offenders, you deprive them of their number one need—attention.

Q. What can we do about a jammer on our repeater?

A. The Amateur Auxiliary incorporates a special function in its program to deal with repeater problems—the Local Interference Committee (LIC). The LIC is organized at the local level to track down repeater jammers and other problem-causers, exert peer pressure to clear up problems, and when problems persist, work with FCC to gather evidence leading to an enforcement action. The LIC is officially sanctioned by the Section Manager, and in the presence of a signed agreement, by the FCC. If you've got a jammer on your hands, contact your Section Manager.

Q. Does the system for shutting down jammers work?

A. Yes. Here's what happened in a recent case in Washington state:

FCC News Release—"Working closely with the Amateur Auxiliary, the Federal Communications Commission (FCC) was able to issue a Notice of Apparent Liability and subsequent Notice of Forfeiture [a fine!] to Mr Billie E. Prell, N7FAQ, of Pasco, Washington.

The action against the amateur was triggered by numerous complaints from other amateur radio operators that Mr Prell was transmitting on 146.04 MHz for the sole purpose of disrupting the communications already in progress on that frequency. The intentional jamming signals were directly observed and identified by members of the Amateur Auxiliary's Local Interference Committee (LIC). The LIC forwarded the pertinent information to the local FCC office for investigation and enforcement."

Q. Recently, our public service net has been plagued with a ham who harasses us—it seems he'll do anything to disrupt our good work. To make matters worse, others join in with catcalls, whistles and other attempts to get rid of the guy. Is this malicious interference, and what can we do about it?

A. Nets are sometimes singled out for abuse because of their perceived "ownership" of a particular frequency. Of course, no individual operator or group has any special privilege to any part of a band.

Although you are suffering a considerable amount of thoughtless remarks, annoying practices and harassment, there may not be malicious interference. To be actionable, interference must be truly malicious. To nail an amateur on a malicious interference charge, Amateur Auxiliary members collect evidence in accordance with the comprehensive guidelines outlined in Chapter 15. The evidence must include dates, times, frequencies, call signs, local field-strength readings and direction-findings of the offending transmissions so that recreations of factual occurrences can be made. Conclusions must not be drawn by the monitors—it is for the FCC to determine whether the evidence, taken together, shows that a rule has been violated and that the accused person did it.

The task before the Auxiliary in a case such as yours is not an easy one: There are numerous stations responding to the primary offending operator with their own jamming transmissions, aggravating the situation enormously. The good news is that evidence gathered in accordance with the guidelines can be relied on by the FCC and used directly in enforcement proceedings. It is no longer necessary for FCC staff to duplicate the monitoring and DFing done by Auxiliary volunteers.

The best course is to try to avoid confrontation. Use extra caution when choosing a frequency to engage your net. Keep your operation legal and strictly above board. If problems persist, apply peer pressure—try to resolve conflicts through negotiation. If you are unsuccessful, contact a representative of the Amateur Auxiliary to the FCC Field Operations Bureau. Don't call FCC—they'll simply refer you to the Auxiliary per standard operating procedure.

WILLFUL OR MALICIOUS INTERFERENCE CLAUSE ADDED TO COMMUNICATIONS ACT

A 1990 measure added prohibitions against willful or malicious interference to the Communications Act of 1934. New Section 333 reads:

Sec. 333. No person shall willfully or maliciously interfere with or cause interference to any radiocommunications of any station licensed or authorized by or under this Act or operated by the United States government.

BUSINESS COMMUNICATIONS

A proper balance must exist in the rules: Amateurs must on the one hand be given the flexibility to achieve the objectives of the amateur service, but on the other, have the degree of protection necessary to prevent exploitation of the service. Amateur Radio should be allowed to use its allocated frequencies unfettered by encroachment from commercial entities. It should not be allowed to be exploited by those who would use them as an alternative to the land mobile, broadcast, maritime, or common carrier radio services.

For this reason, the FCC prohibits an amateur station from transmitting any communication the purpose of which is to facilitate the business or commercial affairs of any party. No amateur station may transmit communications as an alternative to other radio services, except as necessary to providing emergency communications. In an *Order* dated June 29, 1983, the FCC stated that the term "business," in this instance, is used in the broadest context. It includes all types of communications which are intended to facilitate the regular business or commercial affairs of any party, whether individual or organization, whether for-profit or not-for-profit, whether charitable or commercial, and whether government or non-government. By Public Notice titled *Amateur Service International Radiocommunications* dated September 1, 1989, the FCC further elaborated upon the scope of the rules prohibiting business communications: All types of communications related to business activities, including the advertising, soliciting, ordering, furnishing, delivering, accounting or billing of any supplies, materials, or services are prohibited.

COMMUNICATIONS FOR POLICE, AND OTHER PUBLIC SAFETY AGENCIES

Public service is one of the primary reasons for the existence of the Amateur Radio Service. Providing communications assistance to and cooperating with local police departments and other public safety agencies are fine ways to contribute to the welfare of your community. However, hams and their equipment should not be used in lieu of police communications on a routine or day-to-day basis. Amateur participation in police activities should be limited to practice drills for emergency preparedness, actual emergency communications support and occasional augmentation of regular police communications whereby the public is served ("Goblin Patrols" on Halloween and the like).

The whole subject of "public service" communications has some fascinating philosophical overtones. Back in the "good old days" it was easy: if you got paid for it you couldn't do it, and if you didn't, you could. That standard, abandoned by the FCC back in Docket 19245 in the early '70s, would no longer work—in large part because the service we can provide is now so much better than it was, and getting better all the time! There's a demand for our services from people who really should look elsewhere for the solution to their communications needs, and the line separating what we should from what we should not do can be pretty fuzzy.

On the other hand, can we afford to forego the opportunities for positive public exposure of Amateur Radio that service to safety agencies and the media offer, if we're going to excite young people's imaginations? The entire subject of proper use of Amateur Radio in public service and emergency communications is covered in Chapter 13. Third-party traffic is also covered there.

SWAP AND SHOP NETS

The legality of nets where members make arrangements to buy, sell and trade Amateur Radio gear has traditionally been one of the great debates.

Fortunately, the FCC recently dealt with the issue by putting its policy into the rules. You are allowed to inform other amateurs of the availability for sale or trade of ham gear, unless you are trying to make a profit by buying or selling gear on a regular basis. Thus, under these conditions, swap and shop nets are okay.

Keep in mind that it's inappropriate to discuss prices over the air; simply make contact with an interested party on the net, then move to the telephone for the rest of the transaction.

SUMMARY: "IS IT LEGAL?"

Whenever you have a question about the legality of doing something, try to resolve it in the spirit of the rules if you can't find the precise interpretation. For example, you're driving on a city highway at night with your three children in the back seat, and get a flat tire. You pull off into the emergency lane, and realize that your spare is also flat. Your 2-meter hand-held is on the seat next to you; you have no idea where the police call box is. "Should I use the repeater autopatch to call a tow truck? But, that's business communications—the tow truck comes from a commercial company!" There's nothing specifically in the rules that talks about tow truck companies, so you don't know what to do.

Consider the spirit of the rules—you know that ham radio can be used in emergencies, and isn't this sort of an emergency? Your kids and wife are stumbling around in the dark with tractor trailer trucks flying by at 70 mi/h. Pick up your radio and call for help!

Another example: You're talking with your brother in Florida on your weekly 20-meter phone sked. You ask him to contact a mortgage counselor there about the chances of getting a mortgage approved for a retirement condominium on the beach. You tell him about your personal assets, liabilities, the equity and value in your present home. He says okay. Why not? You're not conducting any business; you're just asking him to snoop around a little, right? No big business deal.

But, ask yourself, is this what Amateur Radio is for? Is this conversation consistent with the basis and purpose of Amateur Radio? How would you feel if you came across this conversation in the middle of 20 meters? Answers: not really, not really, and you probably would think that it's inappropriate, and that they should make arrangements by the telephone instead.

Next time you're wondering about whether something's legal or not, first check for the letter of the rules. If you can't find a specific rule, consider the spirit of the rules found in many places, but never more prominently than in the Basis and Purpose of Amateur Radio. Also, use this *Rule Book* to help you decide. We've included many interpretations that have evolved over the years to help you apply the rules to your specific situation. The plain language discussions should also help. If you still can't decide, contact ARRL HQ's Regulatory Information Branch. Its staff is trained in helping amateurs understand and interpret the rules. Contact them at:

ARRL Headquarters
Regulatory Information Branch
225 Main Street
Newington, CT 06111

Don't call the FCC! Usually amateurs contacting FCC do so for emotional reasons. Harmful precedents can be set by an FCC official answering a poorly crafted question. The cure can be far worse than the temporary affliction.

Chapter Eight

Emissions: Modulation, Signals and Information

SINS OF EMISSION

The Commission tried the 1979 World Administrative Radio Conference (WARC 79) emission designators in the Amateur Service from 1985 to 1989. But these designators (such as A1A, J3E, etc) were so confusing, yet over-specific, that hams and otherwise sane engineers couldn't get them right. If you couldn't find the emission designator for some new whizbang modulation scheme, you had to ask the FCC for a special temporary authority (STA) or petition for a permanent rule change. No one loved it.

If It Sounds Like a Duck, You Don't Have to Call it J3E

The FCC is trying something new this time—English. Rather than expressing "telephony" in arcane alphanumerics, Part 97 just says "phone," since we generally know what that is. That approach is being used in the new Part 97 with a cross-reference to the ITU emission designators for those who are at loose ends unless they know which specific emission they're emitting.

To find out what is permitted under the new emission designators, start by looking up the definitions under §97.3(c). For *CW* and *test* emissions, check §97.305(a) and (b), respectively. For other emission designators, check §97.305(c) to find the bands where these emissions are permitted, along with any restrictions and/or additional modes authorized for specific bands, which are located in §97.307(f). The new rules provide new latitude for the experimenter, while preserving the traditional demarcations between RTTY/data and phone/FAX/SSTV operation in the HF bands.

Just an Old Fashioned ID

You won't find this in the new rules, but here's a tip: If you are going to transmit an experimental signal that's permitted by the new rules, bear in mind the needs of other band users. If most hams won't recognize the new modulation method, it is possible that they will conclude that your signal is some kind of commercial intruder. Just like we have a few "repeater police" ready to pounce on you for doing what they consider the wrong thing, there may be some "emission police" who think you're an interloper. If you are going to transmit something new and weird, why not intersperse a few IDs and explain what you're doing in a conventional mode such as CW or phone?

MORE THAN YOU WANTED TO KNOW

As you read the remainder of this chapter, it will be helpful to keep a few definitions in mind:

- *Analog*—Information in continuously variable quantities.
- *Digital*—Information in discrete states.
- *Quantized*—Information whose variables are divided into a finite number of specific values or steps.

Analog is familiar; AM phone and the output of a video camera are examples. So is *digital*; usually the two states are simply on and off. *Quantized* may be new; it is like *analog* in many respects, except that the modulation is not continuously variable but in discrete steps, where each step is assigned a value or meaning. It so happens that the ITU WARC 79 emission designators lump *digital* and *quantized* together under the second symbols 1 or 2 (examples A1A, J2A), while *analog* is separate under the second symbol 3. If you are transmitting an image that is generated by a computer, you are probably emitting a *quantized* signal, not an analog one. The picture has a finite number of steps on its gray scale. An image showing these steps is said to be contoured. Similarly, a computer-generated speech signal is likely *quantized* rather than *analog*, and quantizing noise (gravel or graininess) can be annoying if the steps are too large.

What follows is a mode-by-mode description of what is now permitted under the new rules.

CW

The term *CW* (continuous wave) is used by hams to denote what technically is ICW (interrupted continuous wave), meaning that the carrier is turned on and off with the keying. According to §97.305(a), CW emission, ie, on/off-keyed (OOK) Morse code, can be operated on any frequency in the ham bands.

The old rules specified CW as A1A emission, which means amplitude-modulated telegraphy by on/off keying the main carrier intended for aural reception. In past versions of the rules, the FCC used only A1A to designate CW (on/off keying of the main carrier) but wouldn't have minded if you produced the same result by keying a tone and feeding it into a single-sideband transmitter. But that would have been J2A, which the former rules did not come right out and say was permissible everywhere A1A was. On/off keying of a tone modulating a single-sideband transmitter is now explicitly permitted. You need to have a beat-frequency oscillator (BFO) on to hear the Morse code keyed tone. Also, it is no longer forbidden fruit to copy a CW transmission by other than "aural reception," such as with a computer or by blinking light.

When a carrier is keyed on and off, as in any amplitude modulation, upper and lower (keying) sidebands are generated. The sidebands are above and below the carrier frequency according to the rise and fall times of the keying waveforms. So what's new? Besides transmitting a full carrier, experimenters can reduce or suppress the carrier and can suppress one keying sideband if desired. Possibly experimenters could come up with a way of cutting CW bandwidths in half by suppressing one sideband, maybe even the carrier, leaving one sideband. Don't laugh—it works for SSB phone and some high-speed data modems.

Here's a summary of what the new rules permit under the *CW* emission: International Morse code telegraphy emissions having designators with A, C, H, J or R as the first symbol; 1 as the second symbol; A or B as the third symbol; J2A or J2B. Using the ITU emission designator definitions, that means:

First symbol—type of modulation of the main carrier:

Emission in which the main carrier is amplitude modulated with:

A Double sideband
C Vestigial sideband
H Single sideband, full carrier
J Single sideband, suppressed carrier
R Single sideband, reduced carrier

Second symbol—nature of signals(s) modulating the main carrier:

1 A single channel containing quantized or digital information without the use of a modulating subcarrier

Third symbol—type of information to be transmitted:

A Telegraphy—for aural reception

B Telegraphy—for automatic reception

J2A:

J Single sideband, suppressed carrier

2 A single channel containing quantized or digital information with the use of a modulating subcarrier

A Telegraphy—for aural reception

J2B:

J Single sideband, suppressed carrier

2 A single channel containing quantized or digital information with the use of a modulating subcarrier

B Telegraphy—for automatic reception

MCW

MCW (modulated CW) is produced by modulating a carrier with a tone, then keying the tone or both the tone and the carrier. Most ham rigs don't have this mode built in, in which case you supply the tone with an external tone generator. Unlike CW, you don't need a beat-frequency oscillator (BFO) to hear the tone. This makes it particularly useful for repeater CW IDs.

For many years, MCW was the modulation of choice for emergency transmitters used in aircraft and vessels. MCW occupies a bandwidth wider than that of ordinary CW. With hard keying and square-wave tone modulation, MCW creates such a splatter that it is hard to miss, even with a mistuned receiver, with or without a BFO. MCW, even with soft keying and a clean sine-wave modulating tone, is not generally permitted in the crowded HF ham bands for general communications, for example as a substitute for CW. But there has been, and still is, a special provision in the rules for MCW in the HF bands; that is for code-practice transmissions interspersed with voice announcements in the phone bands. Of course, it isn't MCW unless there is a carrier transmitted, as in the case of tone keying of a double-sideband amplitude-modulated transmitter. If a keyed tone and voice are transmitted alternately over a single-sideband suppressed-carrier transmitter, the Morse transmission looks like CW, and a BFO would be needed in the receiver. See *Phone*, in the following section.

Here's a technical definition of what the new rules permit under the *MCW* emission: Tone-modulated international Morse code telegraphy emissions having designators with A, C, D, F, G or R as the first symbol; 2 as the second symbol; A or B as the third symbol. Using the ITU emission designator definitions, that expands to:

First symbol—type of modulation of the main carrier:

Emission in which the main carrier is amplitude modulated with

A Double sideband

C Vestigial sideband

D Emission in which the main carrier is amplitude and angle modulated either simultaneously or in a pre-established pattern

F Frequency modulation

G Phase modulation

R Single sideband, reduced carrier

Second symbol—nature of signals(s) modulating the main carrier:

2 A single channel containing quantized or digital information with the use of a modulating subcarrier

Third symbol—type of information to be transmitted:

A Telegraphy—for aural reception

B Telegraphy—for automatic reception

PHONE

Phone (short for *telephony*) meant only *analog speech* in the old rules. Now it includes *speech and other sounds*. No, that still doesn't permit music or rock 'n roll with 100% distortion, or old Fido's howls if he can carry a tune. But it does include almost any sound hams might need to transmit.

Alerting and selective calling are explicitly permitted on frequencies authorized for phone. The new rules clearly permit subcarrier tones that are incidental to the operation of the telephony channel. For example, a subcarrier to control the level of the demodulated signal (compandoring) is now permitted—in other words, you can add a pilot tone for amplitude-compandored single sideband (ACSSB) if desired.

And, you can send your station ID by Morse code or other digital means on any frequency where phone operation is permitted, without having to petition the FCC. The key word here is *incidental*: Speech is the main thing, and the tones are supplemental.

You can choose virtually any phone modulation method that can convey speech: double-sideband full carrier, single-sideband full carrier, single-sideband reduced or variable-level carrier, single-sideband suppressed carrier, vestigial sideband, or independent sidebands (a form of multiplexing on one carrier) with one sideband carrying speech, the other having slow-scan TV or facsimile.

You are no longer restricted to analog modulation—*digital* or *quantized* modulation is also permitted, so long as the intelligence being transmitted is telephony. Thus, digital voice is permitted wherever phone operation is authorized. While digital modulation generally involves two states (on and off), quantized modulation consists of stepped levels, where each step is given significance. In some systems, the stair steps could be simply approximations of the analog levels. If there are lots of steps, the ear can't tell the difference; if there aren't enough steps, the speech will sound grainy or even gravelly.

So, how do you get permission to transmit digital or quantized telephony? You already have it. Is there any bandwidth limitation? None according to the new rules, except for the general requirement of "good engineering practice." On the other hand, using excessive bandwidth will get you in immediate trouble with other hams who are trying to share the band with you. So, it is wise to limit bandwidth on the HF bands to that of a single-sideband (analog) radio (roughly 3 kHz) for single-channel speech if possible. The exceptions are that bandwidths on the order of 6 kHz are needed for double-sideband AM phone, for FM phone and independent-sideband transmissions, where each sideband is roughly 3 kHz wide. So, *good engineering practice* in this case boils down to "reasonable and proper bandwidth—don't use more than you need."

Above 902 MHz, §97.305(c) and §97.307(f)(12) of the rules permit multiplexing (MUXing) phone FM modulation of the main carrier. *Good engineering practice* for multiplexing in this case amounts to using no more bandwidth than you need. When in doubt, check with the frequency coordinator in your area to see what sort of protection other adjacent-channel users need.

The following is the technical definition of *phone* emission under the new rules: Speech and other sound emissions having designators with A, C, D, F, G, H, J or R as the first symbol; 1, 2 or 3 as the second symbol; E as the third symbol. Also speech emissions having B as the first symbol; 7, 8 or 9 as the second symbol; E as the third symbol. Using the ITU emission designator definitions, that expands to:

First symbol—type of modulation of the main carrier:
- Emission in which the main carrier is amplitude modulated with
- A Double sideband
- C Vestigial sideband
- D Emission in which the main carrier is amplitude and angle modulated either simultaneously or in a pre-established pattern
- F Frequency modulation
- G Phase modulation
- H Single sideband, full carrier
- J Single sideband, suppressed carrier
- R Single sideband, reduced carrier

Second symbol—nature of signals(s) modulating the main carrier:
- 1 A single channel containing quantized or digital information without the use of a modulating subcarrier
- 2 A single channel containing quantized or digital information with the use of a modulating subcarrier
- 3 A single channel containing analog information

Third symbol—type of information to be transmitted:
- E Telephony

Also:

First symbol—type of modulation of the main carrier:
- B Independent sidebands

Second symbol—nature of signals(s) modulating the main carrier:
- 7 Two or more channels containing quantized or digital information
- 8 Two or more channels containing analog information
- 9 Composite system with one or more channels containing quantized or digital information, together with one or more channels containing analog information

Third symbol—type of information to be transmitted:
- E Telephony

F8E, above 902 MHz:

First symbol—type of modulation of the main carrier:
- F Frequency modulation

Second symbol—nature of signals(s) modulating the main carrier:
- 8 Two or more channels containing analog information

Third symbol—type of information to be transmitted:
- E Telephony

Q. Can I transmit digital speech?

A. Yes. You can transmit either *digital* or *quantized* phone signals. Instead of emitting J3E, the emission designator might be J1E. Transmission of such signals would be in the *phone* bands; it is not considered *data*. Incidentally, *good engineering practice* and good relations with others on the bands would suggest that *digital* or *quantized* phone take up no more bandwidth than a normal analog phone signal.

IMAGE

The word *image* encompasses both television and facsimile. Basically, the new rules permit you to transmit image information using essentially any modulation method. Because image operation, on HF, is within the phone bands, you can alternate image modulation with phone modulation. Or, you can transmit image and phone on the same carrier by using independent-sideband modulation. The bandwidth limitation in this case is essentially the same as for transmitting speech or 3 kHz for a single channel, 6 kHz for double-sideband or two channels of information.

Here is the technical definition of *image* emission under the new rules: Facsimile and television emissions having designators with A, C, D, F, G, H, J or R as the first symbol; 1, 2 or 3 as the second symbol; C or F as the third symbol; and emissions having B as the first symbol; 7, 8 or 9 as the second symbol; W as the third symbol. That translates to the following ITU emission designator definitions:

First symbol—type of modulation of the main carrier:

Emission in which the main carrier is amplitude modulated with

- A Double sideband
- C Vestigial sideband
- D Emission in which the main carrier is amplitude and angle modulated either simultaneously or in a pre-established pattern
- F Frequency modulation
- G Phase modulation
- H Single sideband, full carrier
- J Single sideband, suppressed carrier
- R Single sideband, reduced carrier

Second symbol—nature of signals(s) modulating the main carrier:

- 1 A single channel containing quantized or digital information without the use of a modulating subcarrier
- 2 A single channel containing quantized or digital information with the use of a modulating subcarrier
- 3 A single channel containing analog information

Third symbol—type of information to be transmitted:

- C Facsimile
- F Television (video)

Also:

First symbol—type of modulation of the main carrier:

- B Independent sidebands

Second symbol—nature of signals(s) modulating the main carrier:

- 7 Two or more channels containing quantized or digital information
- 8 Two or more channels containing analog information
- 9 Composite system with one or more channels containing quantized or digital information, together with one or more channels containing analog information

Third symbol—type of information to be transmitted:

- W Combination of the above

"Above" in this case is intended to cover a combination of facsimile or television and telephony by means of independent-sideband (ISB) modulation. ISB modulation with image on one sideband and phone on another has been a part of the rules for years and is permitted in the MF and HF bands. Literally, W in the third symbol of ITU emission designator table included a combination of any of the following types of information:

N No information transmitted
A Telegraphy—for aural reception
B Telegraphy—for automatic reception
C Facsimile
D Data transmission, telemetry, telecommand
E Telephony
F Video

However, when transmitting ISB, it would be prudent to limit the information content of the two independent sidebands to the types of information permitted in that band segment. As *phone* and *image* are usually permitted in the same segments and *CW* is allowed in all bands, it would seem that these are the only emissions permitted for ISB modulation in such segments.

RTTY AND DATA

What's the difference between "Data transmission," or "computer-to-computer communications" and *RTTY*? There may be some gray areas, but here are some characteristics to help you tell gray from gray:

RTTY

Keyboard sending, hard copy or screen presentation, possibly computer buffering
Little or no manipulation or reformatting of text prior to presentation (what is sent is what you get)
Text in Baudot or ASCII
Has no error control (except when using AMTOR)
Message transmission
Asynchronous transmission (ie, start and stop pulses) (except when using AMTOR)

Data

Computer file sending, computer file receiving
Possibly some reorganization of information prior to transmission and probably before presentation
If text, probably in ASCII, Extended ASCII, or foreign language character set
Usually has error detection and/or error correction
Probably packetized transmission
Synchronous transmission (no start and stop pulses)

But in the future, it probably will make little or no difference whether there's a gray area between RTTY and data transmission, since the new rules permit both in the same frequency segments. What types of data transmission are permissible under the new rules? First, you can transmit specified digital codes of Baudot, AMTOR and ASCII, as described in paragraph 97.309(a). Paragraph 97.309(b) provides that a station may use an "unspecified digital code, except to a station in a country with which the United States does not have an agreement permitting the code to be used." It goes on to say that "unspecified digital codes must not be transmitted for the purpose of obscuring the meaning of any communication." The old rules said that any digital code could be used above 50 MHz, but that only Baudot, AMTOR or ASCII could be used below 50 MHz. The new rules don't exactly say it the same way, but look at the limitations §97.305(f)(3) and (4), and how they apply to the authorized emission table in §97.305(c). It is simply another way of telling you to use only specified codes below 50 MHz. A discussion of these codes is found in Chapter 11.

§97.307(f)(5) through (8) provides some new flexibility in digital multiplexing. The main limitations for *RTTY* or *data* signals are signal rate and bandwidth: see Chapter 11.

RTTY and *data* multiplexing is allowed on frequencies above 50.1 MHz within the bandwidth limitations.

RTTY

Here's what the new rules permit under the *RTTY* emission: Narrow-band direct-printing telegraphy emissions having designators with A, C, D, F, G, H, J or R as the first symbol; 1 as the second symbol; B as the third symbol; and emission J2B. In terms of ITU emission designator definitions, that means:

First symbol—type of modulation of the main carrier:
Emission in which the main carrier is amplitude modulated with

- A Double sideband
- C Vestigial sideband
- D Emission in which the main carrier is amplitude and angle modulated either simultaneously or in a pre-established pattern
- F Frequency modulation
- G Phase modulation
- H Single sideband, full carrier
- J Single sideband, suppressed carrier
- R Single sideband, reduced carrier

Second symbol—nature of signals(s) modulating the main carrier:
- 1 A single channel containing quantized or digital information without the use of a modulating subcarrier

Third symbol—type of information to be transmitted:
- B Telegraphy—for automatic reception

J2B:
- J Single sideband, suppressed carrier
- 2 A single channel containing quantized or digital information with the use of a modulating subcarrier
- B Telegraphy—for automatic reception

> ***Q. Can I play my Piccolo?***
> A. *Piccolo* is an RTTY modulation method developed by the British. Instead of representing the 32 positions of an ITA2 code by 32 combinations of 5 pulses, it does so by assigning each a separate (*quantized*) step of carrier frequency when using F1B or modulating tone frequency when using J2B. *Principles and practice of multi-frequency telegraphy*, by JD Ralph, an excellent reference on Piccolo, says it's F1B; we know that J2B sounds like F1B on the air, and both emissions are authorized in Part 97.

Data

The new Part 97 defines the emission designator *data* as "Telemetry, telecommand and computer communications emissions...; D as the third symbol." That agrees closely with the ITU definition of the third emission designator symbol "D," which is: "Data transmission, telemetry, telecommand." The term "computer communications" is simply another way of saying "data transmission." The only problem is that the FCC uses the ITU definition for "telecommand" for the emission designator *data*, and their own definition in §97.3, which is used elsewhere throughout Part 97.

• The ITU defines *telecommand* as: "The use of *telecommunication* for the transmission of signals to initiate, modify or terminate functions of equipment at a distance."

• §97.3 defines *telecommand station* as: "An amateur station that transmits communications to initiate, modify or terminate functions of a space station."

Thus, one must interpret *telecommand* in the ITU sense when referring to emissions and in the FCC §97.3 sense when reading the rest of Part 97. Here's a cross-reference between ITU and FCC Part 97 terminology:

ITU

Telecommand: The use of *telecommunication* for the transmission of signals to initiate, modify or terminate functions of equipment at a distance.

Space Telecommand: The use of *radiocommunication* for the transmission of signals to a *space station* to initiate, modify or terminate functions of equipment on an associated space object, including the *space station*.

FCC

Remote control: The use of a control operator who indirectly manipulates the operating adjustments in the station through a control link to achieve compliance with the FCC Rules.

Telecommand station: An amateur station that transmits communications to initiate, modify or terminate functions of a space station.

Neither *telemetry* nor *space telemetry* is defined in §97.3, but it is clear from §97.207(f) that telemetry is permitted from a space station: "Results of measurements made in the space station, including those related to the function of the station, transmitted by a space station may consist of specially coded messages intended to facilitate communications."

Telemetry is defined by the ITU as "telecommunication for automatically indicating or recording measurements at a distance from the measuring instrument." Telemetry is a little hard to characterize on the air, as it hasn't been used all that much by hams heretofore except from satellites. Paragraph 97.207(f) clearly covers telemetry from satellites and other space stations. Part 97 does not come right out and say that (terrestrial) telemetry is permitted, but then again doesn't say it's prohibited. Certainly, hams have been remotely controlling repeaters for years with an indication back from the repeater station that it understood the command. Think of it this way: If you're going to control something remotely, you better know about its health and welfare before you command it. Once you command it, you'd like to know whether it did what you told it to do. That feedback channel is telemetry. Telemetry is also just measuring anything at a distance, even when you can't remotely control the function. An example of this might be an indication of voltage on a battery charged by solar cells.

Telecommand is the use of telecommunication for the transmission of signals to initiate, modify or terminate functions of equipment at a distance (in other words: remote control). One way to send telecommand or remote-control signals without getting into the realm of unspecified codes would be to use the control characters in ASCII or those positions in Baudot/AMTOR codes not assigned to letters, numerals or fraction bar (/). In terms of ITU emission designators, the following types of emission are permitted for *data* emission: Telemetry, telecommand and computer communications emissions having designators with A, C, D, F, G, H, J or R as the first symbol; 1 as the second symbol; D as the third symbol; and emission J2B. That expands to:

First symbol—type of modulation of the main carrier:

Emission in which the main carrier is amplitude modulated with

- A Double sideband
- C Vestigial sideband
- D Emission in which the main carrier is amplitude and angle modulated either simultaneously or in a pre-established pattern
- F Frequency modulation
- G Phase modulation
- H Single sideband, full carrier
- J Single sideband, suppressed carrier
- R Single sideband, reduced carrier

Second symbol—nature of signals(s) modulating the main carrier:

- 1 A single channel containing quantized or digital information without the use of a modulating subcarrier

Third symbol—type of information to be transmitted:

- D Data transmission, telemetry, telecommand

J2D:

- J Single sideband, suppressed carrier
- 2 A single channel containing quantized or digital information with the use of a modulating subcarrier
- D Data transmission, telemetry, telecommand

Q. Is there a bandwidth limitation for data emission at HF?

A. Not in the rules, except for *good engineering practice*, which applies to everything. However, there are some operational considerations. The HF RTTY/data bands are crowded, and it wouldn't set too well with other hams if you use excessive bandwidth. The practical limitation at HF is imposed by the audio characteristics of the SSB transceivers generally used. Typically, they may have −6 dB audio bandwidths of 2.1 to 2.7 kHz. So, packet-radio bandwidths on the HF bands have been limited to about 2 kHz. For example, the packet frequencies just above 14.100 MHz are spaced every 2 kHz.

Q. Can I use a parallel modem on HF?

A. This refers to a modem that uses several tones, rather than switching between two, and keys them at a slower rate to avoid the effects of multipath (intersymbol) distortion. The emission J2D does not limit the number of tones, it simply limits the transmission to a single channel of information. So, the answer is "yes, if you use J2D emission."

PULSE

Pulse is actually a type of modulation of the main carrier—on a par with amplitude modulation (AM) and angle modulation (a category covering both frequency modulation and phase modulation). Pulses may be modulated in the following ways:

- unmodulated pulses
- pulses modulated in amplitude
- pulses modulated in width/duration
- pulses modulated in position/phase
- pulses in which the carrier is angle modulated during the period of the pulse

Pulse emission also permits transmission of any type of information, namely:

- no information
- telegraphy
- facsimile
- data transmission, telemetry, telecommand
- telephony
- television
- combination of the above (3rd symbol W)
- cases not otherwise covered (3rd symbol X)

Because of its highly impulsive nature, *pulse* is permitted in bands above 902 MHz excluding 1240-1300 MHz and 10.0-10.5 GHz.

SS

Spread Spectrum, or *SS* for short, is a departure from the normal rule of keeping radio-frequency bandwidth as narrow as possible for a given information rate. *SS* deliberately expands the bandwidth; instead of concentrating all the transmitted energy in a tight bandwidth, the energy is spread over a greater bandwidth so that the energy in any one kilohertz is proportionally smaller. The bandwidth expansion amounts to at least 10 times the information bandwidth and may be as much as several hundred times.

The new rules permit the following types of modulation, according to ITU emission designators:

First symbol—type of modulation of the main carrier:

Emission in which the main carrier is amplitude modulated with

A Double sideband
C Vestigial sideband
D Emission in which the main carrier is amplitude and angle modulated either simultaneously or in a pre-established pattern
F Frequency modulation
G Phase modulation
H Single sideband, full carrier
J Single sideband, suppressed carrier
R Single sideband, reduced carrier

Second symbol—nature of signals(s) modulating the main carrier:

X Cases not otherwise covered

Third symbol—type of information to be transmitted:

X Cases not otherwise covered

In other words, you can use any type of modulation of the carrier (except for no modulation or pulse modulation) and can transmit any type of signal and information permitted in the Amateur Radio Service when using SS.

There are some restrictions. First, SS may be used only on bands above 420 MHz. Code, modulation and transmitter power limitations are detailed in §97.311. See also "Spread Spectrum," in Chapter 12.

TEST

When they rewrote the rules, the FCC tried to clear up past uncertainties concerning emission of experimental transmissions and those with no information. "No information" is not necessarily the same as "no modulation," as it is possible to frequency modulate a transmitter with a steady tone that carries no intelligence. You're probably thinking of some QSOs that you felt evidenced no intelligence, but we're talking about really dumb transmissions like unmodulated tones or key-down carriers to tune transmitters or to measure antenna patterns, for example.

The FCC decided to use the emission designator *test* as a catchall category. Technically, *test* is defined as "Emissions containing no information having the designators with N as the third symbol."

There are two basic rules of the road for test emissions. In the paragraph 97.305(c) table, you will note that test emissions are authorized for all amateur bands above 51.0 MHz. As in former versions of the rules, you are permitted to send test signals to a fare-thee-well. It is unclear how other amateurs would welcome your transmitter being key down 24 hours a day forever, but the FCC rules permit it. Below 51.0 MHz, however, paragraph 97.305(b) applies, and the key word is *brief*.

Chapter Nine

A Safari Through the Technical Standards Jungle

The title of this chapter reflects the fear and dread some hams feel when they try to understand the technical standards section of Part 97. Like most of Part 97, the technical standards exist to promote operating techniques that make efficient use of spectrum and minimize interference. Seen in that light, the standards are less intimidating. No one wants to transmit a "dirty" signal, and the standards in Part 97 can help you identify problems that should be solved.

GOOD SIGNALS: 99-44/100 PERCENT PURE

The term "signal purity" is used freely in ham circles, but what does it really mean? Thanks to the clear definitions and standards in Part 97, it's easy to define a "pure" signal.

Section 97.307 spells out the standards FCC expects ham signals to meet. The first paragraph is the most important: *"No amateur station transmission shall occupy more bandwidth than necessary for the information rate and emission type being transmitted, in accordance with good amateur practice."* Simply stated, don't transmit a wide signal when a narrow one will do.

The next paragraph states that *"Emissions resulting from modulation must be confined to the band or segment available to the control operator."* Every modulated signal produces sidebands. You must not operate so close to the band edge that your sidebands extend out of the subband, even if your dial says that your carrier is inside the band. Further: *"Emissions outside the necessary bandwidth must not cause splatter or keyclick interference to operations on adjacent frequencies."* Seems like common sense, doesn't it? The Rules simply codify good operating practice. If your key clicks or over-processed voice signals are causing interference up and down the band, clean it up! You wouldn't ask any less of another ham with a messy signal.

COMMON QUESTIONS AND ANSWERS—BAND EDGES

"How close can I set my dial to the band edge?" is a question asked not only by the beginner, but by experienced amateurs as well. We'll tell you how close you can go to get that rare DX QSL card—and avoid that rare FCC "QSL" card.

Phone

Q. I'm an active HF phone DXer. How close to the band edges can I set my VFO?

A. Many factors are involved. Amateurs commonly consider full-carrier, double-sideband AM signals to be about 6 kHz wide and single-sideband, suppressed-carrier signals to be about 3 kHz wide. Yes, but those bandwidths are probably only 6 dB down, and that isn't what the FCC worries about. Thus, to determine where you may set your VFO in relation to the band edge or band subband edge for your class of license, you'll have to figure out where your signal is attenuated 40 dB. Don't just assume that if your SSB transmitter bandwidth is 3 kHz, then just add a few hundred Hz to be safe. That may be fine, if the shape of the band-limiting filter is sharp enough to attenuate the signal from -6 to -40 dB. If you're going to operate as near as possible to a band edge, then do so after carefully reviewing your equipment specifications if they include such information. Another alternative is to carefully measure the attenuation if you have access to top-notch lab equipment. If you can't do either, then allow a margin of safety for possible inaccuracy of your frequency readout.

Remember, your carrier and all of your sidebands must be confined within the amateur bands and subbands as applicable.

Morse Code

Q. When I operate CW, how close to the band edge can I go?

A. Your transmitter keying envelope rise and fall times determine both the bandwidth of your CW signal and the maximum speed at which you can send and still be received properly. Once set, the rise and fall times (not the keying speed) determine the bandwidth. If your rise and fall times are 5 ms, your signal will have a bandwidth of about 150 Hz, in which case you would have to stay at least 75 Hz from a band edge. If the rise and fall times are 2 ms (fairly typical of commercial transceivers), the bandwidth would be 375 Hz.

TV and Facsimile

Q. Why is fast-scan television not found on the HF bands?

A. Fast-scan television, a mode in which images appear in the same manner as a home broadcast TV, is not found at HF because of bandwidth limitations. Section 97.307(f)(2) states that on any band below 420 MHz "No non-phone emission shall exceed the bandwidth of a communications quality phone emission of the same modulation type." To get across all the information necessary for a fast-moving TV picture, much spectrum is required; so much, in fact, that one fast-scan TV signal could occupy one-fifth of the entire HF spectrum! Bandwidth limits restrict HF TV operation to the slow-scan variety, where images appear as a photograph, or "stop-action," and do not require oodles of band space.

No special bandwidth limits apply above 420 MHz, so you'll find wider bandwidth modes, such as fast-scan television, there. But, remember, in all cases not specifically covered by the rules, the various signals must be used in accordance with good engineering practice. Use modern equipment that is properly adjusted. Conserve spectrum!

SPURIOUS EMISSIONS

Paragraph (c) of §97.307 addresses spurious emission standards. Just what are *spurious emissions* anyway? FCC defines spurious emissions this way: *"An emission, on frequencies outside the necessary bandwidth of a transmission, the level of which may be reduced without affecting the information being transmitted."* Spurious emissions include harmonic emissions, parasitic emissions, intermodulation products and frequency conversion products, but exclude out-of-band emissions.

To fully understand this definition, we need to travel to FCC Part 2 for two more definitions. Necessary bandwidth is defined: *"the width of the frequency band which is just sufficient to ensure the transmission of information at the rate and with the quality required under specified conditions."* An out-of-band emission is: *"Emission on a frequency or frequencies immediately outside the necessary bandwidth which results from the modulation process, but excluding spurious emissions."* Out-of-band emissions are *not necessarily* outside an amateur "band."

Refer to Fig 1. Some of the keying sidebands are outside the "necessary bandwidth." These are out-of-band emissions, but they are *not* considered spurious emissions. On the other hand, we have already seen in §97.307(b) that these sidebands must not interfere with other stations. The harmonics and parasitics shown in Fig 1 *are* spurs, and they must be reduced to the levels specified in Part 97. In §97.307(c), FCC states that all spurious

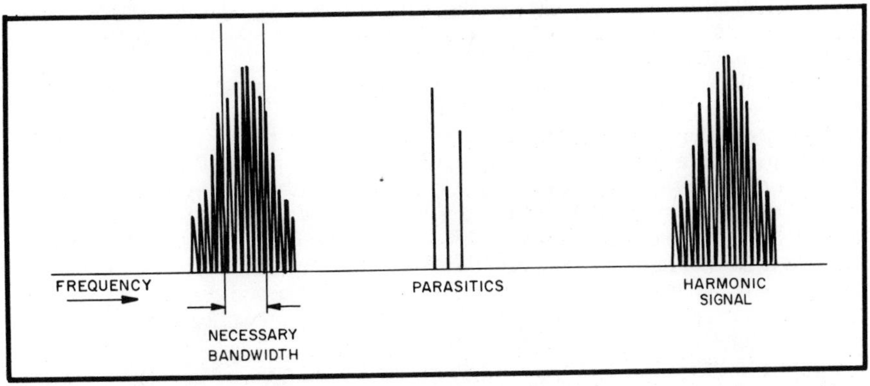

Fig 1—An illustration of *spurious emissions*. Some of the keying sidebands are outside the *necessary bandwidth*. These are considered *out-of-band emissions*, not spurs. The harmonic and parasitic shown here *are* considered spurious emissions; these must be reduced in accordance with §97.307.

emissions must be reduced *"to the greatest extent practicable."* Further, if any spurious emission, including chassis or power line radiation, causes harmful interference to the reception of another radio station, *the licensee of the interfering amateur station* is required to take steps to eliminate the interference. If your spurs are causing interference, it's your job to clean them up. Make sure your transmitter is clean!

How Far is Far Enough?

Now that we know where the spurs are, what do we do with them? FCC is very specific in §97.307(d). If your transmitter or RF power amplifier was built after April 14, 1977, or first marketed after December 31, 1977, and transmits on frequencies below 30 MHz the mean power of any spurious emissions must

- never be more than 50 mW;
- be at least 30 dB below the mean power of the fundamental emission, if the mean power output is less than 5 W; and
- be at least 40 dB below the mean power of the fundamental emission if the mean power output is 5 W or more.

Section 97.307(e) lists the following requirements between 30 and 225 MHz:

- Transmitters with 25 W or less mean output power: spurs must be at least 40 dB below the mean power of the fundamental emission and never greater than 25 μW, but need not be reduced further than 10 μW. This means that the spurs from a 25-W transmitter must be at least 60 dB down to meet the 25 μW restriction.
- Transmitters with more than 25 W mean output power: spurious emissions must be at least 60 dB below the mean power of fundamental emission.

POWER

"An amateur station must use the minimum transmitter power necessary to carry out the desired communication."—Sec. 97.313(a), FCC Rules

Don't run more power than you need.

How closely do radio amateurs adhere to this principle? We all know that in some cases the answer is, not as closely as we should. The FCC has just completed a study that they say confirms this.

According to an FCC release, in late February 1991 Commission field engineers visited 209 amateur stations in various parts of the country. The amateurs who were visited were asked to initiate a contact at the power level normally used, and then to reduce power by approximately one-half.

In three-quarters of the cases, according to the Commission, reducing power did not degrade communications capability. Their conclusion: "Most amateur stations are not operating at minimum power as required by Section 97.313(a)."

The Commission hasn't released the actual study yet, though ARRL has requested a copy. There's a pretty good chance that even if ARRL agrees with the conclusion, it will disagree with how the Commission got there. Except when DXing, most people, when looking for a CQ to answer, look for a signal that's more than 3 dB above the noise; conducting the exercise described in the FCC release doesn't really prove anything.

Still, let's not quibble. We know there are times when we could get along with reduced power. Even for moonbounce you don't *always* need to run the legal limit. Most hams don't own legal-limit equipment and have no interest in doing so. Many enjoy the challenge of QRP operating, and some can boast of making intercontinental contacts at milliwatt levels. Others must run low power for economic or other reasons, but still gain a full measure of enjoyment from Amateur Radio.

When you reduce power, you reduce the impact your operating has on others. Nearby amateurs can use the same band; distant amateurs can use the same or adjacent frequencies. Your electric bill goes down. If the person you're talking to was receiving you well to begin with, all that happens when you reduce power is that his S meter doesn't bounce quite as high.

The Commission thinks reducing power can alleviate RFI/TVI problems. Their study doesn't particularly bear this out: lower power resulted in reduced interference in only one-third of the cases where interference was said to exist, and (while the release is sketchy on this point) stations running 100 watts or less appear no less likely than higher-power stations to be reported as the source of interference. ARRL thinks reducing the maximum power an amateur station runs is an appropriate solution for RFI/TVI only as a voluntary, temporary measure while the right technical solutions are being found and applied.

The Commission does not conclude that a reduction in the maximum power limit is warranted, nor could they have reasonably done so: many legal-limit amateur stations operate without complaint, and there are times when higher power really is needed to overcome poor conditions, high noise levels, or challenging propagation paths.

If the Commission intended its study as a reminder of our obligation under Section 97.313(a), let's accept it as such and operate accordingly. The rules aside, it's the courteous thing to do.

General

In the general case, ham transmitters may never be operated with a peak envelope power (PEP) output of more than 1500 W.

Under FCC "grandfathering" double-sideband full-carrier AM users, were allowed to use the old measure of 1000-W dc input to the transmitter's final amplifier until June 2, 1990. The reason for this "grandfathering" was that the 1500-W PEP output limit meant an approximate 3-dB reduction in maximum power permitted for AM operations. FCC has declined to extend this "grandfathering," and AM operators must observe the new standard.

Novice Bands

Novices and higher-class licensees inhabiting the Novice class subbands on 80, 40 and 15 meters may never operate with a peak envelope power output in excess of 200 W. Novices are limited to 200 watts PEP on their 28-MHz subband, 25 watts PEP on 220 MHz and to 5 watts PEP on 1270 MHz. Other amateurs may use up to 1500 W in the 10-meter Novice band, except Technicians who are also limited to 200 W PEP. All amateurs are limited to 200 watts PEP when operating on the 7.050-7.075 MHz segment in ITU Regions 1 and 3.

Special Restrictions

All amateurs are limited to 200 W PEP on the 30-meter band (10.1-10.15 MHz).

Beacons. These stations are limited to 100 W of peak envelope power output.

70 cm and 33 cm bands. Special 50-W PEP output limits apply to stations operating at these regions when they are located near certain military installations in the US. See §97.313(f) and (g).

COMMON QUESTIONS AND ANSWERS —POWER LIMITS

Q. What is peak envelope power?

A. Peak envelope power (PEP) is the average power supplied to the antenna transmission line by a transmitter during one RF cycle at the crest of the modulation envelope, taken under normal operating conditions.

Q. How do I measure PEP output to determine if my transmitter is operating within FCC rules?

A. The Commission has chosen and published the following standards of measurement: (1) Read an in-line peak-reading RF wattmeter that is properly matched (commercial units are available), and (2) calculate the power using the peak RF voltage as indicated by an oscilloscope or other peak-reading device. Multiply the peak RF voltage by 0.707, square the result and divide by the load resistance (SWR must be 1).

Q. Am I required to have a means of measuring power output from my transmitter?

A. FCC does not require you to provide such measurement equipment and techniques. Hams are simply required to abide by the power limits, period. The standards listed in the previous answer simply indicate how the Commission would measure your transmitter's output during a station inspection.

As a practical matter, most hams don't have to worry about special equipment to check their transmitter's output because they never approach the 1500-W PEP output limit. Many common amateur amplifiers aren't capable of generating this much power. However, if you do have a planet-destroyer amplifier and do operate close to the limit on those rare occasions when you need the extra power, you should be prepared to measure your output along the lines of the standards detailed in the previous answer.

AMPLIFIER BAN AMPLIFIED

In 1978, the Federal Communications Commission banned the manufacture and marketing of any external radio-frequency power amplifier or amplifier kit that is capable of operation on any frequency below 144 MHz unless the FCC has issued a grant of type acceptance for that model amplifier. Since that time, scores of amateurs have written ARRL with questions regarding this ban.

COMMON QUESTIONS AND ANSWERS —AMPLIFIER BAN

Q. Is it illegal to use amplifiers on 10 meters?

A. No, amateurs may use amplifiers capable of operating on 10 meters. While the rules may make it difficult to buy a new amplifier capable of operation on 10 meters, FCC allows amateurs to modify an amplifier to restore or include 10-meter capability. An amateur may modify *no more than one unit of the same model amplifier in any year* without a grant of type acceptance.

Of course, amateurs are permitted to build amplifiers, convert equipment from any other radio service for this use or buy used amplifiers. Nonhams are specifically prohibited from building or modifying amplifiers capable of operation below 144 MHz without FCC type acceptance.

Q. Can a dealer modify amplifiers to restore their 10-meter capability if they are sold only to licensed amateurs?

A. No. These modifications can be performed only by an individual amateur for specific use by the licensed owner of the amplifier at his licensed Amateur Radio station. You *can* ask another amateur to modify the amplifier for you, but you are responsible for ensuring that the equipment complies with all the technical requirements contained in the amateur regulations.

Q. What type of amplifiers may a dealer sell?

A. All external amplifiers capable of operation below 144 MHz must be type accepted by the FCC in order to be marketed. A number of amplifiers, manufactured prior to the April 28, 1978, cutoff date, were issued a waiver of the new regulations.

Q. May I buy or sell a used amateur amplifier that has not been issued either a grant of type acceptance or a waiver, or has been modified so that the grant is no longer valid? What about one that was originally marketed before these regulations were announced, or one that was built from scratch—neither of these two would have a grant nor waiver.

A. You may buy or sell an amplifier under those conditions, but there are restrictions that would be valid regardless of whether the amplifier was capable of operation below 144 MHz. Some amplifiers marketed before April 28, 1978, are covered under the waiver if they are the same model that was granted a waiver. An individual amateur may sell his amplifier regardless of grants or waivers, provided that he sells it only to another amateur operator. He may also sell it to a bona fide amateur equipment dealer. The dealer could sell only those amplifiers that he purchased used from an individual amateur operator, and then only if he sold them to other hams.

While the FCC said it does not require proof of licensing at this time, it is the responsibility of the seller of the equipment, whether he is an individual or a dealer (whoever currently owns the amplifier), to ensure that the buyer is indeed a licensed amateur operator, or a bona fide amateur equipment dealer.

Q. What does type acceptance mean?

A. Type acceptance is an equipment authorization granted by the FCC. It is based on equipment data submitted by the manufacturer and is used to ensure that the equipment will be used in the proper manner of the service for which it has been accepted. This acceptance applies to all identical units marketed by the manufacturer. Amplifiers capable of operating below 144 MHz are the only sort of amateur equipment requiring type acceptance, by the way. Of course, other equipment must meet the FCC standards for purity of emission (§97.307). But the manufacturer of amateur transmitting equipment other than HF amplifiers does not need to submit the "specs" or an actual unit for testing purposes unless the Commission decides the model is not meeting FCC standards, and wants to inspect the equipment.

Q. Under what circumstances would FCC dismiss or deny an application for type acceptance of an external RF amplifier?

A. Some features which may cause a denial are (1) any accessible wiring which, when altered, would permit operation in a manner contrary to FCC rules, (2) circuit boards or similar circuitry to facilitate the addition of components to change the amplifier's operating characteristics in a manner contrary to FCC rules, (3) instructions for operation or modification of the amplifier in a manner contrary to FCC rules, (4) any internal or external controls or adjustments to facilitate operation of the amplifier in a manner contrary to FCC rules, (5) any internal radio-frequency sensing circuitry or any external switch, the purpose of which is to place the amplifier in the transmit mode, (6) the incorporation of more gain than is necessary to operate in the Amateur Radio Service, and (7) any attenuation in the input of the amplifier, which when removed or modified, would permit the amplifier to function at its designed output power when driven by an RF input of less than 50 watts mean power.

Q. Why was the 10-meter ban imposed?

A. FCC said this action had been taken to "stem the flow of large quantities of amplifiers which were being distributed for.. illegal use on frequencies in and around the Citizen's Band Radio Service."

RADIO FREQUENCY INTERFERENCE

Simply put, Amateur Radio is sometimes blamed for causing interference, regardless of the source of the interference. Many complainants believe that they are being interfered with by "that ham down the street," when in fact an amateur station may not be involved at all. Latest FCC figures show that only three percent of RFI complaints result from amateur operation. When a complainant's expensive TV or stereo is experiencing RFI, he is probably not interested in knowing the technical cause of the interference; he simply wants the interference stopped. Many people are confused by the distinction between Amateur Radio and CB. Once you explain to your neighbor what Amateur Radio is, he may be more understanding. The FCC recognizes the cooperation amateurs give in resolving RFI cases. RFI problems can be solved; the keys are information, cooperation and action. The ultimate solution is the incorporation of the required RF immunity during the initial design by the manufacturers and their meeting the voluntary standards. Although the FCC has the authority to legislate standards, it has decided to try the voluntary route first. The Electronic Industries Association has an ongoing program with its member manufacturers toward this goal.

COMMON QUESTIONS AND ANSWERS: RFI

Q. How are RFI problems caused?

A. RFI problems are caused by incompatibility between various electronic systems. The problems generally lie in the following areas:

1) System component design, insufficient shielding or filtering, and/or failure to observe proper installation practices. These are the most probable factors if the device responds to unwanted signals.

2) The proximity of the receiver to the source of the unwanted signal and its lack of immunity in rejection of unwanted signals.

Q. Why is RFI such a big problem?

A. Today we face an interference problem of huge proportions. During fiscal year 1986, the FCC received over 63,000 complaints of RFI to home-entertainment equipment (97% of these complaints involve a service other than the amateur service).

The magnitude of the RFI problem can be attributed to three factors:

1) Rapid growth in the electronics industry has increased the probability of a consumer device being located near an RF source.

2) The use of electronic devices (including TVs, VCRs, radios, video games, and audio tape equipment) by the public has grown at a tremendous rate in recent years so that now, many more devices are subject to interference.

3) Failure of manufacturers in many cases to incorporate in the design of home electronic equipment sufficient filtering or shielding to provide immunity from nearby radio transmitters using these frequencies.

Q. If RFI is such a big problem, why hasn't legislation been enacted to combat RFI?

A. Congress *has* enacted RFI legislation! After 10 years of lobbying by the ARRL, the Communications Amendments Act of 1982 (PL 97-259), was signed into law by President Reagan on September 13, 1982. This law is known as the Goldwater Bill by amateurs because then-Senator Barry Goldwater, K7UGA, was largely responsible for its introduction and passage. The legislative history of the bill, which gave the FCC jurisdiction over RF susceptibility of home electronic equipment, states, in part: "This law clarifies the reservation of exclusive jurisdiction over RFI matters to the Federal Communications Commission. Such matters shall not be regulated by local or state law, nor shall radio transmitting apparatus be subject to local or state regulation as part of any effort to resolve an RFI complaint. The FCC believes that radio operators should not be subject to fines, forfeitures or other liability imposed by any local or state authority as a result of interference appearing in home electronic equipment or systems. Rather, the Committee's intent is that regulation of RFI phenomena shall be imposed only by the Commission." For the time being, the FCC has opted for voluntary standards in place of formal rules and regulations.

Q. What does the Goldwater Bill mean for the radio amateur?

A. The Goldwater Bill gave the FCC the authority to regulate the RFI of home electronic equipment. The FCC didn't have the authority before this legislation was enacted. The FCC and the ARRL are both active in an industry group, in cooperation with the American National Standards Institute (ANSI) which is studying "RF immunity issues." This group, called the Ad Hoc Committee on Pubic Law 97-259 of the Accredited Standards Committee C-63, set an RFI rejection standard for certain home electronic equipment. The voluntary standard provides for TVs and VCRs to reject the field strengths of unwanted signals of not less than 1 volt per meter. This standard was not sufficient for full-power amateur stations under "worst case" conditions but will cover the majority of cases.

Q. Who is ultimately responsible for resolving RFI problems?

A. RFI may result from (1) harmonics, (2) spurious emissions, and (3) fundamental overload. Fundamental overload may produce RFI when the device receiving the interference is inadequately shielded, has unfiltered leads or is located very close to the RF source. If, however, the transmitter is being operated in a completely legal manner and the radiated RF energy on its fundamental frequency is within the limits of FCC regulations, then the interference is probably caused by design deficiencies in the affected device. Typical solutions include filtering and shielding. If the interference is caused by a licensed operating transmitter, its owner has the responsibility to be in compliance with the FCC's rules and regulations. While it is useful to determine in each particular case whether the problem is in the amateur gear or the neighbor's home-entertainment equipment, the best approach to resolving the RFI problems are those which arise in a "no fault" cooperative environment. This is crucial. If blame is the main atmosphere, it's unlikely that the RFI problems will be resolved satisfactorily. In some rare cases, even if the transmitter is 100% "clean" and the device receiving RFI is not at fault, the problem may still remain. Compromise may be the ultimate solution.

Q. What can be done to cure RFI?

A. RFI, in general, will always be a problem, but individual RFI cases can be solved, or at least made bearable for all parties concerned. In trying to be helpful, the amateur may find that his explanations are not welcome. Technical expertise should always be guided by diplomacy and tact in dealing with RFI problems. Cooperation between the parties involved is the most important factor involved in finding a solution. Although RFI is a technical problem, it is also a people problem. Turning that problem into an opportunity depends on three factors: information, cooperation and action. Information is needed to know what to do. The cooperation of the persons involved is essential to resolving the problem. Some kind of action is required to eliminate the RFI. The sooner that happens, the better for everyone involved.

Q. What sources of help are available in resolving RFI problems?

A. The manufacturer of the device is often cooperative in helping the consumer solve RFI problems. A call or letter is well worth while. If no action is taken by the manufacturers, a letter should be sent to Electronic Industries Association (EIA). The address of the EIA is 2001 Eye Street, NW, Washington, DC 20006. The FCC should be contacted only as a last resort.

Several books are available on RFI. One of the best RFI publications is the FCC's *Interference Handbook*, available for $2.50 from the Superintendent of Documents, US Government Printing Office, Washington, DC 20402 or call 202-783-3238. The ARRL publishes a book entitled *Radio Frequency Interference*. This book incorporates some of the FCC text and it is available from HQ for $5 plus $3.00 ($4.00 if shipped by UPS) shipping and handling. *QST* frequently carries articles about RFI. You say you want someone to help you one-on-one in curing your RFI problem? Contact your ARRL Section Manager and he will refer you to an ARRL Technical Specialist in your area.

FCC FORBIDS LOCAL RFI REGULATIONS

ARRL Counsel Chris Imlay, N3AKD, received a letter from FCC General Counsel Robert L. Pettit reaffirming the fact that radio frequency interference (RFI) matters have been preempted by Congress. Imlay had requested an opinion on a Pierre, South Dakota, ordinance regulating RFI.

The letter from the FCC stated that Congress has preempted any concurrent state or local regulation of RFI pursuant to the provisions of the Communications Act. The Act provides that the FCC "may, consistent with the public interest, convenience and necessity, make reasonable regulations (1) governing the [RFI] potential of devices which. . .are capable of emitting radio frequency energy. . .in sufficient degree to cause harmful interference to radio communications. . ." The FCC says the legislation provides explicitly that the Commission has exclusive authority to regulate RFI. Congress declared "the reservation of exclusive jurisdiction to the FCC over matters involving RFI. Such matters shall not be regulated by local or state law, nor shall radio transmitting be subject to local or state regulation as part of any effort to resolve an RFI complaint."

The FCC letter stated that "state laws that require amateurs to cease operations or incur penalties as a consequence of [RFI] thus have been entirely preempted by Congress." The Regulatory Information Branch at ARRL HQ has copies of the "Pettit letter" available for an SASE.

LOW POWER RF DEVICES AND INTERFERENCE

On March 30, 1989, the FCC amended Part 15 of its rules governing radio-frequency devices, which, because of their low power, are not required to be licensed. There is good, bad and ghastly news for radio amateurs.

The good news is that leakage permitted from some "Unintentional" radiating devices (a broad class of devices including radio and TV receivers, VCRs, stereo equipment and the like) will have to be reduced to the more stringent limits now permitted to Class B computing devices which are used in the home.

The bad news is that noncompliant devices of this type are "grandfathered for ten years." Existing TV tuners, for instance, can be designed, built and sold for another decade, having to observe only today's radiation limits. Though the FCC didn't say a word about RFI to consumer devices, the improvements eventually made in front ends of TVs and VCR/TV combinations should result in improved RF rejection, and thus likelihood of RFI complaints, but we'll have to wait until the next century to know!

The ghastly news is that the FCC also adopted seven new "consumer bands" where "Intentional" radiating devices, such as home security systems, garage-door openers, wireless stereo speakers and TV "wireless rabbits" (devices which transfer programs to other TVs and VCRs throughout the house) may operate with higher power than otherwise would be permitted. Four of the specified bands, supposedly selected because Industrial, Scientific and Medical (ISM) devices already operate there, are allocated to the Amateur Radio Service on a primary or secondary basis. These bandes are: 902-920 MHz, 2400-2483.5 (the amateur band here is 2390-2450 MHz), 5725-5875 MHz (hams have 5650-5925 MHz) and 24.00-24.25 GHz (of which 24.00-24.05 is exclusively amateur, the remainder shared).

Manufacturers are not required to include instructions on dealing with interference in consumer guides furnished with their equipment. The only gesture the FCC made toward warning the public about interference is a label stating that the device must not cause interference to any licensed radio service and must accept interference which occurs to it from such services. The second part of this label is not required on radio and TV receivers.

Chapter Ten

Repeaters and Control

In this chapter, we'll try to cut through some of the fog surrounding the rules that apply to repeater operation. Another aspect of VHF FM, the auxiliary station, is discussed in detail. Frequency coordination has become a hot topic in repeater circles lately; we'll look at what the FCC has to say about coordination. The chapter ends with a discussion of band plans and frequency sharing.

DON'T TREAD ON ME

Before we dive into the repeater and auxiliary station rules, a short introduction is in order. Most Sections of Part 97 require interpretation, but no Sections have as many different interpretations as the rules governing repeaters and auxiliary stations. The most important thing to remember is that the *spirit* of the rules is as important (or more so) than the *letter*. As you read the rules, try to keep in mind that they are there to give guidance and *promote* operating practices that do not cause harmful interference, rather than to specifically prohibit activities. Ask yourself whether your on-the-air operations promote the spirit of cooperation that is so important in a *self-regulating* radio service. Remember the first guideline in The Amateur's Code: "The Radio Amateur is CONSIDERATE. . .never knowingly operates in such a way as to lessen the pleasure of others." If you are sure you are following this all-important principle, you will almost always find that your activities are permitted in Part 97.

CONTROL

Before you can understand any of the specialized operating modes in this chapter, we must discuss the concept of *control*. The terms *control operator* and *control point* were introduced in Chapter 6, but the FCC specifically states that control of an Amateur Radio station can be done in one of three very different ways.

Local control is the simplest kind of control. The FCC defines this as "The use of a control operator who directly manipulates the operating adjustments in the station to achieve compliance with the FCC Rules." When you sit in front of your rig and twiddle the knobs, that's local control.

Remote control involves control from a remote point. The FCC calls it "The use of a control operator who indirectly manipulates the operating adjustments in the station through a control link to achieve compliance with the FCC Rules." The key words here are *indirectly* and *control link*. If you wire up a control box so that you can control your station from another room, that's remote control. If you build a DTMF decoder so you can call your shack from a pay phone and key up your transmitter, that's remote control too. The control link is whatever you use to bring the control commands from your hand to the radio. It can be wire, phone line, radio or whatever. If you control your station indirectly, it's remote control.

Section 97.213 sets out a few specific guidelines for remote control:

• *Provision must be incorporated to limit transmissions to no more than three minutes if the control link fails*. This is a common-sense provision. If the control link fails while your transmitter is keyed, the transmitter could be seriously damaged (not to mention all the QRM you'd cause) if there was no three-minute timer.

• *The station must be protected so that unauthorized transmissions cannot be made, willfully or negligently.* This section refers to providing safeguards on your remotely controlled station so that it cannot be used by unauthorized operators. Most remote station operators use DTMF tones or CTCSS systems to limit access to only those people who know the codes. Remember, *you* are responsible for the transmissions from your remote station, just as you are responsible for your home station.

• *A photocopy of the station license and a label with the name, address and telephone number of the station licensee and at least one designated control operator must be posted at the station site.* This makes sure that the FCC will be able to find a responsible person if necessary. If someone uses your remote station to make unauthorized transmissions, the FCC may have to use direction-finding equipment to locate the transmitter. When they travel to the station site, they want to find a card listing your name so they can come knock on your door!

The last type of control is *automatic control*: "The use of devices and procedures for control of a station when it is transmitting so that compliance with the FCC Rules is achieved without the control operator being present at a control point." This is "hands-off" operation; there's nobody home (at the control point). If the repeater is *always* active and retransmits anything that comes along, that's automatic control. Most repeaters operate under automatic control. If you build a station that includes a timer so that it sends your call sign out every two minutes, that's also automatic control. Under Part 97, not all amateur stations can be operated by automatic control. Only space stations, repeaters, stations transmitting RTTY/data emissions above 50 MHz, beacons and some auxiliary stations can be operated automatically. We discussed space stations and beacons in Chapter 12. Let's look at some of the other operations.

REPEATERS

Repeater communication is one of the most popular activities in Amateur Radio today. . . What makes it so popular?

The FCC Rules define a *repeater* as "An amateur station that automatically retransmits the signals of other stations." A repeater normally consists of a trans-

Repeaters combine power and height above average terrain to allow users' signals to be retransmitted over great distances. This repeater site on Sugarloaf Mountain, home of the 146.97 MHz machine, sits at the peak at 4000-plus feet, some 1500 feet above the average terrain in the mountainous region of northwestern Maine.

mitter, receiver, an antenna, a control box and a duplexer (this allows the use of a single antenna for both transmitting and receiving). Operation generally occurs on the VHF amateur bands, although there is some 10-meter repeater activity and repeaters are starting to appear on the UHF and microwave bands. The most popular band for repeaters is 144 MHz (2 meters), with 222 MHz and 450 MHz following in popularity. FM is widely used.

A typical machine sits on top of a mountain or tall building and automatically retransmits signals from small hand-held or mobile rigs. The result is an increase in communications coverage for the user—some repeaters extend coverage to entire states and more! Because of this unique characteristic of repeaters, many other radio services use them. Police and fire departments, forest services, taxis and other land mobile services make great use of repeaters.

Repeater Control

As we've seen from the discussion of control earlier in the chapter, there are many ways to effect control of ham stations. Because repeaters are generally found on hilltops and tall buildings, local control is not practical. Most repeaters operate under automatic control and also provide some sort of control link so that the repeater can be disabled if necessary. Even though no control operator is required, the repeater must operate properly at all times. Make sure procedures and devices are used to prevent unauthorized tampering. Use unpublished control-link frequencies. Put padlocks on your repeater housing. Make sure you get the word quickly if something is wrong, and then have quick access to the repeater turn-off function. Protect your feed lines and antennas whenever possible. FCC has clearly stated in §97.205(e) that "Limiting the use of a repeater to only certain user stations is permissible." This allows you to implement subaudible tone security systems if required to protect the security of your repeater.

A third party participates in amateur communications when you make a phone call with a repeater autopatch. This means that a voice repeater must be locally or remotely controlled and a control operator must be present at the local or remote site when the repeater autopatch is active.

"Ancillary Functions"

In the pre-1989 version of Part 97, FCC was very specific about how repeaters were to be controlled. Section 97.88(e) specifically prohibited controlling a repeater station on its input frequency. The definition of "control" in this case was a bit vague, however. In the 1989 version of Part 97, FCC has attempted to clear up this issue. Unfortunately, the new language also requires some clarification. As this is written, §97.205(e) states "Ancillary functions of a repeater that are available to users on the input channel are not considered remotely controlled functions of the station." Clear as mud, right?

The problem lies in the lack of definition of "ancillary functions." The intent is to allow control of certain functions of the repeater on its input frequency, but which functions? As microprocessor-based repeater controllers proliferate, more and more exotic functions become available to repeater users. Clearly, some functions do not involve "control" of the repeater station. Message mailboxes fall into this category, as do autopatch systems.

Linked systems are another story. Many repeater systems now consist of more than one "machine." FCC has also removed the restriction on repeaters transmitting on more than one frequency in the same band from the same location. This opens the door to even more "octopus-like" repeater systems with multiple receivers and transmitters on several bands. If cross-band link control is not an "ancillary function," it must be done on a frequency authorized for remote-control purposes, and by a radio amateur who is authorized to be the control operator of the repeater. Novice licensees are not permitted to be repeater control operators. If link enabling and disabling is an "ancillary function," control may be effected on the repeater input by any amateur who is permitted to use the repeater (Novices included). This is a complex question; ARRL will be seeking to clarify it in the coming months.

The main point to remember in all this discussion of repeater control is that *you are responsible for the emissions of your repeater at all times*. You must be able to shut the repeater down if there is a problem. If your only means of control is on the repeater input frequency, there may be times when jamming or unintentional interference make this impossible. You should provide an alternate means of control, either by telephone or radio link on another frequency.

Repeater Station Identification

Repeaters may be identified by CW or voice. If an automatic device is used for the CW ID, the sending speed cannot exceed 20 words per minute. The FCC no longer requires that repeaters sign "/R" on CW or "repeater" on voice. Repeaters can also be identified using ASCII, Baudot or AMTOR when that particular code is used for all or part of the communication or when the communication is transmitted in any digital code above 50 MHz. This is why packet TNCs do not need to identify with CW. Amateur fast-scan television repeaters may identify with video as long as the US standard 525-line system is used.

Repeaters are the keys to local communications networks. They automatically retransmit signals from high places, effectively increasing the communications coverage of small, hand-held FM transceivers like K3QEU's here.

Specific Repeater Rules

The main function of this book is to try to explain Part 97 in plain language. Here are some of the specific repeater rules from §97.205:

• *A Novice operator may not be the licensee or control operator of a repeater.* Any other licensed operator may put up a repeater.

• *Specific frequencies are available for repeater operation.* Repeaters may operate on any frequency authorized to the Amateur Radio Service above 29.5 MHz, except for 50.0-51.0, 144.0-144.5, 145.5-146.0, 431.0-433.0 and 435-438 MHz.

• *Two repeater owners must work together to solve an interference problem between them, unless one repeater is coordinated and the other is not.* The licensee of an uncoordinated repeater has primary responsibility for solving an interference problem. This is the FCC's way of recognizing the importance of frequency coordination.

• *You may limit the use of your repeater.* This specifically permits you to operate a "closed" repeater using CTCSS or other systems to limit access. FCC recognizes that a repeater is an Amateur Radio station, licensed to the owner, and that repeater owners may limit the use of their stations.

Another important point to remember is that *a repeater user is not always the control operator*. This is what allows a Novice licensee to use a 222 MHz to 144-MHz linked repeater system. As long as the *input* of the repeater is on a frequency authorized for Novice use, Novices may use the system, even though their signals are being retransmitted on a band where they are not authorized. They are not transmitting on 2 meters, the *repeater station* is. Novices should not be allowed to *enable* the 2-meter link; this may amount to *control* of the repeater. See "Ancillary Functions" discussion.

DIGIPEATERS

With the introduction of packet-radio technology into the Amateur Service, another device has seen widespread use, the *digipeater*. A digipeater receives and retransmits packets. Digipeaters relay signals from other stations and extend the available range for packet communications.

There is a distinction between ordinary repeaters and digipeaters. Digipeaters simply confirm, then pass along data packets; they do not automatically retransmit signals like repeaters do. Digipeaters are not repeaters. Novices are permitted to be control operators for digipeaters, but not for voice repeaters. This allows the Novice packet network to expand and supports digital communications on Novice frequencies.

AUXILIARY STATIONS

When an amateur station is controlled remotely by radio, there is another station involved—the station doing the controlling. This station is called an *auxiliary station*. Here's how the FCC defines an auxiliary station: "An amateur station transmitting communications point-to-point within a system of cooperating amateur stations." There are a few important rules that apply to auxiliary stations:

• *Novice licensees may not put auxiliary stations on the air or be control operators for existing auxiliary stations.* Amateurs with any other class of license may put auxiliary stations on the air or be control operators for auxiliary stations.

• *Auxiliary stations may only transmit in ham bands above and including 220 MHz, except in the segments 431-433 and 435-438 MHz.*

• *Licensees of auxiliary stations causing interference to each other are equally responsible for solving the interference, except where one station is coordinated and the other is not.* Again, this is the FCC's way of recognizing the importance of frequency coordination. We'll discuss this critical topic later in the chapter.

• *An auxiliary station may be automatically controlled only when it is part of*

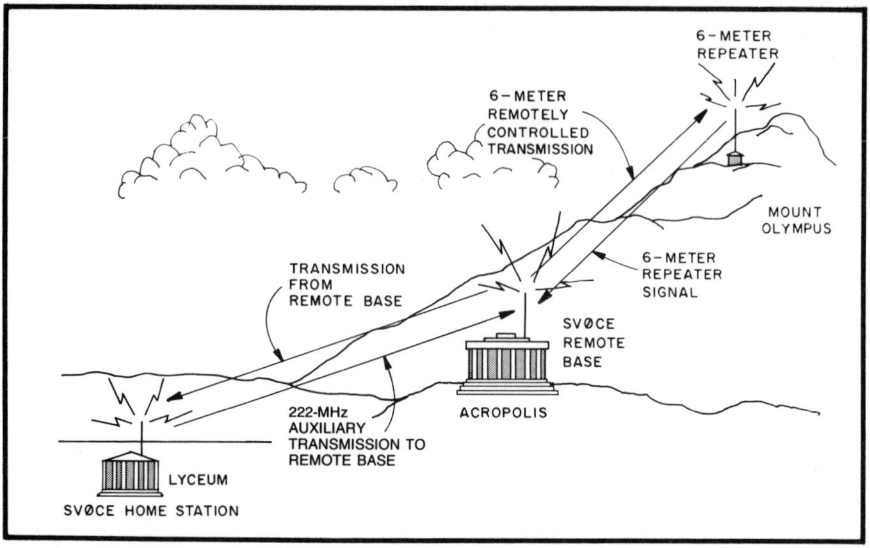

Fig 1—In ancient Athens, Aristotle, SVØCE, used an auxiliary station to remotely control the SVØCE remote base atop the Parthenon. This enabled him to check into the nightly Philosophy Net on the Mount Olympus 6-meter repeater to discuss the issues of the day with fellow hams Theophrastus, Eudemus and Alexander the Great. Notice that 222 signals both to and from the remote base are from auxiliary stations. The 6-meter remote base output is simply a remotely controlled station.

a system that includes an automatically controlled repeater. This means that you can't use a COR-controlled station to retransmit 20-meter signals on 222 MHz if the relay is *on all the time*. If you bring the link up manually with DTMF tones, then it's remotely controlled; that's okay.

The easiest way to explain the operation of an auxiliary station is to use a few examples.

1) Auxiliary stations are used in what have come to be known as "remote bases." A remote base is a station set up, usually in a good location, to relay signals from other stations. One example might be a 50-MHz transceiver linked to a 222-MHz transceiver. Users on 222 MHz have their signals retransmitted on 50 MHz. 50-MHz signals are received and retransmitted on 222. This is shown in Fig 1. When you are transmitting control commands and audio on 222 MHz, your station is an auxiliary station. The 50-MHz transmitter is *not* an auxiliary station; it's an ordinary station under remote control. The 222-MHz transmitter at the remote site that relays 50-MHz signals to you *is* an auxiliary station. It's relaying signals from another band.

It is important to point out that the remotely controlled transmitter or remote base is not a repeater as defined by the FCC rules. This means that an operator controlling a remote base must not operate the remotely controlled transmitter beyond the privileges allowed by his or her license class. (For example, it is acceptable for the 2-meter signals of a Technician class licensee to be repeated on 10 meters if the license class of the repeater's control operator affords operation on the 10-meter repeater subband, but it is *not* acceptable for a Technician to control a remote base with an output on a "non-Technician" frequency. Once again, the reason for this is that the remote base is not a repeater; the person controlling the remote base is the control operator of a conventional amateur station.)

2) Auxiliary stations are used to control simplex autopatch devices. The simplex

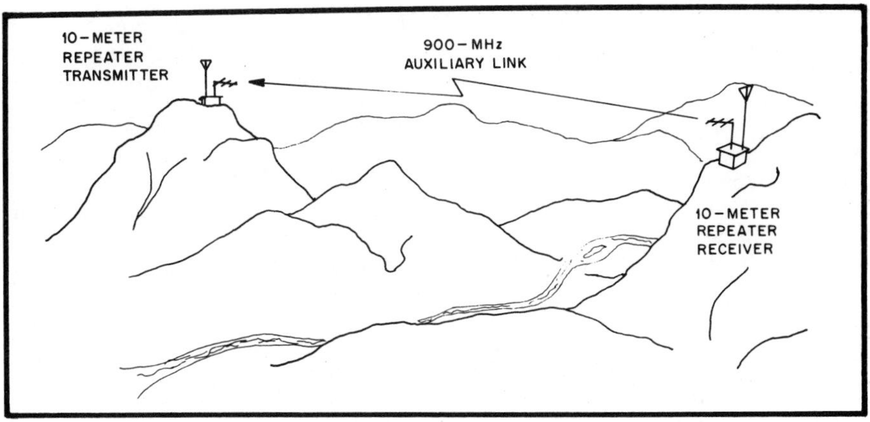

Fig 2—Another use for an auxiliary station. Here, a 900-MHz link relays signals from a 10-meter repeater receiver to the repeater transmitter, located a few miles away.

autopatch ("simpatch") is a box connected to a home station that can connect you to a telephone line. These devices must be used on frequencies authorized for auxiliary stations. You transmit control commands to the simpatch; this makes your station an auxiliary station. The simpatch transmits audio from the phone line; it's also an auxiliary station.

3) Auxiliary stations are used to relay signals between separate parts of a repeater system. Having the repeater receiver and transmitter both at one site can cause problems. These can sometimes be solved with filters and duplexers, but another alternative is to separate the transmitter and receiver. Several 10-meter repeater systems have been constructed using this technique. An auxiliary link on another band can then be used to relay signals from the receiver to the transmitter. This is shown in Fig 2.

FREQUENCY COORDINATION: FCC PR DOCKET 85-22

Coordinating one's choice of frequencies for a repeater has never been a licensing requirement. By early 1985, however, demand for frequencies had grown to the point where even an FCC predisposed to prefer "unregulation" decided something needed to be done. In February 1985, the FCC (in PR Docket 85-22) stated:

> Most of the reported cases of amateur repeater-to-repeater interference appear to involve one or more non-coordinated repeaters. In the past two years we have had to resolve amateur repeater-to-repeater interference disputes in which at least one non-coordinated repeater was involved and in which the parties to the dispute could reach no amicable solution. We attribute the growing number of instances of amateur repeater-to-repeater interference and the need for increased intervention in these matters to the mounting pressure which develops as the desirable repeater frequencies become fully assigned.
>
> When we have intervened in such interference disputes, we have. . . favored the repeater which has been operating in accordance with the recommendation of a local frequency coordinator.
>
> Comments are also sought with regard to whether the FCC should recognize a single national frequency coordinator for the Amateur Radio Service. Such a coordinator could either be an individual national organization or an umbrella organization comprised of local coordination groups. We would expect this type of organization to promulgate coordination (and de-coordination) standards, to facilitate the use of advancing technology, to consider alternative frequency assignments, to consider frequency spacing and repeater separation distances and, in the case of an umbrella organization, to advise local coordinators.

In its comments to PR Docket 85-22, the League proposed these guidelines:

• Preferred status in instances of harmful repeater-to-repeater interference should be granted to amateur repeater operators who have implemented the recommendation of their local or regional volunteer frequency coordinator and are thereby coordinated.

• Frequency coordination should be strongly urged for all amateur stations in repeater, or auxiliary, operation in any geographical area which is served by a frequency coordinator.

• The Commission should not consider alternatives to frequency coordination nor mandate methods of coordination.

• The use of modern technological innovation. . .should be encouraged but not submitted for frequency coordination.

• The Commission should not recognize a single entity, such as a national frequency coordinator for amateur repeater operation. Such coordination activities should be performed by local or regional volunteer frequency coordinators with appropriate support to these coordinators to be provided by the League.

In its Report and Order to PR Docket 85-22, the Commission stated:

> Repeater operation in the Amateur service inherently requires operation on established frequencies. Amateur repeater operation is not frequency agile, as are other types of amateur station operation. As a result, most amateur operators have been willing to voluntarily cooperate to avoid interference to frequencies designed for repeater operation. . .in favor of the greater good, particularly since many amateur repeaters are open to all amateur operators who desire to use them. The cooperation has taken the form of adherence to the determination of local frequency coordinators. While no amateur operator or amateur station "owns" a frequency, this type of coordination is the minimum joint effort by the amateur community needed to facilitate repeater operation. . .
>
> Several coordinators urged us to establish some mechanism to officially recognize local or regional coordinators. Others were concerned about the potential for abuse of power at the local level. Another concern was the exclusive right to coordinate within a geographical area. It is essential that repeater coordinators respond to the broadest base of local amateurs, and consider the concerns not only of repeater owners but also of those users of spectrum affected by repeater operation. Their authority is derived from the voluntary participation of the entire amateur community; their recognition must be derived from the same source. We believe the new rules will assure that a coordinator is representative of all local amateur operators.
>
> Several commenters urged us to abolish closed repeaters in the Amateur service, or, alternatively, to permit coordinators to relegate closed repeaters to secondary status or to give open repeaters preference when coordinating. We are not of the view, as were these commenters, that closed repeaters are any more or less desirable than open repeaters.
>
> We proposed to make non-coordinated repeaters primarily responsible to resolve interference associated with coordinated repeaters. The ARRL commented that we should go even further and make non-coordinated repeaters solely responsible to resolve such interference, and require non-coordinated repeaters to cease operation if the interference is not resolved. Although the focus must be placed in the first instance upon the non-coordinated repeater to resolve such interference, we are adopting our proposed rules which continue to make the coordinated repeater secondarily responsible. This permits local coordinators and the FCC to consider technical alternatives, questions of equity, and spectrum efficiency in reaching the most reasonable solution.

There you have it—the rationale behind the current Part 97 rules that affect amateur repeater coordination. For more information on repeater coordination, see Chapter 2 of *The ARRL Operating Manual*.

BAND PLANS

Band plan is a term you may encounter during your sojourns in the world of repeaters. It refers to an agreement among concerned VHF and UHF operators as to how each VHF and UHF Amateur Radio band should be utilized. The goal of a band plan is to systematically minimize interference between the various modes sharing each band. Besides FM repeater and simplex activity, you can find CW, SSB, AM, OSCAR and R/C (radio control) operations, among others, on these bands.

Most of you who use FM or plan on using FM will probably be using 2 meters. Check the description of the 2-meter band plan in Chapter 5.

In the 144.51-145.49 MHz range, the spacing between the repeater channels is 20 kHz. The first input frequency is 144.51 MHz and the next is 144.53 MHz (144.51 MHz + 20 kHz = 144.53 MHz).

In the 146.01-147.99 MHz range, channel spacing is either 20 or 30 kHz, depending on local policies.

Also, in those areas that utilize the 30-kHz spacing plan, some repeaters will be set up on "splinter" (15-kHz spacing) frequencies, or between two repeater channels. For example, spacing would normally place repeater inputs on 146.01 and 146.04 MHz, but an additional repeater input can be established on 146.025 MHz.

According to the above band plan, the spacing between each repeater input and output is 600 kHz. For example, the input frequency of 146.34 MHz has an output frequency of 146.94 MHz (146.34 MHz + 600 kHz = 146.94 MHz).

The simplex frequencies between 144.90 and 145.10 are currently being used for packet operation, while those between 146.40 and 146.60, and between 147.40 and 147.60 MHz, are channelized for voice-simplex operation. (Note: Select frequencies between 146.40 to 146.60 and 147.40 to 147.60 may also be a repeater input or output.)

A common variation to the band plan is the reversal of the input and output frequencies of those repeaters operating on splinter frequencies, such as 146.625 and 146.315 (not 146.85 and 147.15) MHz. The purpose of this reversal is to reduce cochannel interference.

Under this band plan, repeater pairs on 146 MHz (ie, 146.01/61) will normally have a low input/high output split; that is, the lower frequency (146.01) would be the input and the higher frequency (146.61) would be the output. Conversely, repeater pairs on 147 MHz (ie, 147.81/21) will normally have a high input/low output.

For more information on band plans and repeater operating in your local area, contact your frequency coordinator, listed in the front of the *ARRL Repeater Directory*.

"GOOD AMATEUR PRACTICE"

Got a renegade ham on your hands? You know the type: He operates simplex on the input of the local repeater. Or worse, he puts his repeater on a frequency pair of his choosing despite what the local frequency coordinator has to say. Some renegades enjoy setting up shop on FM in popular EME and terrestrial weak-signal areas, creating havoc with communications of good spectrum citizens.

The renegade writes off his "operation" as being in strict accordance with the letter of the law in Part 97. "Sure, wideband FM is permitted at 144.15—check it out in the regs" and "I was here first—who cares if this happens to be some dumb repeater's input?" are popular retorts from the renegade.

These retorts, however, don't wash with the Commission. Let's take a look at the meaning of good amateur practice, and how it affects operation in accord with nationally recognized band plans.

COMMON QUESTIONS AND ANSWERS —VHF BAND PLANS

Q. How does the Commission feel about the amateur community's own frequency planning and coordination?

A. In a repeater rules proceeding a while back, FCC said:

"The Commission is persuaded by the comments and by observation that regional and national frequency planning and coordination by amateur radio operators themselves can result in the best spectrum utilization appropriate to the service." We'll add that "best spectrum utilization" means amateurs operating in accordance with "good amateur practice"—a requirement found in §97.101 of the Rules.

Q. How does FCC view amateurs who place their repeaters on frequency pairs in disregard of repeater band plans?

A. In an April 27, 1983, letter to a major repeater council, FCC said:

"The only national planning for Amateur Radio Service frequencies that has come to our attention is that done by the American Radio Relay League. The 1982-83 edition of the ARRL Repeater Directory lists over 5600 stations in repeater operation all over the United States and Canada. In view of this widespread acceptance of their band plans, we conclude that any amateur who selects a station transmitting frequency not in harmony with those plans is not operating in accord with good amateur practice. [For example] The ARRL Repeater Directory lists the frequency pair 144.83/145.43 MHz as a repeater channel. Therefore, designation of this channel by the regional frequency coordinator in [an] area is in accord with the ARRL national band plan."

The bottom line is that if stations transmit on frequencies 144.83 or 145.43 (to use the Commission's example above), in a manner that creates interference to coordinated repeaters, then sufficient cause would exist for issuance of an Official Notice of Violation. And, such operation could mean an additional Notice for deliberate and malicious interference.

There are good reasons why simplex operation should be moved from repeater frequencies. The FCC has labeled three: (1) Repeater operation is not permitted on some Amateur Radio bands; (2) on those bands where repeater operation is permitted, such operation is confined to a limited portion—a subband—of the band; and (3) the nature of repeater operation necessitates some form of channelization, haphazard frequency selection would result in poor spectrum use, and constant frequency change is impractical.

Simplex stations do not have such limitations; thus, they have much greater flexibility in frequency choice. They must avoid repeater channels found in widely accepted band plans. Such avoidance constitutes good amateur practice.

Q. Do band plans exist for other bands and activities?

A. Yes; in fact, there are band plans for just about every amateur band.

For example, the 450-MHz band harbors many amateur activities: satellite, television, weak-signal terrestrial and EME communications, and FM and repeater operation. Sure, there's a lot of space in this segment, 420-450 MHz. But there are many activities that would collide with each other if it were not for this plan.

Let's be quick to point out that these plans are not unilateral decisions made in a vacuum. With lots of input from the ARRL VHF Repeater Advisory Committee (VRAC), the VHF/UHF Advisory Committee (VUAC) and other leading groups, they develop and evolve over a period of several years, sometimes decades. Each plan is designed to promote the greatest spectrum efficiency possible.

All amateurs should make every effort to operate in concert with these plans, which have the approval of the ham community and the FCC. In fact, "good amateur practice" dictates compliance with these community standards.

Q. Where can I find copies of band plans?

A. You won't find them in Part 97. As mentioned above, band plans are generated within the amateur ranks, not from the desks of the FCC. You will find these plans in Chapter 5.

Chapter Eleven

Digital Communications: RTTY and Data

In prior editions of the FCC rules, digital communications meant Baudot, AMTOR, ASCII and "any digital code" that might be used (above 50 MHz) for interchange of data between computers, and including packet radio. These are the specific things talked about in this chapter.

Just to keep our dictionaries in sync, however, digital communications is an entire class of emissions that use ones and zeros or discrete (quantized) levels rather than continuously variable quantities as in analog communications. While digital communications is presently associated with computers and machine information transfers, there will be a tendency for some of the older analog modulation techniques to give way to digital techniques for reasons of noise and error reduction. The new rules permit a whole new class of digital emissions for speech and image transmissions. We're not going to discuss them further in this chapter as it would take a clearer crystal ball than anyone has at the moment to see how speech and image digital transmissions will develop among amateurs. As these new modes evolve, it will be increasingly more difficult to tell them apart from packet radio used to transfer computer data. Computers can, after all, be used to generate speech and images.

Back to Baudot, AMTOR, ASCII and digital communications of the kind we've grown to know and love.

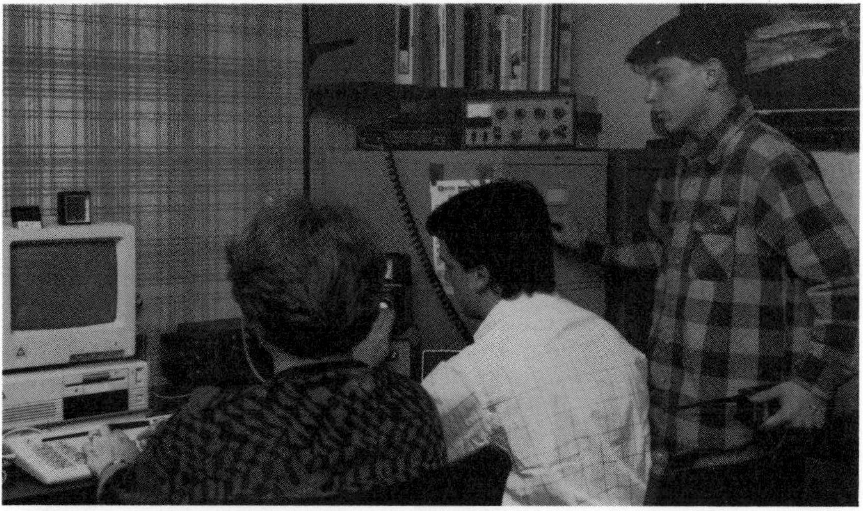

The computer and Amateur Radio: A marriage made in heaven.

RTTY

RTTY is an abbreviation for *radioteletype*. §97.3(c)(7) of the new rules identifies RTTY as *narrow-band direct-printing telegraphy*. It then goes on to name the emission symbols for RTTY; these symbols are explained in Chapter 8.

COMMON QUESTIONS-AND-ANSWERS—RTTY

Q. What does* narrow-band direct-printing *(NB-DP) mean?

A. That is terminology used by the ITU and FCC in other Parts of their rules to mean what we call RTTY. So there you have it—a circular definition!

The bandwidth of an RTTY signal is normally narrower than that of an SSB signal on the MF and HF bands (160-10 meters). The *necessary bandwidth* for a typical 45-baud RTTY signal using frequency-shift keying with a shift of 170 Hz is 249 Hz. For more information on calculating bandwidth, see Chapter 9 of the *The ARRL Handbook*.

Direct-printing means that the originating station formats the message to print out on a page of paper (hard copy). Of course, the receiving operator could elect to display the incoming message on a computer screen. Or, the receiving station computer could simply store the information in memory and never print it out. Nevertheless, the original intent was to produce page copy at the receiving end.

Q. What is Baudot?

A. Baudot is the more familiar name for a 5-bit code known worldwide as International Telegraph Alphabet No. 2 (ITA2). Its formal definition is found in International Telegraph and Telephone Consultative Committee (CCITT) Recommendation F.1, Division C. Combinations of ones and zeros in 5 bits can produce 32 different positions. Each position is assigned a graphic character or a machine control function. By having two cases (letters and figures), all the letters of the Latin alphabet, numerals and many commonly used punctuation marks can be accommodated. For a table showing the bit patterns and their assignments, see Chapter 19 of *The ARRL Handbook*.

Q. What is AMTOR?

A. AMTOR is an acronym meaning *AM*ateur *T*eleprinting *O*ver *R*adio. It is an adaptation of *SITOR*, used in the maritime service. The term *TOR* has caught on as a generic reference to these kinds of systems. Its formal definition may be found in International Radio Consultative Committee (CCIR) Recommendations 476-2 (1978), 476-3 (1982), 476-4 (1986) or 625 (1986). The bit patterns and their assignments are given in Chapter 19 of *The ARRL Handbook*.

One important ingredient in TOR is its 7-bit code. For example, the bit sequences for the letter A (and hyphen in figure case) is 1000111, and for B (? in figure case) is 1110010. Note that both bit sequences have four 1s and three 0s; this is true for all TOR code combinations. This is done to provide a method of error detection at the receiving station. If anything but the correct four 1s, three 0s combination is received, the receiving station knows there was an error in reception.

Another feature is a mode called *A*utomatic *R*epeat re*Q*uest (*ARQ*), also called Mode A. This is a protocol that calls for the sending station to transmit three characters, then wait for an ACKnowledgement, then three more characters, and so forth. If the four 1s, three 0s combination is not received, then an ACK is not given, and the sending station repeats the three characters until an ACK is received.

There is also a Mode B which uses *F*orward *E*rror *C*orrection (*FEC*). Mode B is used for transmissions from one point to more than one receiving station—situations where it would be impractical to wait for an ACK from each receiving station. In the FEC mode, each block of three characters is simply sent twice in a one-way transmission. The theory is that the receiving station equipment will accept characters having the correct 4/3 ratio and reject the others, and each character gets two chances to be received. Mode B is useful for bulletin transmissions and roundtables where ACKs are not feasible.

Q. Is AMTOR a form of "RTTY"?

A. You bet. It is simply RTTY with built-in error-control techniques, as explained above.

Q. What is ASCII?

A. Officially, ASCII is what §97.309(a)(3) calls the American National Standards Institute X3.4-1977. The rules also permit International Telegraph and Telephone Consultative Committee (CCITT) Recommendation T.50, International Alphabet No. 5 (IA5), or International Organization for Standardization, International Standard ISO 646 (1983), which are simply international forms of ASCII.

Practically, ASCII is a 7-unit coded character set having 128 code combinations. A table showing the character set is given in Chapter 19 of *The ARRL Handbook*.

Q. Are code extensions permissible?

A. §97.309(a) of the rules also permits extensions as provided for in CCITT Recommendation T.61 (Malaga-Torremolinos, 1984). These extensions provide for additional graphic symbols and diacritical marks used for foreign languages. None of these special characters would come up in everyday English-language text, but they're there just in case. Of course, permission to use code extensions does not relieve a station of identifying properly using the basic character set. That's just the same idea as for phone, in which you can chat in a foreign language, but you must identify in English or international phonetics so others on the band can understand.

PACKET RADIO

Packet radio is simply a packaging method for transmission. The basic idea is to break up a message into small transmission blocks, called packets. Depending on the speed of transmission, a packet may last only a fraction of a second or several seconds. The length may vary, but a typical packet might contain a line of text, a header showing who it came from and where it's going to and a trailer with error-control bits.

As in AMTOR Mode A, an ARQ protocol is used. As a result, packet radio is presently best suited for point-to-point communication. FEC protocols are not in present use but will likely be developed for bulletin dissemination and roundtable applications.

COMMON QUESTIONS-AND-ANSWERS—PACKET RADIO

Q. But is packet radio legal?

A. Yes. Wherever *data* emission is permitted in the amateur band frequency segments in §97.305(c), packet radio may be used. You won't find a mention of packet radio, as such, in the rules except in §97.109(d). It specifies that the AX.25 Amateur Packet-Radio Link-Layer Protocol, version 2.0 or compatible, must be used when a station is retransmitting third-party traffic under automatic control on frequencies above 50 MHz.

Q. Where can I read more about packet radio?

A. Chapter 19 of the *The ARRL Handbook* has a technical description of packet radio, and *The ARRL Operating Manual* has operating information. A good general booklet is *Your Gateway to Packet Radio*. The ARRL also publishes *QEX*, which is available by subscription; check *QST* magazine or write ARRL HQ for ordering information.

UNSPECIFIED DIGITAL CODES

Above 50 MHz where *data* and *RTTY* emissions are permitted, *unspecified* digital codes may be used in communication between stations licensed by the FCC. Baudot, AMTOR and ASCII are specified in the rules, so *unspecified* includes everything else. There is a provision for using unspecified codes when communicating with stations in other countries that have an agreement with the United States to that effect. However, there are no such agreements in effect as of this writing. Unspecified digital codes must not be used to obscure the meaning of any communication.

AUTOMATIC CONTROL OF DATA AND RTTY STATIONS

Q. Is it legal?

A. Yes. An amateur station may be under automatic control when transmitting digital communications on frequencies 50 MHz and above.

§97.109(d) continues a restriction relating to third-party traffic, as follows: "No station may be automatically controlled while transmitting third-party traffic, except a station retransmitting digital packet radio communications on the 6 m and shorter wavelength bands. Such stations must be using the American Radio Relay League, Inc. *AX.25 Amateur Packet-Radio Link-Layer Protocol, Version 2.0*, October 1984 (or compatible). The retransmitted messages must originate at a station that is being locally or remotely controlled."

In addition, the ARRL Board of Directors has been studying the merits of operation under automatic control at frequencies below 50 MHz. If the Board considers it in the best interests of the service to do so, the ARRL may petition the FCC for amendment of the rules.

For the past several years, there has been a special temporary authority (STA) requested by the ARRL to allow for experimentation with automatic control of certain stations engaged in automatic forwarding of traffic. This operation, known as SKIPNET, has served as a test bed for experiments with message-forwarding protocols and station-control techniques.

MODULATION METHODS FOR DATA AND RTTY

Former versions of the rules specified the emission symbol F1B, meaning frequency-shift of the main carrier with automatically received telegraphy, for *RTTY*. It was generally understood that packet-radio transmissions could operate wherever F1B was permitted, even though the third symbol in F1B technically should have been "D." Also, it was understood that alternative means of generating a frequency-shift-keyed signal, such as feeding audio-frequency-shift-keyed (AFSK) tones into a single-sideband transmitter, would produce the equivalent effect on the air as F1B. Finally, a careful review of previous editions of the rules would lead one to conclude that a ham wouldn't land in the hoosegow if the FSK or AFSK were replaced by PSK or APSK (phase-shift).

If you were enjoying some sense of forbidden fruit by violating the technical definition of F1B, then you may be disappointed in the new rules. All this is perfectly OK now. Just read the technical definitions of *data* and *RTTY* in §97.3(f). For a plain-English translation, see Chapter 8.

COMMON QUESTIONS-AND-ANSWERS— DATA, RTTY MODULATION METHODS

Q. Is it permissible to modulate an FM voice transmitter with data or RTTY?

A. It depends on the frequency. It is presently permissible only where *data* or *RTTY* emissions are authorized above 50 MHz. This type of transmission is commonly used in the VHF bands because of the ready availability of FM transceivers.

Some amateurs have expressed a desire to operate using this mode in the 10-meter band above 29.0 MHz. While FM voice is specifically authorized as a mode, neither *data* nor *RTTY* are permitted on 10 meters except in the 28.0-28.3 MHz segment.

Q. Are there any speed limits or bandwidth constraints for data or RTTY?

A. Yes, at least below 450 MHz. The limits break down as follows:

Frequency Range	*Speed Limit for Specified Codes of Baudot, AMTOR, ASCII*	*Maximum Bandwidth for Unspecified Codes*
1.80 - 24.93 MHz	300 bauds	Not permitted
28.0 - 28.3 MHz	1200 bauds	Not permitted
50.1 - 148 MHz	19.6 kilobauds	20 kHz
222 - 450 MHz	56 kilobauds	100 kHz
Above 902 MHz	No speed limit	No bandwidth limit

The maximum bandwidth, in this case, is the "width of a frequency band outside of which the mean power of the total emission is attenuated at least 26 dB below the mean power of the total emission, including allowances for transmitter drift or Doppler shift." Where no speed or bandwidth limits are stated, above, the basic rule is to stay within the ham band. But there's another practical matter: Other hams using the band won't be pleased if you are using the entire band. It would be a good idea to check the appropriate band plan and contact your area frequency coordinator to see just how much bandwidth your peers would like you to occupy.

Chapter Twelve

Specialized Operating

Every ham should understand the FCC Rules that apply to ordinary everyday operating. There are some specialized operating modes, however, that don't come up as topics of conversation during the usual 75-meter ragchew. In this chapter, we'll talk about some of those modes.

We'll discuss amateur stations in space; Part 97 of the FCC's rules defines both a *space station* and an *earth station*. *Telecommand* operation, as defined in Part 97, is the special preserve of designated earth stations that control the functions of space stations. *Beacons* are a useful part of our continuing efforts to use our bands to maximum advantage. This chapter contains information to help you understand what you must do if you want to put a beacon on the air. Finally, we'll look at what the FCC Rules say about *spread spectrum* operations.

LOST IN SPACE

When you build a repeater, you try to put the antenna on a tall tower or on top of a tall building. The higher you get the antenna, the better coverage your repeater will have. What about a repeater with an antenna more than *50 kilometers* high? You'd expect it to have great coverage, right? An amateur satellite may not be more than a repeater in space with a very large footprint on the earth. Except for geostationary orbits, satellites don't stay in one spot, either. They cross international "borders" all the time. A satellite is obviously not your average amateur station.

Microsat represents the latest generation in a long line of OSCAR satellites.

In 1971, member nations of the International Telecommunication Union (ITU) sat down at the conference table to fashion regulations for the burgeoning commercial and noncommercial satellite technologies. Rules were needed for international coordination of satellite frequencies, locations and purposes given the proliferation of hardware floating virtually over every nation on earth. The 1971 Space WARC (World Administrative Radio Conference) delegates arrived at a number of agreements and requirements, and the FCC was obligated to carry them out. Accordingly, the Amateur Radio Service witnessed the introduction of a new subpart in Part 97: the

Amateur-Satellite Service (ASAT). The Amateur-Satellite Service rules have now been integrated into Part 97. As with other sections of the rules, FCC has taken steps to bring the space operations section of Part 97 into close accord with the ITU regulations.

Part 97 defines a *space station* as "An amateur station located more than 50 km above the Earth's surface." This obviously includes amateur satellites, and also includes any amateur operation from the Space Shuttle, the Soviet MIR space station and any future operations by astronauts in space. Section 97.207 details a few special rules that apply to space stations:

• *Only an amateur station licensed to an Amateur Extra Class licensee can be a space station.* Any licensed ham can be the control operator of a space station, however. This means that the amateur gear on board OSCAR 27 must be licensed to an Extra Class ham, but once the satellite is in orbit, any other ham can be allowed to control it. Control operator privileges are subject to the limitations of the control operator's license, of course. If you have a Technician class license, you can't control a satellite on a 15-meter uplink outside the 15-meter Technician subband.

• *It must be possible to make the space station stop transmitting if the FCC orders this.* This is done by *telecommand*, another type of specialized operation we'll look at later in the chapter. All this means is that the FCC wants to make sure that someone can shut off OSCAR 29's transmitter if it's interfering with the guidance system on the Jupiter 2 as it leaves for Alpha Centauri. Common sense, eh?

• *A space station may automatically retransmit the radio signals of Earth stations and other space stations.* An amateur satellite wouldn't be very useful without this provision.

• *Space stations are exempt from some rules that apply to ordinary amateur stations.* Space stations do not have to identify themselves, and space stations are permitted to transmit one-way communications. If space stations transmit the results of measurements made in the station they may use special codes to facilitate communications without worrying about the "codes and ciphers" provisions in Part 97.

• *Space stations may transmit only on frequencies authorized in Part 97.* Table 1 shows the transmit frequencies authorized to space stations by §97.207(c)(2).

• *The licensee of a space station must notify the FCC.* This is an important part of placing an amateur satellite in orbit. Notification allows the FCC to keep track of US-licensed amateur satellites so that it can respond to any interference complaints registered with the ITU. A satellite is an "international" station, and its licensee must remember that he has international responsibilities. FCC specifies *when* they must be notified in Part 97, but rather than spell out *what* information must be provided, FCC defers to the ITU Regulations. The appropriate sections of the ITU regs are available from ARRL HQ. If you see a space station in your future, these rules are *required reading*!

The FCC must be notified four times:

1) No less than 27 months before the space station will begin transmissions. This notification must include the information specified in Appendix 4 of the ITU regs. This includes the name of the satellite, the date it will commence operations, the name and address of the organization responsible for the satellite and the satellite's orbital parameters (where it will travel in space). Notification must also include technical information about any radio links the satellite will use; earth-to-space, space-to-earth and space-to-space as appropriate.

2) The FCC must be notified again no less than five months before the space station starts transmitting. This time Appendix 3 is the relevant part of the ITU Regulations. This notification must include much more detailed information about the RF links the space station will use.

3) Once the space station is in space and operating, you have seven days to let the FCC know your station has commenced in-space operation. This notice must update the pre-space notifications. For example, you must tell the FCC if the 23-cm

Table 1

Frequencies Authorized to Space Stations

Bands	
Wavelength	*Frequency*
40 m	7.0-7.1 MHz
20 m	14.00-14.25 MHz
17 m	18.068-18.168 MHz
15 m	21.00-21.45 MHz
12 m	24.89-24.99 MHz
10 m	28.0-29.7 MHz
2 m	144-146 MHz
70 cm	435-438 MHz
23 cm	1260-1270 MHz
13 cm	2400-2450 MHz
9 cm	3.40-3.41 GHz Regions 2 and 3 only
5 cm	5.83-5.85 GHz space-to-earth only
3 cm	10.45-10.50 GHz
1.2 cm	24.00-24.05 GHz
6 mm	47.0-47.2 GHz
4 mm	75.5-81.0 GHz
2 mm	142-149 GHz
1 mm	241-250 GHz

Table 2

Frequencies Authorized to Earth and Telecommand Stations

Bands	
Wavelength	*Frequency*
40 m	7.0-7.1 MHz
20 m	14.00-14.25 MHz
17 m	18.068-18.168
15 m	21.00-21.45 MHz
12 m	24.89-24.99 MHz
10 m	28.0-29.7 MHz
2 m	144-146 MHz
70 cm	435-438 MHz
23 cm	1260-1270 MHz earth-to-space only
13 cm	2400-2450 MHz
9 cm	3.40-3.41 GHz Regions 2 and 3 only
5 cm	5.65-5.67 GHz earth-to-space only
3 cm	10.45-10.50 GHz
1.2 cm	24.00-24.05 GHz
6 mm	47.0-47.2 GHz
4 mm	75.5-81.0 GHz
2 mm	142-149 GHz
1 mm	241-250 GHz

transponder on your satellite has failed or the 13-cm telemetry transmitter is only operating at half power.

4) Finally, when the satellite fails or the Shuttle lands and space operation is terminated, you must notify the FCC within three months. If the FCC orders you to terminate space operation, you must let them know that you have complied no later than 24 hours after the operation ends.

EARTH STATIONS

The FCC defines an *Earth station* as "An amateur station located on, or within 50 km of, the Earth's surface intended for communications with space stations or with other Earth stations by means of one or more objects in space." Any radio amateur can be the control operator of an Earth station, subject to the limitations of his license class. Some specific transmitting frequencies are authorized for Earth stations; these are shown in Table 2.

(SPACE) TELECOMMAND STATIONS

FCC defines a *telecommand station* as "An amateur station that transmits communications to initiate, modify or terminate functions of a space station." The definitions of a space station and an earth station follow the ITU regulations fairly closely, but here the FCC makes a significant departure from the ITU definitions and even from definitions in the FCC's own Part 2. ITU defines *telecommand* as "The use of telecommunication for the transmission of signals to initiate, modify or terminate functions of equipment at a distance." A separate definition is provided for *space telecommand*: "The use of radiocommunication for the transmission of signals to a space station to initiate, modify or terminate functions of equipment on an associated space object, including the space station."

It doesn't make a lot of difference what you call it, as long as you realize that Part 97 means "control of a space station" when the rules say "telecommand." Again, there are a few special rules in §97.211 that apply to a telecommand station:

• *Any amateur station may be a telecommand station.* Only stations designated by the licensee of the space station may transmit commands to that station, however. This is a simple precaution that protects the space station from unauthorized control. This privilege is also limited by the privileges of the operator's license class. Like the space station control operator requirements, if you have a Technician class license, you can't control a (space) telecommand station on 20 meters.

• *A telecommand station may transmit special codes intended to obscure the meaning of telecommand messages.* This also protects the space station from unauthorized control commands. One wrong command could turn an expensive satellite into just another piece of orbiting space junk!

• *Telecommand stations may transmit only on frequencies authorized in Part 97.* Table 3 shows the frequencies authorized for (space) telecommand operation in §97.211(c).

REMOTE CONTROL OF MODEL CRAFT

We talked about remote control of an amateur station (§97.213) in Chapter 10. Amateurs are also permitted to use radio links to control "model craft." Section 97.215 details the restrictions on this kind of operation:

• *Station identification is not required for transmission directed only to the model craft.* The control transmitter must bear a label indicating the station's call sign and the licensee's name and address.

• *Control signals are not considered codes and ciphers.*

• *Transmitter power cannot exceed one watt.*

BEACONS

A beacon station is simply a transmitter that alerts listeners to its presence. In the Radionavigation Service, beacons are used to provide navigational guidance. In the Amateur Service, beacons are used primarily for the study of radio-wave propagation—to allow amateurs to tell when a band is open to different parts of the country or world. Accordingly, FCC defines a *beacon*: "An amateur station transmitting communications for the purposes of observation of propagation and reception or other related experimental activities."

Section 97.203 addresses beacon operation. A few key points:

• *Automatically controlled beacon stations are limited to the frequencies shown in Table 3.* Beacons that are manually controlled are not subject to the same restrictions as automatically controlled beacons.

• *The transmitter power of a beacon must not exceed 100 W.*

• *Any license class, except Novice, can operate a beacon station.*

Table 3

Frequencies Authorized for Automatically controlled Beacon Stations

28.20	-	28.30	MHz
50.06	-	50.08	MHz
144.275	-	144.300	MHz
222.05	-	222.06	MHz
432.300	-	432.400	MHz
all amateur bands above 450 MHz			

In response to a request from ARRL based on membership input, the FCC recently moved the 2-meter and 70-cm automatic control beacon subbands from 144.05-144.06 MHz and 432.07-432.08 MHz to 144.275-144.300 MHz and 432.300-432.400 MHz. The League requested the change based on the fact that the old subbands were completely within the portions of each band used for weak-signal communications. "The presence of powerful beacons has. . .resulted in interference to moonbounce and other weak-signal amateur experimentation. Overall, it would better serve the needs of weak-signal experimenters to have the beacons outside the band segments primarily used for weak-signal communications and experimentation."

SPREAD SPECTRUM

Most people think of an "efficient" communications system as one that crams the most information into the smallest possible spectrum space. We hams have been taught for years that "wide" means "bad" as far as radio signals go. Spread-spectrum (SS) techniques take the exact opposite approach: The signal is spread out over a very wide bandwidth.

The *ARRL Handbook* contains a detailed technical description of spread-spectrum techniques in Chapter 21, so we will not go into much technical detail here. It is sufficient to say that SS uses digital techniques to spread a signal out over a wide bandwidth in such a way that the signal can be recovered by a receiver that is expecting the SS signal. The signal may be spread so far that it becomes invisible to a conventional receiver. This has obvious military applications. Another benefit of SS systems is that the "despreading" process can reject undesired signals—even signals much stronger than the desired communications. Again, this makes SS a popular military antijamming technique.

SS communications are permitted on the 70-cm (420-MHz) band and all amateur frequencies above this band. There are two types of SS that amateurs are allowed to use. *Frequency hopping (FH)* spread spectrum uses a binary sequence to switch the transmit frequency many times per second. If the receiver is synchronized to the transmitter, it can follow the hopping and the system becomes transparent to the users. To avoid interference to and from conventional users of a band, the time the transmitter stays on any one frequency must be kept very short. This time (called the *dwell time*) is typically less than 10 milliseconds.

Direct sequence (DS) spread spectrum uses a very fast bit stream to spread the energy of the carrier over a wide band of frequencies. This binary sequence is called *pseudonoise (PN)*. Again, the transmitter and receiver must use the same synchronized sequence, but once they are in sync the system becomes transparent to the user.

The FCC rules for spread-spectrum operation are fairly complicated, and a bit intimidating at first. As you read through the rules, however, you'll find that they merely spell out the parameters that must be followed to ensure that everyone uses the same kind of SS. The rules were written to make it easy for FCC to monitor this new mode. FCC also hopes to minimize interference complaints and to make those few that do arise easier to deal with. Let's look at a few highlights of §97.311:

- *SS communications are authorized only between points within areas regulated by the FCC.* This means that under the current rules, you can't use SS to work your buddy in Canada, even if Canadian hams are permitted to use SS.
- *SS communications must not be used for the purposes of obscuring the meaning of any communication.* A pretty obvious provision, but one FCC wanted to spell out, given the potentials of SS techniques.
- *Stations transmitting SS communications must not cause interference to other stations, and must accept interference from stations employing other authorized emissions.* This says that for now, SS is a "second-class citizen" on the ham bands. Your complaints that the local repeater is interfering with your SS communications

will fall on deaf ears at FCC. On the other hand, if your SS communications are interfering with the Orange Tabby Swap'n'Shop Net, *you* will be told to cease and desist. FCC does state in this provision that unintentionally triggering a carrier-operated repeater is not considered harmful interference. It's still not a good idea, however. If you cause this kind of interference when operating frequency-hopping SS, back off on your dwell time on any particular frequency. Tests in the Washington, DC area showed that fast FH-SS with short dwell times can operate on the inputs of repeaters without "kerchunking" or causing noticeable interference in the outputs of the repeaters.

- *Only certain spreading sequences may be used.* This allows the FCC to monitor SS communications.
- *Detailed records of SS operations must be kept.* These records must be kept for one year following the last entry, and must contain enough information to allow the FCC to demodulate your SS signals. Section 97.311(e) spells out all the information that must be recorded to meet these requirements.
- *SS transmitter power must not exceed 100 W.*

The rules may seem a bit excessive, but they're there to allow experimentation while they protect other users of the ham bands where SS is allowed. With time, FCC may relax these restrictions and allow SS to take its place with all the other "first-class" emissions.

SUMMARY

Part 97 allows for some unconventional operating modes and techniques. Feel free to widen your horizons and experiment with some of them, but remember that *you* are responsible for understanding the rules that pertain to anything you are doing on the air. It's an old cliche, but "ignorance of the law is no excuse." Read the appropriate Sections of Part 97 until you are sure that you are following the letter *and* the spirit of the rules. If you have questions, the Regulatory Information Branch at ARRL HQ is here to help.

Chapter Thirteen

Serving the Public

EMERGENCY COMMUNICATION: IS IT LEGAL?

Of course, all *emergency* communications are legal. Yet, because of folklore and secondhand anecdotes, emergency and public-service communications have become a confusing topic for many amateurs. A surprising number seem to believe that much of our public-service and disaster communications are illegal.

Some Examples

During August and September 1987, nearly *700 square miles* of California forest lands were destroyed by wildfire, causing the evacuation of tens of thousands of mountain residents. Hundreds of ham operators provided support communications for the US Forest Service, the California Department of Forestry, the American Red Cross and other relief agencies.

Once the fires were out, several hams were heard asking, "Were we legal? Or, were we conducting the regular business of these relief agencies?" That this question was asked at all, under the circumstances, illustrates the confusing interpretations of FCC rules within the amateur fraternity.

In some instances, the misunderstandings about emergency communications have tarnished the image of Amateur Radio. At a recent 200-mile bike ride, a "sag wagon" with Amateur Radio communications arrived on the scene of a serious accident; a volunteer paramedic had already arrived to administer first aid.

Due to the extent of the injuries, the paramedic asked to confer with a physician who happened to be in the vicinity of net control. Strangely, the net control refused to allow the physician to speak directly over the radio. In spite of complicated medical terminology and the potential for mistakes, the net control operator insisted on verbally relaying each message. The control operator said he wasn't sure if it would be legal for the paramedic to speak directly with the physician.

Unfortunately, this paramedic is a volunteer with a search and rescue group that *needs* Amateur Radio support. But, based on this unfortunate incident, they have chosen to avoid ham radio because, the paramedic said, "It's unreliable."

At another bike tour, open to the public and sponsored by a local bike club, several hams told the ham radio coordinator that helping the bike club was not legal for ham radio—yet seven of the 2500 riders suffered major injuries requiring paramedic or helicopter air ambulance response. Ham radio proved essential to the safety of the riders.

N4ALE, a member of the Athens (Georgia) Radio Club, provides communications support during "The Gambler," a 50-km bicycle race held to benefit a local homeless shelter. The course winds through the estate of entertainer Kenny Rogers, hence the name "The Gambler." Amateurs provide communications support in such events to promote safe observance and participation by the public.

So What is Legal, Anyway?

For the most part, the confusion is not really in the FCC rules, but in the amateur community and their understanding and interpretation of the FCC rules.

Somewhere in the chain of ham-radio folklore, facts about emergency communications have become distorted. At times, hams have written to the FCC asking about a hypothetical situation. Unfortunately, this may result in a hasty legal opinion, formed without consideration of all necessary factual details, when in fact, the FCC would prefer for us to be self-regulating and to resolve operational issues by ourselves.

When the FCC releases a *Report and Order* in a rule-making proceeding, it usually includes a discussion of why the new rule was written. Sometimes, these explanations appear at odds with, or to incompletely explain, the regulations.

To help us understand what we can and cannot do, we must have a good understanding of each of the following three principles:

1) Business communications
2) Emergency communications
3) Public-event communications

Business Communications

As we've seen in Chapter 7, business communications are expressly forbidden within the Amateur Radio Service. Amateur Radio exists for several good reasons, including public-service and technical experimentation. If routine business communications were allowed, any business could license its employees and swamp our 2-meter band with kilowatt repeaters and continuous communications where we would not be welcome. (This has already happened in the General Mobile Radio Service, a "mixed use" service for both personal and business use.)

Because of this prohibition on business communications, the FCC has added a carefully worded exception for use during times of emergency, allowing Amateur Radio operators to conduct whatever type of communication is needed. You can't use your station to "facilitate the business or commercial affairs of any party," or as an "alternative to other authorized radio services, *except as necessary to providing emergency communications*." Note the words "any party"—the FCC rules make no distinction between for-profit and non-profit businesses. You can't conduct the *regular* business of a charitable organization, such as providing mobile communications for a food bank in its daily collection of surplus food.

You can, however, assist at a 10-km running race sponsored by the food bank (or a for-profit business) when your involvement is for the primary benefit of the general public, even if there is an incidental benefit to the sponsor. For example, where the communications are related to the safety of the attendees and participants, the primary beneficiary is the general public, not the sponsor of the event.

Emergency Communications

An important exception to the business communications prohibition is the case of emergency communications, that is, communications "in connection with the immediate safety of human life and immediate protection of property when normal communication systems are not available." The difficulty is the interpretation of what constitutes an immediate threat to life or property.

During an emergency, you may use your radio in any manner that is appropriate. Even though putting out fires or providing disaster assistance may be the *regular* business of your fire department or of the American Red Cross, in these situations an emergency affecting the immediate safety of life and property has occurred, and your Amateur Radio participation is not only allowed, but encouraged.

When Does a Situation Become an Emergency?

The key words that define an emergency are "immediate safety of human life and immediate protection of property when normal communication systems are not available." Obvious examples of an emergency include natural disasters—such as tornadoes, hurricanes, blizzards, floods—and other forms of severe weather, forest fires, landslides and earthquakes. All of these typically cause immediate danger to both life and property and outages of normal communication systems (telephones and public-safety radio systems).

A train derailment causing this toxic chemical spill posed an immediate threat to life in the Miamisburg, Ohio, area recently. Hams provided communications support to police, fire and other public-safety services.

Under these guidelines, assisting the Forest Service during a wildfire, allowing a physician to use your radio or performing Red Cross disaster assessment are all legitimate Amateur Radio operations.

Other situations, though, are less clear cut. For example, you spot a motorist, stranded along a suburban highway. Can you call for help on the repeater autopatch? At first this hardly seems like an emergency, but it may be a real danger to the stranded motorist.

In 1988, a San Francisco Bay Area mother and daughter were killed when their disabled automobile was struck from behind. They were parked well off on the right side of the freeway, emergency flashers on, hood up, in broad daylight. Could you have called for a tow truck? Of course. Pick up your hand-held and call! See Chapter 7 for more discussion of this example.

At the scene of an accident, can you hand your radio to an unlicensed person, such as a fire chief? Yes. As long as you remain the control operator, this is merely standard third-party operation. In fact, this is usually the most efficient way to provide communications to an agency during an emergency. Rather than relay the message yourself, why not put the sender and the recipient on the radio? This eliminates errors and is much more efficient.

PUBLIC EVENTS COMMUNICATIONS

The FCC encourages public-service activities within Amateur Radio. A fundamental principle found in the very first FCC rule in Part 97 is "Recognition and enhancement of the value of the amateur service to the public as a voluntary non-commercial communications service..."

Much of the confusion over ham-radio public-service communications stems both from a confusing Report and Order issued by the FCC in 1983 and from a letter written to the FCC in 1984 regarding support of the New York City Marathon.

WA2YII helps the amateur communications effort at the largest running race in the world, the New York City Marathon. The Herculean effort is coordinated each year by ARRL Hudson Division Director Steve Mendelsohn, WA2DHF.

One of the purposes of the amateur network had been to inform the general public, and possibly the news media, of the race status via a public address system at each mile marker. Clearly, this amounted to using Amateur Radio for purposes that are prohibited by the rules.

The letter basically asked if it was okay for the ham network to be broadcast over a public address system. Quite correctly, the FCC replied that reporting the position of lead runners via the amateur network and the public-address system ran afoul of the prohibition on broadcasting to the public.

But contrary to widespread belief, the FCC did *not* prohibit amateurs from assisting at events where there are paid participants. Acceptable activities, the FCC wrote, are not determined "by the profit objectives of the sponsor, nor by the pay status of other participants...Although some communications transmitted could incidentally benefit a sponsor, we do not view such communications as violations of the rules where their main purpose is to provide a service to the public."

Further, and again contrary to popular

opinion, the FCC did *not* rule that, in general, it is illegal to transmit lead-runner position reports. At many races, the race director needs to know the locations of the lead runners, the "pack" and the last runners so he can correctly position the first aid, ambulance and water-support crews. If that is indeed the purpose of lead-runner reports, then this function is in the interest of runner and spectator safety and is a legal function for the Amateur Radio Service. Where position reports are intended for a PA broadcast, an alternative radio service must be used—see "Alternatives to the Amateur Radio Service" elsewhere in this chapter.

Other examples of public service include bike races and tours, parades, air shows, festivals, games and other activities that use your services to benefit the public.

However, not all public-service activities are allowed. For example, using ham radio to coordinate ticket sales at a public festival is forbidden since this is clearly a business function. On the other hand, using ham radio to coordinate supplies for an open-to-the-public, 100-mile bike tour is permissible because such supplies, even if they include food, are essential to the well-being, health and safety of the riders.

Can You Use Tactical Call Signs?

Tactical call signs are often used when working with other agencies during an emergency, or during large public-service activities. For example, during a running race, names like "finish line," "Mile 1," "Mile 2," "First Aid 1," and "Water truck" quickly identify each function and eliminate confusion when working with other agencies, such as a fire department, where amateur call signs are meaningless.

The use of tactical call signs in no way relieves you of the obligation to identify your operation under the FCC's rules for normal station identification. You must still give your FCC-assigned call sign at the end of your communication, and at least every 10 minutes during the contact.

Can You Receive Payment for Your Amateur Radio Assistance?

No. The FCC regulations prohibit payment for the use of an Amateur Radio station.

Note that this rule does not prohibit you from being reimbursed for incidental expenses unrelated to your radio communication. If you assist at a disaster scene 100 miles from your home, you are not prohibited from receiving reimbursement for out-of-pocket travel expenses unrelated to your radio communication. For example, if as an American Red Cross Disaster Services Volunteer, you are flown to the scene of a disaster where you happen to use Amateur Radio as part of the relief effort, you are not required to pay your own airfare. For more discussion of the prohibition on compensation, see Chapter 7.

What Does The FCC Think About Public Service?

In 1983, the FCC issued a Report and Order concerning business operations and the various radio services that it regulates. The Order, unfortunately, confused many people, causing ARRL to ask the FCC for clarification. Here's a portion of the FCC response to ARRL Counsel Chris Imlay, N3AKD.

"We want to emphasize that the Order does not prohibit amateur radio operators from participating in the routine events of traditional public service activities. For example, amateur radio operators may provide communications for municipal parades, marathons, walkathons, Eye Bank activities and the like. Although they may incidentally "benefit" the sponsor, their main purpose is to provide a service to the public which is the real beneficiary. Direct promotion to assist in the sale of a sponsor's product would, of course, be forbidden. Although it is not feasible to give you a list of every type of activity for which amateur licensees might be called on to provide communications assistance, we do want to assure that we concur in all the examples that you mention in your letter, including the permissibility of public service communications for neighborhood bike races, fireworks displays and the Olympic games. We agree that an amateur licensee's providing public service communications enhances any event which a particular organization offers as a part of its normal functions.

The Order was not intended to impose any new restrictions or to cut back on what amateur operators have legitimately been doing all along. What was intended was to alert the amateur community to the fact that the Amateur Radio Service should not be used in lieu of other radio services for the transmission of business messages. I think that we can all agree that a businessman, who also happens to be an amateur radio operator, should not use amateur radio facilities to call his office about details that surround his business transactions. On the other hand, the same businessman should feel free to use his amateur radio station if a member of his family becomes ill, if there is a safety factor in traveling on the highway, such as the need for a tow truck, etc . . ."—James C. McKinney, Chief, Private Radio Bureau

These points were further clarified in a letter from former FCC Private Radio Bureau Chief Robert Foosaner to Stephen Mendelsohn, WA2DHF, regarding amateur participation in the New York City Marathon:

This is in response to your letter of October 15, 1984, concerning providing amateur radio communications at the New York Road Runners Club marathon. The Commission addressed the matter of business communications in the Amateur Radio Service in the Order released July 12, 1983. You will note that the term business communications, as defined in [the rules], is used in the broadest context. It includes all types of communications which are intended to facilitate the regular business affairs of any party, whether for-profit or not-for-profit, etc. Thus, the determination as to the types of amateur radio communications that your group could provide at a marathon would not be affected by the profit objectives of the sponsor, nor by the pay status of other participants.

A fundamental guideline that should be observed in these instances is also stated in the Order: ". . .the Amateur Radio Service should not be used as an alternative to the land mobile, broadcast, maritime or common carrier radio services, all of which have been established by appropriate regulatory processes." To the extent that these other radio services can be used to perform the necessary communications, such communications should not be transmitted by amateur radio.

[The rules] which prohibit business communications by amateur radio, do not prohibit amateur radio operators from participating in a marathon as a public service activity. Although some communications transmitted could incidentally benefit a sponsor, we do not view such communications as violations of the rules where their main purpose is to provide a service to the public.

In your letter you describe three specific services which amateur radio could provide. The first is a medical network, by which race authorities could be notified of a runner's need for medical attention. This medical network is, of course, acceptable.

The second service is logistical. Amateur radio operators would provide the communications necessary to facilitate the public's safe observation of the event. Clearly there is benefit to the race sponsor, but it is incidental; the principal beneficiaries of this would be the runners and the public.

Finally, there is the lead-runner position network. As you acknowledge, the purpose of this is to facilitate a system whereby the public, including, presumably, the news media, are informed of the progress of the race via amateur radio. This runs afoul of [the rules], which prohibits the dissemination of radio communications intended to be received by the public. If you wish to provide this service, we recommend you do it on commercial frequencies with other equipment. Amateur radio operators could participate in this phase, but not by virtue of their amateur licenses.

Please inform your group that their licenses are not endangered by participating in the marathon. They have my support and my personal thanks for serving the public.

What Congress Says About Amateur Radio's Public-Service Efforts

One of the last pieces of business accomplished by the Congress in 1988 was a nice little resolution expressing its feelings about the volunteer public-service work of radio amateurs:

SENSE OF CONGRESS

The Congress finds that—

(1) more than four hundred and thirty-five thousand radio amateurs in the United States are licensed by the Federal Communications Commission upon examination in radio regulations, technical principles, and the international Morse code;

(2) by international treaty and the Federal Communications Commission regulations, the amateur is authorized to operate his or her station in a radio service in intercommunications and technical investigations solely with a personal aim and without pecuniary interest;

(3) among the basic purposes for the Amateur Radio Service is the provision of voluntary, noncommercial radio service, particularly emergency communications; and

(4) volunteer amateur radio emergency communications services have consistently and reliably been provided before, during, and after floods, tornadoes, forest fires, earthquakes, blizzards, train wrecks, chemical spills, and other disasters.

It is the sense of the Congress that—

(1) it strongly encourages and supports the Amateur Radio Service and its emergency communications efforts; and

(2) Government agencies shall take into account the valuable contributions made by amateur radio operators when considering actions affecting the Amateur Radio Service.

Alternatives to the Amateur Radio Service

Running race organizers and fire departments do not have "ham radio problems"—they have communications problems. To them, ham radio is just a telephone. They are asking for your help because they need your expert assistance to solve a communications problem; that you use ham radio frequencies to meet their need is only incidental to them. At times, particularly when business-like functions are requested, alternatives to the Amateur Radio Service may be more appropriate.

When a group asks for a function that we cannot perform legally under current FCC regulations, we typically say we cannot help them. We then miss out on an important training opportunity and we diminish our public-service role in the eyes of our local community.

But if we view ourselves as reliable communications problem solvers, we must do better. There is nothing in the rules prohibiting us, if properly licensed, from using another radio service for the communications that we are not authorized to perform as amateurs. Operational techniques on frequency bands allocated to other services can be just as professional and valuable as on the ham bands.

At some events you need to keep in touch with a key group of organizers, such as event directors, head of first aid, and so on. One approach has been to have a ham accompany them continuously and to provide a radio when needed. Obviously, this is people intensive and a more convenient solution would be to hand the key person a simple, nonham radio, hand-held or beeper.

Another example is that of the festival which needs to coordinate ticket sales. For these events, an alternative is to use business-radio-service transceivers.

Aside from the Citizens Band, there are three other services that could help. Low-cost, short-range, 49-MHz FM hand-held radios are available from several suppliers. These radios cover ¼ to ½ mile with a clean FM signal and are useful for short-range communications.

The General Mobile Radio Service operates on 16 FM channels at 462 MHz and 467 MHz. This service provides for both personal and business communication using relatively low cost radios.

Portable and mobile cellular radiotelephone equipment should not be overlooked; anyone who can operate a telephone can use a cellular radiophone. Disadvantages are that cellular systems often don't work outside of metropolitan areas or in mountainous terrain, and they are expensive.

These alternate radio systems and other business systems should be suggested to those who ask for functions inappropriate for the Amateur Radio Service. In some instances, these radios can be purchased at low cost, provided by the sponsor of the event, or are available for rent or loan from various sources (see the telephone book Yellow Pages).

DISASTER COMMUNICATIONS

If an emergency strikes a widespread area, disrupting the normal lines of communication, the FCC engineer-in-charge of the area may designate certain frequencies for use by stations assisting the stricken area only. All amateur transmission with, or within, the designated area conducted on the FCC-designated emergency frequencies must pertain directly to relief work, emergency service or the establishment and maintenance of efficient networks for handling emergency traffic. The FCC may also set forth further special conditions and rules during the communications emergency.

Also, the Commission may designate certain amateur stations to police the emergency frequencies, warning noncomplying stations operating there. The emergency conditions imposed by the FCC can be lifted only by the FCC or its authorized representative. Amateurs desiring a declaration of a communication emergency should contact the FCC engineer-in-charge of the area concerned.

In any case, however, when normal communications systems are overloaded, damaged or disrupted because a disaster has occurred, or is likely to occur, you can always provide essential communications needs, and facilitate relief actions. If you're in an area not regulated by the FCC, you can still provide these services, but only

Following the great Mexico City Earthquake in 1985, the county of San Diego, California, awarded a handsome commendation to the amateur community for its communications support of the relief effort. ARRL officials WA6WZO and W6INI accept the award on behalf of the amateur community.

in accord with an international resolution: ITU Resolution #640 (see Appendix).

A station in, or within 92.6 km of Alaska, can use SSB (suppressed or reduced carrier) on 5.1675 kHz to provide emergency communications along with Alaska private-fixed stations. Power must not exceed 150 W.

Good Amateur Practice in Disasters: A Case Study

During Hurricane Gilbert, which devastated the island of Jamaica in the Caribbean in September 1988, amateurs learned a number of lessons that should help us provide better communications in future disaster situations:

- Communications channels in support of damage assessment and disaster relief agencies were slow to be established, and in some cases had to be established outside the amateur bands. (Incredibly, some amateur stations even followed these officially designated stations outside the bands, without authorization!)
- Preoccupation with welfare inquiry traffic got in the way of higher priority communication. The Red Cross placed a moratorium on inquiries to Jamaica for several days; this provided time for outbound welfare messages to be sent, each of which could potentially head off at least one, and perhaps many, inquiries. Accepting inquiry traffic before there is any way to handle it raises false hopes and clogs the system.
- In a disaster, control belongs to those in the affected area; they are in the best position to know the priorities. Those of us who are fortunate enough to be outside the disaster area are there to support *them*, not the other way around.
- In providing information to the media, we must make sure what is being passed along is authentic, and not unsubstantiated hearsay.

General Considerations In Emergencies

- Use your receiver more, your transmitter less. The tendency to transmit rather than listen causes excessive QRM.
- Monitor emergency net frequencies.
- Listen to W1AW for the latest bulletin and news: phone on the hour, RTTY at 15 past the hour, CW on the half hour.

RACES

Founded in 1952 with the help of the ARRL, the Radio Amateur Civil Emergency Service is fed and cared for by the Federal Emergency Management Administration (FEMA). RACES works principally at the local level through local and state civil defense agencies organized by state government to provide emergency communications in the event the FCC authorizes its use.

Emergency communications preparation is rapidly becoming one of the top priorities for many radio amateurs. Government agencies are beginning to realize the potential service that hams who are familiar with emergency communications procedures can provide.

COMMON QUESTIONS-AND-ANSWERS: RACES

Q. What is RACES, and what does it have to do with me?

A. The Radio Amateur Civil Emergency Service, as part of the Amateur Radio Service, provides radio communications for civil defense purposes only, during periods of local, regional or national civil emergencies. These emergencies are not limited to war-related activities, but can include natural disasters such as fires, floods and earthquakes. It is important to note that RACES operation is authorized only by the FCC after it is requested by a local, state or federal official, and is strictly limited to official civil defense activities in the event of an emergency communications situation.

Q. Does this mean that I can volunteer as a RACES station?

A. At the present time there is a freeze on the issuance of new RACES licenses. RACES operation is conducted by amateurs using their own primary station licenses, and by existing RACES stations.

Q. Then to volunteer as a RACES control operator, all I need is a valid Amateur Radio license?

A. Well, not quite. You must also be officially enrolled in a civil defense organization. Contact your local CD office for information and applications.

Q. While engaged in RACES operation, does my license class limit me as to frequency use?

A. Yes. Operator privileges in RACES are dependent upon, and identical to, those for the class of license held in the Amateur Radio Service.

Q. What frequencies are available to an operator conducting communications in RACES?

A. All of the authorized frequencies and emissions allocated to the Amateur Radio Service are also available to RACES on a shared basis. But in the event that RACES is activated by the FCC following a request from a local, state or federal official, Amateur Radio stations engaged in RACES operation will be limited to the frequencies listed in the table below. Additionally, there are specific operating limitations with respect to these frequencies. At this point, it should be noted that in all cases not specifically covered by the RACES rules, amateurs engaging in RACES operation will be governed by the provisions of the rules governing Amateur Radio stations and operators.

RACES Frequencies

kHz		*MHz*	
1800-1825	3984-4000	10.10 -10.15	
		14.047-14.053	52-54
1975-2000	7079-7125	14.220-14.230	
3500-3550	7245-7255	14.331-14.350	144.50-145.71
3930-3980		21.047-21.053	146-148
		21.228-21.267	
		28.550-28.750	
		29.237-29.273	1240-1300
		29.450-29.650	2390-2450
		50.350-50.750	

Q. As an operator in RACES, what types of other stations can I communicate with?

A. As a RACES operator, you may communicate with: (1) Another RACES station, (2) Amateur Radio stations certified as being registered with a civil defense organization, (3) stations of the US Government authorized by the responsible agency to conduct communications with stations engaged in RACES operation and (4) any other station in any other service regulated by the FCC, whenever that station is authorized by the Commission to exchange communications with stations in RACES operation.

Q. Is there anything else I should keep in mind while engaged in RACES operation?

A. It is important to bear in mind that any communication you make while operating in RACES must be specifically authorized by the civil defense organization for the area served. Furthermore, RACES stations may transmit only civil defense communication of the following types: Messages concerning impending or actual conditions jeopardizing public safety, or national defense or security during periods of civil emergencies including: (1) messages directly concerning the immediate safety and protection of life, property and the maintenance of law and order; the alleviation of human suffering and need, and the combating of armed attack or sabotage; (2) messages directly concerning the accumulation and dissemination of public information or instructions to the civilian population.

Q. Can we hold practice RACES drills?

A. Yes. Also permitted are communications for the purpose of training (drills and tests) when necessary to establish and maintain the orderly and efficient operation of RACES as ordered by the responsible civil defense organization. However, these communications must not exceed a total time of one hour per week. With the approval of the chief officer for emergency planning in your state, however, such tests and drills may be conducted for a period not to exceed 72 hours no more than twice in any calendar year.

Q Why are there limits on RACES drills?

A. In 1976, the Commission limited the use of RACES station drills and tests to one hour a week. A factor in its decision was that under the guise of RACES drills and tests, improper use was being made of amateur frequencies for local government land mobile communications. The intervening years have proven that the drill and test limitation has been effective in curbing that type of misuse. Recently, the FCC decided that there are certain circumstances when a longer RACES drill or test exercise is justified and can be accommodated without inviting misuse of the amateur frequencies. As a result, the FCC put into the rules the exception to the one hour limit described above.

Q. I thought the emergency communications aspect of Amateur Radio was provided for in ARES. What is the difference between RACES and ARES?

A. This is an important distinction. ARES, the Amateur Radio Emergency Service, is the "emergency" division of the ARRL Field Organization. It consists of licensed amateurs who have voluntarily registered their qualifications and equipment for communication duty in the event of a disaster. Every licensed amateur, regardless of membership in ARRL or any other local or national organization, is eligible for membership in ARES. ARES is administered by the League on a local, section-wide and national basis. RACES, on the other hand, is sponsored by the federal government and is under the jurisdiction of the FCC. It is a means by which amateurs may serve civil defense agencies in disaster communications on an organized basis, using their own bands and, to a large extent, their own equipment. It is intended that RACES, when properly authorized, will remain on the air in the event of any officially declared emergency, although the rest of Amateur Radio may be silenced.

RACES is a separate entity from ARES, although ARRL advocates dual membership in and cooperative efforts between both groups whenever possible. Also, the Federal Emergency Management Agency has recommended that civil defense organizations throughout the country affiliate with already-existing ARES groups in their state.

THIRD-PARTY TRAFFIC

Communications on behalf of third parties has been a part of Amateur Radio from its earliest beginnings in the United States. The very basis for the formation of the League in 1914 was to organize amateurs to relay messages on one another's behalf in order to overcome the limited range of the amateur stations of the day. In that simpler time, there was essentially no limit to the content of such messages nor on whose behalf the messages could be sent.

It was not until the 1930's that international limitations were placed on amateur traffic, at the insistence of European governments for whom the telecommunications monopoly was a source of considerable revenue. While handling messages or providing communications for material compensation always has been prohibited in Amateur Radio, it was not until 1972 that the FCC specifically prohibited "business communications" in Docket 19245 and thus began to regulate amateur traffic on the basis of its content. Amateurs, for the first time, were in the position of having to evaluate the content of the messages they were relaying.

It was true that the permissive rules in force prior to 1972 left Amateur Radio open to possible commercial exploitation; well-meaning amateurs anxious to be of service could be persuaded to operate their stations for someone else's commercial or private benefit, as long as they themselves were not compensated for providing the service. At the time this abuse was more hypothetical than real, but the years since 1972 have brought increased communications capabilities to amateur stations as well as increased demands for certain kinds of services on behalf of third parties. By and large, while there have been some difficulties arising from the unavoidable "grey area" between business and personal communications and from occasional overzealous interpretations of what constitutes business communications, the prohibition on non-emergency business communications in Amateur Radio has not caused serious problems for amateur licensees. However, the FCC is currently taking another look at the third-party traffic rules as part of its effort to resolve some problems it perceives on the amateur bands. The privilege *is* tenuous at best, and it is important that amateurs obey the letter and spirit of the third-party traffic rules in order to keep it.

What exactly is third-party traffic?

Third-party traffic is Amateur Radio communication by or under the supervision of the control operator at an Amateur Radio station to another Amateur Radio station on behalf of anyone other than the control operator. A third-party message is one the control operator (first party) of your station sends to another station (second party) for anyone else (third party). Third-party messages include those that are spoken, written, keystroked, keyed, photographed or otherwise originated by or for a third party, and transmitted by your Amateur Radio station live or delayed. A third party may also be a person permitted by the control operator to participate in Amateur Radio communications.

Third-party traffic is one of the so-called "gray" areas where there is much room for interpretation. The following discussion will hopefully clarify this area of the rules.

Table 1

International Third-Party Traffic—Proceed with Caution

Occasionally, DX stations may ask you to handle a third-party message to a friend or relative in the States. This is all right as long as the US has signed an official Third-Party Traffic Agreement with that particular country, or the third party is a licensed amateur. The traffic must be noncommercial and of a personal, unimportant nature. During an emergency, our State Department will often work out a special temporary agreement with the country involved, but in normal times, never handle traffic without first making sure it is legally permitted.

US Amateurs May Handle Third-Party Traffic With:

C5	The Gambia	TI	Costa Rica
CE	Chile	V2	Antigua and Barbuda
CO	Cuba	V3	Belize
CP	Bolivia	V4	St Christopher and Nevis
CX	Uruguay	V6	Federated States of Micronesia
D6	Federal Islamic Republic of Comoros	VE	Canada
EL	Liberia	VK	Australia
GB*	United Kingdom	VR6**	Pitcairn Island
HC	Ecuador	XE	Mexico
HH	Haiti	YN	Nicaragua
HI	Dominican Republic	YS	El Salvador
HK	Colombia	YV	Venezuela
HP	Panama	ZP	Paraguay
HR	Honduras	3D6	Swaziland
J3	Grenada	4U1ITU	ITU, Geneva
J6	St Lucia	4U1VIC	VIC, Vienna
J7	Dominica	4X	Israel
J8	St Vincent and the Grenadines	6Y	Jamaica
JY	Jordan	8R	Guyana
LU	Argentina	9G	Ghana
OA	Peru	9L	Sierra Leone
PY	Brazil	9Y	Trinidad and Tobago
TG	Guatemala		

*Third-party traffic permitted between US amateurs and special-events stations in the United Kingdom having the prefix GB only, with the exception that GB3 stations are not included in this agreement.

**Since 1970, there has been an informal agreement between the United Kingdom and the US, permitting Pitcairn and US amateurs to exchange messages concerning medical emergencies, urgent need for equipment or supplies, and private or personal matters of island residents.

Please note that the Region 2 Division of the International Amateur Radio Union (IARU) has recommended that international traffic on the 20- and 15-meter bands be conducted on the following frequencies:

14.100-14.150 MHz
14.250-14.350 MHz
21.150-21.200 MHz
21.300-21.450 MHz

The IARU is the alliance of Amateur Radio Societies from around the world; Region 2 comprises Member-Societies in North, South and Central America, and the Caribbean.

Note: At the end of an exchange of third-party traffic with a station located in a foreign country, an FCC-licensed amateur must also transmit the call sign of the foreign station as well as his own call.

There are three main types of third-party traffic. The first deals with *third-party messages*, those sent via traffic nets or other means. Message fairs and displays at shopping malls provide sources for this type of routine messages. Not all messages are as formal as this, however. A third-party message may be no more than a "Gee, you're in Birmingham, please say hello to Tyrone Shoelaces for me..."

The second type of third-party traffic deals with *phone-line interconnection*, or so-called "phone patch" and "autopatch." These operations allow third parties to communicate directly with second and first parties via the telephone system. The third type of third-party traffic is the *direct participation* by interested third parties in actual Amateur Radio communication. The rules provide for this type of operation as long as the control operator supervises the third party and makes transmitter adjustments to ensure proper operation. At no time may a control operator leave a third party unattended at a transmitter that is on the air. Such an act would amount to a serious relinquishing of control duties. Also, the rules prohibit participation in this type of third-party traffic by a prior amateur whose license was revoked; suspended for less than the balance of the license term and the suspension is still in effect; suspended for the balance of the license term and relicensing has not taken place; surrendered for cancellation following notice of revocation, suspension or monetary forfeiture proceedings; or who is the subject of a cease and desist order which relates to amateur operation and is still in effect.

The third-party traffic rules are quite clear: *International third-party traffic* is prohibited. The only exceptions are (1) in cases where the US has a special third-party agreement with another country (a list of these countries appears in the accompanying sidebar); (2) the third party is a licensed amateur eligible to be the control operator of the station; and (3) in cases of emergency where there is an immediate threat to lives and property.

Third-party traffic involving *material compensation* to any party is not allowed. Third-party traffic involving *business communications* is not permitted unless for a bona fide emergency. See "Business Communications," Chapter 7.

COMMON QUESTIONS AND ANSWERS —THIRD PARTY TRAFFIC

Q. Our traffic net often serves as an outlet for incoming and outgoing international traffic. Is this legal, and what regulations should we be aware of?

A. The handling of international third-party traffic is forbidden except where the country has a third-party agreement with the United States, or where the third party is a licensed amateur.

Messages have to be limited to those of a technical nature and to personal remarks that are not important enough to justify use of the public telephone.

Q. What about the legality of sending a message to a nonprofit organization such as the ARRL HQ?

A. Chances are, such a message could be construed to be facilitating the normal business affairs of the League. In this case, the League is a "business," and by sending the message DID NOT GET MY APRIL *QST* X 73, you are involving material compensation and the commercial affairs of HQ. The same applies to requests for the *Repeater Directory*, contest forms, operating aids and so forth. Don't send a message to FCC via the National Traffic System asking for 500 610 forms!

Q. How about a message requesting medical supplies from the Red Cross during an emergency? Wouldn't this message be considered to be facilitating the normal course of business of the Red Cross?

A. The key word is emergency. Emergency communications must relate directly to the immediate safety of life of individuals or to the immediate protection of property. In an emergency situation, the FCC does not prohibit US amateurs from handling traffic relating to the saving of life and property. Requests for emergency supplies from a Red Cross center would be permitted under these circumstances. Normally, however, such communications would not be permitted.

Q. What if I'm talking to someone in a country with whom we have a third-party agreement, and he wants to talk with a relative in my town. I don't speak their language—what do I do?

A. You have two choices: You can tell the relative what he can and cannot talk about, and hope he understands—and complies! However, the better choice is to decline to cooperate, including terminating the conversation in progress, if you think there is a possibility that the communication may be questionable. There are two reasons for this. You may have your license revoked for allowing illegal traffic to pass through your station. But on a broader scale, isn't it better to risk hurting someone's feelings than to risk the revocation of a third-party agreement? It could happen, if a telecommunication authority in another country decides that its amateurs are conducting illegal traffic.

Q. I have a General class license. I'd like to retransmit a Technician licensee's 2-meter signal in the 20-meter General phone band. Is this legal?

A. When a Technician's signals enter the 14-MHz band at a General class licensee's station, the operation involves third-party traffic to the General class licensee. Such operation is permitted under the Rules, which do not specify the manner in which the third-party traffic is received for relay: by mail, telephone, in person or by 2 meters.

Q. May a Novice legally use a 222-MHz repeater that is crossband-linked to 2 meters?

A. Yes, so long as the Novice's transmitter is operating within the Novice-authorized frequency bands, and the link is full-time, or activated by a Technician or higher-class control operator. (A word of caution: if the link can be turned on and off by the repeater user, then this would put the Novice in control of a 2-meter repeater, which is not allowed.)

Q. When I checked into a traffic net the other night, I was asked to handle a message originated in the US and bound for a person living in a country that does not have a third-party agreement with the US. I realize, of course, that I must not relay the message via a ham in that country. But, may I route it for ultimate delivery to a ham in another country that holds an agreement with the US and with the addressee's country?

A. Yes. The FCC, and the third-party-traffic rules, are concerned with the borders of the countries involved. That is, as far as you're concerned, the third-party message crosses the US border, and the border of the second party's country that holds an agreement with the US. The FCC is not concerned about the location of the message's origination or destination; they are concerned with the manner in which the third-party traffic is handled over the air.

Q. Is it okay to send third-party traffic to a ham in France for another ham there?

A. Yes. Recently, the FCC adopted the policy of many other countries, including that of the United Kingdom's Department of Trade and Industry:

"Third Party Traffic should be regarded under two separate headings:
- the passing of messages on behalf of other licensed radio amateurs; and
- the passing of messages on behalf of non-licensed people or organizations."

Thus, where third-party traffic is normally prohibited between the US and other countries, where the third party is an amateur and eligible to be the control operator of the station, the third-party traffic is permitted.

PHONE PATCH AND AUTOPATCH GUIDELINES

Radio amateurs in the United States enjoy a great privilege: the ability to interconnect their individual stations and repeaters with the public telephone system. The wisdom of the federal government in permitting, and even in defending, this freedom has been demonstrated time and again. There is no way to calculate the value of the lives and property that have been saved by the intelligent use of phone patch and autopatch facilities in emergency situations. The public interest has been well served by amateurs with interconnect capabilities.

As with any privilege, this one can be abused, and the penalty for abuse could be the loss of the privilege for all amateurs. What constitutes abuse of phone patch and autopatch privileges? In the absence of specific regulations governing their use, the answer to this question depends on one's perspective. Consider these facts: To other amateurs, phone patching activities that result in unnecessary frequency congestion or which appear as a commercialization of Amateur Radio operation are an abuse of their privilege to engage in other forms of amateur activities.

To the telephone company, which needs to protect its massive investment in capital equipment, anything that endangers its equipment, its personnel or its revenues is an abuse.

To the FCC, which is responsible for the efficient use of the radio spectrum by the services it regulates, any radiocommunication that could be handled more appropriately by wire is an unnecessary use of a valuable resource.

To the commercial suppliers of radiocommunication for business purposes (Radio Common Carriers), competition from a noncommercial service constitutes a possible threat to their livelihood.

At one time or another, threats to radio amateur's interconnect privileges have come from each of these sources. And threats may come from another quarter: the governments of certain nations that prohibit amateurs from handling third-party messages internationally in competition with government-owned telecommunications services. If illegal phone patching to and from their countries cannot be controlled, they reason, the solution may be to ban all international third-party traffic by amateurs and to permit no such special arrangements.

The question facing amateurs is this: Should phone patches and autopatches be subject to reasonable voluntary restraints, thereby preserving most of our traditional flexibility, or should we risk forcing our government to define for us specifically what we can and cannot do? Experience has shown very clearly that when specific regulations are established, both innovation and flexibility are likely to suffer.

The Amateur Radio Service is not a common carrier, and its primary purpose is not the handling of routine messages on behalf of nonamateurs. However, third-party communications as an incidental part of Amateur Radio adds an important dimension to our public-service capability.

It is the policy of the League to safeguard the prerogative of amateurs to interconnect their stations, including repeaters, to the public telephone system. An important element of this defense is encouraging amateurs to maintain a high standard of legal and ethical conduct in their patching activities. It is to this end that these guidelines are addressed. They are based on several sets of standards that have been in use of several years on a local or regional basis throughout the country. The ideas they represent have widespread support within the amateur community. All amateurs are urged to observe these standards carefully so our traditional freedom from government regulation may be preserved as much as possible.

1) International phone patches must be conducted only when there is a special third-party agreement between the countries concerned. The only exceptions are when the immediate safety of life or property is endangered, or where the third party is a licensed amateur eligible to be a control operator of the station.

2) Phone patches or autopatches involving the business affairs of any party must not be conducted at any time. The content of any patch should be such that it is clear to any listener that business communications is not involved. Particular caution must be observed in calling any business telephone. Calls to place an order for a commercial product must not be made, nor may calls be made to one's office to receive or to leave business messages. However, calls made in the interests of highway safety, such as for the removal of injured persons from the scene of an accident or for the removal of a disabled vehicle from a hazardous location, are permitted.

3) All interconnections must be made in accordance with telephone company tariffs. If you have trouble obtaining information about them from your telephone company representatives, the tariffs are available for public inspection at your telephone company office.

4) Phone patches and autopatches should never be made solely to avoid telephone toll charges. Phone patches and autopatches should never be made when normal telephone service could just as easily be used.

5) Third parties should not be retransmitted until the responsible control operator has explained the nature of Amateur Radio to them. Control of the station must never be relinquished to an unlicensed person. Permitting a person you don't know very well to conduct a patch in a language you don't understand amounts to relinquishing control.

6) Phone patches and autopatches must be terminated immediately in the event of any illegality or impropriety.

7) Autopatch facilities must not be used for broadcasting. If a repeater has the capability of transmitting information, such as weather reports, which is of interest to the general public, such transmissions must occur only when requested by a licensed amateur and must not conform to a specific time schedule. The retransmission of radio signals from other services is not permitted in the Amateur Radio Service.

8) Station identification must be strictly observed. In particular, US stations conducting international phone patches must identify in English at least once every 10 minutes, and must also give their call sign and the other station's call sign at the end of the exchange of transmissions.

9) In selecting frequencies for phone patch work, the rights of other amateurs must be considered. In particular, patching on 20 meters should be confined to the upper portion of the 14,200-14,350 kHz segment in accordance with the IARU Region 2 recommendation.

10) Phone patches and autopatches should be kept as brief as possible, as a courtesy to other amateurs; the amateur bands are intended to be used primarily for communication among radio amateurs.

11) If you have any doubt as to the legality or advisability of a patch, don't make it.

Compliance with these guidelines will help ensure that our interconnection privilege will continue to be available in the future, which will in turn help us contribute to the public interest.

THE NET GAME

Nets are on-the-air clubs, folks coming together to discuss or engage in favorite activities of mutual interest. There are nets for traffic handlers, ragchewers, computer fans, DXers, historians, aviators, philosophers, county hunters and hosts more for countless other hams.

Nets meet regularly on prearranged days, times and frequencies, and can attract scores of members and passersby at any time. One merely must open the pages of the ARRL *Net Directory* to see just how much formal net activity exists for public-service-minded hams alone!

COMMON QUESTIONS AND ANSWERS—NETS

Q. I noticed that there are quite a few nets meeting regularly on 75 meters. Do these nets have exclusive rights to a specific frequency?

A. There is nothing in the Rules that recognizes a net's special privilege to any specific frequency. It's generally a case of first come, first served. Before starting a net, the net-control station should take precautions to avoid using a frequency occupied by other stations. This should be accomplished by asking politely "Is this frequency in use?" Conversely, individual operators should ask the same question before engaging in operation to determine if another QSO or net is in progress on that frequency.

The bottom line is that no one owns a frequency. Whoever is on any given frequency first should, if possible, be protected from interference by other stations. Net-control stations should tell their charges that the net will convene on the prearranged net frequency "plus or minus the QRM," for example.

Q. If I am in QSO with another ham on a net frequency prior to net time, am I supposed to move to accommodate the net when it convenes?

A. Because there are so many hams on one frequency during a net, there must be a regularly scheduled, prearranged net frequency and time. Remember: These net members must find the net in the first place. Net operations are a bit more unwieldy than individual operations because nets involve so many stations. It is far easier for individuals to look out for nets than it is for nets to move 10 or 100 hams to other frequencies in a crowded band. There are no hard-and-fast rules concerning this policy. Indeed, it is not formally recognized by FCC as "good amateur practice." It's simply a matter of courtesy, nothing more. After all, nets are good ways to meet and exchange ideas with other hams having similar interests; and they occupy only one frequency. Many hams making use of but one frequency is efficient and sound spectrum usage.

Q. How does one identify while engaged in net operations?

A. The rules say you must identify you station once every 10 minutes. The problem is that most net check-ins are idle for 10 or more minutes at a time. Thus, most check-ins give their call after every transmission or brief communication on the net to ensure that they will not have to identify while another station is transmitting.

If you're handling third-party traffic with a foreign ham on the net, you must also give his or her station's call sign as part of your ID.

Q. In the United States there are many nets that cater to hams selling and buying their ham radio equipment. Are these so-called "swap-and-shop" nets legal?

A. Yes, within certain constraints. See Chapter 7 for a discussion of swap-and-shop nets.

Q. Where can I find a list of traffic and emergency communications nets?

A. The ARRL publishes a *Net Directory,* available for $1 from ARRL HQ.

Chapter Fourteen

Regulation: The Big Picture

R*aised on Radio.* This is an apt title song on an album by the rock group "Journey." Everyone reading this book has been "raised on radio." Whether it be AM, FM or shortwave, radio goes everywhere. Radio is manifested in just about every nook and cranny in the modern world. A myriad of radio services exists for the needs of individuals, business, government, science and others. Even though the Amateur Radio Service is richly endowed with a wide range of bands, Amateur Radio occupies only a small part of the total available space. Nevertheless, the electromagnetic spectrum is a limited resource; each kilohertz is precious to those competing interests that lay claim to it. Unlike natural resources, fortunately, the spectrum is a nondepletable resource—one that if misused can be restored to normal as soon as the misuse stops. Each day gives us a new opportunity to use the spectrum efficiently and intelligently.

You might be thinking at this point: Who decides where Amateur Radio frequencies will be, or, for that matter, where my favorite AM or FM broadcast station will be? With the proliferation of these competing radio services within the physical confines of the radio spectrum comes the need for controls. Without such controls, chaos would reign supreme with the various radio services colliding with each other. Not surprisingly, controls have developed over the years, implemented at both the international and domestic levels. The International Telecommunication Union (ITU) has the vital role of dividing up the range of communications frequencies for the entire world. Based on the demonstrated or perceived needs of different services, which include commercial broadcast, land mobile and private radio (including Amateur Radio), member-nations of the ITU decide which radio services will be given which band of frequencies. Once that's done, the government regulators for each particular country take over.

INTERNATIONAL REGULATION OF THE SPECTRUM

Nations sign all sorts of treaties and agreements (international communications, nuclear arms, ozone depletion and so on) to bring some order to international relationships. As mentioned above, without these agreements, anarchy would prevail. Although it's fair to say that many of these agreements aren't worth the paper they're written on, think how bad the international scene could be *without* such understandings. Interestingly enough, those affecting Amateur Radio have proved quite effective over the years. These must be *inter*national in scope, because as every radio amateur knows, radio waves know no geographical or political boundaries—they don't stop for customs inspections!

Amateur Radio frequency band allocations just don't happen. Band allocation proposals must survive a maze of national agencies and the ITU as well as the gamut of other spectrum users. The ITU allocates portions of the radio spectrum to various services vying for their own slice of the pie. It fashions regulations designed to reduce potential interference problems.

The process occurs at the international conference table. Member-nations' delegates bring their countries' official positions to the table. They debate the merits of these positions, taking into consideration changes in technologies since the previous conference and the need for each administration. They finally arrive at an International Table of Allocations and international Radio Regulations. Amateur Radio is provided for in Article 32 of those regulations (see the Appendix).

For example, in 1979, a World Administrative Radio Conference (WARC) was held in Geneva, Switzerland. This conference was the first in 20 years to take a top-to-bottom look at the ITU Radio Regulations and the international Table of Frequency Allocations. As a result, a new Table was generated, and other changes in the Radio Regulations of the ITU were made. The United States, a world leader in the telecommunications arena, was an active participant in the conference. Years of preparation culminated in sweeping changes that affect radio services worldwide, at least until the next WARC.

So, the international Radio Regulations of the ITU affect all radio amateurs. The US has a responsibility to make rules that are consistent with these international agreements. Once the international allocations have been decided, it's up to the Federal Communications Commission (FCC) to decide the best way to allocate frequency bands to those services using them in the US. The FCC is the governing body in the US when it comes to Amateur Radio. The Communications Act of 1934, as amended, is the chief tool by which the US carries out its obligations to the world's telecommunications community; through the authority delegated to the FCC by Congress in the Communications Act, the FCC was then able to adopt a body of rules to deal with communications. Part 97 (officially cited as 47 CFR [Code of Federal Regulations] §97) of the FCC rules governs Amateur Radio.

The International Telecommunication Union

The origins of the ITU trace back to the invention of the telegraph in the 19th century. To establish an international telegraph network, it was necessary to reach agreement on uniform message handling and technical compatibility. Bordering European countries worked out some bilateral agreements. This eventually led to creation of the ITU (which then stood for the International *Telegraph* Union) at Paris in 1865 by the first International Telegraph Convention, which reached agreement on basic regulations. The founding of the ITU is celebrated each year on May 17; watch *QST* for special operating activities commemorating the event. The ITU currently has a membership of 166 countries.

Starting with a conference in Berlin in 1906, attention focused on how to divide the radio spectrum by specific uses to minimize interference. In 1927, the ITU Washington Radio Conference of 27 maritime states was the beginning of international regulation of Amateur Radio. At the conference, the Table of Frequency Allocations (see Chapter 5) was adopted and six harmonically related bands from 1.715 to 60 MHz were allocated to amateurs. Some of the amateur bands were revised at this and subsequent conferences held in Cairo (1938), Atlantic City (1947) and Geneva (1959), in consideration of the needs of other radio services.

In 1932, a Telegraph and Telephone Conference and a Radiotelegraph Conference in Madrid merged into a single International Telecommunication Convention. The Radio Regulations resulting from this conference, among other things, explicitly prohibited amateurs from handling international third-party messages unless specifically permitted by the two countries involved. Under the new Part 97, US amateurs may now exchange third-party messages on behalf of licensed amateurs anywhere in the world; when it comes to *nonlicensed* third parties, however, traffic may be handled *only* with the countries listed in the table in Chapter 13. These countries have signed formal third-party traffic agreements with the US.

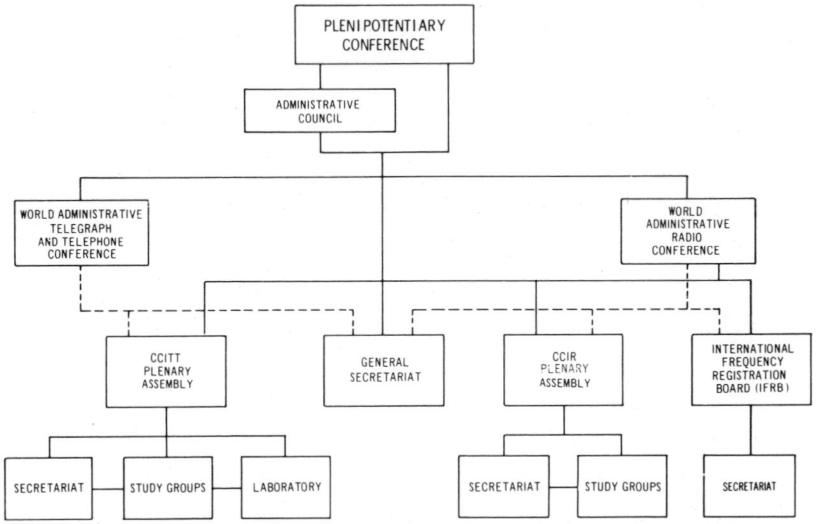

Fig 1—Organization chart of the International Telecommunication Union (ITU).

At the Atlantic City conference in 1947, substantial changes were made in the ITU organization. The ITU became a specialized agency of the United Nations (now the oldest such agency) and ITU headquarters was transferred from Berne to Geneva, Switzerland. The internal structure of the ITU is shown in Fig 1. Have you heard 4U1ITU on the air lately? This is the amateur station on-line at ITU HQ in Geneva; 4U1ITU, which counts as a separate country for DXCC, is active on all bands/modes, particularly in DX contests.

The ITU has Plenipotentiary Conferences every five or six years; plenipotentiary means that the conference is fully authorized to do any and all work of the ITU. The conferences determine general policies, review the work of the Union, revise the Convention if necessary, elect the members of the Union that are to serve on the Administrative Council, and elect the Secretary General, the Deputy Secretary General, Directors of the International Radio Consultative Committees (CCIR) and the members of the International Frequency Registration Board (IFRB). The last such conference was held in Nairobi, Kenya, in 1982.

The CCIR studies technical and operating questions, and issues recommendations relating to radio communication. The CCIR organization is shown in Fig 2. Amateurs have had a longstanding interest in the CCIR deliberative process. The League monitors, and makes input through, Study Group 8—Mobile, Radiodetermination and Amateur Services.

The International Telegraph and Telephone Consultative Committee (CCITT) studies technical, operating and tariff questions, and issues recommendations relating to telegraphy and telephony. The organization structure of the CCITT Study Group is shown in Fig 3.

Among other things, the international Morse code is specified in CCITT Recommendation F.1. Amateurs paid little attention to CCITT until the advent of packet radio, which sent people scurrying for international data-communications recommendations. The AX.25 packet-radio protocol, for example, is based on CCITT Recommendation X.25

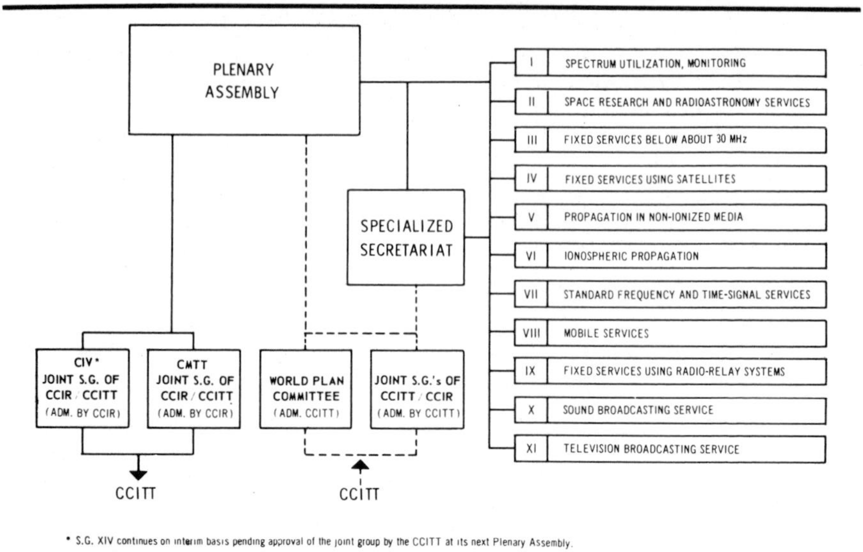

Fig 2—Organization chart of the International Radio Consultative Committee (CCIR).

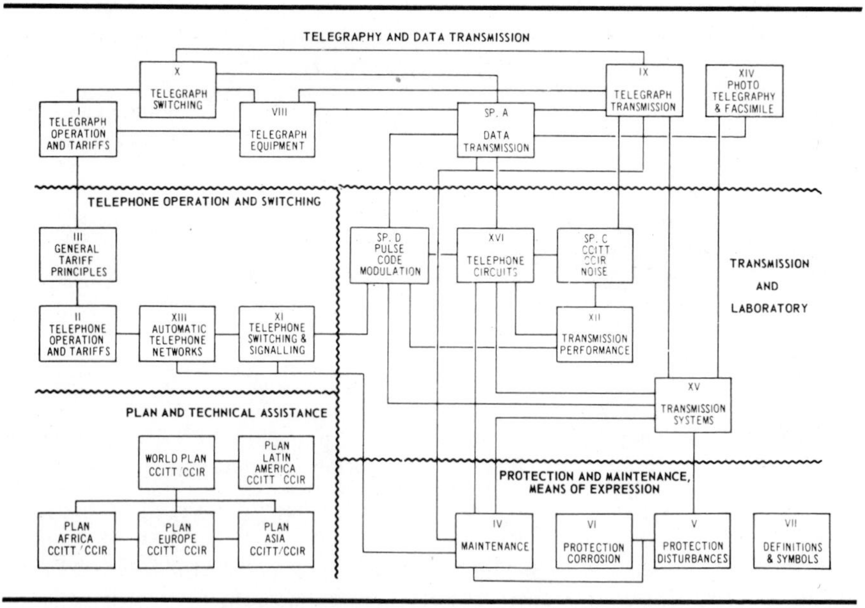

Fig 3—Organization chart of the International Telegraph and Telephone Consultative Committee (CCITT) Study Groups.

World Administrative Radio Conferences

The job of a WARC is to revise the ITU Radio Regulations. Conferences that had limited agendas considering space and radio astronomy matters and had some effects on the Amateur-Satellite Service were held in 1963, 1971 and 1977. WARC-79 was the last conference to go over *the complete set* of ITU Radio Regulations and culminated in three new amateur allocations at 10, 18 and 24 MHz (see below). Specialized conferences are held about twice a year, but most have limited agendas and do not have the power to change the rules or allocations of the Amateur Service.

Amateur Radio's unified voice at these international conferences are coordinated through the International Amateur Radio Union (IARU), a federation of national Amateur Radio societies (like the League) representing the interests of two-way Amateur Radio communications worldwide. Founded in Paris in 1925, the IARU is governed by a Constitution and Bylaws, with the International Secretariat located at ARRL HQ in Newington. The IARU has three regional organizations: Region 1—Africa, Europe, USSR, Middle East (excluding Iran) and Mongolia; Region 2—North and South America, including Hawaii and the Johnston and Midway Islands; Region 3—the rest of Asia and Oceania. To date, the IARU has 126 member-societies.

The IARU did not wait until the last minute in terms of gearing up for what turned out to be the historic WARC-79. As early as 1963, ARRL President Herbert Hoover, Jr, W6ZH, recognized that preparations had to begin for the next WARC. Efforts were already underway in Europe to strengthen Region 1 of the IARU. Wearing his other hat as IARU president, Mr Hoover launched a program to develop Amateur Radio in the new nations of Africa. These efforts continued under Mr Hoover's successor, Robert W. Denniston, WØDX. The Intruder Watch (now known as the ARRL Interference Reporting System—AIRS) was created to document the interference from nonamateur stations suffered by amateurs in their exclusive bands. WØDX also developed a personal rapport with a number of amateurs outside North America who were destined to play important roles in the IARU. When Noel Eaton, VE3CJ, became IARU president, the three regional organizations assumed a greater importance in the functioning of the Union; extensive efforts were undertaken to improve the liaison between what is now the International Secretariat and the member-societies, and more importantly, to bolster the societies' efforts to influence their governments. An International Working Group was established in 1976 to advise on WARC preparations. This group became the nucleus of the IARU Team which went to Geneva in 1979.

FCC preparations for WARC-79 were well underway in 1974. Remember, it was the FCC's responsibility to determine the long-term requirements of *all* non-Federal government users; Amateur Radio was only a small part of this mosaic. The FCC accomplished its objective through a series of Notices of Inquiry in FCC Docket 20271 soliciting comments, and through temporary Advisory Committees established for each service. (For more information on how the FCC does its job, see "Domestic Regulation," below.)

The FCC made special efforts to encourage public participation in the formulation and discussion of WARC-related issues. Surprisingly enough when you consider all the commercial frequencies that were up for grabs, no group was more active in this process than the nation's radio amateurs. Hundreds of individuals and clubs submitted comments at several stages of the proceeding, supplementing those of the League and the FCC's own Advisory Committee for Amateur Radio. The League's comments alone totaled nearly 200 pages!

The resultant 560-page Report and Order set forth the FCC's proposals. It was said to represent the combined thinking and agreement of the FCC and the various agencies of the Federal government. This document was then forwarded to the Department of State with the recommendation that it be made the official US proposal for WARC-79. Through the efforts of organized amateurs in the US, principally the

League, the official US position was very favorable as far as Amateur Radio was concerned.

Formal adoption of WARC objectives for Amateur Radio came at a series of meetings of the IARU Regions in 1975-76. IARU Region 3 led off in March 1975 by adopting objectives which essentially mirrored those of the four-man US study group. A month later, Region 1 adopted very similar objectives, except that those below 10 MHz were more modest. Region 2 followed, in April 1976, by endorsing the objectives previously adopted by Region 3. WARC-79 was the first conference for which the world's amateurs adopted a *common* position in this way.

In conjunction with the Region 2 Conference in April 1976, IARU President VE3CJ had convened a meeting with representatives of the three IARU regional organizations and several member-societies. One idea emerging from this meeting was a need for a worldwide IARU working group to assist in guiding the preparatory work. This working group met several times over the following two years. One of their important products was a model position paper in English, French and Spanish, which IARU member-societies could use as a basis for their own formal submissions to their governments. Even more important were the efforts by IARU member-societies to get Amateur Radio representatives on their national delegations. This was successful in 17 countries, including the US.

The basic approach, basic strategies and organization used in preparing Amateur Radio for WARC-79 proved to be sound. When the Final Acts of the Conference were signed in December 1979, Amateur Radio emerged not only with its present bands intact but with important new allocations at 10.1-10.15, 18.068-18.168 and 24.89-24.99 MHz (see Chapter 5 for details) as well! Further, there were relaxation of restrictions on some of the existing amateur bands, and additional segments were earmarked for amateur satellite work. WARC-79 was a tremendous team effort on the part of many, many persons who had the faith and the vision to work successfully toward a common goal. The degree of success is attributable almost entirely to the intensive preparation conducted by the IARU. The IARU Geneva Team was led by VE3CJ, the late Vic Clark, W4KFC, Richard Baldwin, W1RU, and David Sumner, K1ZZ.

Future WARCs

The IARU member-societies are preparing for WARC-92. Some preparatory work involves attending ITU meetings to get to know the issues and those persons who will become decision-making delegates. WARC-preparatory travel to IARU conferences is reinforcing the necessity of adequate liaison with government telecommunications officials and support for the goals adopted by the IARU Administrative Council. For more information on the work of the IARU, contact ARRL HQ.

DOMESTIC REGULATION OF THE SPECTRUM

With a copy of the Final Acts clutched firmly in hand, WARC delegates return home and their governments implement the accords. In the US, once the Senate advises and consents to ratification, this task falls upon the FCC and the National Telecommunications and Information Administration—NTIA (see below). When Senate ratification of WARC-79 finally occurred in 1983, FCC began amending its rules to bring them into line with the new international Radio Regulations.

Federal Communications Commission

What is the FCC? Well, it's the outfit that issues you your license, for one thing! The FCC is the US government agency charged with regulating interstate and foreign communication involving radio, television, wire cable and satellite. The FCC does

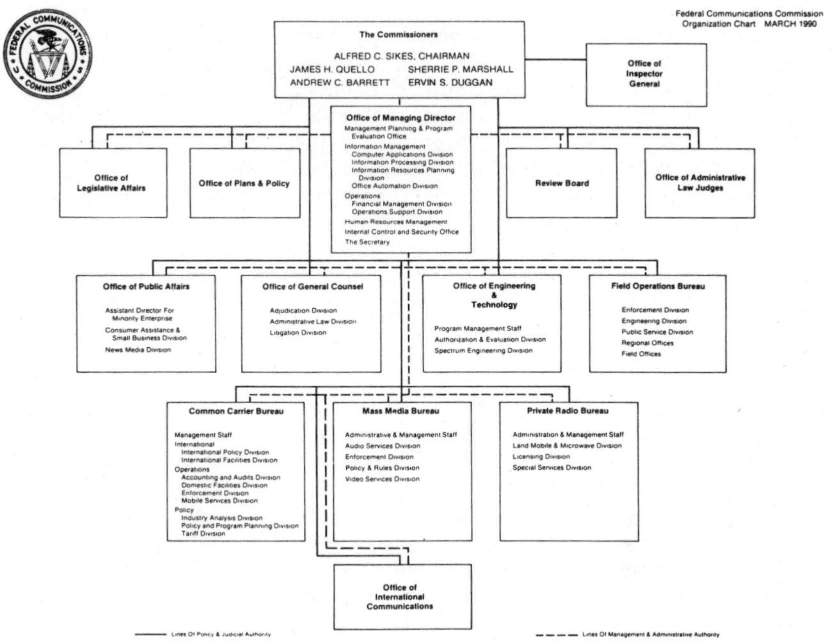

Fig 4—Organization chart of the Federal Communications Commission (FCC).

not function like any other government department; it is a sovereign Federal agency created by Congress and, as such, reports directly to Congress, although its members are appointed by the President.

In the early days of radio regulation, jurisdiction over wire and radio communications at various times was handled by the Department of Commerce, Post Office Department, Interstate Commerce Commission and the Federal Radio Commission. Technological developments and interference problems, however, necessitated coordination of these functions into a single agency. The Communications Act, signed by President Roosevelt on June 19, 1934, created the Federal Communications Commission for that purpose (see "The Early Days," below).

Today's FCC allocates bands of frequencies to non-government communications services and assigns frequencies to individual stations. It licenses and regulates stations and operators, and regulates common carriers in interstate and foreign communications by telegraph, telephone and satellite. For a specific description of the FCC's Congressionally authorized powers, see the extracts from the Communications Act, below. One job it does *not* do is regulate Federal government radio operations; this is done by the NTIA, under delegated authority from the President.

The FCC consists of five Commissioners appointed by the President with the approval of the Senate. No Commissioner can have a financial interest in any FCC-regulated business. Appointments are for five years, except when filling an unexpired term. One of the Commissioners is designated Chairman by the President. The Chairman's tenure during his or her term of office is at the pleasure of the President.

As with many federal agencies, the Commissioners function "collegially" (ie, one man—one vote), supervising all FCC activities, with substantial delegation of responsibilities to FCC staff. The Chairman is responsible for the overall administration of the internal affairs of the FCC and sets the basic agenda for the agency; otherwise, as noted above, he, like his fellow commissioners, has only one vote in formal policy decisions. The internal structure of the FCC is shown in Fig 4.

Policy determinations are made by the Commission as a whole. FCC practices conform to the Communications Act of 1934, as amended, the Administrative Procedure Act, as amended, and other applicable laws.

The FCC cooperates with other agencies such as various government agencies involved with radio and wire communication in international and domestic matters. It also cooperates with radio-user groups such as the League.

FCC regulation of radio includes consideration of applications for construction permits and license for all classes of non-government stations, and frequency, power and call-sign assignments. The FCC is involved in authorization of communications circuits, modification and renewal of licenses, and inspection of transmitting equipment and regulation of its use. The FCC has enforcement powers and may levy fines in cases of noncompliance with its rules. In sum, the FCC carries out the Communications Act. The complete text of the Communications Act would occupy many pages; see the Appendix for those sections that are the most applicable to Amateur Radio. Note particularly Sections 324, 325, 333 and 705 and the penalties outlined in Sections 501 and 502.

Of course, the FCC has authority over the Amateur Radio Service, but it also concerns itself with a number of other services. These include Aviation (aircraft and ground); Marine (ship and coastal); and Public Safety (police, fire, forestry conservation, highway maintenance, local government, special emergency and state guard). FCC holds jurisdiction over Industrial Services including business, forest products, manufacturers, motion pictures, petroleum, power, relay press, special industrial and telephone maintenance. The Land Transportation Services cover railroad, passenger and truck, taxicab and automobile emergency communications. Other services include Personal (CB), Disaster, Experimental and Common Carrier. This latter service covers a wide range of communications including paging, land mobile, microwave relay, broadcast relay, and international radiotelephone and telegraph.

As we've seen, the FCC is charged with taking care of communications provisions of treaties and international agreements to which the US is a party ("party" meaning the US is a nation that signed on the dotted line). Under Department of State auspices, the FCC participates in related international conferences. FCC licenses radio and cable circuits from the US to foreign ports and regulates the operating companies. It also licenses the radio stations on American planes and ships in international service, and, under international agreements and upon request, inspects the radio equipment of foreign vessels touching US ports. In addition, it is the medium for resolving cases of interference between domestic and foreign radio stations.

The FCC is required "to study new uses for radio, provide for experimental uses of frequencies, and generally encourage the larger and more effective use of radio in the public interest." Cooperation is maintained with government and commercial research activities. The FCC operates a laboratory at Laurel, Maryland. It also carries out studies to provide information on complex questions facing the FCC and the telecommunications industry as a whole.

Wire and radio communications facilities used to aid the national defense form one of the basic requirements of the Communications Act. The President has delegated some of these functions to the FCC. Among other things, the FCC supervises the Emergency Broadcast System to notify and instruct the public in the event of enemy attack.

The functions relating to assignment of frequencies to radio stations belonging to, and operated by, the US government were assigned to the Assistant Secretary of Commerce for Communications and Information (who also holds the title of NTIA Administrator). See Fig 5 for the internal structure of NTIA. Among its various functions, NTIA performs the following:

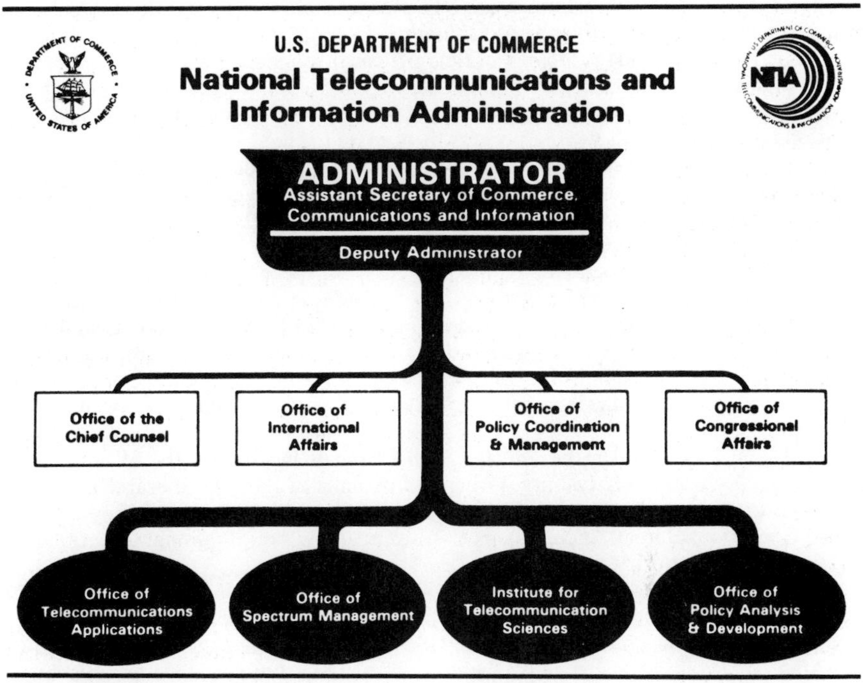

Fig 5—Organization chart of the National Telecommunications and Information Administration (NTIA).

- coordinates telecommunications activities of the Executive Branch (ie, the President and the Cabinet);
- develops plans, policies and programs relating to international telecommunications issues;
- coordinates preparations for US participation in international telecommunications conferences and negotiations;
- develops, in cooperation with the FCC, a long-range plan for improved management of all electromagnetic spectrum resources, including jointly determining the National Table of Frequency Allocations;
- conducts telecommunications research and development.

Working alongside the NTIA is another related government entity, the Interdepartment Radio Advisory Committee, IRAC. IRAC traces back to a mutual agreement of government departments on June 1, 1922. The NTIA appoints the officers of IRAC. IRAC includes representatives of the various Cabinet departments, agencies and armed services, and assists the NTIA administrator in assigning frequencies to US government radio stations and in developing and executing plans, procedures, and technical criteria. The FCC must coordinate any actions with IRAC that might affect the Federal government's use of the radio spectrum.

Internal Structure of the FCC

FCC staff is organized on a functional basis. There are four operating bureaus—Mass Media, Common Carrier, Field Operations and Private Radio—and seven staff offices—Managing Director, Engineering and Technology, Public Affairs, Plans and

Policy, General Counsel, Administrative Law Judges and the Review Board. Its headquarters are in two buildings in Washington, DC.

The FCC field staff is located in field offices throughout the country. The field staff engages for the most part in engineering work. This includes monitoring the radio spectrum to see that station operations meet technical requirements, inspecting stations of all types and issuing permits or licenses to those found qualified. It also locates and closes unauthorized transmitters, furnishes radio bearings for aircraft or ships in distress, locates sources of interference and suggests remedial measures. The field staff also performs special engineering work for other government agencies and obtains and analyzes technical data for FCC use.

Where precisely does Amateur Radio fit into the FCC's scheme of things? Amateur Radio is administered by the FCC's Private Radio Bureau (PRB), specifically the PRB Special Services Division and its Personal Radio Branch. Amateur Radio is considered private because it is a two-way service for individuals for private, strictly noncommercial reasons, unlike broadcasting which serves a mass audience or common-carrier services (such as the telephone system) which provide a communications service for hire.

Also included under the Private Radio Bureau heading is the all-important Licensing Division in Gettysburg. Other components of the FCC hierarchy of most concern to Amateur Radio are the Office of Engineering and Technology and the Field Operations Bureau, including its Enforcement Division, Regional Offices, Field Offices and Monitoring Stations.

The fact that additional bands were allocated to Amateur Radio at WARC-79 clearly points to the significance attached to the Amateur Service by the international telecommunications community. In the US, the FCC attaches the same importance to Amateur Radio as evidence by the amount of spectrum space we are allocated. But most amateurs take nothing for granted; continued adherence to the good-amateur-practice standard is absolutely necessary to maintain the allocations as they now exist.

Deregulation

The League is only one of many representatives of the various radio services affected by FCC actions. For example, the National Cable Television Association (NCTA) and the National Association of Broadcasters (NAB) are others who represent their respective "industries." All these recognized the FCC's trend towards eliminating unnecessary rules, ie, "deregulation," particularly during the Reagan administration. A mandate has been passed down to regulatory agencies that the people should have less intrusion into their lives by the Federal government, with the marketplace philosophy—based on individual initiative and free enterprise—prevailing whenever possible.

Under FCC Chairman Mark Fowler, a Reagan appointee, deregulation accelerated. Fowler ultimately resigned in the spring of 1987, after serving as FCC Chairman for six years, longer than any other chairman. His replacement was another advocate of deregulation, Dennis Patrick, who was an FCC commissioner prior to his elevation as Chairman. President Bush picked Alfred C. Sikes, who had been serving as the NTIA Administrator (see discussion of the NTIA earlier in this chapter), as the current chairman following Mr Patrick's resignation. The Bush Administration is expected to follow the deregulatory course of the preceding administration.

One of the most momentous occurrences in the history of deregulation was the enactment of the Communications Amendments Act of 1982 (Public Law 97-259), which opened the door to sweeping changes in the Amateur Service and placed the primary responsibility for protecting the future of Amateur Radio where it belongs: on we amateurs ourselves. Signed into law by President Reagan in September 14, 1982, PL 97-259 amended the Communications Act in several critical areas (all of which have been incorporated into the new Part 97), as follows:

• Authority was vested in the FCC to regulate the susceptibility of electronic equipment to RFI;

• the Amateur Service was exempted from the "secrecy of communications" provisions of §705 of the Communications Act. This cleared the way for a more active role on the part of amateurs to police our own bands;

• Because of this exemption, the FCC was legally authorized to use volunteers to monitor the bands for rules violations and convey information to FCC personnel. This formed the basis for the creation of the League's Amateur Auxiliary to the FCC's Field Operations Bureau (see Chapter 15);

• FCC was authorized to use volunteers in preparing and administrating exams, which led the League (and others) to become Volunteer Examiner Coordinators and coordinating exams throughout the US and overseas (see Chapter 2); and

• The term of an amateur license became 10 years (increased from five) to reduce the administrative burden on the FCC and amateur licensees.

History was made again in February 1987 when, in response to an ARRL proposal, the FCC adopted "Novice Enhancement," which gave Novices SSB privileges on 10 meters, and new privileges on 220 and 1270 MHz.

So, in the main, deregulation has been very positive for the entire telecommunications field, and the League has, for the most part, supported the FCC's deregulatory actions in Amateur Radio, since we amateurs have demonstrated time and again our ability to keep our own shop in order. In recent years, we have seen the FCC eliminate logging requirements, simplify station ID, permit ASCII, AMTOR, packet and other digital codes, Novice Enhancement and so on, all culminating in the adoption of a new Part 97, which is the subject of this edition of the *Rule Book*.

HOW DOES THE FCC MAKE RULES?

As we have seen, the FCC is the government agency charged to regulate the telecommunications services in the US. Less familiar, however, is the *process* by which the FCC makes these rules. For example, how did the new Part 97 come into being? Do they simply come out of thin air or are they conjured up by a psychic or channeller? Or are they just handed down to us from those who "know better"? The answer is a resounding no; we amateurs have a right to directly participate in the rule-making procedure. As American citizens, we can and do have a profound effect on which rules are added, dropped or modified.

The Administrative Procedure Act

The population growth and sociological and technical advances in the US, particularly since World War 1, brought about ever-increasing demands for government services. Examples included aviation, radio, medicine, and many, many others. Recognizing that it had neither the facilities, time nor expertise to administer and regulate such diverse fields, the US Congress established administrative agencies; broad duties, powers and enforcement tools were delegated to each agency. Many of these agencies are "hybrid" in that they are not explicitly under the executive branch (the President) or the legislative branch (Congress), but, like the FCC, somewhere in between.

It was not long before the Courts recognized that the rules, regulations and polices of these agencies had the force and effect of law just as though enacted by Congress. However, persons affected by these rules as well as the courts expressed concern over the manner by which the rules were adopted, amended and enforced. This culminated in the 1946 enactment by Congress of the Administrative Procedure Act, which (along with certain sections of the Communications Act itself that affect FCC procedures only) sets forth specific procedures that all administrative agencies must follow in adopting and amending their rules. The Act also set forth the procedures to be followed in adjudicatory (ie, trial-like) hearings. The complete text of the Act can be found starting at 5 USC [United States Code] §552.

Insofar as rule making is concerned (and a rule making pertains to a process like PR Docket No. 88-139, which led to the adoption of the new Part 97), the essential provisions of the Act are (1) public notice of the proposal in the *Federal Register*, and (2) the right of interested persons to submit written comments. This is "notice-and-comment" rule making. Certain rules, primarily those relating to agency organization and internal operation, are not subject to the notice-and-comment procedure. Also, prior notice need not be given if an agency for good cause finds that the notice and comment procedure is impractical, unnecessary or contrary to the public interest. Overall, rules may be adopted, amended or repealed by an agency on its own initiative, or may be requested by an interested person by the filing of a petition for rule making. An example of the former would be the Part 97 rewrite, an example of the latter would be the League's petition for Novice Enhancement. Obviously, rules changes in Part 97 have originated by *both* modes.

Petitions for Rule Making

Believe it or not, the requirements for initiating a rule-making procedure are relatively simple and straightforward. Any interested person may petition the FCC for the adoption, amendment or repeal of a rule or regulation. The petition should be addressed to the Secretary, Federal Communications Commission, Washington, DC 20554, and typed on 8½ by 11-inch paper, preferably double spaced. The petition should set forth the text or substance of the proposed rule, or the rule sought to be amended or repealed, together with all facts, views, arguments and data deemed to support the action requested. The petition should indicate how the interests of the petitioner will be affected. The sidebar shows the proper caption for a petition.

Amateurs should be mindful of three things when filing a petition (or submitting comments about someone else's petition) to the FCC. The first thing the FCC is interested in is your individual experience, ie, your credibility, in the areas covered by the petition. Such experience should, presumably, shed new light on issues or questions raised. Secondly, the FCC is interested in an unemotional rendition of the facts—"Just the facts, ma'am," as Sgt Joe Friday used to say. Your submission should explain the facts briefly, but fully. Explain your position and present evidence to support that position. Third, be aware that the FCC is interested in *specifics*. If, for example, part of a present rule is acceptable to you and other parts are unacceptable, you must state this. In addition, you should state other opinions and how the public would be better served by your own position. Comment only on a specific issue. When you file comments on a petition originated by someone else, restrict your comments

---

Caption Format To Be Used for Petiton or Formal Comments

Before the
FEDERAL COMMUNICATIONS COMMISSION
Washington, DC 20554

In the Matter of	)	
	)	
Amendment of Section 97.—	)	
(Insert rule number if an	)	RM-
amendment is	)	
proposed, and the	)	
subject matter of the	)	
Amateur Radio Service.)	)	

---

only to the issue raised in that petition. Don't use that as a vehicle for submitting a new proposal which should be reserved for a future petition of your own.

If the FCC, in making a preliminary review of a petition, concludes that it meets these minimum requirements (or that a waiver of the requirements is warranted), then it will issue a "Public Notice" entitled "Petition for Rulemaking Filed," giving the file number (RM-), the name of the petitioner, the date of filing and a brief summary of the proposal. Such notices are not printed in the *Federal Register*, but all those relating to Amateur Radio are summarized in ARRL publications such as *QST* and *The ARRL Letter*; the public notice is available for inspection at FCC HQ. Some petitions that plainly do not warrant FCC consideration are not given RM-file-numbers and are usually dismissed by an FCC bureau chief under delegated authority. Any interested person may file a statement in support of or in opposition to a petition for rule making not later than 30 days from issuance of the Public Notice. Replies to supporting or opposing statements are due not later than 15 days after the filing of such statements.

Notice of Proposed Rule Making

Rule making involving Amateur Radio matters usually falls under the jurisdiction of the FCC's Private Radio Bureau. Petitions involving amateur matters are processed by the Personal Radio Branch of PRB. If a petition has merit, a draft (ie, not finalized) Notice of Proposed Rule Making (NPRM) may be submitted by the PRB Chief to the Commissioners for their consideration. If it is adopted for release—which requires a majority vote by the Commissioners—a Docket Number will be assigned (eg, the Part 97 rewrite matter was originally designated "PR Docket No. 88-139"), and the entire NPRM will be released to the public and published in the *Federal Register* for comments.

Depending on the FCC's workload, its priorities and the amount of interest shown by concerned parties, several months or even years may elapse between the release of an NPRM and when the FCC reaches a final decision, if at all. For example, the Part 97 rewrite NPRM was adopted by the FCC on their own initiative on March 24, 1988, but the final version was not put to bed until May 31, 1989 (with the actual text not released to the public until June 9).

As required by the Administrative Procedure Act, the NPRM must set forth a statement of the time, place and nature of public rule-making proceedings, a reference to the legal authority under which the rule is proposed, and either the terms or substance of the proposed rule or a description of the subjects and issues involved. Deadlines for filing comments and reply comments are given (reply comments are those that are filed in response *not* to the underlying NPRM but to the comments that were filed *in response to* the underlying NPRM, which are available to the public at the FCC's public reference room in Washington, assuming, again that you're in the neighborhood). The NPRM must, of course, be published in the *Federal Register*. Interested persons have an opportunity to participate in the proceeding through the submission of data, views or arguments in writing.

If you are filing comments in an NPRM (such as when the FCC released its Part 97 proposal), use the caption format shown above, making sure that you put the appropriate Docket number at the top. Had you commented on the Part 97 NPRM, you would have made sure to put "PR Docket No. 88-139" at the top of the first page. If you wanted to be real slick, you could also have put "Reorganization and Deregulation of Part 97 of the Rules Governing the Amateur Radio Service" right underneath the words "In the Matter of" as well.

When you write your comments, follow the same content guidelines we discussed above with respect to petitions for rule making (ie, list your credentials, be fact-specific and on point). When you comment on an active NPRM, the FCC wants you to send in an original and four copies for a total of five documents (always make an additional copy for your own personal records). If you want to be sure that each FCC commissioner gets a personal copy, send five additional copies. So, if you want to have all bases covered, your envelope to the FCC must contain a total of 10 documents, the original and nine copies. The same rules apply for filing reply comments.

All comments are reviewed by the FCC staff and play a role in the ultimate decision made by the FCC itself. Therefore, it's important to get them in by deadline.

HOW FCC RULES ARE MADE

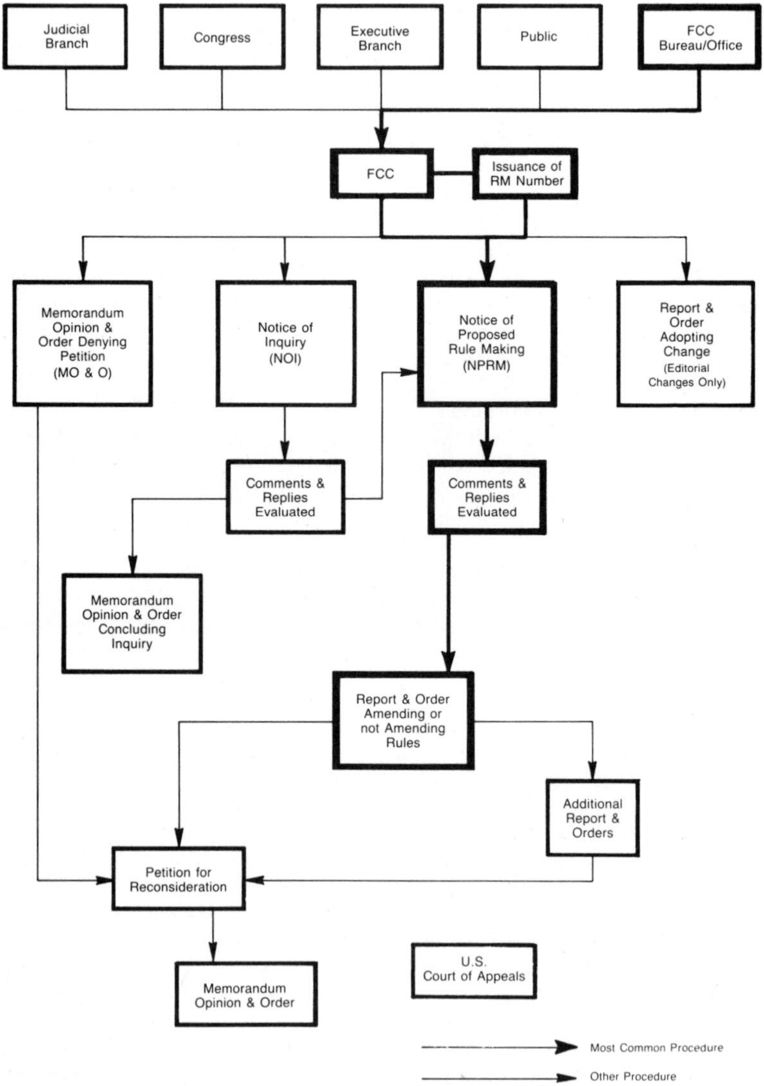

Adapted from the
FCC Communicator, September 1975

Comments not filed may not be considered by the FCC in its deliberations. For example, the comment deadline in the Part 97 rewrite NPRM was August 31, 1988, with reply comments due October 31, 1988. However, because of the complexity of the subject matter, the League on behalf of the entire amateur community petitioned for a 90-day extension, which was granted by the FCC to allow for the broadest possible input (the new comment and reply comment deadline became November 29, 1988 and January 31, 1989 respectively).

Generally, the FCC would not be receptive to such extensions, and the original comment deadlines are strictly adhered to. However, under the Administrative Procedure Act and FCC rules, a person who has missed a comment deadline may prepare comments anyway, filing with them another document titled "Motion for Leave to Submit Late-Filed Comments." If the Motion shows good cause (ie, your excuse is convincing!) as to the lateness of the filing, and if the matter is not too far along on the FCC staff work schedule, your comments may be accepted. Don't count on either an extension or your individual motion being granted, however. If the FCC is considering a matter that you feel is important, make sure you type up your comments and get them in the mail well in advance of the deadline.

Occasionally, a Notice of Inquiry (NOI) may be issued or combined with an NPRM. An NOI will set forth the FCC's concern over a particular matter and solicit comments and suggestions for the world at large as to whether adoption, amendment or repeal of a rule may be desirable. The same notice and comment procedures are followed with NOIs as with NPRMs.

Copies of FCC NPRMs concerning Amateur Radio are usually available from ARRL HQ for an SASE. Summaries or the word-for-word text of NPRMs are printed in the *Federal Register*, which is available in most local libraries. Listen to W1AW and watch *QST*, *The ARRL Letter* and other ham publications for information on the latest FCC happenings concerning Amateur Radio. Copies of FCC documents may be obtained, for a fee, from the FCC's contractor for records duplication: The International Transcription Service, Room 140, 2100 M St NW, Washington, DC 20037, phone 202-857-3800.

The Report and Order

Once all the comments are reviewed, (for amateur matters, this is usually done by the Personal Radio Branch of PRB), a draft Report and Order will be prepared by that branch and submitted to the Chief of PRB. Then the document must work its way up the hierarchy, surviving checkpoints along the way. A draft Report and Order must be approved at each level within the Bureau, and then coordinated with other interested Bureaus or Offices within the FCC before formally being presented to the Commissioners for their consideration and approval. A Report and Order is just what it sounds like—the Commission issues a detailed Report of its findings and an Order is issued based on the judgment of the Commissioners (as recommended by the staff).

As with the Part 97 rewrite Report and Order adopted May 31, 1989, specific rules changes are listed. Revisions of the Report and Order take place right up to the moment it is adopted by the FCC Commissioners, usually after due consideration by the Commissioners at an "Open Meeting," a regular meeting of the Commissioners that has a published agenda and is open to the public. During these open meetings, FCC staff members most familiar with the subject at hand will make the presentation. The Commissioners may decide to adopt the Report and Order as presented to them by the staff, order the staff to make specific revisions in the document and then adopt it, or terminate the NPRM without amending any rule or taking any action (this occurred on May 21, 1989, when the Commissioners terminated the PRB-3 Special Call Sign Proposal *without* action).

The rule or rules finally adopted need not be identical to the original proposal. The Courts have held that there must merely be some relationship between the proposal and the rule finally adopted, and that the FCC must have considered all the relevant comments that were submitted. The Administrative Procedure Act requires that there must be a concise general statement of the basis and purpose incorporated in the rules. Sometimes, these "concise" statements of why the FCC did what it did are anything but, indeed often going on and on in excruciating detail. What the FCC is doing is putting all its cards on the table to show it made a rational decision—this is done to avoid both any problems with Congress (which can exert pressure on the FCC since Congress controls the FCC's appropriations, ie, the purse strings) as well as judicial review of their decision (see "Court Appeals," below). The FCC tends to be sensitive to Congress and the Courts, so it carefully frames its Reports and Orders and the like so that it has stated its case as persuasively as possible.

Generally, a Report and Order is the end of the line for a particular rules change. The rules become law under the Administrative Procedure Act 30 days after publication in the *Federal Register*. As noted above with respect to the Part 97 rewrite chronology (or the Novice Enhancement proposal, PR Docket 86-161, which was released in April 1986 after an ARRL petition filed in June 1985, and not adopted by the FCC until February 1987), the process often takes years, depending on the FCC's workload, agenda and priorities.

Incidentally, legal scholars refer to notice-and-comment rule making as "informal rule making." It seems weird to call a process *informal* when there is an extensive paper trail of petitions, NPRM, comments/reply comments and a Report and Order. But it's called informal to distinguish it from *formal* rule making, which generally involves all the above steps, plus a full-blown trial-like oral hearing with various witnesses providing testimony on the record and such. Obviously, the FCC prefers from a logistical standpoint to use the notice-and-comment procedure in which it only has to consider written submissions; in legal jargon, this is often termed deciding a matter by "taking it on the papers." Formal rule making occurs most often during high-profile commercial broadcasting matters and other "big bucks" situations where, for political and other reasons, making a decision without oral testimony would be unsatisfactory. Remember, too, that Amateur Radio is a comparatively small part of the FCC's responsibilities.

Due Process

You might be wondering at this point why this process takes so long and even if it's all worth it. Well, as has been said many times, this is the price we pay for democracy. We are saddled with these elaborate and often slow procedures because we have a free society. All interested persons have an opportunity to hear and to be heard on a given issue—it's called due process of law, which is embodied in the US Constitution. These tedious procedures that allow for public participation at the expense of speedy decision making are viewed as desirable in our system. It's one of the fundamental characteristics that distinguishes us from the totalitarian regimes around the world, and makes the US the world leader in freedom.

Petitions for Reconsideration

Section 405 of the Communications Act, as amended, affords "a person aggrieved or whose interests are adversely affected" by an order (a new or amended rule, etc) the right to petition the FCC for reconsideration. The petitioner must state specifically why the FCC's action should be changed. A Petition for Reconsideration must be filed within 30 days of the date of the public notice of the final FCC action, which generally means within 30 days of its publication in the *Federal Register*.

A Petition for Reconsideration usually is referred to the same Bureau as prepared the original Report and Order. From a practical standpoint, it is virtually impossible to obtain a favorable action on a Petition for Reconsideration if no new facts are presented. Occasionally, however, if the petitioner shows good cause, the FCC may grant the Petition for Reconsideration and modify the earlier order.

The format and number of copies required for reconsideration petitions are the same as described above, although they may not exceed 25 double-spaced typewritten pages. Oppositions to Petitions for Reconsideration are limited to 10 doubled-spaced typewritten pages.

The effective date of a new or amended rule is not automatically postponed by the filing of a Petition for Reconsideration. If a stay of the effective date of the rule or amendment is desired, the petitioner must specifically request it in a "Motion to Stay" and must show good cause (such as irreparable harm) why the rule should not go into effect.

Court Appeals

Judicial review of an FCC decision may be sought under §402(a) of the Communications Act and §§701-706 of the Administrative Procedure Act, as long as review is sought over a *final* decision. The court may either affirm (approve) the action of an agency like the FCC, or reverse it or send it back to the FCC for further consideration.

Generally, the court will be quite deferential to an agency such as the FCC, because of the technical nature of the communications world, so the chances of the aggrieved person prevailing on appeal are remote. The standard the Court uses is whether the agency action is "arbitrary, capricious or an abuse of discretion." If the Court can find a reasonable or rational basis for an agency action (which is, again, why FCC Report and Orders try to address every conceivable issue), no abuse of discretion will be found. A Court might set aside a rule-making action if, for example, the FCC exceeded the authority delegated to it by Congress or under the Constitution, if it failed to properly follow its notice-and-comment procedures and the like, or acted in a way that was not supported by the substantial evidence that it had gathered on the record (ie, the agency's factfinding was unreasonable) or in the event there was a prejudicial error.

As mentioned, the Court generally follows a policy of not substituting its judgment for that of the agency because of the agency's presumed expertise in that field. Moreover, the Courts are much more comfortable with issues of law (procedure, applicability of statutes, and so on) and are reluctant to address the facts and the details of the particular controversy. The standard for evaluating a question of fact would be whether the FCC's action was supported by substantial evidence on the record; in questions of law, the Court would be much more inclined to substitute its own judgment for that of the FCC or another agency. As such, in a factual determination, the Courts will rarely go beyond the facts and evidence already put on the record during the agency rule making.

In the relatively rare event that the Court remands a rule-making matter back to the FCC for further consideration or proceedings, it will usually be handled by the same Bureau that put it together originally.

It is clear from this discussion that Petitions for Reconsideration and appeals to the Courts are not guaranteed to bring about changes in rules adopted in the rule-making process. Often the most practical course is to file a *new* petition for rule making after experience has been gained with the new or amended rules and it can be demonstrated that the rule, as amended, is not working out as planned and therefore not in the best interests of the amateur community.

Adjudication

In those isolated cases where a licensee would be the subject of an FCC enforcement action, he would have a right to hearing under the Administrative Procedure Act before an FCC Administrative Law Judge. This is a trial-type hearing called an "adjudication." See Chapter 15 for a discussion of cooperative efforts that occur between the FCC and the ARRL in rules enforcement.

The FCC and You

This chapter talks about how it's your right as an American citizen to participate in the FCC's rule-making process. At this point, we're not trying to undercut your right to participate in the process, but please think before you leap. That is, please exercise common sense. For example, say you've been ragchewing on the same 75-meter frequency and at the same time with the same stations for 364 uninterrupted, blissful days. On day 365, you can't complete your contact because of QRM from a contest. You do *not* then run to your computer to draft a petition to the FCC to prohibit contesting. That would be totally out of proportion to such a temporary situation.

A responsibility of our tradition of self-regulation that has been discussed in this *Rule Book* means that at all times we must minimize our tendency to complain and/or formally petition the FCC for narrow or overly restrictive rules interpretations, particularly for emotional reasons. This may result in unfavorable precedents being set that will actually be harmful to the Amateur Radio Service. The FCC's response may be a hasty or uninformed legal opinion by an FCC functionary who may not have the benefit of real-world operating experience. This opinion would be rendered in good faith, to be sure, but you can expect that it would be formulated without consideration of all the necessary details. FCC staff faces a formidable workload and they are doing the best they can under the circumstances; indeed, the FCC wants us to resolve our operational issues by ourselves, which is provided for within the latitude of the new Part 97.

In terms of a rule making that already is pending, or in a highly important, significant situation where you as a radio amateur feel it's crucial to submit a petition for rule making on your own, it is best that you contact the League *first*. The ARRL acts as a clearinghouse for all rule-making matters and painstakingly works towards gauging a consensus on an issue *before* formally contacting the FCC. The League is a representative democracy; when the League determines that such a consensus exists, it then initiates proposals for the good of the Amateur Service, such as the ARRL petition for rule making that culminated in Novice Enhancement. The League also monitors *all* FCC proposals whether they directly or indirectly affect Amateur Radio, publicizes them extensively in *QST*, *The ARRL Letter* and elsewhere, and submits comments on behalf of the amateur community on each and every one where appropriate. It also encourages individual amateurs to file comments on important matters, too.

Before you participate in an FCC proceeding, contact the Regulatory Information Branch at ARRL HQ or your ARRL Director to find out what the status of a particular issue is, and whether your comments are vitally needed to achieve a positive outcome or whether, in some cases, your involvement would be unnecessary.

Summary

New editions of the *FCC Rule Book* are published frequently to keep pace with the changes in the rules themselves. The rules have evolved over time, and will continue to evolve. The rules are dynamic because Amateur Radio is dynamic—constantly changing to meet and create new methods and technologies to better serve individuals and society at large.

also monitors *all* FCC proposals whether they directly or indirectly affect Amateur Radio, publicizes them extensively in *QST*, *The ARRL Letter* and elsewhere, and submits comments on behalf of the amateur community on each and every one where appropriate. It also encourages individual amateurs to file comments on important matters, too, such as the grassroots support enlisted in the 220-MHz matter.

Before you participate in an FCC proceeding, contact the Regulatory Information Department at ARRL HQ or your ARRL Director to find out what the status of a particular issue is, and whether your comments are vitally needed to achieve a positive outcome or whether, in some cases, your involvement would be unnecessary.

Summary

New editions of the *FCC Rule Book* are published to keep pace with the changes in the rules themselves. The rules have evolved over time, and will continue to evolve. The rules are dynamic because Amateur Radio is dynamic—constantly changing to meet and create new methods and technologies to better serve individuals and society at large.

Chapter Fifteen

Rules Compliance, the Amateur Auxiliary and You

Among the many significant aspects of the Communications Amendments Act of 1982 passed by Congress and signed by the President is one which authorizes the FCC to use amateur volunteers to monitor the airwaves for rules violations. This is a crucial factor in maintaining order and the traditional high standards on the amateur bands, as governmental belt-tightening does not and will not provide the FCC's Field Operations Bureau (FOB) with the necessary resources to monitor the amateur bands to any great extent. Moreover, the Volunteer Examiner Program has caused an influx of operators into the Amateur Radio Service, creating an even greater potential need for monitoring of amateur band activity.

Here's what Congress said when finalizing the bill:

> The Amateur Radio Service has been praised for being self-regulated. The Commission has reported that less time has been devoted to monitoring and regulating the Amateur Service than to any other service because of its self-policing and discipline.
>
> One primary purpose of the Conference Substitute is to provide the Federal Communications Commission with the authority to implement various programs which will result in improvements in administration of the Amateur Radio Service and to cut the costs thereof. It will further allow the Amateur Radio Service to continue its tradition as the most self-regulated radio service in the United States, and to become to some extent self-administered, requiring even less expenditure to government time and effort than in the past.

THE AMATEUR AUXILIARY

When they implemented volunteer monitoring, the FCC's Field Operations Bureau recognized the value of the organized and disciplined amateur community through its membership organization, ARRL. They recognized the long history and tradition of the ARRL's Official Observer (OO) program and the League's extensive Field Organization.

To make good use of it, the FOB created the Amateur Auxiliary. FOB and ARRL signed an agreement outlining the objectives and nature of the program and the commitment by ARRL to administer it.

The Amateur Auxiliary addresses both *maintenance monitoring* and *amateur-to-amateur interference* (sometimes misnamed malicious interference). Maintenance monitoring is conducted through the enhanced OO program, while local amateur-to-amateur interference is handled by specifically authorized *Local Interference Committees*. These committees, where sanctioned by the ARRL Section Manager, can enter into local cooperative agreements with the FCC Regional Director or Engineer-In-Charge for the geographical area concerned by simply "localizing" the language in the national agreement.

ARRL sections are the focal point for liaison and the primary communications channel between organized amateurs and FCC's Field Operations Bureau offices. The Amateur Auxiliary is administered by the League's Section Managers and OO Coordinators with support from ARRL HQ.

General Objectives/Concepts

The general objectives of the Amateur Auxiliary are to:

1) Foster a wider knowledge of and better compliance with laws, rules and regulations governing the Amateur Radio Service;

2) Extend the concepts of self-regulation and self-administration of the Service;

3) Enhance the opportunity for individual amateurs to contribute to the public welfare as outlined in the basis and purpose of the Amateur Radio Service;

4) Enable the Field Operations Bureau of FCC to efficiently and effectively utilize its manpower and resources.

The role of the Amateur Auxiliary is to give technical and operational advice and other assistance to amateurs and others who are receptive. The task is not to find fault but to identify causes and effects, and to find ways to achieve solutions. *The mission is not direct enforcement*. Because the boundary between observation and enforcement is not always obvious, mature judgment is clearly required of the Auxiliary members and its leadership. The Auxiliary, to be viable and effective, must avoid the appearance of enforcement. It must also avoid the appearance of having a vested interest in any specific type of amateur operations or of being highly sympathetic to amateur groups which advocate specific activities or causes.

Training and Certification

Only those amateurs who have successfully demonstrated a thorough knowledge of and skill in volunteer monitoring will be enrolled as members of the Amateur Auxiliary. You must pass an exam covering information contained in this book and other training materials.

The appointment procedure is as follows:

1) All Official Observer and Local Interference Committee Chairman appointment inquiries are sent to the Section Manager (SM), since all OO appointments are initiated by the Section Manager or the SM's designee, the OO Coordinator (OOC).

2) The SM (or OOC) sends an appointment card, FSD-211, to ARRL HQ, indicating "RECOMMENDATION."

3) ARRL HQ sends the prospective OO this book, other supplementary literature and an open-book examination paper. After the candidate reviews the material, he or she returns the exam to ARRL HQ for grading.

4) The OO is notified that he or she has successfully completed the training and exam, or sent a re-test with subject areas needing further study pointed out. A copy of this notification goes to the Section Manager who then sends the official appointment certificate to the new OO.

5) ARRL HQ sends initial supplies to the new OO.

Regional Monitoring Stations

There will be situations, particularly at HF, that will transcend section boundaries. Because of this, another level in the Amateur Auxiliary is required. This higher level involves the *Regional Monitoring Stations* (RMS). A limited number of amateurs with impeccable credentials (including letters of recommendation from League officials) will be considered for the regional monitoring function.

Regional Monitoring Stations are appointed by the ARRL President, after their application is approved by the concerned ARRL Directors and Section Managers. RMSs are in charge of a wide geographic area, similar in scope to areas covered by FCC monitoring stations. Inquiries regarding appointment as a Regional Monitoring

Station should be sent to the Field Services Manager at ARRL HQ.

OOs and Section Managers can call upon the appropriate Regional Monitoring Station for assistance in complex cases in the course of Auxiliary operations. The RMS works closely with the FCC FOB monitoring stations on those cases that require action beyond the routine maintenance monitoring of the Official Observer. The RMS deals primarily with instances of flagrant and repeated noncompliance with substantive regulations. Along with direct consultation with the FCC's FOB, the RMS has a "heavy-duty" advisory notice (FSD-214) for use with more difficult problems. But, again, the thrust is to bring about *voluntary resolution* of the problem by the individual in violation. The RMS may also assist local interference committees coping with a difficult case of true malicious interference or harassment.

It is important to note that an accused rule violator has certain constitutional rights in the context of any administrative proceeding involving the possible suspension or revocation of his amateur license or other sanction. These rights include a hearing, if requested, and the opportunity to cross-examine any person who has submitted evidence against him. All evidence used by the FCC in enforcement situations must be made available to the accused, including the identity of the RMS. It is thus *not* possible, to keep the identity of the RMS confidential in a proceeding where forfeiture, license revocation, or suspension is the potential result. The RMS may be called upon to testify at a hearing and must be available for cross-examination by the accused or the attorney for the accused as to the basis for the accusation and the means by which the RMS obtained that information. It is important that all RMS personnel be well schooled in the gathering, preserving and presentation of evidence to FCC for use in possible revocation hearings.

Compliance Levels

The overall objective of the Amateur Auxiliary is to bring about a satisfactory level of compliance in the Amateur Radio Service. To determine compliance trends, Amateur Auxiliary data is quantified and analyzed at ARRL HQ. This helps the Amateur Auxiliary pinpoint those areas in need of greater or less attention and also enables the Auxiliary to report the impact of the program to the FCC. This accountability will enable the Auxiliary to continually sharpen skills and maximize efforts, and thus direct energies to those areas where it will do the most good.

Expectations

The Auxiliary must avoid creating the perception that the program will cure all the ills that abound on the air. Some of these ills are clear violations, others are not; the ability to differentiate is important. The general amateur public must not think volunteer monitoring can solve all these on-the-air problems (both real and perceived). For example, certain cases of malicious interference and harassment are prevalent on repeaters in some parts of the country. These evils cannot be cured swiftly or easily. Much evidence gathering is involved: this can be a time-consuming process.

Even more difficult for many amateurs to understand is how to deal with those advocates of "free thinking"; hams who don't comply with gentlemen's agreements, and so on. These individualists delight in creating chaos. Unfortunately, such types feed on the ignorance of others and thrive on baiting the listening audience into discussions of who is going to call the monitoring station first, who had the frequency first, and so on. Often the individualists are far better versed in the rules and regulations than those who confront them on the air. Too often this leads to frustration manifested by catcalls, whistles, carriers and general chaos on the frequency—exactly the desired effect. This continues to fan the flames, and can lead to the situation where the true violations are now being perpetrated by the hams in the audience. To expect the Auxiliary to solve such problems is not realistic. The Auxiliary should avoid becoming embroiled in such controversy.

Technical Standards

With different technical backgrounds amongst the participants in the Amateur Auxiliary, this book cannot begin to try to present a comprehensive technical base. There are many technical publications already in existence that can do this. But the level of technical expertise exhibited by the amateur community is well known, and will no doubt be tapped in staffing the Amateur Auxiliary. Here, we'll mention some of the areas that perhaps deserve greater attention, offer a few precautions and list some references that may serve two purposes: (1) benefit the OO in acquiring and improving technical knowledge of the specifics involved in volunteer monitoring; and (2) help the OO to effectively respond to those who receive OO Advisory Notices and seek advice and authoritative literature.

What to Watch for and Some Precautions

The OO program is intended to note discrepancies and call them to the attention of those who very often are unaware of the discrepancy or who do not realize that what they are doing is potentially in violation. For example, it is quite common for an amateur to be unaware of a harmonic or spurious signal outside the amateur bands strong enough to be heard in distant places. Novice licensees are especially prone to this discrepancy, so it is appropriate to listen on second and third harmonic multiples of the Novice bands. It is often surprising how many signals can be heard, and usually Novices are most grateful to be notified. Higher-grade licensees, especially those running increased power, are also far from immune to excessive harmonic radiation.

Often the operator of a station with key clicks and chirp on his CW signals is unaware they exist. Broad signals, with by-products of splatter and distortion, are frequent on the phone bands, while FM signals are prone to overdeviation. These are all technical difficulties that can be watched for and are subject to notification. The recipient will almost always appreciate the notification.

Key clicks and phone splatter can also result when a receiver is overloaded by extremely strong signals, however, especially those radiated locally. Be careful to make sure you are not sending a notice to someone merely because his signal is strong, causing clicks or splatter at your location which would not be noticeable at a distance. Even with one-hop skip, a signal can be strong enough to overload some receivers. Sometimes a local condition can make a signal sound as though it is ac-modulated. Occasionally, strange mixing effects caused by strong local signals can cause "birdies" where no signal actually exists. Images are also frequently present in receivers without proper shielding or isolation between stages; these effects are also more pronounced with strong local signals. Improperly shielded IF stages can cause a receiver to produce what sounds like commercial operation in the amateur bands. Whenever you hear a signal where it shouldn't be, always consider that it could possibly be your equipment. Check it out carefully, and don't send the OO advisory card until you are sure you're right.

References

The OO candidate must be familiar with the following references from the *ARRL Handbook*. References pertain to the 1989 edition, but other recent editions are also applicable:

Code Transmission: 19-2 through 19-9
Single-Sideband Transmission: 18-1 through 18-17
Frequency Modulation and Repeaters: 18-18 through 18-25
Digital Communications: 19-9 through 19-49

Newer editions of the *ARRL Handbook* feature a chapter devoted exclusively to monitoring and direction finding. This chapter is a substantial asset to Amateur Auxiliary activities, and, in fact, was written with the Amateur Auxiliary program in mind.

OFFICIAL OBSERVER ADVISORY NOTICE

Radio: ____________________, your call was heard calling/working ______________ at ______________ UTC.

Date: __________ 198 __ Frequency ______________ kHz. Mode ________. Your RST ________.

The following is noted in the interest of maintaining Amateur Radio's reputation for good operating/technical practices: 1☐ FREQUENCY INSTABILITY 2☐ CHIRP 3☐ SPURIOUS 4☐ HARMONIC 5☐ HUM 6☐ KEY CLICKS 7☐ BROAD SIGNAL 8☐ DISTORTED AUDIO 9☐ OVER DEVIATION 10☐ OUT OF BAND 11☐ IMPROPER ID 12☐ LANGUAGE 13☐ CAUSING INTERFERENCE 15☐ CARRIER 20☐ OTHER

Remarks: ____

____

____

Please refer to FCC Regulation ______________. Please take a few minutes to determine what equipment factors or operating practices might have contributed to this apparent departure from the rule or the good amateur practice standard. The intent of this notice is to alert you to the above noted operating condition. NO REPLY IS NECESSARY. The undersigned ARRL Official Observer has fulfilled this helping role by simply alerting you, and is not *required* to reply to any correspondence. Thank you for your attention and any cooperative efforts to enhance the high standards of the Amateur Radio Service which we all share with pride.

FSD-213(685) Signature ______________________ Call ______________

From (print) ______________________

____

____

To:

____

____

____

The Official Observer program is sponsored by **the American Radio Relay** League, 225 Main **Street, Newington, CT 06111,** U.S.A., to help **amateurs help each other.** For over 50 years, **this volunteer program has aided** thousands of **amateurs to maintain their** transmitting equipment **and operating procedures** in compliance **with the regulations. The OO** program is a function **of the Amateur Auxiliary** of the FCC's Field **Operations** Bureau **in accordance** with Public **Law 97-259. High standards** of operation **benefit** the entire **amateur** community. Your **continued cooperation is** appreciated.

Fig 1—Official Observer Advisory Notice.

Official Observer Advisory Notice

The primary notification tool of the OO is the Official Observer Advisory Notice, form FSD-213. See Fig 1. This card is used to notify stations of operating discrepancies. A space is provided for reference to the appropriate FCC regulation. The OO should research the regulation in question to be sure it applies.

Official Observers should avoid sending a notice to someone interfering with them or a net or repeater they are operating on. This is not generally good for relations with the amateurs the program is trying to serve. Even when an interfering station has key clicks or chirps or is splattering badly, it is best not to take the chance of giving the impression that the notice arises from your personal interest. (On the other hand, there is no harm in asking another Observer to take an independent look if you continue to observe the clicks or chirp.) *Make your advisories strictly the result of detached objective monitoring where you are not otherwise personally involved.*

Avoid any hint of enforcement. Before amateurs can be receptive to your help, you must have a clear understanding of your role as one who offers technical and operational *advice*. You can go a long way to fostering the kind of rapport necessary to bring about behavioral change (a) if you understand your proper role; and (b) if your entire demeanor and manner of conducting OO business is beyond reproach, totally objective and delivered in the spirit of assistance. Remember: You are not an enforcer; you are an advisor and helper.

Project a friendly spirit on your advisory notices. Your objective is to bring about compliance with the regulations by friendly persuasion. Write a message in the remarks section to detail the infraction in an objective, friendly manner. Add a personal note to soften the blow of the OO advisory. Words like: "I hope this report will be of help to you. 73" can go a long way to bring about good results.

What to do With a Difficult Case?

The Official Observer is usually involved with maintenance monitoring, ie scanning the bands to assist in *maintaining* the high reputation of self-regulation that the Amateur Service has earned. Occasionally, the OO will encounter the somewhat more controversial or unprofessional side of amateur operations, such as obscenity, indecency, profanity, false signals or willful or malicious interference. A great deal of tact must be used when you send notices for these discrepancies. In fact, the wisdom of sending notices for isolated instances is open to question at times. An alternative may be to simply document the incident and if there is no recurrence over a reasonable period, then forget it. Consider it a momentary aberration.

If such a case develops into a full-fledged prolonged case of amateur-to-amateur interference or other substantive violation, then it can become a case beyond the scope of the individual OO. If this is an HF case, like interference caused to or by nets, then the Official Observer would almost certainly refer such difficult cases to a higher level of response by the Amateur Auxiliary. Consultation with the section OO Coordinator is then in order and, at the discretion of the Coordinator, the Amateur Auxiliary Regional Monitoring Station may be contacted.

Under no circumstances should the OO initiate direct contact with the FCC monitoring station. Decision to make such contact is made at a higher level. Only the most extreme cases will be brought to the attention of the Field Operations Bureau, and then only under the professional guidance of the FCC personnel in strict accordance with the established referral policy of the Auxiliary.

Petty cases of interference should be solved by amateurs and not referred to the FCC. Historically, FCC prosecution of just a few such hard-core cases has had a marked positive effect on the behavior of those who might deliberately abuse our privileges. Short of FCC involvement, the RMS can advise the offender with a "heavy-duty" advisory notice; this should be used by the RMS before any FCC referral is made.

Definitions of Interference

The malicious interference problem can be viewed from the standpoint of the frequency involved. The high-frequency bands are long-haul communication frequencies where interference will likely be originating from many miles away. This is the problem which has in the past affected ECARS, MIDCARS and WESCARS, international emergency traffic handling, interference to other nets and other types of activities associated with HF. Here, long-range detection systems must be employed.

Interference on the VHF and UHF bands is usually related to repeater operation. Because repeaters operate on fixed frequencies, they are easy to disrupt. This presents a temptation to the type of person who commits malicious interference. The interference problem can be discussed from the viewpoint of the severity and type of interference involved. While term "malicious interference" is freely used, this is only one of the different types of amateur-to-amateur interference that can occur. There are four in all.

Inadvertent Interference: The first is one we have probably all been guilty of at one time or another. Because of inattention, heedlessness, negligence or some other reason, the offender is unaware that he is creating interference. He may not be able to hear the station he is interfering with, or as happens with repeaters, a station may simultaneously key up more than one repeater. This is a very common occurrence in large metropolitan areas. Also, the inadvertent or unintentional offender may be a new amateur who has not yet been indoctrinated in good amateur operating procedures.

In any case, inadvertent or unintentional interference does not represent a major problem to the Amateur Radio Service. Education seems to be the best solution.

Careless Interference: The second type of amateur-to-amateur interference is careless interference. By this we mean not premeditated or recurring. While this type of interference falls into the deliberate category, it is usually short-lived and caused by temporary eruptions of temper. A person might become a bit hot under the collar and tell someone off or refuse to relinquish a frequency when it seems the proper thing to do. When this person cools off and thinks about his actions, he is likely to be a bit ashamed of himself. The type of person committing this interference does not intend to repeat it. Although the occurrence is unfortunate and serious FCC enforcement actions might take place, the Amateur Radio Service in general will not experience repeated interference from this individual.

Harassment: The third type of interference is classified as harassment. Here we begin to deal with the more serious aspects of interference. Here, also, the Auxiliary begins to show more interest. This person is likely to do anything short of destroying life and property to make life miserable for his victims. Harassment is usually a never-ending program. It ranges all the way from the kerchunker on a repeater to the jammer who uses foul language or any other means he can think of to disrupt operations on the air.

Malicious Interference: Although we have spoken freely of malicious interference, only the fourth and last category of interference is the truly malicious type. The malicious interference offender intends to damage people or things. The offender actively follows victims as they change frequency in attempts to get away from the interference.

Local Interference Committees

Interference problems generated on VHF or UHF repeaters are primarily local problems requiring local resolution. The Amateur Auxiliary mechanism for dealing with any local amateur-to-amateur interference is the Local Interference Committee (LIC).

The Local Interference Committee is within the purview of the Section Manager's overall Amateur Auxiliary program. The Local Interference Committee gains official standing through the Section Manager. It is, in effect, a "group appointment" of the Section Manager, with specific authorization to deal with local problems of amateur-to-amateur interference.

The prospective Committee makes a brief written proposal to the Section Manager outlining the nature of the Committee structure. This proposal should include the following key elements:

1) Statement of purpose and reference to participation in the Amateur Auxiliary.
2) Area of jurisdiction or specific task, including a statement of impartiality.
3) Any appropriate operating instructions.
4) How long committee plans to operate.
5) Name of the Members of the Committee, with a designated Chairman.
6) Space for the Committee Chairman's signature.
7) Space for Section Manager's signature of authorization.
8) Space for FCC field facility supervisor's signature (this is optional).

The FCC sign-off (an option) constitutes a "local FCC-ARRL agreement." With FCC agreement, Local Interference Committees may work directly with the appropriate FCC field facility under the terms of that agreement. However, the initial contact on a particular problem must first be conducted with the knowledge and consent of the OO Coordinator. FCC has indicated a strong desire to initiate agreements with Local Interference Committees as an effective means of dealing with VHF repeater discrepancies. The Local Interference Committee may also call upon the assistance of the Regional Monitoring Station through the OO Coordinator.

As a participant in the overall Amateur Auxiliary response, the Chairman of the LIC should be aware of the policies described in this chapter. The chairman is subject to the same certification/examination procedure as an OO; he must demonstrate familiarity with the contents of this book and other training materials. The Chairman is in turn responsible for ensuring that each member of the Committee has the appropriate level of knowledge and understanding.

An OO may be asked to participate as a member of the Committee; this does not necessarily imply any special standing. OOs should be especially attentive to definitions, recognize the different types of interference, and most importantly know when the problem cannot be handled by an individual. Part of being a good OO is knowing when you have to call on other volunteer amateurs for help. The Amateur Auxiliary concept is a team effort.

The Make-Up of the Committee

LIC members should be amateurs with experience in the installation and operation of repeater systems. Amateurs with VHF and/or UHF direction-finding equipment and experience are also very helpful. Members of the committee should preferably be selected by an area council of radio clubs, if such an organization exists, or by the clubs particularly interested in VHF, UHF and repeater operations if there is no council. The organization of the committee would be determined by the council, clubs, or committee members. The prime criterion for membership is that the members of the committee must be respected and accepted by the general amateur community in the area.

Whenever possible, at least one attorney, preferably an Amateur Radio operator, experienced with criminal trial practice and rules of evidence, should be a member of or available to the committee. The chairman is the only member who should contact the local or area FCC field office.

General Procedures—LICs

Complaints of deliberate interference are received and investigated by the committee. The investigation might include preparation of audio-tape recordings of the interfering or objectionable transmissions, oscilloscope photos and other recordings showing the switching characteristics of the carrier, and results of direction-finding investigations. Wherever possible, all material should be sufficiently detailed and complete so it can be used in further investigations by the FCC field engineers, in formal hearings held by the FCC, or in any court action conducted by law enforcement agencies and offices.

Some FCC field offices find such recordings helpful; some do not use them at all. Clearly, you should direct your activities toward what is most useful to your local or area FCC field office.

The chairman of your committee should report informally to the FCC field office on the status of all active investigations being conducted by the committee. All materials obtained by the committee during its investigation should be made available to the Commission if this is requested. The FCC may also seek the assistance of the committee when appropriate.

If such committees are to be effective, their investigations, as well as those of the FCC, must be *confidential*. The committees must be willing and able to *resist demands* for action from amateurs who are not familiar with what is being done.

Specific Procedures—LICs

Documentation. An objective of the local interference committee is to provide total documentation of a case of interference. This documentation may include tape recordings of the interference (if appropriate), direction-finding bearings, times, frequencies, dates and other pertinent data. One useful method of providing this information is to use a portable tape recorder, not only to record the interference, but to add the above information on the tape as progress is made toward finding the source of the interference. This information may have to be transcribed into written form if your local or area FCC office prefers written documentation.

Direction Finding. Information on direction-finding techniques can be found in the *ARRL Handbook*. Once you find a technique that works for you, perfection of that technique requires lots of practice. In short, you must get to know your equipment. Fashion your equipment based on other successful direction finders and then use it as often as possible. DF your friends, people holding normal QSOs and other signal sources. Don't be afraid to try something new or to develop a new idea.

Communications. When more than one station is DFing a source of interference, there must be communication between the DFing stations. For interference occurring on two meters, the following table lists different forms of communication in the order of security:

1) Telephone.
2) Non 2-meter simplex.
3) Non 2-meter repeater.
4) 2-meter simplex.
5) 2-meter repeater.
6) The channel being interfered with.

Confrontation. Let's assume that you successfully DF the source of the interference. What next? It is difficult to make a specific recommendation, because what works in one instance may not work in another.

In some cases, confrontation will solve the problem. Once the person causing the interference loses his anonymity, he will often stop jamming. If you are going after a person who is known to be violent, however, it would not be wise to knock on his door to discuss the problem with him.

A milder form of confrontation is to write the jammer a letter. This avoids a direct confrontation and the threat of violence that can take place at a face-to-face meeting. The letter should deal strictly with the facts, stating dates, times, content of the interfering transmission and other pertinent data. It should clearly state that you know the source of the interference but should not make any specific accusations. It is best if an attorney-member of the committee can write this letter.

The FCC. Suppose you have been unsuccessful in terminating the interference. Your next recourse is to go to the local or regional FCC field office for assistance. Have an objective, detailed and airtight case. Only the chairman or designated spokesman of the interference committee should contact the FCC, and any and all evidence accumulated by the committee should be turned over to the Commission. This evidence, whether in the form of tapes or written notes, should be neat and orderly. The FCC engineer handling the case is apt to give it more complete attention if the information at his disposal is easy to read and utilize.

Follow-Up. Even if the FCC launches an immediate investigation of the case, results may be slow in coming. In the meantime, you should not wait around for the FCC to solve the problem. You should continue to document the case! Documentation of repeated occurrences of the interference will go a long way toward proving maliciousness and intent. Intent is very hard to establish, but one way of doing so is to document repeated interference of a malicious nature by one individual. This documentation should, in turn, be handed over to the FCC. The FCC is far more likely to aggressively pursue the case if it is aware that the interference is still going on.

Functions and Referral Procedure

The guiding principles that accompany bringing a matter to the FCC's attention are: (1) All other avenues of Amateur Auxiliary response have been exhausted; (2) the matter is being referred to the FCC's attention with the full expectation that the matter is so serious that the FCC will take action; (3) the Amateur Auxiliary will continue to provide the FCC with documentation and cooperate with the FCC until resolution; and (4) the referral procedure calls for "in house" checks—prior to calling in the FCC—to confirm that the referral is indeed warranted.

Here is a word-and-graphic breakdown (Figs 2 through 5) of the functions of each tier of the Amateur Auxiliary and the necessary safeguard hurdles that must be negotiated prior to referral to the next highest rung on the ladder.

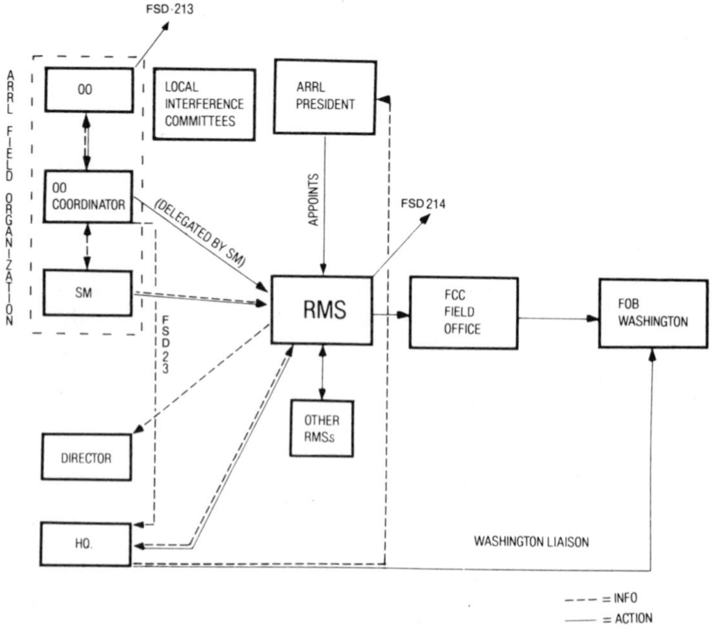

Fig 2—Amateur Auxiliary organizational chart: Referral of HF discrepancies.

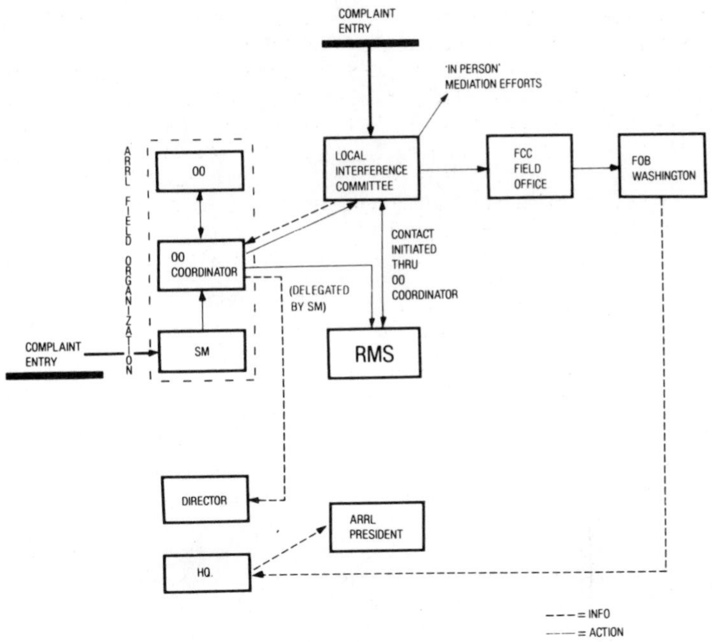

Fig 3—Amateur Auxiliary organizational chart: Referral of VHF discrepancies.

Official Observer:

1) Identifies technical and operating discrepancies.
2) Sends OO advisory notices.
3) May function as a member of a Local Interference Committee (with no special standing).
4) Reports to the OO Coordinator.
5) Refers problem cases to the OO Coordinator.
6) Collects evidence under the supervision of the OO Coordinator and/or Regional Monitoring Station (if such has been assigned to the problem).

Local Interference Committee:

1) Identifies technical and operating discrepancies, especially on VHF/UHF (eg repeaters).
2) Utilizes "in person" mediation/resolution efforts.
3) Reports to the OO Coordinator.
4) Requests RMS assistance via the OO Coordinator.
5) *In the presence of a local signed agreement* with the local FCC Engineer-in-charge or FCC monitoring station (approved by the Section Manager), may initiate contact with the appropriate FCC official upon advice from the OO Coordinator and notification of the affected ARRL Director.
6) Does field work and evidence collection as directed by FCC in accordance with the terms of the local agreement.

OO Coordinator:

1) Reports to the Section Manager.
2) Receives reports from the OOs and Local Interference Committees.

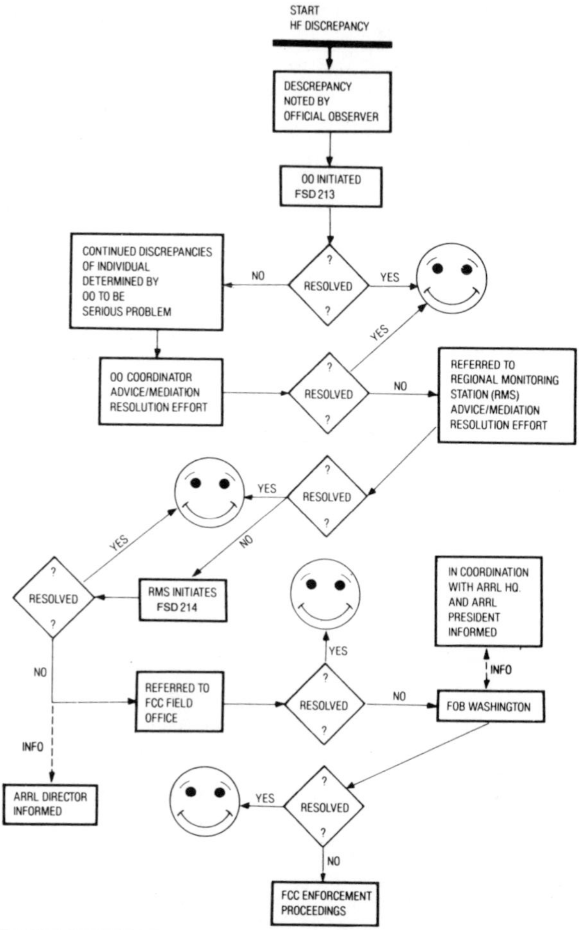

Fig 4—Typical HF complaint flowchart.

3) Forwards record/reports (FSD-23) to Headquarters.

4) Appoints OOs (when so delegated by the SM).

5) Makes referrals to the Regional Monitoring Station.

6) Assists Local Interference Committees in evidence gathering (where appropriate).

7) Assists OOs in evidence gathering under the supervision of the RMS.

8) Ensures that any FCC referrals by the Local Interference Committees are done under his consent and notification of the affected ARRL Director.

9) Contacts ARRL HQ for advise on assistance in technical or administrative matters.

Regional Monitoring Station:

1) Assists the OO as referred by the OO Coordinator (initiates FSD-214, Advisory Notice of Radio Station Conditions, as appropriate).

2) Assists the Local Interference Committee as referred by the OO Coordinator.

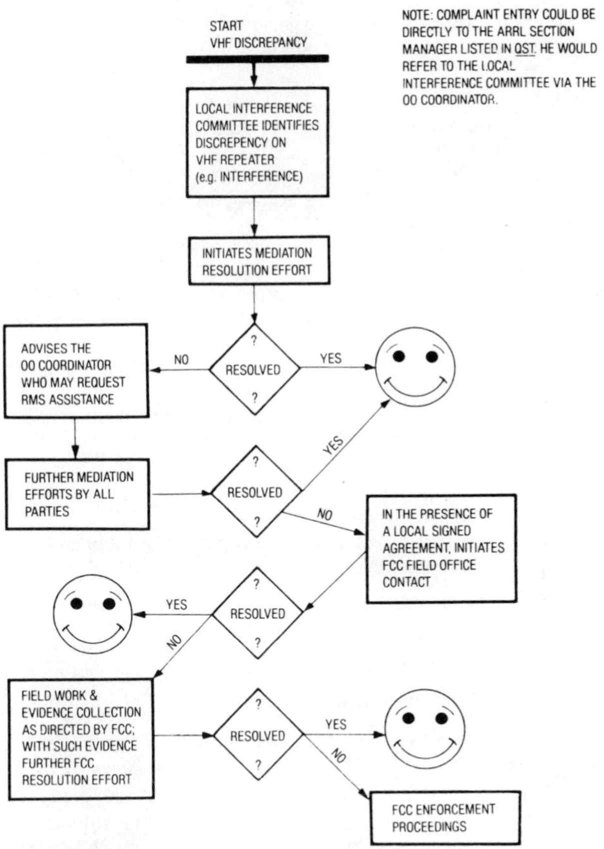

Fig 5—Typical VHF repeater complaint flowchart.

3) Supervises OO Coordinators and assists Local Interference Committees in monitoring/evidence collection procedures.

4) Is the decision maker on making referral to FCC after appropriate notification of the affected Division Director, primarily for HF discrepancies.

5) Acts as a facilitator between Headquarters and the local FCC office in making Headquarters referrals to the Field Operations Bureau in Washington.

6) Supplies activity reports to Headquarters on a timely basis.

Section Manager:

1) Oversees the activities of the OO Coordinator.

2) Is the contact point for FCC-initiated inquiries.

3) Ensures that the affected Division Director is kept informed of FCC referred cases.

4) Appoints OO Coordinator and OOs (may be delegated to Coordinator) upon notification by Headquarters of certification.

5) Authorizes (in writing) Local Interference Committees.

Division Director:

1) Is kept informed of hard-core cases under FCC review.

2) Offers mediation advice to the Amateur Auxiliary where appropriate.

Headquarters:

1) Provides all support materials (forms, newsletters, postage, etc.) for conducting the Amateur Auxiliary.

2) Upon recommendation for appointment of an OO by the Section Manager (or delegated OO Coordinator) provides training materials and certifies to the SM successful completion of training.

3) Maintains a data base of records in accordance with provisions of this Guide.

4) Conducts critical review of the program in concert with the Field Operations Bureau in Washington and implements appropriate enhancement in accordance with Board policy.

5) Refers difficult cases from the RMS to the Field Operations Bureau in Washington where appropriate.

6) Advises the ARRL President of difficult cases being referred to the Field Operations Bureau, Washington.

ARRL President:

1) Appoints Regional Monitoring Stations.

2) Is advised by Headquarters of hard-core cases brought to the attention of the Field Operations Bureau in Washington.

Evidence Gathering

As an OO or RMS, you must conduct monitoring activities and assemble information in such a way that it is (1) useful evidence in cases of repeated or intentional rule violations, in which it may be used later in license suspension or revocation hearings, and (2) available should you have to protect yourself against a defamation (libel or slander) action. Although both of these situations will be rare, it is difficult to predict, in any given situation, what the outcome of an Auxiliary report will be. You must prepare each OO report as though you will be called on to testify at an FCC hearing as to your actions which gave rise to the enforcement proceedings.

Prior to the enactment of the Communications Amendments Act of 1982, amateurs were unable to provide voluntary monitoring services to the government, or to disclose to third parties what was heard on the air. Now, those limitations have been removed, and the evidence gathered by volunteers can be relied on by the FCC and used directly in enforcement proceedings. It is no longer necessary for FCC staff to duplicate the monitoring and DFing done by volunteers.

To make sure the evidence is useful, and at the same time protect yourself against a lawsuit based on an accusation that you made defamatory remarks about another amateur, you must first restrict all monitoring activities to squarely fit within the statutory authority granted to the FCC by the Communications Amendments Act of 1982. These are as follows:

(I) The detection of improper Amateur Radio transmissions;

(II) The conveyance to Commission personnel of information which is essential to the enforcement of the Communications Act or regulations prescribed by the FCC, relating to the Amateur Radio Service; and

(III) The issuance of advisory notices to persons who apparently have violated any provision of the Act or regulations prescribed by the FCC relating to the Amateur Radio Service.

Agreement Between
The Federal Communications Commission
Field Operations Bureau
and
The American Radio Relay League, Inc.
with respect to amateur volunteers

1. The Field Operations Bureau (FOB) of the Federal Communications Commission (FCC) and the American Radio Relay League, Inc. (ARRL) agree to cooperate in a joint effort to improve rules compliance in the Amateur Radio Service, as provided for in Public Law 97.259 (The Communications Amendments Act of 1982).

The objectives of this program are to foster a wider knowledge of and better compliance with laws, rules and regulations governing the Amateur Radio Service, to extend the concepts of self-regulation and self-administration of the Service, while enabling the Field Operations Bureau to efficiently and effectively use its manpower and services.

The FOB has entered into this agreement with the ARRL to avail itself of the services of the League's Field Organization. FOB may elect to enter into other agreements.

Regional Monitoring Stations, or other members of the ARRL Field Organization, as directed by ARRL procedures in each case, are the focal points for liaison and the primary communications channel between organized amateurs and the FOB field facilities. This program, the foundation of which will be the ARRL Official Observers, will be known as the Amateur Auxiliary to the Field Operations Bureau. FOB's Regional Directors are responsible for the overview and the direction of the Amateur Auxiliary program in their regions, in conjunction with designated ARRL field officials, and will jointly review local policies, practices and procedures, and work together, looking to achieve solutions to problems and regional consistency in accordance with FOB's manual for the Amateur Auxiliary which contains basic overall guidance.

2. Under this specific Amateur Auxiliary agreement, FCC personnel and amateur volunteers may interact to perform the following functions:

a. maintenance monitoring of the Amateur Radio Service frequencies

b. fostering wider knowledge of the rules

c. responding to complaints/allegations and developing procedures which emphasize cooperative "no fault" solutions, and if and when impasses occur, aid and encourage development of solutions through independent mediation

d. signal identification/source location in support of FOB field facilities

e. courtesy Amateur Radio station evaluation (this function can only be activated upon specific approval of an FOB Regional Director)

f. FOB enforcement support (this function can only be activated upon specific approval of an FOB Regional Director)

g. other specific projects as appropriate (information collection, support during emergency operations and so forth).

3. In order for the provisions of paragraph two (2) of this Agreement to be applied in a location where the need is identified by the parties, the FCC field facility supervisor and the designated ARRL Field Organization official may agree to implement any of the functions of the Amateur Auxiliary as outlined above, provided approval for national implementation of that function has been granted and appropriate training material has been prepared, and the appropriate ARRL official has authorized such action as to the specific case under consideration.

4. All prospective members of the Amateur Auxiliary will be required to undergo a training and certification procedure administered by ARRL, and successful completion of such training/certification will be required for enrollment.

5. The above outlined cooperative program is hereby agreed to by the signatories and is in force as of the date indicated below. This agreement may be amended by mutual agreement of both parties and will remain in effect until terminated. FCC/FOB and ARRL will periodically review this agreement and coordinate such revisions as may be necessary. Upon 90 days written notice, this agreement may be terminated by either party.

____________	____________	____________
Date	for FCC	for ARRL

Any activities not aimed specifically at one of these purposes exceeds the statutory authority of the monitor and may result in having evidence gathered under such circumstances ruled inadmissible as having been provided by an "incompetent" witness. That is to say, you are able to testify only to those things you personally witnessed in connection with detecting improper amateur transmissions, conveying information essential to enforcement or in preparing and issuing advisory notices to amateurs.

For a comprehensive set of guidelines for gathering evidence, contact The Amateur Auxiliary Coordinator at ARRL HQ.

PART 97—AMATEUR RADIO SERVICE

97.309 RTTY and data emission codes.
97.311 SS emission types.
97.313 Transmitter power standards.
97.315 Type acceptance of external RF power amplifiers.
97.317 Standards for type acceptance of external RF power amplifiers.

Subpart E—Providing Emergency Communications

97.401 Operation during a disaster.
97.403 Safety of life and protection of property.
97.405 Station in distress.
97.407 Radio amateur civil emergency service.

Subpart F—Qualifying Examination Systems

97.501 Qualifying for an amateur operator license.
97.503 Element standards.
97.505 Element credit.
97.507 Preparing an examination.
97.509 Administering an examination.
97.511 Technician, General, Advanced, and Amateur Extra Class operator license examination.
97.513 Novice Class operator license examination.
97.515 Volunteer examiner requirements.
97.517 Volunteer examiner conduct.
97.519 Coordinating examination sessions.
97.521 VEC qualifications.
97.523 Question pools.
97.525 Accrediting VEs.
97.527 Reimbursement for expenses.

Appendix 1 Places where the amateur service is regulated by the FCC.

Appendix 2 VEC Regions.

Subpart A—General Provisions

§97.1 Basis and purpose.

The rules and regulations in this Part are designed to provide an amateur radio service having a fundamental purpose as expressed in the following principles:

(a) Recognition and enhancement of the value of the amateur service to the public as a voluntary noncommercial communication service, particularly with respect to providing emergency communications.

(b) Continuation and extension of the amateur's proven ability to contribute to the advancement of the radio art.

(c) Encouragement and improvement of the amateur service through rules which provide for advancing skills in both the communication and technical phases of the art.

(d) Expansion of the existing reservoir within the amateur radio service of trained operators, technicians, and electronics experts.

(e) Continuation and extension of the amateur's unique ability to enhance international goodwill.

§97.3 Definitions.

(a) The definitions of terms used in Part 97 are:

(1) *Amateur operator*. A person holding a written authorization to be the control operator of an amateur station.

(2) *Amateur radio services*. The amateur service, the amateur-satellite service and the radio amateur civil emergency service.

(3) *Amateur — satellite service*. A radiocommunication service using stations on Earth satellites for the same purpose as those of the amateur service.

(4) *Amateur service*. A radiocommunication service for the purpose of self-training, intercommunication and technical investigations carried out by amateurs, that is, duly authorized persons interested in radio technique solely with a personal aim and without pecuniary interest.

(5) *Amateur station*. A station in an amateur radio service consisting of the apparatus necessary for carrying on radiocommunications.

(6) *Automatic control*. The use of devices and procedures for control of a station when it is transmitting so that compliance with the FCC Rules is achieved without the control operator being present at a control point.

(7) *Auxiliary station*. An amateur station transmitting communications point-to-point within a system of cooperating amateur stations.

(8) *Bandwidth*. The width of a frequency band outside of which the mean power of the total emission is attenuated at least 26 dB below the mean power of the total emission, including allowances for transmitter drift or Doppler shift.

(9) *Beacon*. An amateur station transmitting communications for the purposes of observation of propagation and reception or other related experimental activities.

(10) *Broadcasting*. Transmissions intended for reception by the general public, either direct or relayed.

(11) *Control operator*. An amateur operator designated by the licensee of a station to be responsible for the transmissions from that station to assure compliance with the FCC Rules.

(12) *Control point*. The location at which the control operator function is performed.

(13) *CSCE*. Certificate of successful completion of an examination.

(14) *Earth station*. An amateur station located on, or within 50 km of, the Earth's surface intended for communications with space stations or with other Earth stations by means of one or more other objects in space.

(15) *EIC*. Engineer in Charge of an FCC Field Facility.

(16) *External RF power amplifier*. A device capable of increasing power output when used in conjunction with, but not an integral part of, a transmitter.

(17) *External RF power amplifier kit*. A number of electronic parts, which, when assembled, is an external RF power amplifier, even if additional parts are required to complete assembly.

(18) *FAA*. Federal Aviation Administration.

(19) *FCC*. Federal Communications Commission.

(20) *Frequency coordinator*. An entity, recognized in a local or regional area by amateur operators whose stations are eligible to be auxiliary or repeater stations, that recommends transmit/receive channels and associated operating and technical parameters for such stations in order to avoid or minimize potential interference.

(21) *Harmful interference*. Interference which endangers the functioning of a radionavigation service or of other safety services or seriously degrades, obstructs or repeatedly interrupts a radiocommunication service operating in accordance with the Radio Regulations.

(22) *Indicator*. Words, letters or numerals appended to and separated from the call sign during the station identification.

(23) *Information bulletin*. A message directed only to amateur operators consisting solely of subject matter of direct interest to the amateur service.

(24) *International Morse code*. A dot-dash code as defined in International Telegraph and Telephone Consultative Committee (CCITT) Recommendation F.1 (1984), Division B, I. Morse code.

(25) *ITU*. International Telecommunication Union.

(26) *Line A*. Begins at Aberdeen, WA, running by great circle arc to the intersection of 48°N, 120°W, thence along parallel 48°N, to the intersection of 95°W, thence by great circle arc through the southernmost point of Duluth, MN, thence by great circle arc to 45°N, 85°W, thence southward along meridian 85°W, to its intersection with parallel 41°N, thence along parallel 41°N, to its intersection with meridian 82°W, thence by great circle arc through the southernmost point of Bangor, ME, thence by great circle arc through the southernmost point of Searsport, ME, at which point it terminates.

(27) *Local control*. The use of a control operator who directly manipulates the operating adjustments in the station to achieve compliance with the FCC Rules.

(28) *National Radio Quiet Zone*. The area in Maryland, Virginia and West Virginia Bounded by 39° 15′N on the north, 78° 30′W on the east, 37° 30′N on the south and 80° 30′W on the west.

(29) *Physician*. For the purposes of this Part, a person who is licensed to practice in a place where the amateur service is regulated by the FCC, as either a Doctor of Medicine (MD) or a Doctor of Osteopathy (DO).

(30) *Question pool*. All current examination questions for a designated written examination element.

(31) *Question set*. A series of examination questions on a given examination selected from the question pool.

(32) *Radio Regulations*. The latest ITU *Radio Regulations* to which the United States is a party.

(33) *RACES* (radio amateur civil emergency service). A radio service using amateur stations for civil defense communications during periods of local, regional or national civil emergencies.

(34) *Remote control*. The use of a control operator who indirectly manipulates the operating adjustments in the station through a control link to achieve compliance with the FCC Rules.

(35) *Repeater*. An amateur station that automatically retransmits the signals of other stations.

(36) *Space station*. An amateur station located more than 50 km above the Earth's surface.

(37) *Spurious emission*. An emission, on frequencies outside the necessary bandwidth of a transmission, the level of which may be reduced without affecting the information being transmitted.

(38) *Telecommand station*. An amateur station that transmits communications to initiate, modify or terminate functions of a space station.

(39) *Third party communications*. A message from the control operator (first party) of an amateur station to another amateur station control operator (second party) on behalf of another person (third party).

(40) *VE*. Volunteer examiner.

(41) *VEC*. Volunteer-examiner coordinator.

(b) The definitions of technical symbols used in this Part are:

(1) *EHF* (extremely high frequency). The frequency range 30-300 GHz.

(2) *HF* (high frequency). The frequency range 3-30 MHz.

(3) *Hz*. Hertz.

(4) *m*. Meters

(5) *MF* (medium frequency). The frequency range 300-3000 kHz.

(6) *PEP* (peak envelope power). The average power supplied to the antenna transmission line by a transmitter during one RF cycle at the crest of the modulation envelope taken under normal operating conditions.

(7) *RF*. Radio frequency.

(8) *SHF* (super-high frequency). The frequency range 3-30 GHz.

(9) *UHF* (ultra-high frequency). The frequency range 300-3000 MHz.

(10) *VHF* (very-high frequency). The frequency range 30-300 MHz.

(11) *W*. Watts.

(c) The following terms are used in this Part to indicate emission types. Refer to §2.201 of the FCC Rules, *Emission, modulation and transmission characteristics*, for information on emission type designators.

(1) *CW*. International Morse code telegraphy emissions having designators with A, C, H, J or R as the first symbol; 1 as the second symbol; A or B as the third symbol; and emissions J2A and J2B.

(2) *Data*. Telemetry, telecommand and computer communications emissions having designators with A, C, D, F, G, H, J or R as the first symbol; 1 as the second symbol; D as the third symbol; and emission J2D. Only a digital code of a type specifically authorized in this Part may be transmitted.

(3) *Image*. Facsimile and television emissions having designators with A, C, D, F, G, H, J or R as the first symbol; 1, 2 or 3 as the second symbol; C or F as the third symbol; and emissions having B as the first symbol; 7, 8 or 9 as the second symbol; W as the third symbol.

(4) *MCW*. Tone-modulated international Morse code telegraphy emissions having designators with A, C, D, F, G, H or R as the first symbol; 2 as the second symbol; A or B as the third symbol.

(5) *Phone*. Speech and other sound emissions having designators with A, C, D, F, G, H, J or R as the first symbol; 1, 2 or 3 as the second symbol; E as the third symbol. Also speech emissions having B as the first symbol; 7, 8 or 9 as the second symbol; E as the third symbol. MCW for the purpose of performing the station identification procedure, or for providing telegraphy practice interspersed with speech. Incidental tones for the purpose of selective calling or alerting or to control the level of a demodulated signal may also be considered phone.

(6) *Pulse*. Emissions having designators with K, L, M, P, Q, V or W as the first symbol; 0, 1, 2, 3, 7, 8, 9 or X as the second symbol; A, B, C, D, E, F, N, W or X as the third symbol.

(7) *RTTY*. Narrow-band direct-printing telegraphy emissions having designators with A, C, D, F, G, H, J or R as the first symbol; 1 as the second symbol; B as the third symbol; and emission J2B. Only a digital code of a type specifically authorized in this Part may be transmitted.

(8) *SS*. Spread-spectrum emissions using bandwidth-expansion modulation emissions having designators with A, C, D, F, G, H, J or R as the first symbol; X as the second symbol; X as the third symbol. Only a SS emission of a type specifically authorized in this Part may be transmitted.

(9) *Test*. Emissions containing no information having the designators with N as the third symbol. Test does not include pulse emissions with no information or modulation unless pulse emissions are also authorized in the frequency band.

§97.5 Station license required.

(a) When a station is transmitting on any amateur service frequency from a geographic location within 50 km of the Earth's surface where the amateur service is regulated by the FCC, the person having physical control of the apparatus must hold an FCC-issued written authorization for an amateur station.

(b) When a station is transmitting on any amateur service frequency from a location within 50 km of the Earth's surface and aboard any vessel or craft that is documented or registered in the United States, the person having physical control of the apparatus must hold an FCC-issued written authorization for an amateur station.

(c) When a station is transmitting on any amateur-satellite service frequency from a location more than 50 km above the Earth's surface aboard any craft that is documented or registered in the United States, the person having physical control of the apparatus must hold an FCC-issued written authorization for an amateur station.

(d) The types of written authorizations that permit amateur station operation where the amateur service is regulated by the FCC are:

(1) An operator/primary station license (FCC Form 660) issued to the person by the FCC. A primary station license is issued only to a person, together with an operator license on the same document. Every amateur operator licensed by the FCC must have one, but only one, primary station license. Except a representative of a foreign government, any person who qualifies by examination is eligible to apply for an operator/primary station license.

(2) A club station license (FCC Form 660) issued to the person by the FCC. A club station license is issued only to the person who is the license trustee designated by an officer of the club. The trustee must hold an FCC-issued Amateur Extra, Advanced, General, or Technician operator license. The club must be composed of at least two persons and must have a name, a document of organization, management and a primary purpose devoted to amateur service activities consistent with this Part.

(3) A military recreation station license (FCC Form 660) issued to the person by the FCC. A military recreation station license is issued only to the person who is the license custodian designated by the official in charge of the United States military recreational premises where the station is situated. The custodian must not be a representative of a foreign government. The custodian need not hold an amateur operator license.

(4) A RACES station license (FCC Form 660) issued to the person by the FCC. A RACES station license is issued only to the person who is the license custodian designated by the official responsible for the governmental agency served by that civil defense organization. The custodian must not be a representative of a foreign government. The custodian must be the civil defense official responsible for coordination of all civil defense activities in the area concerned. The custodian need not hold an amateur operator license.

(5) A reciprocal permit for alien amateur licensee (FCC Form 610-AL) issued to the person by the FCC. A reciprocal permit for alien amateur licensee is issued only to a person who is a citizen of a country with which the United States has arrangements to grant reciprocal operating permits to visiting alien amateur operators. The person must be a citizen of the same country that issued the amateur service license. No person who is a citizen of the United States, regardless of any other citizenship also held, is eligible for a reciprocal permit for alien amateur licensee. No person holding an FCC-issued amateur service license will be issued a reciprocal permit for alien amateur licensee.

(6) An amateur service license issued to the person by the Government of Canada. The person must be a Canadian citizen.

(e) The written authorization for an amateur station authorizes the use in accordance with the FCC Rules of all transmitting apparatus under the physical control of the station licensee at points where the amateur service is regulated by the FCC. The original written authorization document or a photocopy thereof must be retained at the station.

§97.7 Control operator required.

When transmitting, each amateur station must have a control operator. Only a person holding one of the following documents may be the control operator of a station:

(a) An operator/primary station license (FCC Form 660) issued to the person by the FCC.

(b) A reciprocal permit for alien amateur licensee (FCC Form 610-AL) issued to the person by the FCC.

(c) An amateur service license issued to a Canadian citizen by the Government of Canada.

§97.9 Operator license.

(a) There are 5 classes of operator licenses: Novice, Technician, General, Advanced and Amateur Extra. An operator license authorizes the holder to be the control operator of a station with the privileges of the operator class specified on the license. The license document or a photocopy thereof must be in the personal possession of the licensee at all times when the person is the control operator of a station.

(b) A person holding a Novice, Technician, General, or Advanced Class operator license who has properly filed with the FCC an application for a higher operator class which has not yet been acted upon, and who holds a CSCE indicating that the person completed the necessary examinations within the previous 365 days is authorized to exercise the rights and privileges of the higher operator class.

§97.11 Stations aboard ships or aircraft.

(a) The installation and operation of an amateur station on a ship or aircraft must be approved by the master of the ship or pilot in command of the aircraft.

(b) The station must be separate from and independent of all other radio apparatus installed on the ship or aircraft, except a common antenna may be shared with a voluntary ship radio installation. The station's transmissions must not cause interference to any other apparatus installed on the ship or aircrarft.

(c) The station must not constitute a hazard to the safety of life or property. For a station aboard an aircraft, the apparatus shall not be operated while the aircraft is operating under Instrument Flight Rules, as defined by the FAA, unless the station has been found to comply with all applicable FAA Rules.

§97.13 Restrictions on station locations.

(a) Before placing an amateur station on land of environmental importance or that is significant in American history, architecture or culture, the licensee may be required to take certain actions prescribed by §§1.1301-1.1319 of the FCC Rules.

(b) A station within 1600 m (1 mile) of an FCC monitoring facility must protect that facility from harmful interference. Failure to do so could result in imposition of operating restrictions upon the amateur station by an EIC pursuant to §97.121 of this Part. Geographical coordinates of the facilities that require protection are listed in §0.121(c) of the FCC Rules.

§97.15 Station antenna structures.

(a) Unless the amateur station licensee has received prior approval from the FCC, no antenna structure, including the radiating elements, tower, supports and all appurtenances, may be higher than 61 m (200 feet) above ground level at its site.

(b) Unless the amateur station licensee has received prior approval from the FCC, no antenna structure, at an airport or heliport that is available for public use and is listed in the *Airport Directory* of the current *Airman's Information Manual* or in either the *Alaska* or *Pacific Airman's Guide and Chart Supplement*; or at an airport or heliport under construction that is the subject of a notice or proposal on file with the FAA, and except for military airports, it is clearly indicated that the airport will be available for public use; or at an airport or heliport that is operated by the armed forces of the United States; or at a place near any of these airports or heliports, may be higher than:

(1) 1 m above the airport elevation for each 100 m from the nearest runway longer than 1 km within 6.1 km of the antenna structure.

(2) 2 m above the airport elevation for each 100 m from the nearest runway shorter than 1 km within 3.1 km of the antenna structure.

(3) 4 m above the airport elevation for each 100 m from the nearest landing pad within 1.5 km of the antenna structure.

(c) An amateur station antenna structure no higher than 6.1 m (20 feet) above ground level at its site or no higher than 6.1 m above any natural object or existing manmade structure, other than an antenna structure, is exempt from the requirements of paragraphs (a) and (b) of this Section.

(d) Further details as to whether an aeronautical study and/or obstruction marking and lighting may be required, and specifications for obstruction marking and lighting, are contained in Part 17 of the FCC Rules, *Construction, Marking, and Lighting of Antenna Structures*. To request approval to place an antenna structure higher than the limits specified in paragraphs (a), (b) and (c) of this Section, the licensee must notify the FAA on FAA Form 7460-1 and the FCC on FCC Form 854.

(e) Except as otherwise provided herein, a station antenna structure may be erected at heights and dimensions sufficient to accommodate amateur service communications. [State and local regulation of a station antenna structure must not preclude amateur service communications. Rather, it must reasonably accommodate such communications and must constitute the minimum practicable regulation to accomplish the state or local authority's legitimate purpose. *See* PRB-1, 101 FCC 2d, 952 (1985) for details.]

§97.17 Application for new license.

(a) Any qualified person is eligible to apply for an amateur service license.

(b) Each application for a new operator/primary station license must be made on FCC Form 610. Each application for a reciprocal permit for alien amateur licensee must be made on FCC Form 610-A. No new license for a club, military recreation, or RACES station will be issued.

(c) Each application for a new operator/primary station license and each application involving a change in operator class must be submitted to the VEs administering the qualifying examination.

(d) Any qualified person is eligible to apply for a reciprocal permit for alien amateur licensee. The application must be submitted to the FCC, P.O. Box 1020, Gettysburg, PA 17326.

(e) No person shall obtain or attempt to obtain, or assist another person to obtain or attempt to obtain, an operator license or reciprocal permit for alien amateur licensee by fraudulent means.

(f) A call sign will be assigned systematically to each station. The FCC will issue public announcements detailing the policies and procedures of the call sign assignment system. The FCC will not grant any request for a specific call sign.

§97.19 Application for a renewed or modified license.

(a) Each application for a renewed or modified operator/primary station license must be made on FCC Form 610. Each application for a renewed or modified club, military recreation or RACES station license must be made on FCC Form 610-B. A reciprocal permit for alien amateur licensee is not renewable. A new reciprocal permit may be issued upon proper application.

(b) Each application for a renewed or modified amateur service license must be accompanied by a photocopy of the license document or the original document, unless it has been lost, mutilated or destroyed. Each application for a modified operator license involving a change in operator class must be submitted to the VEs administering the qualifying examination. All other applications must be submitted to: FCC, P.O. Box 1020, Gettysburg, PA 17326.

(c) When the licensee has submitted a timely application for renewal of an unexpired license (between 60 and 90 days prior to the end of the license term is recommended), the licensee may continue to operate until the disposition of the application has been determined. If a license expires, application for renewal may be made during a grace period of 2 years after the expiration date. During this grace period, the expired license is not valid. A license renewed during the grace period must be dated as of the date of the renewal.

§97.21 Mailing address and station location.

Each application for an amateur service license and each application for a reciprocal permit for alien amateur licensee must show a mailing address and a station location (the addresses may be the same) in an area where the amateur service is regulated by the FCC. The mailing address must be one where the licensee can receive mail delivery by the United States Postal Service. The station location must be a place where a station can be physically located. (A post office box, rural delivery service number, or general delivery is unsuitable as a station location.)

§97.23 License term.

(a) An amateur service license is normally issued for a 10-year term.

(b) A reciprocal permit for alien amateur licensee is normally issued for a 1-year term.

§97.25 FCC modification of station license.

(a) The FCC may modify a station license, either for a limited time or for the duration of the term thereof, if it determines:

(1) That such action will promote the public interest, convenience and necessity; or

(2) That such action will promote fuller compliance with the provisions of the Communications Act of 1934, as amended, or of any treaty ratified by the United States.

(b) When the FCC makes such a determination, it will issue an order of modification. The order will not become final until the licensee is notified in writing of the proposed aciton and the grounds and reasons therefor. The licensee will be given reasonable opportunity of no less than 30 days to protest the modification; except that, where safety of life or property is involved, a shorter period of notice may be provided. Any protest by a licensee of an FCC order of modification will be handled in accordance with the provisions of 47 U.S.C. §316.

§97.27 Replacement license.

Each licensee or permittee whose original document is lost, mutilated or destroyed must request a replacement. The request must be made to: FCC, P.O. Box 1020, Gettysburg, PA 17326. A statement of how the document was lost, mutilated or destroyed must be attached to the request. A replacement license must bear the same expiration date as the license that it replaces.

Subpart B—Station Operation Standards

§97.101 General standards.

(a) In all respects not specifically covered by FCC Rules each amateur station must be operated in accordance with good engineering and good amateur practice.

(b) Each station licensee and each control operator must cooperate in selecting transmitting channels and in making the most effective use of the amateur service frequencies. No frequency will be assigned for the exclusive use of any station.

(c) At all times and on all frequencies, each control operator must give priority to stations providing emergency communications, except to stations transmitting communications for training drills and tests in RACES.

(d) No amateur operator shall willfully or maliciously interfere with or cause interference to any radio communication or signal.

§97.103 Station licensee responsibilities.

(a) The station licensee is responsible for the proper operation of the station in accordance with the FCC Rules. When the control operator is a different amateur operator than the station licensee, both persons are equally responsible for proper operation of the station.

(b) The station licensee must designate the station control operator. The FCC will presume that the station licensee is also the control operator, unless documentation to the contrary is in the station records.

(c) The station licensee must make the station and the station records available for inspection upon request by an FCC representative. When deemed necessary by an EIC to assure compliance with the FCC Rules, the station licensee must maintain a record of station operations containing such items of information as the EIC may require in accord with §0.314(x) of the FCC Rules.

§97.105 Control operator duties.

(a) The control operator must ensure the immediate proper operation of the station, regardless of the type of control.

(b) A station may only be operated in the manner and to the extent permitted by the privileges authorized for the class of operator license held by the control operator.

§97.107 Alien control operator privileges.

(a) The privileges available to a control operator holding an amateur service license issued by the Government of Canada are:

(1) The terms of the *Convention Between the United States and Canada (TIAS no. 2508) Relating to the Operation by Citizens of Either Country of Certain Radio Equipment or Stations in the Other country;*

(2) The operating terms and conditions of the amateur service license issued by the Government of Canada; and

(3) The applicable provisions of the FCC Rules, but not to exceed the control operator privileges of an FCC-issued Amateur Extra Class operator license.

(b) The privileges available to a control operator holding an FCC-issued reciprocal permit for alien amateur licensee are:

(1) The terms of the agreement between the alien's government and the United States;

(2) The operating terms and conditions of the amateur service license issued by the alien's government;

(3) The applicable provisions of the FCC Rules, but not to exceed the control

operator privileges of an FCC-issued Amateur Extra Class operator license; and

(4) None, if the holder of the reciprocal permit has obtained an FCC-issued operator/primary station license.

(c) At any time the FCC may, in its discretion, modify, suspend, or cancel the amateur service privileges within or over any area where radio services are regulated by the FCC of any Canadian amateur service licensee or alien reciprocal permittee.

§97.109 Station control.

(a) Each amateur station must have at least one control point.

(b) When a station is being locally controlled, the control operator must be at the control point. Any station may be locally controlled.

(c) When a station is being remotely controlled, the control operator must be at the control point. Any station may be remotely controlled.

(d) When a station is being automatically controlled, the control operator need not be at the control point. Only stations transmitting RTTY or data emissions on the 6 m or shorter wavelength bands, and stations specifically designated elsewhere in this Part may be automatically controlled. Automatic control must cease upon notification by an EIC that the station is transmitting improperly or causing harmful interference to other stations. Automatic control must not be resumed without prior approval of the EIC.

(e) No station may be automatically controlled while transmitting third-party communications, except a station retransmitting digital packet radio communications on the 6 m and shorter wavelength bands. Such stations must be using the American Radio Relay League, Inc. *AX.25 Amateur Packet — Radio Link — Layer Protocol, Version 2.0*, October 1984 (or compatible) which is available from the American Radio Relay League, Inc., 225 Main St, Newington, CT 06111. The retransmitted messages must originate at a station that is being locally or remotely controlled.

§97.111 Authorized transmissions.

(a) An amateur station may transmit the following types of two-way communications:

(1) Transmissions necessary to exchange messages with other stations in the amateur service, except those in any country whose administration has given notice that it objects to such communications. The FCC will issue public notices of current arrangements for international communications;

(2) Transmissions necessary to exchange messages with a station in another FCC-regulated service while providing emergency communications;

(3) Transmissions necessary to exchange messages with a United States government station, necessary to providing communications in RACES; and

(4) Transmissions necessary to exchange messages with a station in a service not regulated by the FCC, but authorized by the FCC to communicate with amateur stations. An amateur station may exchange messages with a participating United States military station during an Armed Forces Day Communications Test.

(b) In addition to one-way transmissions specifically authorized elsewhere in this Part, an amateur station may transmit the following types of one-way communications:

(1) Brief transmissions necessary to make adjustments to the station;

(2) Brief transmissions necessary to establishing two-way communications with other stations;

(3) Transmissions necessary to remotely control a device from a distant location;

(4) Transmissions necessary to providing emergency communications;

(5) Transmissions necessary to assisting persons learning, or improving proficiency in, the international Morse code; and

(6) Transmissions necessary to disseminate information bulletins.

§97.113 Prohibited transmissions.

(a) No amateur station shall transmit any communication the purpose of which is to facilitate the business or commercial affairs of any party. No station shall transmit communications as an alternative to other authorized radio services, except as necessary to providing emergency communications. A station may, however, transmit communications to:

(1) Facilitate the public's safe observation of, or safe participation in, a parade, race, marathon or similar public gathering. No amateur station shall transmit communications concerning moving, supplying and quartering observers and participants for any sponsoring organization unless the principal beneficiary of such communications is the public and any benefit to the sponsoring organization is incidental.

(2) Inform other amateur operators of the availability of apparatus normally used in an amateur station, including such apparatus for sale or trade. This exception is not authorized to any person seeking to derive a profit by buying or selling such apparatus on a regular basis.

(b) No station shall transmit messages for hire or for material compensation, direct or indirect, paid or promised. The control operator of a club station, however, may accept compensation for such periods of time during which the station is transmitting telegraphy practice or information bulletins provided that:

(1) The station transmits the telegraphy practice and information bulletins for at least 40 hours per week;

(2) The station schedules operations on all amateur service MF and HF bands using reasonable measures to maximize coverage;

(3) The schedule of normal operating times and frequencies is published at least 30 days in advance of the actual transmissions; and

(4) The control operator does not accept any direct or indirect compensation for periods during which the station is transmitting any other material.

(c) No station shall transmit communications in order to engage in any form of broadcasting, nor to engage in any activity related to program production or newsgathering for broadcasting purposes. A station may, however, transmit communications to convey news information about an event for dissemination to the public when the following conditions are present:

(1) The information involves the immediate safety of life of individuals or the immediate protection of property;

(2) The information is directly related to the event;

(3) The information cannot be transmitted by any other means because normal communications systems have been disrupted or because there are no other communication systems available at the place where the information is originated; and

(4) Other means of communication could not be reasonably provided before or at the time of the event.

(d) No station shall transmit: music; radiocommunications or messages for any purpose, or in connection with any activity, that is contrary to federal, state, or local law; messages in code or ciphers where the intent is to obscure the meaning (except where specifically excepted elsewhere in this Part); obscene, indecent, or profane words, language, or meaning; and/or false or deceptive messages or signals.

(e) No station shall retransmit programs or signals emanating from any type of radio station other than an amateur station, except communications originating on United States Government frequencies between a space shuttle and its associated Earth stations. Prior approval for such retransmissions must be obtained from the National Aeronautics and Space Administration. Such retransmissions must be for the exclusive use of amateur operators.

(f) No amateur station, except an auxiliary, repeater or space station, may automatically retransmit the radio signals of other amateur stations.

§97.115 Third party communications.

(a) An amateur station may transmit messages for a third party to:

(1) Any station within the jurisdiction of the United States.

(2) Any station within the jurisdiction of any foreign government whose administration has made arrangements with the United States to allow amateur stations to be used for transmitting international communications on behalf of third parties. No station shall transmit messages for a third party to any station within the jurisdiction of any foreign government whose administration has not made such an arrangement. This prohibition does not apply to a message for any third party who is eligible to be a control operator of the station.

(b) The third party may participate in stating the message where:

(1) The control operator is present at the control point and is continuously monitoring and supervising the third party's participation; and

(2) The third party is not a prior amateur service licensee whose license was revoked; suspended for less than the balance of the license term and the suspension is still in effect; suspended for the balance of the license term and relicensing has not taken place; or surrendered for cancellation following notice of revocation, suspension or monetary forfeiture proceedings. The third party may not be the subject of a cease and desist order which relates to amateur service operation and which is still in effect.

(c) At the end of an exchange of international third party communications, the station must also transmit in the station identification procedure the call sign of the station with which a third party message was exchanged.

§97.117 International communications.

Transmissions to a different country, where permitted, shall be made in plain language and shall be limited to messages of a technical nature relating to tests, and, to remarks of a personal character for which, by reason of their unimportance, recourse to the public telecommunications service is not justified.

§97.119 Station identification.

(a) Each amateur station, except a space station or telecommand station, must transmit its assigned call sign on its transmitting channel at the end of each communication, and at least every 10 minutes during a communication, for the purpose of clearly making the source of the transmissions from the station known to those receiving the transmissions. No station may transmit unidentified communications or signals, or transmit as the station call sign, any call sign not authorized to the station.

(b) The call sign must be transmitted with an emission authorized for the transmitting channel in one of the following ways:

(1) By a CW emission. When keyed by an automatic device used only for identification, the speed must not exceed 20 words per minute;

(2) By a phone emission in the English language. Use of a phonetic alphabet as an aid for correct station identification is encouraged;

(3) By a RTTY emission using a specified digital code when all or part of the communications are transmitted by a RTTY or data emission;

(4) By an image emission conforming to the applicable transmission standards, either color or monochrome, of §73.682(a) of the FCC Rules when all or part of the communications are transmitted in the same image emission; or

(5) By a CW or phone emission during SS emission transmission on a narrow bandwidth frequency segment. Alternatively, by the changing of one or more

parameters of the emission so that a conventional CW or phone emission receiver can be used to determine the station call sign.

(c) An indicator may be included with the call sign. It must be separated from the call sign by the slant mark or by any suitable word that denotes the slant mark. If the indicator is self-assigned, it must be included after the call sign and must not conflict with any other indicator specified by the FCC Rules or by any prefix assigned to another country.

(d) When the operator license class held by the control operator exceeds that of the station licensee, an indicator consisting of the call sign assigned to the control operator's station must be included after the call sign.

(e) When the control operator is a person who is exercising the rights and privileges authorized by §97.9(b) of this Part, an indicator must be included after the call sign as follows:

(1) For a control operator who has requested a license modification from Novice Class to Technician Class: KT;

(2) For a control operator who has requested a license modification from Novice or Technician Class to General Class: AG;

(3) For a control operator who has requested a license modification from Novice, Technician, or General Class operator to Advanced Class: AA; or

(4) For a control operator who has requested a license modification from Novice, Technician, General, or Advanced Class operator to Amateur Extra Class: AE.

(f) When the station is transmitting under the authority of a reciprocal permit for alien amateur licensee, an indicator consisting of the appropriate letter-numeral designating the station location must be included before the call sign issued to the station by the licensing country. When the station is transmitting under the authority of an amateur service license issued by the Government of Canada, a station location indicator must be included after the call sign. At least once during each intercommunication, the identification announcement must include the geographical location as nearly as possible by city and state, commonwealth or possession.

§97.121 Restricted operation.

(a) If the operation of an amateur station causes general interference to the reception of transmissions from stations operating in the domestic broadcast service when receivers of good engineering design, including adequate selectivity characteristics, are used to receive such transmissions, and this fact is made known to the amateur station licensee, the amateur station shall not be operated during the hours from 8 p.m. to 10:30 p.m., local time, and on Sunday for the additional period from 10:30 a.m. until 1 p.m., local time, upon the frequency or frequencies used when the interference is created.

Subpart C—Special Operations

§97.201 Auxiliary station.

(a) Any amateur station licensed to a holder of a Technician, General, Advanced or Amateur Extra Class operator license may be an auxiliary station. A holder of a Technician, General, Advanced or Amateur Extra Class operator license may be the control operator of an auxiliary station, subject to the privileges of the class of operator license held.

(b) An auxiliary station may transmit only on the 1.25 m and shorter wavelength bands, except the 431-433 MHz and 435-438 MHz segments.

(c) Where an auxiliary station causes harmful interference to another auxiliary station, the licensees are equally and fully responsible for resolving the interference unless one station's operation is recommended by a frequency coordinator and the other station's is not. In that case, the licensee of the non-coordinated auxiliary station has primary responsibility to resolve the interference.

(d) An auxiliary station may be automatically controlled only when it is part of a system that includes a repeater station also being automatically controlled.

(e) An auxiliary station may transmit one-way communications.

§97.203 Beacon station.

(a) Any amateur station licensed to a holder of a Technician, General, Advanced or Amateur Extra Class operator license may be a beacon. A holder of a Technician, General, Advanced or Amateur Extra Class operator license may be the control operator of a beacon, subject to the privileges of the class of operator license held.

(b) A beacon must not concurrently transmit on more than 1 channel in the same amateur service frequency band, from the same station location.

(c) The transmitter power of a beacon must not exceed 100 W.

(d) A beacon may be automatically controlled while it is transmitting on the 28.20-28.30 MHz, 50.06-50.08 MHz, 144.275-144.300 MHz, 222.05-222.06 MHz or 432.300-432.400 MHz segments, or on the 33 cm and shorter wavelength bands.

(e) Before establishing an automatically controlled beacon in the National Radio Quiet Zone or before changing the transmitting frequency, transmitter power, antenna height or directivity, the station licensee must give written notification thereof to the Interference Office, National Radio Astronomy Observatory, P.O. Box 2, Green Bank, WV 24944.

(1) The notification must include the geographical coordinates of the antenna, antenna ground elevation above mean sea level (AMSL), antenna center of radiation above ground level (AGL), antenna directivity, proposed frequency, type of emission, and transmitter power.

(2) If an objection to the proposed operation is received by the FCC from the National Radio Astronomy Observatory at Green Bank, Pocahontas County, WV, for itself or on behalf of the Naval Research Laboratory at Sugar Grove, Pendleton County, WV, within 20 days from the date of notification, the FCC will consider all aspects of the problem and take whatever action is deemed appropriate.

(f) A beacon must cease transmissions upon notification by an EIC that the station is operating improperly or causing undue interference to other operations. The beacon may not resume transmitting without prior approval of the EIC.

(g) A beacon may transmit one-way communications.

§97.205 Repeater station.

(a) Any amateur station licensed to a holder of a Technician, General, Advanced or Amateur Extra Class operator license may be a repeater. A holder of a Technician, General, Advanced or Amateur Extra Class operator license may be the control operator of a repeater, subject to the privileges of the class of operator license held.

(b) A repeater may receive and retransmit only on the 10 m and shorter wavelength frequency bands except the 28.0-29.5 MHz, 50.0-51.0 MHz, 144.0-144.5 MHz, 145.5-146.0 MHz, 431.0-433.0 MHz and 435.0-438.0 MHz segments.

(c) Where the transmissions of a repeater cause harmful interference to another repeater, the two station licensees are equally and fully responsible for resolving the interference unless the operation of one station is recommended by a frequency coordinator and the operation of the other station is not. In that case, the licensee of the noncoordinated repeater has primary responsibility to resolve the interference.

(d) A repeater may be automatically controlled.

(e) Ancillary functions of a repeater that are available to users on the input channel are not considered remotely controlled functions of the station. Limiting the use of a repeater to only certain user stations is permissible.

(f) Before establishing a repeater in the National Radio Quiet Zone or before changing the transmitting frequency, transmitter power, antenna height or directivity, or the location of an existing repeater, the station licensee must give written notification thereof to the Interference Office, National Radio Astronomy Observatory, P.O. Box 2, Green Bank, WV 24944.

(1) The notification must include the geographical coordinates of the station antenna, antenna ground elevation above mean sea level (AMSL), antenna center of radiation above ground level (AGL), antenna directivity, proposed frequency, type of emission, and transmitter power.

(2) If an objection to the proposed operation is received by the FCC from the National Radio Astronomy Observatory at Green Bank, Pocahontas County, WV, for itself or on behalf of the Naval Research Laboratory at Sugar Grove, Pendleton County, WV, within 20 days from the date of notification, the FCC will consider all aspects of the problem and take whatever action is deemed appropriate.

§97.207 Space station.

(a) Any amateur station licensed to a holder of an Amateur Extra Class operator license may be a space station. A holder of any class operator license may be the control operator of a space station, subject to the privileges of the class of operator license held by the control operator.

(b) A space station must be capable of effecting a cessation of transmissions by telecommand whenever such cessation is ordered by the FCC.

(c) The following frequency bands and segments are authorized to space stations:

(1) The 17 m, 15 m, 12 m and 10 m bands, 6 mm, 4 mm, 2 mm and 1 mm bands; and

(2) The 7.0-7.1 MHz, 14.00-14.25 MHz, 144-146 MHz, 435-438 MHz, 1260-1270 MHz and 2400-2450 MHz, 3.40-3.41 GHz, 5.83-5.85 GHz, 10.45-10.50 GHz and 24.00-24.05 GHz segments.

(d) A space station may automatically retransmit the radio signals of Earth stations and other space stations.

(e) A space station may transmit one-way communications.

(f) Results of measurements made in the space station, including those related to the function of the station, transmitted by a space station may consist of specially coded messages intended to facilitate communications.

(g) The licensee of each space station must give two written, pre-space station notifications to the Private Radio Bureau, FCC, Washington, DC 20554. Each notification must be in accord with the provisions of Articles 11 and 13 of the Radio Regulations.

(1) The first notification is required no less than 27 months prior to initiating space station transmissions and must specify the information required by Appendix 4 and Resolution No. 642 of the Radio Regulations.

(2) The second notification is required no less than 5 months prior to initiating space station transmissions and must specify the information required by Appendix 3 and Resolution No. 642 of the Radio Regulations.

(h) The licensee of each space station must give a written, in-space station notification to the Private Radio Bureau, FCC, Washington, DC 20554, no later than 7 days following initiation of space station transmissions. The notification must update the information contained in the pre-space notification.

(i) The licensee of each space station must give a written, post-space station notification to the Private Radio Bureau, FCC, Washington, DC 20554, no later than 3 months after termination of the space station transmissions. When the termination is ordered by the FCC, notification is required no later than 24 hours after termination.

§97.209 Earth station.

(a) Any amateur station may be an Earth station. A holder of any class operator license may be the control operator of an Earth station, subject to the privileges of the class of operator license held by the control operator.

(b) The following frequency bands and segments are authorized to Earth stations:

(1) The 17 m, 15 m, 12 m and 10 m bands, 6 mm, 4 mm, 2 mm, and 1 mm bands; and

(2) The 7.0-7.1 MHz, 14.00-14.25 MHz, 144-146 MHz, 435-438 MHz, 1260-1270 MHz and 2400-2450 MHz, 3.40-3.41 GHz, 5.65-5.67 GHz, 10.45-10.50 GHz and 24.00-24.05 GHz segments.

§97.211 Telecommand station.

(a) Any amateur station designated by the licensee of a space station is eligible to transmit as a telecommand station for that space station, subject to the privileges of the class of operator license held by the control operator.

(b) A telecommand station may transmit special codes intended to obscure the meaning of telecommand messages to the station in space operation.

(c) The following frequency bands and segments are authorized to telecommand stations:

(1) The 17 m, 15 m, 12 m and 10 m bands, 6 mm, 4 mm, 2 mm and 1 mm bands; and

(2) The 7.0-7.1 MHz, 14.00-14.25 MHz, 144-146 MHz, 435-438 MHz, 1260-1270 MHz and 2400-2450 MHz, 3.40-3.41 GHz, 5.65-5.67 GHz, 10.45-10.50 GHz and 24.00-24.05 GHz segments.

(d) A telecommand station may transmit one-way communications.

§97.213 Remote control of a station.

An amateur station may be remotely controlled where:

(a) There is a radio or wireline control link between the control point and the station sufficient for the control operator to perform his/her duties. If radio, the control link must use an auxiliary station. A control link using a fiber optic cable or another telecommunication service is considered wireline.

(b) Provisions are incorporated to limit transmission by the station to a period of no more than 3 minutes in the event of malfunction in the control link.

(c) The station is protected against making, willfully or negligently, unauthorized transmissions.

(d) A photocopy of the station license and a label with the name, address, and telephone number of the station licensee and at least one designated control operator is posted in a conspicuous place at the station location.

§97.215 Remote control of model craft.

An amateur station transmitting signals to control a model craft may be operated as follows:

(a) The station identification procedure is not required for transmissions directed only to the model craft, provided that a label indicating the station call sign and the station licensee's name and address is affixed to the station transmitter.

(b) The control signals are not considered codes or ciphers intended to obscure the meaning of the communication.

(c) The transmitter power must not exceed 1 W.

Subpart D—Technical Standards

§97.301 Authorized frequency bands.

The following transmitting frequency bands are available to an amateur station located within 50 km of the Earth's surface, within the specified ITU Region, and outside any area where the amateur service is regulated by any authority other than the FCC.

(a) For a station having a control operator holding a Technician, General, Advanced or Amateur Extra Class operator license:

Wavelength band	**ITU Region 1**	**ITU Region 2**	**ITU Region 3**	**Sharing requirements See §97.303, Paragraph:**
VHF	*MHz*	*MHz*	*MHz*	
6 m	—	50-54	50-54	(a)
2 m	144-146	144-148	144-148	(a)
1.25 m	—	222-225	—	(a), (b)
UHF	*MHz*	*MHz*	*MHz*	
70 cm	430-440	420-450	420-450	(a), (b), (f)
33 cm	—	902-928	—	(a), (b), (g)
23 cm	1240-1300	1240-1300	1240-1300	(j)
13 cm	2300-2310	2300-2310	2300-2310	(a), (b), (j)
-do-	2390-2450	2390-2450	2390-2450	(a), (b), (j)
SHF	*GHz*	*GHz*	*GHz*	
9 cm	—	3.3-3.5	3.3-3.5	(a), (b), (k), (l)
5 cm	5.650-5.850	5.650-5.925	5.650-5.850	(a), (b), (m)
3 cm	10.00-10.50	10.00-10.50	10.00-10.50	(b), (c), (i), (n)
1.2 cm	24.00-24.25	24.00-24.25	24.00-24.25	(a), (b), (i), (o)
EHF	*GHz*	*GHz*	*GHz*	
6 mm	47.0-47.2	47.0-47.2	47.0-47.2	
4 mm	75.5-81.0	75.5-81.0	75.5-81.0	(b), (c), (h)
2.5 mm	119.98-120.02	119.98-120.02	119.98-120.02	(k), (p)
2 mm	142-149	142-149	142-149	(b), (c), (h), (k)
1 mm	241-250	241-250	241-250	(b), (c), (h), (q)
—	above 300	above 300	above 300	(k)

(b) For a station having a control operator holding an Amateur Extra Class operator license:

Wavelength band	**ITU Region 1**	**ITU Region 2**	**ITU Region 3**	**Sharing requirements See §97.303, Paragraph:**
MF	*kHz*	*kHz*	*kHz*	
160 m	1810-1850	1800-2000	1800-2000	(a), (b), (c)

HF	MHz	MHz	MHz	
80 m	3.50-3.75	3.50-3.75	3.50-3.75	(a)
75 m	3.75-3.80	3.75-4.00	3.75-3.90	(a)
40 m	7.0-7.1	7.0-7.3	7.0-7.1	(a)
30 m	10.10-10.15	10.10-10.15	10.10-10.15	(d)
20 m	14.00-14.35	14.00-14.35	14.00-14.35	
17 m	18.068-18.168	18.068-18.168	18.068-18.168	
15 m	21.00-21.45	21.00-21.45	21.00-21.45	
12 m	24.89-24.99	24.89-24.99	24.89-24.99	
10 m	28.0-29.7	28.0-29.7	28.0-29.7	

(c) For a station having a control operator holding an Advanced Class operator license:

Wavelength band	**ITU Region 1**	**ITU Region 2**	**ITU Region 3**	**Sharing requirements See §97.303, Paragraph:**
MF	*kHz*	*kHz*	*kHz*	
160 m	1810-1850	1800-2000	1800-2000	(a), (b), (c)
HF	*MHz*	*MHz*	*MHz*	
80 m	3.525-3.750	3.525-3.750	3.525-3.750	(a)
75 m	3.775-3.800	3.775-4.000	3.775-3.900	(a)
40 m	7.025-7.100	7.025-7.300	7.025-7.100	(a)
30 m	10.10-10.15	10.10-10.15	10.10-10.15	(d)
20 m	14.025-14.150	14.025-14.150	14.025-14.150	
-do-	14.175-14.350	14.175-14.350	14.175-14.350	
17 m	18.068-18.168	18.068-18.168	18.068-18.168	
15 m	21.025-21.200	21.025-21.200	21.025-21.200	
-do-	21.225-21.450	21.225-21.450	21.225-21.450	
12 m	24.89-24.99	24.89-24.99	24.89-24.99	
10 m	28.0-29.7	28.0-29.7	28.0-29.7	

(d) For a station having a control operator holding a General Class operator license:

Wavelength band	**ITU Region 1**	**ITU Region 2**	**ITU Region 3**	**Sharing requirements See §97.303, Paragraph:**
MF	*kHz*	*kHz*	*kHz*	
160 m	1810-1850	1800-2000	1800-2000	(a), (b), (c)
HF	*MHz*	*MHz*	*MHz*	
80 m	3.525-3.750	3.525-3.750	3.525-3.750	(a)
75 m	—	3.85-4.00	3.85-3.90	(a)
40 m	7.025-7.100	7.025-7.150	7.025-7.100	(a)
-do-	—	7.225-7.300	—	(a)
30 m	10.10-10.15	10.10-10.15	10.10-10.15	(d)
20 m	14.025-14.150	14.025-14.150	14.025-14.150	
-do-	14.225-14.350	14.225-14.350	14.225-14.350	
17 m	18.068-18.168	18.068-18.168	18.068-18.168	
15 m	21.025-21.200	21.025-21.200	21.025-21.200	
-do-	21.30-21.45	21.30-21.45	21.30-21.45	
12 m	24.89-24.99	24.89-24.99	24.89-24.99	
10 m	28.0-29.7	28.0-29.7	28.0-29.7	

(e) For a station having a control operator holding a Novice Class operator license, or a Technician Class operator license plus a CSCE indicating that the person passed element 1(A), 1(B), or 1(C), or a Technician Class operator license issued before February 14, 1991:

Wavelength band	**ITU Region 1**	**ITU Region 2**	**ITU Region 3**	**Sharing requirements See §97.303, Paragraph:**
HF	*MHz*	*MHz*	*MHz*	
80 m	3.675-3.725	3.675-3.725	3.675-3.725	(a)
40 m	7.050-7.075	7.10-7.15	7.050-7.075	(a)
15 m	21.10-21.20	21.10-21.20	21.10-21.20	
10 m	28.1-28.5	28.1-28.5	28.1-28.5	

(f) For a station having a control operator holding a Novice Class operator license:

Wavelength band	**ITU Region 1**	**ITU Region 2**	**ITU Region 3**	**Sharing requirements See §97.303, Paragraph:**
VHF	*MHz*	*MHz*	*MHz*	
1.25 m	—	222.10-223.91	—	(a), (b)
UHF	*MHz*	*MHz*	*MHz*	
23 cm	1270-1295	1270-1295	1270-1295	(i)

§97.303 Frequency sharing requirements.

The following is a summary of the frequency sharing requirements that apply to amateur station transmissions on the frequency bands specified in §97.301 of this Part. (For each ITU Region, each frequency band allocated to the amateur service is designated as either a secondary service or a primary service. A station in a secondary service must not cause harmful interference to, and must accept interference from, stations in a primary service. See §§2.105 and 2.106 of the FCC Rules, *United States Table of Frequency Allocations* for complete requirements.)

(a) Where, in adjacent ITU Regions or Subregions, a band of frequencies is allocated to different services of the same category, the basic principle is the equality of right to operate. The stations of each service in one region must operate so as not to cause harmful interference to services in the other Regions or Subregions. *(See* ITU *Radio Regulations,* No. 346 (Geneva, 1979).)

(b) No amateur station transmitting in the 1900-2000 kHz segment, the 70 cm band, the 33 cm band, the 13 cm band, the 9 cm band, the 5 cm band, the 3 cm band, the 24.05-24.25 GHz segment, the 76-81 GHz segment, the 144-149 GHz segment and the 241-248 GHz segment shall cause harmful interference to, nor is protected from interference due to the operation of, the Government radiolocation service.

(c) No amateur station transmitting in the 1900-2000 kHz segment, the 3 cm band, the 76-81 GHz segment, the 144-149 GHz segment and the 241-248 GHz segment shall cause harmful interference to, nor is protected from interference due to the operation of, stations in the non-Government radiolocation service.

(d) No amateur station transmitting in the 30 meter band shall cause harmful interference to stations authorized by other nations in the fixed service. The licensee of the amateur station must make all necessary adjustments, including termination of transmissions, if harmful interference is caused.

(e) Reserved

(f) In the 70 cm band:

(1) No amateur station shall transmit from north of Line A in the 420-430 MHz segment.

(2) The 420-430 MHz segment is allocated to the amateur service in the United States on a secondary basis, and is allocated in the fixed and mobile (except aeronautical mobile) services in the International Table of allocations on a primary basis. No amateur station transmitting in this band shall cause harmful interference to, nor is protected from interference due to the operation of, stations authorized by other nations in the fixed and mobile (except aeronautical mobile) services.

(3) The 430-440 MHz segment is allocated to the amateur service on a secondary basis in ITU Regions 2 and 3. No amateur station transmitting in this band in ITU Regions 2 and 3 shall cause harmful interference to, nor is protected from interference due to the operation of, stations authorized by other nations in the radiolocation service. In ITU Region 1, the 430-440 MHz segment is allocated to the amateur service on a co-primary basis with the radiolocation service. As between these two services in this band in ITU Region 1, the basic principle that applies is the equality of right to operate. Amateur stations authorized by the United States and radiolocation stations authorized by other nations in ITU Region 1 shall operate so as not to cause harmful interference to each other.

(4) No amateur station transmitting in the 449.75-450.25 MHz segment shall cause interference to, nor is protected from interference due to the operation of stations in, the space operation service and the space research service or Government or non-Government stations for space telecommand.

(g) In the 33 cm band:

(1) No amateur station shall transmit from within the States of Colorado and Wyoming, bounded on the south by latitude 39° N, on the north by latitude 42° N, on the east by longitude 105° W, and on the west by longitude 180° W.[1] This band is allocated on a secondary basis to the amateur service subject to not causing harmful interference to, and not receiving protection from any interference due to the operation of, industrial, scientific and medical devices, automatic vehicle monitoring systems or Government stations authorized in this band.

(2) No amateur station shall transmit from those portions of the States of Texas and New Mexico bounded on the south by latitude 31° 41′ N, on the north by latitude 34° 30′ N, on the east by longitude 104° 11′ W, and on the west by longitude 107° 30′ W.

(h) No amateur station transmitting in the 23 cm band, the 3 cm band, the 24.05-24.25 GHz segment, the 76-81 GHz segment, the 144-149 GHz segment and the 241-248 GHz segment shall cause harmful interference to, nor is protected from interference due to the operation of, stations authorized by other nations in the radiolocation service.

(i) In the 1240-1260 MHz segment, no amateur station shall cause harmful interference to, nor is protected from interference due to the operation of, stations in the radionavigation-satellite service.

(j) In the 13 cm band:

(1) The amateur service is allocated on a secondary basis in all ITU Regions. In ITU Region 1, no amateur station shall cause harmful interference to, and is not protected from interference due to the operation of, stations authorized by other nations in the fixed service. In ITU Regions 2 and 3, no station shall cause harmful interference to, and is not protected from interference due to the operation of, stations authorized by other nations in the fixed, mobile and radiolocation services.

(2)In the United States, the 2300-2310 MHz segment is allocated to the amateur

[1]Waived July 2, 1990, to permit amateurs in the restricted areas to transmit in the following segments: 902.0-902.4, 902.6-904.3, 904.7-925.3, 925.7-927.3, and 927.7-928.0 MHz.

service on a co-secondary basis with the Government fixed and mobile services. In this segment, the fixed and mobile services must not cause harmful interference to the amateur service. No amateur station transmitting in the 2400-2450 MHz segment is protected from interference due to the operation of industrial, scientific and medical devices on 2450 MHz.

(k) No amateur station transmitting in the 3.332-3.339 GHz and 3.3458-3525 GHz segments, the 2.5 mm band, the 144.68-144.98 GHz, 145.45-145.75 GHz and 146.82-147.12 GHz segments and the 343-348 GHz segment shall cause harmful interference to stations in the radio astronomy service. No amateur station transmitting in the 300-302 GHz, 324-326 GHz, 345-347 GHz, 363-365 GHz and 379-381 GHz segments shall cause harmful interference to stations in the space research service (passive) or Earth exploration-satellite service (passive).

(l) In the 9 cm band:

(1) In ITU Regions 2 and 3, the band is allocated to the amateur service on a secondary basis.

(2) In the United States, the band is allocated to the amateur service on a co-secondary basis with the non-Government radiolocation service.

(3) In the 3.3-3.4 GHz segment, no amateur station shall cause harmful interference to, nor is protected from interference due to the operation of, stations authorized by other nations in the radiolocation service.

(4) In the 3.4-3.5 GHz segment, no amateur station shall cause harmful interference to, nor is protected from interference due to the operation of, stations authorized by other nations in the fixed and fixed-satellite service.

(m) In the 5 cm band:

(1) In the 5.650-5.725 GHz segment, the amateur service is allocated in all ITU Regions on a co-secondary basis with the space research (deep space) service.

(2) In the 5.725-5.850 GHz segment, the amateur service is allocated in all ITU Regions on a secondary basis. No amateur station shall cause harmful interference to, nor is protected from interference due to the operation of, stations authorized by other nations in the fixed-satellite service in ITU Region 1.

(3) No amateur station transmitting in the 5.725-5.875 GHz segment is protected from interference due to the operation of industrial, scientific and medical devices operating on 5.8 GHz.

(4) In the 5.650-5.850 GHz segment, no amateur station shall cause harmful interference to, nor is protected from interference due to the operation of, stations authorized by other nations in the radiolocation service.

(5) In the 5.850-5.925 GHz segment, the amateur service is allocated in ITU Region 2 on a co-secondary basis with the radiolocation service. In the United States, the segment is allocated to the amateur service on a secondary basis to the non-Government fixed-satellite service. No amateur station shall cause harmful interference to, nor is protected from interference due to the operation of, stations authorized by other nations in the fixed, fixed-satellite and mobile services. No amateur station shall cause harmful interference to, nor is protected from interference due to the operation of, stations in the non-Government fixed-satellite service.

(n) In the 3 cm band:

(1) In the United States, the 3 cm band is allocated to the amateur service on a co-secondary basis with the non-government radiolocation service.

(2) In the 10.00-10.45 GHz segment in ITU Regions 1 and 3, no amateur station shall cause interference to, nor is protected from interference due to the operation of, stations authorized by other nations in the fixed and mobile services.

(o) No amateur station transmitting in the 1.2 cm band is protected from interference due to the operation of industrial, scientific and medical devices on 24.125 GHz. In the United States, the 24.05-24.25 GHz segment is allocated to the amateur service on a co-secondary basis with the non-government radiolocation and Government and non-government Earth exploration-satellite (active) services.

(p) The 2.5 mm band is allocated to the amateur service on a secondary basis. No amateur station transmitting in this band shall cause harmful interference to, nor is protected from interference due to the operation of, stations in the fixed, inter-satellite and mobile services.

(q) No amateur station transmitting in the 244-246 GHz segment of the 1 mm band is protected from interference due to the operation of industrial, scientific and medical devices on 245 GHz.

§97.305 Authorized emission types.

(a) An amateur station may transmit a CW emission on any frequency authorized to the control operator.

(b) A station may transmit a test emission on any frequency authorized to the control operator for brief periods for experimental purposes, except that no pulse modulation emission may be transmitted on any frequency where pulse is not specifically authorized.

(c) A station may transmit the following emission types on the frequencies indicated, as authorized to the control operator, subject to the standards specified in §97.307(f) of this part.

Wavelength band	Frequencies	Emission types authorized	Standards See §97.307(f) Paragraph:
MF			
160 m	Entire band	RTTY, data	(3)
-Do-	-Do-	Phone, image	(1), (2)
HF			
80 m	Entire band	RTTY, data	(3), (9)
75 m	Entire band	Phone, image	(1), 2)
40 m	7.000-7.100 MHz	RTTY, data	(3), (9)
-Do-	7.075-7.100 MHz	Phone, image	(1), (2), (9), (11)
-Do-	7.100-7.150 MHz	RTTY, data	(3), (9)
-Do-	7.150-7.300 MHz	Phone, image	(1), (2)
30 m	Entire band	RTTY, data	(3)
20 m	14.00-14.15 MHz	RTTY, data	(3)
-Do-	14.15-14.35 MHz	Phone, image	(1), (2)
17 m	18.068-18.110 MHz	RTTY, data	(3)
-Do-	18.110-18.168 MHz	Phone, image	(1), (2)
15 m	21.0-21.2 MHz	RTTY, data	(3), (9)
-Do-	21.20-21.45 MHz	Phone, image	(1), (2)
12 m	24.89-24.93 MHz	RTTY, data	(3)
-Do-	24.93-24.99 MHz	Phone, image	(1), (2)
10 m	28.0-28.3 MHz	RTTY, data	(4)
-Do-	28.3-28.5 MHz	Phone, image	(1), (2), (10)
-Do-	28.5-29.0 MHz	Phone, image	(1), (2)
-Do-	29.0-29.7 MHz	Phone, image	(2)
VHF			
6 m	50.1-51.0 MHz	RTTY, data	(5)
-Do-	-Do-	MCW, phone, image	(2)
-Do-	51.0-54.0 MHz	RTTY, data, test	(5), (8)
-Do-	-Do-	MCW, phone, image	(2)
2 m	144.1-148.0 MHz	RTTY, data, test	(5), (8)
-Do-	-Do-	MCW, phone, image	(2)
1.25 m	Entire band	RTTY, data, test	(6), (8)
-Do-	-Do-	MCW, phone, image	(2)

UHF			
70 cm	entire band	MCW, phone, image, RTTY, data, SS, test	(6), (8)
33 cm	entire band	MCW, phone, image, RTTY, data, SS, test pulse	(7), (8), (12)
23 cm	entire band	MCW, phone, image, RTTY, data, SS, test	(7), (8), (12)
13 cm	entire band	MCW, phone, image, RTTY, data, SS, test pulse	(7), (8), (12)
SHF			
9 cm	entire band	MCW, phone, image, RTTY, data, SS, test, pulse	(7), (8), (12)
5 cm	entire band	MCW, phone, image, RTTY, data, SS, test, pulse	(7), (8), (12)
3 cm	entire band	MCW, phone, image, RTTY, data, SS, test,	(7), (8), (12)
1.2 cm	entire band	MCW, phone, image RTTY, data, SS, test, pulse	(7), (8), (12)
EHF			
6 mm	entire band	MCW, phone, image, RTTY, data, SS, test, pulse	(7), (8), (12)
4 mm	entire band	MCW, phone, image, RTTY, data, SS, test, pulse	(7), (8), (12)
2.5 mm	entire band	MCW, phone, image, RTTY, data, SS, test, pulse	(7), (8), (12)
2 mm	entire band	MCW, phone, image, RTTY, data, SS, test, pulse	(7), (8), (12)
1 mm	entire band	MCW, phone, image, RTTY, data, SS, test, pulse	(7), (8), (12)
—	above 300 GHz	MCW, phone, image, RTTY, data, SS, test, pulse	(7), (8), (12)

§97.307 Emission standards.

(a) No amateur station transmission shall occupy more bandwidth than necessary for the information rate and emission type being transmitted, in accordance with good amateur practice.

(b) Emissions resulting from modulation must be confined to the band or segment available to the control operator. Emissions outside the necessary bandwidth must not cause splatter or keyclick interference to operations on adjacent frequencies.

(c) All spurious emissions from a station transmitter must be reduced to the greatest extent practicable. If any spurious emission, including chassis or power line radiation, causes harmful interference to the reception of another radio station, the licensee of the interfering amateur station is required to take steps to eliminate the interference, in accordance with good engineering practice.

(d) The mean power of any spurious emission from a station transmitter or external RF power amplifier transmitting on a frequency below 30 MHz must not exceed 50 mW and must be at least 40 dB below the mean power of the fundamental emission. For a transmitter of mean power less than 5 W, the attenuation must be at least 30 dB. A transmitter built before April 15, 1977, or first marketed before January 1, 1978, is exempt from this requirement.

(e) The mean power of any spurious emission from a station transmitter or external RF power amplifier transmitting on a frequency between 30-225 MHz must be at least 60 dB below the mean power of the fundamental. For a transmitter having a mean power of 25 W or less, the mean power of any spurious emission supplied to the antenna transmission line must not exceed 25 uW and must be at least 40 dB below the mean power of the fundamental emission, but need not be reduced below the power of 10 uW. A transmitter built before April 15, 1977, or first marketed before January 1, 1978, is exempt from this requirement.

(f) The following standards and limitations apply to transmissions on the frequencies specified in §97.305(c) of this Part.

(1) No angle-modulated emission may have a modulation index greater than 1 at the highest modulation frequency.

(2) No non-phone emission shall exceed the bandwidth of a communications quality phone emission of the same modulation type. The total bandwidth of an independent sideband emission (having B as the first symbol), or a multiplexed image and phone emission, shall not exceed that of a communications quality A3E emission.

(3) Only a RTTY or data emission using a specified digital code listed in §97.309(a) of this Part may be transmitted. The symbol rate must not exceed 300 bauds, or for frequency-shift keying, the frequency shift between mark and space must not exceed 1 kHz.

(4) Only a RTTY or data emission using a specified digital code listed in §97.309(a) of this Part may be transmitted. The symbol rate must not exceed 1200 bauds. For frequency-shift keying, the frequency shift between mark and space must not exceed 1 kHz.

(5) A RTTY, data or multiplexed emission using a specified digital code listed in §97.309(a) of this Part may be transmitted. The symbol rate must not exceed 19.6 kilobauds. A RTTY, data or multiplexed emission using an unspecified digital code under the limitations listed in §97.309(b) of this Part also may be transmitted. The authorized bandwidth is 20 kHz.

(6) A RTTY, data or multiplexed emission using a specified digital code listed in §97.309(a) of this Part may be transmitted. The symbol rate must not exceed 56 kilobauds. A RTTY, data or multiplexed emission using an unspecified digital code under the limitations listed in §97.309(b) of this Part also may be transmitted. The authorized bandwidth is 100 kHz.

(7) A RTTY, data or multiplexed emission using a specified digital code listed in §97.309(a) of this Part or an unspecified digital code under the limitations listed in §97.309(b) of this Part may be transmitted.

(8) A RTTY or data emission having designators with A, B, C, D, E, F, G, H, J or R as the first symbol; 1, 2, 7 or 9 as the second symbol; and D or W as the third symbol is also authorized.

(9) A station having a control operator holding a Novice or Technician Class operator license may only transmit a CW emission using the international Morse code.

(10) A station having a control operator holding a Novice or Technician Class operator license may only transmit a CW emission using the international Morse code or phone emissions J3E and R3E.

(11) Phone and image emissions may be transmitted only by stations located in ITU Regions 1 and 3, and by stations located within ITU Region 2 that are west of 130° West longitude or south of 20° North latitude.

(12) Emission F8E may be transmitted.

§97.309 RTTY and data emission codes.

(a) Where authorized by §97.305(c) and 97.307(f) of this Part, an amateur station may transmit a RTTY or data emission using the following specified digital codes:

(1) The 5-unit, start-stop, International Telegraph Alphabet No. 2 code, defined in International Telegraph and Telephone Consultative Committee Recommendation F.1, Division C.

(2) The 7-unit code, specified in International Radio Consultative Committee Recommendation CCIR 476-2 (1978), 476-3 (1982), 476-4 (1986) or 625 (1986).

(3) The 7-unit code, defined in American National Standards Institute X3.4-1977 or International Alphabet No. 5, defined in International Telegraph and Telephone Consultative Committee Recommendation T.50 or in International Organization for Standardization, International Standard ISO 646 (1983), and extensions as provided for in CCITT Recommendation T.61 (Malaga-Torremolinos, 1984).

(b) Where authorized by §§97.305(c) and 97.307(f) of this Part, a station may transmit a RTTY or data emission using an unspecified digital code, except to a station in a country with which the United States does not have an agreement permitting the code to be used. RTTY and data emissions using unspecified digital codes must not be transmitted for the purpose of obscuring the meaning of any communication. When deemed necessary by an EIC to assure compliance with the FCC Rules, a station must:

(1) Cease the transmission using the unspecified digital code;

(2) Restrict transmission of any digital code to the extent instructed;

(3) Maintain a record, convertible to the original information, of all digital communications transmitted.

§97.311 SS emission types.

(a) SS emission transmissions by an amateur station are authorized only for communications between points within areas where the amateur service is regulated by the FCC. SS emission transmissions must not be used for the purpose of obscuring the meaning of any communication.

(b) Stations transmitting SS emission must not cause harmful interference to stations employing other authorized emissions, and must accept all interference caused by stations employing other authorized emissions. For the purposes of this paragraph, unintended triggering of carrier operated repeaters is not considered to be harmful interference.

(c) Only the following types of SS emission transmissions are authorized (hybrid SS emissions transmissions involving both spreading techniques are prohibited):

(1) Frequency hopping where the carrier of the transmitted signal is modulated with unciphered information and changes frequency at fixed intervals under the direction of a high speed code sequence.

(2) Direct sequence where the information is modulo-2 added to a high speed code sequence. the combined information and code are then used to modulate the RF carrier. The high speed code sequence dominates the modulation function, and is the direct cause of the wide spreading of the transmitted signal.

(d) The only spreading sequences that are authorized are from the output of one binary linear feedback shift register (which may be implemented in hardware or software).

(1) Only the following sets of connections may be used:

Number of stages in shift register	*Taps used in feedback*
7	7,1
13	13, 4, 3, 1
19	19, 5, 2, 1

(2) The shift register must not be reset other than by its feedback during an individual transmission. The shift register output sequence must be used without alteration.

(3) The output of the last stage of the binary linear feedback shift register must be used as follows:

(i) For frequency hopping transmissions using x frequencies, n consecutive bits from the shift register must be used to select the next frequency from a list of frequencies sorted in ascending order. Each consecutive frequency must be selected by a consecutive block of n bits. (Where n is the smallest integer greater than $\log_2$ x.)

(ii) For direct sequence transmissions using m-ary modulation, consecutive blocks of $\log_2$ m bits from the shift register must be used to select the transmitted signal during each interval.

(e) The station records must document all SS emission transmissions and must be retained for a period of 1 year following the last entry. The station records must include sufficient information to enable the FCC, using the information contained therein, to demodulate all transmissions. The station records must contain at least the following:

(1) A technical description of the transmitted signal;

(2) Pertinent parameters describing the transmitted signal including the frequency or frequencies of operation and, where applicable, the chip rate, the code rate, the spreading function, the transmission protocol(s) including the method of achieving synchronization, and the modulation type;

(3) A general description of the type of information being conveyed, (voice, text, memory dump, facsimile, television, etc.);

(4) The method and, if applicable, the frequency or frequencies used for station identification; and

(5) The date of beginning and the date of ending use of each type of transmitted signal.

(f) When deemed necessary by an EIC to assure compliance with this Part, a station licensee must:

(1) Cease SS emission transmissions;

(2) Restrict SS emission transmissions to the extent instructed; and

(3) Maintain a record, convertible to the original information (voice, text, image, etc.) of all spread spectrum communications transmitted.

(g) The transmitter power must not exceed 100 W.

§97.313 Transmitter power standards.

(a) An amateur station must use the minimum transmitter power necessary to carry out the desired communications.

(b) No station may transmit with a transmitter power exceeding 1.5 kW PEP. Until June 2, 1990, a station transmitting emission A3E is exempt from this requirement provided the power input (both RF and direct current) to the final amplifying stage supplying RF power to the antenna feed line does not exceed 1 kW, exclusive of power for heating the cathodes of vacuum tubes.

(c) No station may transmit with a transmitter power exceeding 200 W PEP on:

(1) The 3.675-3.725 MHz, 7.10-7.15 MHz, 10.10-10.15 MHz and 21.1-21.2 MHz segments;

(2) The 28.1-28.5 MHz segment when the control operator is a Novice or Technician operator; or

(3) The 7.050-7.075 MHz segment when the station is within ITU Regions 1 or 3.

(d) No station may transmit with a transmitter power exceeding 25 W PEP on the VHF 1.25 m band when the control operator is a Novice operator.

(e) No station may transmit with a transmitter power exceeding 5 W PEP on the UHF 23 cm band when the control operator is a Novice operator.

(f) No station may transmit with a transmitter power exceeding 50 W PEP on the UHF 70 cm band from an area specified in footnote US7 to §2.106 of the FCC Rules, unless expressly authorized by the FCC after mutual agreement, on a case-by-case basis, between the EIC of the applicable field facility and the military area frequency coordinator at the applicable military base. An Earth station or telecommand station, however, may transmit on the 435-438 MHz segment with a maximum of 611 W effective radiated power (1 kW equivalent isotropically radiated power) without the authorization otherwise required. The transmitting antenna elevation angle between the lower half-power (−3 dB relative to the peak or antenna bore sight) point and the horizon must always be greater than 10°.

(g) No station may transmit with a transmitter power exceeding 50 W PEP on the 33 cm band from within 241 km of the boundaries of the White Sands Missile Range. Its boundaries are those portions of Texas and New Mexico bounded on the south by latitude 31° 41′ North, on the east by longitude 104° 11′ West, on the north by latitude 34° 30′ North, and on the west by longitude 107° 30′ West.

§97.315 Type acceptance of external RF power amplifiers.

(a) No more than 1 unit of 1 model of an external RF power amplifier capable of operation below 144 MHz may be constructed or modified during any calendar year by an amateur operator for use at a station without a grant of type acceptance. No amplifier capable of operation below 144 MHz may be constructed or modified by a non-amateur operator without a grant of type acceptance from the FCC.

(b) Any external RF power amplifier or external RF power amplifier kit (see §2.815 of the FCC Rules), manufactured, imported or modified for use in a station or attached at any station must be type accepted for use in the amateur service in accordance with Subpart J of Part 2 of the FCC Rules. This requirement does not apply if one or more of the following conditions are met:

(1) The amplifier is not capable of operation on frequencies below 144 MHz. For the purpose of this part, an amplifier will be deemed to be incapable of operation below 144 MHz if it is not capable of being easily modified to increase its amplification characteristics below 120 MHz and either:

(i) The mean output power of the amplifier decreases, as frequency decreases from 144 MHz, to a point where 0 dB or less gain is exhibited at 120 MHz; or

(ii) The amplifier is not capable of amplifying signals below 120 MHz even for brief periods without sustaining permanent damage to its amplification circuitry.

(2) The amplifier was manufactured before April 28, 1978, and has been issued a marketing waiver by the FCC, or the amplifier was purchased before April 28, 1978, by an amateur operator for use at that amateur operator's station.

(3) The amplifier was:

(i) Constructed by the licensee, not from an external RF power amplifier kit, for use at the licensee's station; or

(ii) Modified by the licensee for use at the licensee's station.

(4) The amplifier is sold by an amateur operator to another amateur operator or to a dealer.

(5) The amplifier is purchased in used condition by an equipment dealer from an amateur operator and the amplifier is further sold to another amateur operator for use at that operator's station.

(c) A list of type accepted equipment may be inspected at FCC headquarters in Washington, DC, or at any FCC field location. Any external RF power amplifier appearing on this list as type accepted for use in the amateur service may be marketed for use in the amateur service.

§97.317 Standards for type acceptance of external RF power amplifiers.

(a) To receive a grant of type acceptance, the amplifier must satisfy the spurious emission standards of §97.307(d) or (e) of this Part, as applicable, when the amplifier is:

(1) Operated at its full output power;

(2) Placed in the "standby" or "off" positions, but still connected to the transmitter; and

(3) Driven with at least 50 W mean RF input power (unless a higher drive level is specified).

(b) To receive a grant of type acceptance, the amplifier must not be capable of operation on any frequency or frequencies between 24 MHz and 35 MHz. The amplifier will be deemed incapable of such operation if it:

(1) Exhibits no more than 6 dB gain between 24 MHz and 26 MHz and between 28 MHz and 35 MHz. (This gain will be determined by the ratio of the input RF driving signal (mean power measurement) to the mean RF output power of the amplifier); and

(2) Exhibits no amplification (0 dB gain) between 26 MHz and 28 MHz.

(c) Type acceptance may be denied when denial would prevent the use of these amplifiers in services other than the amateur service. The following features will result in dismissal or denial of an application for type acceptance:

(1) Any accessible wiring which, when altered, would permit operation of the amplifier in a manner contrary to the FCC Rules;

(2) Circuit boards or similar circuitry to facilitate the addition of components to change the amplifier's operating characteristics in a manner contrary to the FCC Rules;

(3) Instructions for operation or modification of the amplifier in a manner contrary to FCC Rules;

(4) Any internal or external controls or adjustments to facilitate operation of the amplifier in a manner contrary to the FCC Rules;

(5) Any internal RF sensing circuitry or any external switch, the purpose of which is to place the amplifier in the transmit mode;

(6) The incorporation of more gain in the amplifier than is necessary to operate in the amateur service; for purposes of this paragraph, the amplifier must:

(i) Not be capable of achieving designed output power when driven with less than 50 W mean RF input power;

(ii) Not be capable of amplifying the input RF driving signal by more than 15 dB, unless the amplifier has a designed transmitter power of less than 1.5 kW (in such a case, gain must be reduced by the same number of dB as the transmitter power relationship to 1.5 kW; This gain limitation is determined by the ratio of the input RF driving signal to the RF output power of the amplifier where both signals are expressed in peak envelope power or mean power);

(iii) Not exhibit more gain than permitted by paragraph (c)(6)(ii) of this Section when driven by an RF input signal of less than 50 W mean power; and

(iv) Be capable of sustained operation at its designed power level;

(7) Any attenuation in the input of the amplifier which, when removed or modified, would permit the amplifier to function at its designed transmitter power when driven by an RF frequency input signal of less than 50 W mean power; or

(8) Any other features designed to facilitate operation in a telecommunication service other than the Amateur Radio Services, such as the Citizens Band (CB) Radio Service.

Subpart E—Providing Emergency Communications

§97.401 Operation during a disaster.

(a) When normal communication systems are overloaded, damaged or disrupted because a disaster has occurred, or is likely to occur, in an area where the amateur service is regulated by the FCC, an amateur station may make transmissions necessary to meet essential communication needs and facilitate relief actions.

(b) When normal communication systems are overloaded, damaged or disrupted because a natural disaster has occurred, or is likely to occur, in an area where the amateur service is not regulated by the FCC, a station assisting in meeting essential communication needs and facilitating relief actions may do so only in accord with ITU Resolution No. 640 (Geneva, 1979). The 80 m, 75 m, 40 m, 30 m, 20 m, 17 m, 15 m, 12 m, and 2 m bands may be used for these purposes.

(c) When a disaster disrupts normal communication systems in a particular area, the FCC may declare a temporary state of communication emergency. The declaration will set forth any special conditions and special rules to be observed by stations during the communication emergency. A request for a declaration of a temporary state of emergency should be directed to the EIC in the area concerned.

(d) A station in, or within 92.6 km of, Alaska may transmit emissions J3E and R3E on the channel at 5.1675 MHz for emergency communications. The channel must be shared with stations licensed in the Alaska-private fixed service. The transmitter power must not exceed 150 W.

§97.403 Safety of life and protection of property.

No provision of these rules prevents the use by an amateur station of any means of radiocommunication at its disposal to provide essential communication needs in connection with the immediate safety of human life and immediate protection of property when normal communication systems are not available.

§97.405 Station in distress.

(a) No provision of these rules prevents the use by an amateur station in distress of any means at its disposal to attract attention, make known its condition and location, and obtain assistance.

(b) No provision of these rules prevents the use by a station, in the exceptional circumstances described in paragraph (a), of any means of radiocommunications at its disposal to assist a station in distress.

§97.407 Radio amateur civil emergency service.

(a) No station may transmit in RACES unless it is an FCC-licensed primary, club, or military recreation station and it is certified by a civil defense organization as registered with that organization, or it is an FCC-licensed RACES station. No person may be the control operator of a RACES station, or may be the control operator of an amateur station transmitting in RACES unless that person holds a FCC-issued amateur operator license and is certified by a civil defense organization as enrolled in that organization.

(b) The frequency bands and segments and emissions authorized to the control operator are available to stations transmitting communications in RACES on a shared basis with the amateur service. In the event of an emergency which necessitates the invoking of the President's War Emergency Powers under the provisions of Section 706 of the Communications Act of 1934, as amended, 47 U.S.C. §606, RACES stations and amateur stations participating in RACES may only transmit on the following frequencies:

(1) The 1800-1825 kHz, 1975-2000 kHz, 3.50-3.55 MHz, 3.93-3.98 MHz, 3.984-4.000 MHz, 7.079-7.125 MHz, 7.245-7.255 MHz, 10.10-10.15 MHz, 14.047-14.053 MHz, 14.22-14.23 MHz, 14.331-14.350 MHz, 21.047-21.053 MHz, 21.228-21.267 MHz, 28.55-28.75 MHz, 29.237-29.273 MHz, 29.45-29.65 MHz, 50.35-50.75 MHz, 52-54 MHz, 144.50-145.71 MHz, 146-148 MHz, 2390-2450 MHz segments;

(2) The 1.25 m, 70 cm and 23 cm bands; and

(3) The channels at 3.997 MHz and 53.30 MHz may be used in emergency areas when required to make initial contact with a military unit and for communications with military stations on matters requiring coordination.

(c) A RACES station may only communicate with:

(1) Another RACES station;

(2) An amateur station registered with a civil defense organization;

(3) A United States Government station authorized by the responsible agency to communicate with RACES stations;

(4) A station in a service regulated by the FCC whenever such communication is authorized by the FCC.

(d) An amateur station registered with a civil defense organization may only communicate with:

(1) A RACES station licensed to the civil defense organization with which the amateur station is registered;

(2) The following stations upon authorization of the responsible civil defense official for the organization with which the amateur station is registered:

(i) A RACES station licensed to another civil defense organization;

(ii) An amateur station registered with the same or another civil defense organization;

(iii) A United States Government station authorized by the responsible agency to communicate with RACES stations; and

(iv) A station in a service regulated by the FCC whenever such communication is authorized by the FCC.

(e) All communications transmitted in RACES must be specifically authorized by the civil defense organization for the area served. Only civil defense communications of the following types may be transmitted:

(1) Messages concerning impending or actual conditions jeopardizing the public safety, or affecting the national defense or security during periods of local, regional, or national civil emergencies;

(2) Messages directly concerning the immediate safety of life of individuals, the immediate protection of property, maintenance of law and order, alleviation of human suffering and need, and the combating of armed attack or sabotage;

(3) Messages directly concerning the accumulation and dissemination of public information or instructions to the civilian population essential to the activities of the civil defense organization or other authorized governmental or relief agencies; and

(4) Communications for RACES training drills and tests necessary to ensure the establishment and maintenance of orderly and efficient operation of the RACES as ordered by the responsible civil defense organization served. Such drills and tests may not exceed a total time of 1 hour per week. With the approval of the chief officer for emergency planning in the applicable State, Commonwealth, District or territory, however, such tests and drills may be conducted for a period not to exceed 72 hours no more than twice in any calendar year.

Subpart F—Qualifying Examination Systems

§97.501 Qualifying for an amateur operator license.

An applicant must pass an examination for the issuance of a new amateur operator license and for each change in operator class. Each applicant for the class of operator license specified below must pass, or otherwise receive examination credit for, the following examination elements:

(a) Amateur Extra Class operator: Elements 1(C), 2, 3(A), 3(B), 4(A), and 4(B);
(b) Advanced Class operator: Elements 1(B) or 1(C), 2, 3(A), 3(B), and 4(A);
(c) General Class operator: Elements 1(B) or 1(C), 2, 3(A), and 3(B);
(d) Technician Class operator: Elements 2 and 3(A);
(e) Novice Class operator: Elements 1(A) or 1(B) or 1(C), and 2.

§97.503 Element standards.

(a) A telegraphy examination must be sufficient to prove that the examinee has the ability to send correctly by hand and to receive correctly by ear texts in the international Morse code at not less than the prescribed speed, using all the letters of the alphabet, numerals 0-9, period, comma, question mark, slant mark and prosigns ar, bt and sk.

(1) Element 1(A): 5 words per minute;
(2) Element 1(B): 13 words per minute;
(3) Element 1(C): 20 words per minute.

(b) A written examination must be such as to prove that the examinee possesses the operational and technical qualifications required to perform properly the duties of an amateur service licensee. Each written examination must be comprised of a question set as follows:

(1) Element 2: 30 questions concerning the privileges of a Novice Class operator license. The minimum passing score is 22 questions answered correctly.

(2) Element 3(A): 25 questions concerning the additional privileges of a Technician Class operator license. The minimum passing score is 19 questions answered correctly.

(3) Element 3(B): 25 questions concerning the additional privileges of a General Class operator license. The minimum passing score is 19 questions answered correctly.

(4) Element 4(A): 50 questions concerning the additional privileges of an Advanced Class operator license. The minimum passing score is 37 questions answered correctly.

(5) Element 4(B): 40 questions concerning the additional privileges of an Amateur Extra Class operator license. The minimum passing score is 30 questions answered correctly.

(c) The topics and number of questions required in each question set are listed below for the appropriate examination element:

Topics	*Element:* 2	*3(A)*	*3(B)*	*4(A)*	*4(B)*
(1) FCC rules for the amateur radio services	10	5	4	6	8
(2) Amateur station operating procedures	2	3	3	1	4
(3) Radio wave propagation characteristics of amateur service frequency bands	1	3	3	2	2

(4) Amateur radio practices	4	4	5	4	4
(5) Electrical principles as applied to amateur station equipment	4	2	2	10	6
(6) Amateur station equipment circuit components	2	2	1	6	4
(7) Practical circuits employed in amateur station equipment	2	1	1	10	4
(8) Signals and emissions transmitted by amateur stations	2	2	2	6	4
(9) Amateur station antennas and feed lines	3	3	4	5	4

§97.505 Element credit.

(a) The administering VEs must give credit as specified below to an examinee holding any of the following documents:

(1) An unexpired (or within the grace period) FCC-issued amateur operator license: The least elements required for the license held. For a Technician Class operator license issued before March 21, 1987, credit must also be given for Element 3(B).

(2) A CSCE: Each element the CSCE indicates the examinee passed within the previous 365 days.

(3) A photocopy of a FCC Form 610 which was submitted to the FCC indicating the examinee qualified for a Novice Class operator license within the previous 365 days: Elements 1(A) and 2.

(4) An unexpired (or expired less than 5 years) FCC-issued commercial radiotelegraph operator license or permit: Element 1(C).

(5) A current, or expired but within the grace period for renewal, Novice, Technician plus a CSCE indicating that the person passed Element 1(A) or 1(B). Technician issued before February 14, 1991. General, or Advanced Class operator license, and a Form 610 containing:

(i) A physician's certification stating that because the person is an individual with a severe handicap, the person is unable to pass a 13 or 20 words per minute telegraphy examination: and

(ii) A release signed by the person permitting disclosure to the FCC of medical information pertaining to the person's handicap: Element 1(C).

(b) No examination credit, except as herein provided, shall be allowed on the basis of holding or having held any other license.

§97.507 Preparing an examination.

(a) Each telegraphy message and each written question set administered to an examinee must be prepared by a VE holding an FCC-issued Amateur Extra Class operator license. A telegraphy message or written question set, however, may also be prepared for the following elements by a VE holding an FCC-issued operator license of the Class indicated:

(1) Element 3(B): Advanced Class operator.

(2) Elements 1(A) and 3(A): Advanced or General Class operator.

(3) Element 2: Advanced, General or Technician Class operator.

(b) Each question set administered to an examinee must utilize questions taken from the applicable question pool.

(c) Each telegraphy message and each written question set administered to an examinee for a Technician, General, Advanced, or Amateur Extra Class operator license must be prepared, or obtained from a supplier, by the administering VEs according to instructions from the coordinating VEC.

(d) The preparation of each telegraphy message and each written question set administered to an examinee for a Novice Class operator license is the responsibility of the administering VEs. The telegraphy message and written question set may be obtained by the administering VEs from a supplier.

(e) A telegraphy examination must consist of a message sent in the international Morse code at no less than the prescribed speed for a minimum of 5 minutes. The message must contain each required telegraphy character at least once. No message known to the examinee may be administered in a telegraphy examination. Each 5 letters of the alphabet must be counted as 1 word. Each numeral, punctuation mark and prosign must be counted as 2 letters of the alphabet.

§97.509 Administering an examination.

(a) Each examination for an amateur operator license must be administered at a location and a time specified by the administering VEs. Each administering VE must be present and observe the examinee throughout the entire examination. The administering VEs are responsible for the proper conduct and necessary supervision of each examination. The administering VEs must immediately terminate the examination upon failure of the examinee to comply with their instructions.

(b) Each examinee must comply with the instructions given by the administering VEs.

(c) No examination that has been compromised shall be administered to any examinee. Neither the same telegraphy message nor the same question set may be readministered to the same examinee.

(d) Passing a telegraphy receiving examination is adequate proof of an examinee's ability to both send and receive telegraphy. The administering VEs, however, may also include a sending segment in a telegraphy examination.

(e) Upon completion of each examination element, the administering VEs must immediately grade the examinee's answers. The administering VEs are responsible for determining the correctness of the examinee's answers.

(f) When the examinee is credited for all examination elements required for the operator license sought, the administering VEs must certify on the examinee's application form that the applicant is qualified for the license and report the basis for the qualification.

(g) When the examinee does not score a passing grade on an examination element, the administering VEs must return the application form to the examinee and inform the examinee of the grade.

(h) The administering VEs must accommodate an examinee whose physical disabilities require a special examination procedure. The administering VEs may require a physician's certification indicating the nature of the disability before determining which, if any, special procedures must be used.

(i) The FCC may:

(1) Administer any examination element itself;

(2) Readminister any examination element previously administered by VEs, either itself or under the supervision of VEs designated by the FCC; or

(3) Cancel the operator and station licenses of any licensee who fails to appear for readministration of an examination when directed by the FCC, or who does not successfully complete any required element which is readministered. In an instance of such cancellation, the person will be issued operator and station licenses consistent with completed examination elements that have not been invalidated by not appearing for, or by failing, the examination upon readministration.

§97.511 Technician, General, Advanced and Amateur Extra Class operator license examination.

(a) Each session where an examination for a Technician, General, Advanced or Amateur Extra Class operator license is administered must be coordinated by a VEC. Each administering VE must be accredited by the coordinating VEC.

(b) Each examination for a Technician Class operator license must be administered by 3 administering VEs, each of whom must hold an FCC-issued Amateur Extra or Advanced Class operator license.

(c) Each examination for a General, Advanced or Amateur Extra Class operator license must be administered by 3 administering VEs, each of whom must hold an FCC-issued Amateur Extra Class operator license.

(d) The administering VEs must make a public announcement before administering an examination for Technician, General, Advanced or Amateur Extra Class operator license. The number of candidates at any examination may be limited.

(e) The administering VEs must issue a CSCE to an examinee who scores a passing grade on an examination element.

(f) Within 10 days of the administration of a successful examination for the Technician, General, Advanced or Amateur Extra Class operator license, the administering VEs must submit the application to the coordinating VEC. If telegraphy element credit is claimed under Section 97.505(a)(5), the physician's certification and the patient's release on the license application, Form 610, must be completed.

§97.513 Novice Class operator license examination.

(a) Each examination for a Novice Class operator license must be administered by 2 VEs. The VEs do not have to be accredited by a VEC. Each administering VE must hold a current FCC-issued Amateur Extra, Advanced or General Class operator license.

(b) Within 10 days of the administration of a successful examination for a Novice Class operator license, the administering VEs must submit the application to: FCC, P.O. Box 1020, Gettysburg, PA 17326.

§97.515 Volunteer examiner requirements.

(a) Each administering VE must be at least 18 years of age.

(b) Any person who owns a significant interest in, or is an employee of, any company or other entity that is engaged in the manufacture or distribution of equipment used in connection with amateur station transmissions, or in the preparation or distribution of any publication used in preparation for obtaining amateur licenses, is ineligible to be an administering VE. An employee who does not normally communicate with that part of an entity engaged in the manufacture or distribution of such equipment, or in the preparation or distribution of any publication used in preparation for obtaining amateur operator licenses, is eligible to be an administering VE.

(c) No person may be a VE if that person's amateur station license or amateur operator license has ever been revoked or suspended.

(d) No VE may administer an examination to that VE's spouse, children, grandchildren, stepchildren, parents, grandparents, stepparents, brothers, sisters, stepbrothers, stepsisters, aunts, uncles, nieces, nephews, and in-laws.

§97.517 Volunteer examiner conduct.

No VE may administer or certify any examination by fraudulent means or for monetary or other consideration including reimbursement in any amount in excess of that permitted. Violation of this provision may result in the revocation of the VE's amateur station license and the suspension of the VE's amateur operator license.

§97.519 Coordinating examination sessions.

(a) A VEC must coordinate the efforts of VEs in preparing and administering examinations.

(b) At the completion of each examination session coordinated, the coordinating VEC must collect the applications and test results from the administering VEs. The coordinating VEC must screen and forward all applications for qualified examinees within 10 days of their receipt from the administering VEs to: FCC, P.O. Box 1020, Gettysburg, PA 17326.

(c) Each VEC must make any examination records available to the FCC, upon request.

§97.521 VEC qualifications.

No organization may serve as a VEC unless it has entered into a written agreement with the FCC. The VEC must abide by the terms of the agreement. In order to be eligible to be a VEC, the entity must:

(a) Be an organization that exists for the purpose of furthering the amateur service;

(b) Be capable of serving as a VEC in at least the VEC region (see Appendix 2) proposed;

(c) Agree to coordinate examinations for Technician, General, Advanced, and Amateur Extra Class operator licenses;

(d) Agree to assure that, for any examination, every examinee qualified under these rules is registered without regard to race, sex, religion, national origin or membership (or lack thereof) in any amateur service organization;

(e) Not be engaged in the manufacture or distribution of equipment used in connection with amateur station transmissions, or in the preparation or distribution of any publication used in preparation for obtaining amateur licenses, unless a persuasive showing is made to the FCC that preventive measures have been taken to preclude any possible conflict of interest.

§97.523 Question pools.

All VECs must cooperate in maintaining one question pool for each written examination element. Each question pool must contain at least 10 times the number of questions required for a single examination. Each question pool must be published and made available to the public prior to its use for making a question set. Each question on each VEC question pool must be prepared by a VE holding the required FCC-issued operator license, *See* §97.507(a) of this Part.

§97.525 Accrediting VEs.

(a) No VEC may accredit a person as a VE if:

(1) The person does not meet minimum VE statutory qualifications or minimum qualifications as prescribed by this Part;

(2) The FCC does not accept the voluntary and uncompensated services of the person;

(3) The VEC determines that the person is not competent to perform the VE functions; or

(4) The VEC determines that questions of the person's integrity or honesty could compromise the examinations.

(b) Each VEC must seek a broad representation of amateur operators to be VEs. No VEC may discriminate in accrediting VEs on the basis of race, sex, religion or national origin; nor on the basis of membership (or lack thereof) in an amateur service organization; nor on the basis of the person accepting or declining to accept reimbursement.

§97.527 Reimbursement for expenses.

(a) VEs and VECs may be reimbursed by examinees for out-of-pocket expenses incurred in preparing, processing, administering, or coordinating an examination for a Technician, General, Advanced, or Amateur Extra operator license.

(b) The maximum amount of reimbursement from any one examinee for any one examination at a particular session regardless of the number of examination elements taken must not exceed that announced by the FCC in a Public Notice. (The basis for the maximum fee is $4.00 for 1984, adjusted annually each January 1 thereafter for changes in the Department of Labor Consumer Price Index.)

(c) No reimbursement may be accepted by any VE for preparing, processing, or administering an examination for a Novice operator license.

(d) Each VE and each VEC accepting reimbursement must maintain records of out-of-pocket expenses and reimbursements for each examination session. Written certifications must be filed with the FCC each year that all expenses for the period from January 1 to December 31 of the preceding year for which reimbursement was obtained were necessarily and prudently incurred.

(e) The expense and reimbursement records must be retained by each VE and each VEC for 3 years and be made available to the FCC upon request.

(f) Each VE must forward the certification by January 15 of each year to the coordinating VEC for the examinations for which reimbursement was received. Each VEC must forward all such certifications and its own certification to the FCC on or before January 31 of each year.

(g) Each VEC must disaccredit any VE failing to provide the certification. The VEC must advise the FCC on January 31 of each year of any VE that it has disaccredited for this reason.

Appendix 1—Places where the amateur service is regulated by the FCC.

In ITU Region 2, the amateur service is regulated by the FCC within the territorial limits of the 50 United States, District of Columbia, Caribbean Insular areas [Commonwealth of Puerto Rico, United States Virgin Islands (50 islets and cays) and Navassa Island], and Johnston Island (Islets East, Johnston, North and Sand) and Midway Island (Islets Eastern and Sand) in the Pacific Insular areas.

In ITU Region 3, the amateur service is regulated by the FCC within the Pacific Insular territorial limits of American Samoa (seven islands), Baker Island, Commonwealth of Northern Mariannas Islands, Guam Island, Howland Island, Jarvis Island, Kingman Reef, Palmyra Island (more than 50 islets) and Wake Island (Islets Peale, Wake and Wilkes).

Appendix 2—VEC Regions.

1. Connecticut, Maine, Massachusetts, New Hampshire, Rhode Island and Vermont.
2. New Jersey and New York.
3. Delaware, District of Columbia, Maryland and Pennsylvania.
4. Alabama, Florida, Georgia, Kentucky, North Carolina, South Carolina, Tennessee and Virginia.
5. Arkansas, Louisiana, Mississippi, New Mexico, Oklahoma and Texas.
6. California.
7. Arizona, Idaho, Montana, Nevada, Oregon, Utah, Washington and Wyoming.
8. Michigan, Ohio and West Virginia.

9. Illinois, Indiana and Wisconsin.

10. Colorado, Iowa, Kansas, Minnesota, Missouri, Nebraska, North Dakota and South Dakota.

11. Alaska

12. Caribbean Insular areas.

13. Hawaii and Pacific Insular areas.

APPENDICES

APPENDIX 1

Communications Act of 1934 extracts

The Communications Act of 1934

The complete text of the Communications Act of 1934 would occupy many pages. The only parts given are those most applicable to Amateur Radio station licensing and regulations in this country. Note particularly Sections 324, 325 and 705 and the penalties outlined in Sections 501 and 502.

Be it enacted by the Senate and House of Representatives of the United States of America in Congress assembled,

Section 1. For the purpose of regulating interstate and foreign commerce in communication by wire and radio so as to make available, so far as possible, to all the people of the United States, a rapid, efficient, nationwide and worldwide wire and radio communication service with adequate facilities at reasonable charges, for the purpose of the national defense, for the purpose of promoting safety of life and property through the use of wire and radio communication, and for the purpose of securing a more effective execution of this policy by centralizing authority heretofore granted by law to several agencies and by granting additional authority with respect to interstate and foreign commerce in wire and radio communication there is hereby created a commission to be known as the "Federal Communications Commission," which shall be constituted as hereinafter provided, and which shall execute and enforce the provisions of this Act.

Section 2.(a) The provisions of the Act shall apply to all interstate and foreign communication by wire or radio and all interstate and foreign transmission of energy by radio, which originates and/or is received within the United States, and to all the licensing and regulating of all radio stations as hereinafter provided; but it shall not apply to persons engaged in wire or radio communication or transmission in the Canal Zone, or to wire or radio communications or transmission wholly within the Canal Zone. . .

Section 4.(a) The Federal Communications Commission (in this Act referred to as the "Commission") shall be composed of five commissioners appointed by the President, by and with the advice and consent of the Senate, one of whom the President shall designate as chairman.

Section 4.(f)

(4)(A) The Commission, for purposes of preparing any examination for an amateur station operator license, may accept and employ the voluntary and uncompensated services of any individual who holds an amateur station operator license of a higher class than the class license for which the examination is being prepared. In the case of examinations for the highest class of Amateur station operator license, the Commission may accept and employ such services of any individual who holds such class of license.

(B) The Commission, for purposes of administering any examination for an amateur station operator license, may accept and employ the voluntary and uncompensated services of any individual who holds an amateur station operator license of a higher class than the class license for which the examination is being conducted. In the case of examinations for the highest class of amateur station operator license, the Commission may accept and employ such services of any individual who holds such class of license. Any person who owns a significant interest in, or is an employee of, any company or other entity which is engaged in the manufacture or distribution of equipment used in connection with Amateur Radio transmissions, or in the preparation or distribution of any publication used in preparation for obtaining amateur station operator licenses, shall not be eligible to render any service under this subparagraph.

(C)(i) The Commission, for purposes of monitoring violations of any provision of this Act (and of any regulation prescribed by the Commission under this Act) relating to the Amateur Radio Service, may—

(I) recruit and train any individual licensed by the Commission to operate an amateur station; and

(II) accept and employ the voluntary and uncompensated services of such individual.

(ii) The Commission, for purposes of recruiting and training individuals under clause (i) and for purposes of screening, annotating, and summarizing violation reports referred under clause (i), may accept and employ the voluntary and uncompensated services of any amateur station operator organization.

(iii) The functions of individuals recruited and trained under this subparagraph shall be limited to—

(I) the detection of improper Amateur Radio transmissions;

(II) the conveyance to Commission personnel of information which is essential to the enforcement of this Act (or regulations prescribed by the Commission under this Act) relating to the Amateur Radio Service; and

(III) issuing advisory notices, under the general direction of the Commission, to persons who apparently have violated any provision of this Act (or regulations prescribed by the Commission under this Act) relating to the Amateur Radio Service.

Nothing in this clause shall be construed to grant individuals recruited and trained under this subparagraph any authority to issue sanctions to violators or to take an enforcement action other than any action which the Commission may prescribe by rule.

(J)With respect to the acceptance of voluntary uncompensated services for the preparation, processing, or administration of examinations for amateur station operator licenses pursuant to subparagraph (A) or (B) of this paragraph, individuals, or organizations which provide or coordinate such authorized volunteer services may recover from examinees reimbursement for out-of-pocket costs. The total amount of allowable cost reimbursement per examinee shall not exceed $4, adjusted annually every January 1 for changes in the Department of Labor Consumer Price Index. Such individuals and organizations shall maintain records of out-of-pocket expenditures and shall certify annually to the Commission that all costs for which reimbursement was obtained were necessarily and prudently incurred.

Section 301. It is the purpose of this Act, among other things, to maintain the controls of the United States over all the channels of interstate and foreign radio transmission; and to provide for the use of such channels, but not the ownership thereof, by persons for limited periods of time, under licenses granted by Federal authority, and no such license shall be construed to create any right, beyond the terms, conditions and periods of the license. No person shall use or operate any appartus for the transmission of energy or communications or signals by radio. . . except under and in accordance with this Act and with a license in that behalf granted under the provisions of this Act.

Section 302.(a) The Commission may, consistent with the public interest, convenience and necessity, make reasonable regulations (1) governing the interference potential of devices which in their operation are capable of emitting radio frequency energy. . . in sufficient degree to cause harmful interference to radio communications and (2) establishing minimum performance standards for home electronic equipment and systems to reduce their susceptiblity to interference from radio frequency energy. Such regulations shall be applicable to the manufacture, import, sale, offer for sale, or shipment of such devices and home electronic equipment and systems, and to the use of such devices. (b) No person shall manufacture, import, sell, offer for sale, or ship device or home electronic equipment and systems, or use devices which fail to comply with regulations promulgated pursuant to this section.

Section 303. Except as otherwise provided in this Act, the Commission from time to time, as public convenience, interest or necessity requires, shall—

a) Classify radio stations

b) Prescribe the nature of the service to be rendered...

c) Assign bands of frequencies...

d) Determine the location of stations...

e) Regulate the kind of apparatus to be used with respect to its external effects and the purity and sharpness of the emissions from each station and from the apparatus therein.

f) Make such regulations not inconsistent with law as it may deem necessary to prevent interference between stations and to carry out the provisions of this Act: *Provided, however,* that changes in the frequencies, authorized power, or in the times of operation of any station, shall not be made without the consent of the station licensee unless, after a public hearing, the Commission shall determine that such changes will promote public convenience or interest or will serve public necessity, or the provisions of this Act will be more fully complied with;

g) Study new uses for radio, provide for experimental uses of frequencies, and generally encourage the larger and more effective use of radio in the public interest;

j) Have authority to make general rules and regulations requiring stations to keep such records...as it may deem desirable...

l)1) Have authority to prescribe the qualifications of station operators...and to issue licenses to persons who are found to be qualified by the commission and who otherwise are legally eligible for employment in the United States... 2) Notwithstanding paragraph (1) of this subsection, an individual to whom a radio station is licensed under the provisions of this Act may be issued an operator's license to operate that station. 3) In addition to amateur operator licenses which the Commission may issue to aliens pursuant to paragraph (2) of this subsection, and notwithstanding Section 301 of this Act and paragraph (1) of this subsection, the Commission may issue authorizations, under such conditions and terms as it may prescribe to permit an alien licensed by his government as an Amateur Radio operator to operate his Amateur Radio station licensed by his government in the United States, its possessions, and the Commonwealth of Puerto Rico provided there is in effect a multilateral or bilateral agreement, to which the United States and the alien's government are parties, for such operation on a reciprocal basis by United States Amateur Radio operators. Other provisions of this Act and of the Administrative Procedure Act shall not be applicable to any request or application for or modification, suspension or cancellation of any such authorization.

m)1) Have authority to suspend the license of any operator upon proof sufficent to satisfy the Commission that the licensee—(A) has violated or caused, aided, or abetted the violation of, any provision of any Act, treaty or convention binding on the United States, which the Commission is authorized to administer, or any regulation made by the Commission under any such Act, treaty or convention; or (B) has failed to carry out a lawful order of the master or person lawfully in charge of the ship or aircraft on which he is employed; or (C) has willfully damaged or permitted radio apparatus or installations to be damaged; or (D) has transmitted superfluous radio communications or signals or communications containing profane or obscene words, language or meaning, or has knowingly transmitted—(1) false or deceptive signals or communications; or (2) a call signal or letter which has not been assigned by proper authority to the station he is operating; or (E) has willfully or maliciously interfered with any other radio communications or signals; or (F) has obtained or attempted to obtain, or has assisted another to obtain or attempted to obtain, an operator's license by fraudulent means.

2) No order of suspension of any operator's license shall take effect until fifteen days' notice in writing thereof, stating the cause for the proposed suspension has been given to the operator licensee who may make written application to the Commission at any time within said fifteen days for a hearing upon such order...

n) Have authority to inspect all radio installations...

o) Have authority to designate call letters of all stations.

p) Have authority to cause to be published such call letters.

q) Have authority to require the painting and/or illumination of radio towers if and when in its judgment such towers constitute, or there is a reasonable possibility that they may constitute, a menace to air navigation.

r) Make such rules and regulations...to carry out the provisions of this Act, or any international radio or wire communications treaty or convention...

Section 308. (b) All applications for station licenses, or modifications or renewals thereof, shall set forth such facts as the Commission by regulation may prescribe as to the citizenship, character, and financial, technical, and other qualifications of the applicant to operate the station; the ownership and location of the proposed station and of the stations, if any, with which it is proposed to communicate; the frequencies and the power desired to be used; the hours of the day or other periods of time during which it is proposed to operate the station; the purposes for which the station is to be used; and such other information as it may require. The Commission, at any time after the filing of such original application and during the term of any such licenses, may require from an applicant or licensee further written statements of fact to enable it to determine whether such original application should be granted or denied or such license revoked. Such application and/or such statement of fact shall be signed by the applicant and/or licensee.

Section 310.(a) The station license required under this Act shall not be granted to or held by any foreign government or the representative thereof. (c) In addition to amateur station licenses which the Commission may issue to aliens pursuant to this Act, the Commission may issue authorizations, under such conditions and terms as it may prescribe, to permit an alien licensed by his government as an Amateur Radio operator to operate his Amateur Radio station licensed by his government in the United States, its possessions, and the Commonwealth of Puerto Rico provided there is in effect a bilateral agreement between the United States and the alien's government for such operation on a reciprocal basis by United States Amateur radio operators. Other provisions of this Act and of the Administrative Procedure act shall not be applicable to any request or application for or modification, suspension or cancellation of any such authorization.

Section 312.(a) The Commission may revoke any station license or construction permit—

(1) for false statements knowingly made either in the application or in any statement of fact which may be required pursuant to Section 308;

(2) because of conditions coming to the attention of the Commission which would warrant it in refusing to grant a license or permit on an original application;

(3) for willful or repeated failure to operate substantially as set forth in the license;

(4) for willful or repeated violation of, or willful or repeated failure to observe any provision of this Act or any rule or regulation of the Commission authorized by this Act or by a treaty ratified by the United States;

(5) for violation of or failure to observe any final cease and desist order issued by the Commission under this section;

(6) for violation of section 1304, 1343, or 1464 of title 18 of the United States Code; or

(b) Where any person (1) has failed to operate substantially as set forth in a license (2) has violated or failed to observe any of the provisions of this Act, or section 1304, 1343, or 1464 of title 18 of the United States Code,or (3) has violated or failed to observe any rule or regulation of the Commission authorized by this Act or by a treaty ratified by the United States, the Commission may order such person to cease and desist from such action.

(c) Before revoking a license or permit pursuant to subsection (a), or issuing a cease and desist order pursuant to subsection (b),the Commission shall serve upon the licensee, permittee, or person involved an order to show cause why an order of revocation or a cease and desist order should not be issued. Any such order to show cause, shall contain a statement of the matters with respect to which the Commission is inquiring and shall call upon said licensee, permitee, or person to appear before the Commission at a time and place stated in the order, but in no event less than thirty days after the receipt of such order, and give evidence upon the matter specified therein; except that where safety of life or property is involved, the Commission may provide in the order for a shorter period. If after hearing, or a waiver thereof, the Commission determines that an order of revocation or a cease and desist order should issue, it shall issue such order, which shall include a statement of the findings of the Commission and the grounds and reasons therefor and specify the effective date of the order, and shall cause the same to be served on said licensee, permittee, or person.

(d) In any case where a hearing is conducted pursuant to the provisions of this section, both the burden of proceeding with the introduction of evidence and the burden of proof shall be upon the Commission.

(e) The provisions of section 9(b) of the Administrative Procedure Act which apply with respect to the institution of any proceeding for the revocation of a license or permit shall apply also with the respect to the institution, under this section, of any proceeding for the issuance of a cease and desist order.

(f) For the purposes of this section:

(1) The term "willful," when used with reference to the commission or omission of any act, means the conscious and deliberate commission or omission of such act, irrespective of any intent to violate any provision of this Act or any rule or regulation of the Commission authorized by this Act or by a treaty ratified by the United States.

(2) The term "repeated," when used with reference to the commission or omission of any act, means the commission or omission of such act more than once or, if such commission or omission is continuous, for more than one day.

Section 318. The actual operation of all transmitting apparatus in any radio station for which a station license is required by this Act shall be carried on only by a person holding an operator's license issued hereunder. No person shall operate any such apparatus in such station except under and in accordance with an operator's license issued to him by the Commission...

Section 321... (b) All radio stations, including Government stations and stations on board foreign vessels when within the territorial waters of the United States, shall give absolute priority to radio communications or signals relating to ships in distress.

Section 324. In all circumstances, except in case of radio communications, or signals relating to vessels in distress, all radio stations, including those owned and operated by the United States, shall use the minimum amount of power necessary to carry out the communication desired.

Section 325. (a) No person within the jurisdiction of the United States shall knowingly utter or transmit, or cause to be uttered or transmitted, any false or fraudulent signal of distress, or communication relating thereto, nor shall any broadcasting station rebroadcast the program or any part thereof of another broadcasting station without the express authority of the originating station.

Section 333. No person shall willfully or maliciously interfere with or cause interference to any radiocommunications or any station licensed or authorized by or under this Act or operated by the United State government.

Section 501. Any person who willfully and knowingly does or causes or suffers to be done any act, matter or thing, in this Act prohibited or declared to be unlawful, or who willfully or knowingly omits or fails to do any act, matter or thing in this Act required to be done, or willfully or knowingly causes or suffers such omission or failure, shall, upon conviction thereof, be punished for such offense, for which no penalty (other than a forfeiture) is provided by this Act, by a fine of not more than $10,000 or by imprisonment for a term not exceeding two years, or both...

Section 502. Any person who willfully or knowingly violates any rule, regulation, restriction or condition made by the Commission under authority of this act, or any rules, regulation, restriction or condition made or imposed by any international radio or wire communications treaty or convention, or regulations annexed thereto, to which the United States is or may hereafter become a party, shall, in addition to any other penalties provided by law, be punished, upon conviction thereof, by a fine of not more than $500 for each and every day during which such offense occurs...

Section 503...(b) Any person who is determined by the Commission, in accordance with paragraph (3) or (4) of this subsection, to have—(A) willfully or repeatedly failed to comply substantially with the terms and conditions of any license, permit, certificate, or other instrument or authorization issued by the Commission; (B) willfully or repeatedly failed to comply with any of the provisions of this Act or of any rule, regulation, or order...shall be liable to the United States for a forfeiture penalty...

(2) The amount of any forfeiture penalty determined under this subsection shall not exceed $2000 for each violation. Each day of a continued violation shall constitute a separate offense...

Section 705...No person receiving or assisting in receiving, or transmitting or assisting in transmitting, any interstate or foreign communication by wire or radio shall divulge or publish the existence, contents, substance, purport, effect or meaning thereof,...to any person other than the addressee, his agent or attorney...or in response to a subpoena issued by a court of competent jurisdiction, or on demand or other lawful authority...and no person not being entitled thereto shall receive or assist in receiving any interstate or foreign communication by wire or radio and use the same or any information therein contained for his own benefit or for the benefit of another not entitled thereto...This section shall not apply to the receiving, divulging, publishing or utilizing the contents of any radio communication, which is transmitted by any station for the use of the general public, which relates to ships, aircraft, vehicles or persons in distress or which is transmitted by an amateur radio station or by a citizens band radio operator...

Section 706...(c) Upon proclamation by the President that there exists war or a threat of war or a state of public peril or disaster or other national emergency, or in order to preserve the neutrality of the United States, the President...may suspend or amend, for such time as he may see fit, the rules and regulations applicable to any or all stations...within the jurisdiction of the United States as prescribed by the Commission, and may cause the closing of any station for radio communication ...and the removal therefrom of its apparatus and equipment, or he may authorize the use or control of any such station...and/or its apparatus and equipment by any department of the Government under such regulations as he may prescribe, upon just compensation to the owners...

APPENDIX 2

International Radio Regulations.

Article 1—Terms and Definitions

Section III. Radio Services

§3.34 *Amateur Service:*

A *radiocommunication service* for the purpose of self-training, intercommunication and technical investigations carried out by amateurs, that is, by duly authorized persons interested in radio technique solely with a personal aim and without pecuniary interest.

§3.35 *Amateur-Satellite Service:*

A *radiocommunications* service using *space stations* on earth *satellites* for the same purposes as those of the *amateur service.*

Article 32—Amateur Service and Amateur-Satellite Service

Section I. Amateur Service

§1. Radiocommunications between amateur stations of different countries shall be forbidden if the administration of one of the countries concerned has notified that it objects to such radiocommunications.

§2. (1) When transmissions between amateur stations of different countries are permitted, they shall be made in plain language and shall be limited to messages of a technical nature relating to tests and to remarks of a personal character for which, by reason of their unimportance, recourse to the public telecommunications service is not justified.

(2) It is absolutely forbidden for amateur stations to be used for transmitting international communications on behalf of third parties.

(3) The preceding provisions may be modified by special arrangements between the administrations of the countries concerned.

§3. (1) Any person seeking a license to operate the apparatus of an amateur station shall prove that he is able to send correctly by hand and to receive correctly by ear texts in Morse code signals. The administrations concerned may, however, waive this requirement in the case of stations making use exclusively of frequencies above 30 MHz.

(2) Administrations shall take such measures as they judge necessary to verify the operational and technical qualifications of any person wishing to operate the apparatus of an amateur station.

§4. The maximum power of amateur stations shall be fixed by the administrations concerned, having regard to the technical qualifications of the operators and to the conditions under which these stations are to operate.

§5. (1) All the general rules of the Convention and of these Regulations shall apply to amateur stations. In particular, the emitted frequency shall be as stable and as free from spurious emissions as the state of technical development for such stations permits.

(2) During the course of their transmissions, amateur stations shall transmit their call sign at short intervals.

Section II. Amateur-Satellite Service

§6. The provisions of Section I of this Article shall apply equally, as appropriate, to the Amateur-Satellite Service.

§7. Space stations in the Amateur-Satellite Service operating in bands shared with other services shall be fitted with appropriate devices for controlling emissions in the event that harmful interference is reported in accordance with the procedure laid down in Article 22. Administrations authorizing such space stations shall inform the IFRB and shall ensure that sufficient earth command stations are established before launch to guarantee that any harmful interference which might be reported can be terminated by the authorizing administration.

APPENDIX 3

Classification of Emissions

§2.201 Emission, modulation, and transmission characteristics.

The following system of designating emission, modulation, and transmission characteristics shall be employed.

(a) Emissions are designated according to their classification and their necessary bandwidth.

(b) A minimum of three symbols are used to describe the basic characteristics of radio waves. Emissions are classified and symbolized according to the following characteristics.

(1) First symbol—type of modulation of the main carrier;
(2) Second symbol—nature of signal(s) modulating the main carrier;
(3) Third symbol—type of information to be transmitted.

Note: A forth and fifth symbol are provided for additional information and are shown in Appendix 6, Part A of the ITU Radio Regulations. Use of the fourth and fifth symbol is optional. Therefore, the symbols may be used as described in Appendix 6, but are not required by the Commission.

(c) First symbol—types of modulation of the main carrier:

(1) Emission of an unmodulated carrier.. N
(2) Emission in which the main carrier is amplitude-modulated (including cases where sub-carriers are angle-modulated):
—Double-sideband.. A
—Single-sideband, full carrier.. H
—Single-sideband, reduced or variable level carrier........................... R
—Single-sideband, suppressed carrier.. J
—Independent sidebands.. B
—Vestigial sideband... C
(3) Emission in which the main carrier is angle-modulated:
—Frequency modulation... F
—Phase modulation... G

Note: Whenever frequency modulation "F" is indicated, Phase modulation "G" is also acceptable.

(4) Emission in which the main carrier is amplitude and angle-modulated either simultaneously or in a pre-established sequence........................ D
(5) Emission of pulses:[1]
—Sequence of unmodulated pulses... P
—A sequence of pulses:
—Modulated in amplitude... K
—Modulated in width/duration.. L

[1]Emissions where the main carrier is directly modulated by a signal which has been coded into quantized form (e.g. pulse code modulation) should be designated under (2) or (3).

—Modulated in position/phase.. M
—In which the carrier is angle-modulated during the period of the pulse.. Q
—Which is a combination of the foregoing or is produced by other means.. V

(6) Cases not covered above, in which an emission consists of the main carrier modulated, either simultaneously or in a pre-established sequence, in a combination of two or more of the following modes: amplitude, angle, pulse.. W
(7) Cases not otherwise covered.. X

(d) Second Symbol—nature of signal(s) modulating the main carrier:

(1) No modulating signal.. 0
(2) A single channel containing quantized or digital information without the use of a modulating subcarrier, excluding time-division multiplex.......... 1
(3) A single channel containing quantized or digital information with the use of a modulating subcarrier, excluding time-division multiplex.......... 2
(4) A single channel containing analogue information.............................. 3
(5) Two or more channels containing quantized or digital information........ 7
(6) Two or more channels containing analogue information...................... 8
(7) Composite system with one or more channels containing quantized or digital information, together with one or more channels containing analogue information.. 9
(8) Cases not otherwise covered.. X

(e) Third Symbol—type of information to be transmitted:[2]

(1) No information transmitted.. N
(2) Telegraphy—for aural reception.. A
(3) Telegraphy—for automatic reception.. B
(4) Facsimile.. C
(5) Data transmission, telemetry, telecommand.. D
(6) Telephony (including sound broadcasting).. E
(7) Television (video).. F
(8) Combination of the above.. W
(9) Cases not otherwise covered.. X

(f) Type *B* emission: As an exception to the above principles, damped waves are symbolized in the Commission's rules and regulations as type *B* emission. The use of type B emissions is forbidden.

(g) Whenever the full designation of an emission is necessary, the symbol for that emission, as given above, shall be preceded by the necessary bandwidth of the emission as indicated in §2.202(b)(1).

APPENDIX 4

Convention Between Canada and the United States of America, Relating to the operation by Citizens of Either Country of Certain Radio Equipment or Stations in the Other Country (Effective May 15, 1952)

Article III

It is agreed that persons holding appropriate amateur licenses issued by either country may operate their amateur stations in the territory of the other country under the following conditions:

(a) Each visiting amateur may be required to register and receive a permit before operating any amateur station licensed by his government.

(b) The visiting amateur will identify his station by:

(1) Radiotelegraph operation. The amateur call sign issued to him/her by the licensing country followed by a slant (/) sign and the amateur call sign prefix and call area number of the country he is visiting.

(2) Radiotelephone operation. The amateur call sign in English issued to him by the licensing country followed by the words, "fixed" "portable" or "mobile," as appropriate, and the amateur call sign prefix and call area number of the country he is visiting.

(c) Each amateur station shall indicate at least once during each contact with another station its geographical location as nearly as possible by city and state or city and province.

(d) In other respects the amateur station shall be operated in accordance with the laws and regulations of the country in which the station is temporarily located.

APPENDIX 5

Extracts from the international Radio Regulations.

Resolution No. 640

Relating to the International Use of Radiocommunications, in the Event of Natural Disasters, in Frequency Bands Allocated to the Amateur Service.

Considering

a) that in the event of natural disaster normal communication systems are frequently overloaded, damaged, or completely disrupted.

b) that rapid establishment of communications is essential to facilitate worldwide relief actions.

c) that the amateur bands are not bound by international plans or notification procedures, and are therefore well adapted for short-term use in emergency cases.

d) that international disaster communications would be facilitated by temporary use of certain frequency bands allocated to the amateur service.

e) that under those circumstances the stations of the amateur service because of their widespread distribution and their demonstrated capacity in such cases, can assist in meeting essential communication needs.

f) the existence of national and regional amateur emergency networks using frequencies throughout the bands allocated to the amateur service.

g) that in the event of a natural disaster, direct communications between amateur stations and other stations might enable vital communications to be carried out until normal communications are restored.

Recognizing

that the rights and responsibilities for communications in the event of a natural disaster rest with the administrations involved.

Resolves

1. that the bands allocated to the amateur service which are specified in No. 510 may be used by administrations to meet the needs of international disaster communications.

2. that such use of these bands shall be only for communications in relation to relief operations in connection with natural disasters.

3. that the use of specified bands allocated to the amateur service by non-amateur stations for disaster communications shall be limited to the duration of the emergency and to the specific geographical areas as defined by the responsible authority of the affected country.

4. that disaster communications shall take place within the disaster area and between the disaster area and the permanent headquarters of the organization providing relief.

5. that such communications shall be carried out only with the consent of the administration of the country in which the disaster has occurred.

6. that relief communications provided from outside the country in which the disaster has occurred shall not replace existing national or international amateur emergency networks.

7. that close cooperation is desirable between amateur stations and the stations of other radio services which may find it necessary to use amateur frequencies in disaster communications.

8. that such international relief communications shall avoid, as far as practicable, interference to the amateur service networks.

Invites Administrations

1. to provide for the needs of international disaster communications.

2. to provide for the needs of emergency communications with their national regulations.

APPENDIX 6

Extracts from the international Radio Regulations.

Resolution No. 641

Relating to the use of the Frequency Band 7000-7100 kHz

Considering

a) that the sharing of frequency bands by amateur and broadcasting services is undesirable and should be avoided.

b) that it is desirable to have worldwide exclusive allocations for these services in Band 7.

c) that the band 7000-7100 kHz is allocated on a worldwide basis exclusively to the amateur service.

Resolves

that the broadcasting service shall be prohibited from the band 7000-7100 kHz and that the broadcasting stations operating on frequencies in this band shall cease such operation.

APPENDIX 7

Extracts from the international Radio Regulations.

Resolution No. 642

Relating to the Bringing into Use of Earth Stations in the amateur-satellite service.

Recognizing

that the procedures of Articles 11 and 13 are applicable to the amateur-satellite service.

Recognizing Further

a) that the characteristics of each station in the amateur-satellite service vary widely.

b) that space stations in the amateur-satellite service are intended for multiple access by amateur earth stations in all countries.

c) that coordination among stations in the amateur and Amateur Satellite services is accomplished without the need for formal procedures.

d) that the burden of terminating any harmful interference is placed upon the administration authorizing a space station in the amateur-satellite service pursuant to the provisions of No. 2741 of the Radio Regulations.

Notes

that certain information specified in Appendices 3 and 4 cannot reasonably be provided for earth stations in the amateur-satellite service.

Resolves

1. that when an administration (or one acting on behalf of a group of named administrations) intends to establish a satellite system in the amateur-satellite service and wishes to publish information with respect to earth stations in the system it may:

1.1 communicate to the IFRB all or part of the information listed in Appendix 3; the IFRB shall publish such information in a special section of its weekly circular requesting comments to be communicated within a period of four months after the date of publication.

1.2 notify under Nos. 1488 to 1491 all or part of the information listed in Appendix 3; the IFRB shall record it in a special list.

2. that this information shall include at least the characteristics of a typical amateur earth station in the amateur-satellite service having the facility to transmit signals of the space station to initiate, modify, or terminate the functions of the space station.

APPENDIX 8

§2.815 External radio frequency power amplifiers.

(a) As used in this part, an external radio frequenccy power amplifier is any device which, (1) when used in conjunction with a radio transmitter as a signal source is capable of amplification of that signal, and (2) is not an integral part of a radio transmitter as manufactured.

(b) After April 27, 1978, no person shall manufacture, sell or lease, offer for sale or lease (including advertising for sale or lease), or import, ship, or distribute for the purpose of selling or leasing or offering for sale or lease, any external radio frequency power amplifier or amplifier kit capable of operation on any frequency or frequencies between 24 and 35 MHz.

NOTE: For purposes of this part, the amplifier will be deemed incapable of operation between 24 and 35 MHz if:

(1) The amplifier has no more than 6 decibels of gain between 24 and 26 MHz and between 28 and 35 MHz. (This gain is determined by the ratio of the input RF driving signal (mean power measurement) to the mean RF output power of the amplifier.); and

(2) The amplifier exhibits no amplification (0 decibels of gain) between 26 and 28 MHz.

(c) No person shall manufacture, sell or lease, offer for sale or lease (including advertising for sale or lease) or import, ship or distribute for the purpose of selling or leasing or offering for sale or lease, any external radio frequency power amplifier or amplifier kit capable of operation on any frequency or frequencies below 144 MHz unless the amplifier has received a grant of type acceptance in accordance with Subpart J of this part and Subpart C of Part 97 or other relevant parts of this chapter. No more than 10 external radio frequency power amplifiers or amplifier kits may be constructed for evaluation purposes in preparation for the submission of an application for a grant of type acceptance.

NOTE: For the purposes of this part, an amplifier will be deemed incapable of operation below 144 MHz if the amplifier is not capable of being easily modified to increaqse its amplification characteristics below 120 MHz, and either:

(1) The mean output power of the amplifier decreases, as frequency decreases from 144 MHz, to a point where 0 decibels or less gain is exhibited at 120 MHz and below 120 MHz, or

(2) The amplifier is not capable of even short periods of operation below 120 MHz without sustaining permanent damage to its amplification circuitry.

(d) The proscription in paragraph (b) of this section shall not apply to marketing, as defined in that paragraph, by a licensed amateur radio operator to another licensed amateur radio operator of an external radio frequency power amplifier fabricated in not more than one unit of the same model in a calendar year by that operator provided the amplifier is for the amateur operator's personal use at his licensed amateur radio station and the requirements of §§97.315 and 97.317 of this chapter are met.

(e) The proscription in paragraph (c) of this section shall not apply in the marketing, as defined in that paragraph, by a licensed amateur radio operator to another licensed amateur radio operator of an external radio frequency power amplifier if the amplifier is for the amatuer radio operator's personal use at his licensed amateur radio station and the requirements of §§97.315 or 97.317 of this chapter are met.

APPENDIX 9

§2.314 Additional authority delegated.

(x) When deemed necessary by the Engineer-in-Charge of a Commission field facility to assure compliance with the Rules, a station licensee shall maintain a record of such operating and maintenance records as may be necessary to resolve conditions of interference or deficient technical operation.

APPENDIX 10

§0.121 Location of field installations.

(a) Field offices are located throughout the United States. For the address and phone number of the closest office contact the Field Operations Bureau or see the U.S. Government Manual.

(b) Protected field offices are located at the following geographical coordinates:

Allegan, Michigan
42°36′20″ N. Latitude
84°57′20″ W. Longitude
Anchorage, Alaska
61°09′43″ N. Latitude
149°59′55″ W. Longitude
Belfast, Maine
44°26′42″ N. Latitude
69°04′58″ W. Longitude
Canandaigua, New York
42°54′48″ N. Latitude
77°15′59″ W. Longitude
Douglas, Arizona
31°30′02″ N. Latitude
109°39′12″ W. Longitude
Ferndale, Washington
48°57′21″ N. Latitude
122°33′13″ W. Longitude
Grand Island, Nebraska
40°55′21″ N. Latitude
98°25′42″ W. Longitude
Kingsville, Texas
27°26′29″ N. Latitude
97°53′00″ W. Longitude
Laurel, Maryland
39°09′54″ N. Latitude
76°49′17″ W. Longitude
Livermore, California
37°43′30″ N. Latitude
121°45′12″ W. Longitude
Powder Springs, Georgia
33°51′44″ N. Latitude
84°43′26″ W. Longitude
Sabana Seca, Puerto Rico
18°27′23″ N. Latitude
66°13′37″ W. Longitude
Santa Isabel, Puerto Rico
18°00′26″ N. Latitude
66°22′32″ W. Longitude
Vero Beach, Florida
27°36′21″ N. Latitude
80°38′06″ W. Longitude
Waipahu, Hawaii
21°22′45″ N. Latitude
157°59′54″ W. Longitude

Memorandum Opinion and Order in PRB-1

Here's the full text of FCC's Memorandum Opinion and Order in PRB-1. If you require an "official" copy of PRB-1 for use in a legal proceeding, you may cite the *Federal Register:* 50 FR 38813.

Before the Federal Communications Commission Washington, DC 20554	FCC 85-506 36149

In the Matter of	)	
	)	
Federal preemption of state and	)	PRB-1
local regulations pertaining	)	
to Amateur radio facilities.	)	

MEMORANDUM OPINION AND ORDER

Adopted: September 16, 1985 ; Released: September 19, 1985

By the Commission: Commissioner Rivera not participating.

Background

1. On July 16, 1984, the American Radio Relay League, Inc. (ARRL) filed a Request for Issuance of a Declaratory Ruling asking us to delineate the limitations of local zoning and other local and state regulatory authority over Federally-licensed radio facilities. Specifically, the ARRL wanted an explicit statement that would preempt all local ordinances which provably preclude or significantly inhibit effective reliable amateur radio communications. The ARRL acknowledges that local authorities can regulate amateur installations to insure the safety and health of persons in the community, but believes that those regulations cannot be so restrictive that they preclude effective amateur communications.

2. Interested parties were advised that they could file comments in the matter.[1] With extension, comments were due on or before December 26, 1984,[2] with reply comments due on or before January 25, 1985[3] Over sixteen hundred comments were filed.

Local Ordinances

3. Conflicts between amateur operators regarding radio antennas and local authorities regarding restrictive ordinances are common. The amateur operator is governed by the regulations contained in Part 97 of our rules. Those rules do not limit the height of an amateur antenna but they require, for aviation safety reasons, that certain FAA notification and FCC approval procedures must be followed for antennas which exceed 200 feet in height above ground level or antennas which are to be erected near airports. Thus, under FCC rules some amateur antenna support structures require obstruction marking and lighting. On the other hand, local municipalities or governing bodies frequently enact regulations limiting antennas and their support structures in height and location, e.g. to side or rear yards, for health, safety or aesthetic considerations. These limiting regulations can result in conflict because the effectiveness of the communications that emanate from an amateur radio station are directly dependent upon the location and the height of the antenna. Amateur operators maintain that they are precluded from operating in certain bands allocated for their use if the height of their antennas is limited by a local ordinance.

4. Examples of restrictive local ordinances were submitted by several amateur

operators in this proceeding. Stanley J. Cichy, San Diego, California, noted that in San Diego amateur radio antennas come under a structures ruling which limits building heights to 30 feet. Thus, antennas there are also limited to 30 feet. Alexander Vrenios, Mundelein, Illinois wrote that an ordinance of the Village of Mundelein provides that an antenna must be a distance from the property line that is equal to one and one-half times its height. In his case, he is limited to an antenna tower for his amateur station just over 53 feet in height.

5. John C. Chapman, an amateur living in Bloomington, Minnesota, commented that he was not able to obtain a building permit to install an amateur radio antenna exceeding 35 feet in height because the Bloomington city ordinance restricted "structures" heights to 35 feet. Mr. Chapman said that the ordinance, when written, undoubtedly applied to buildings but was now being applied to antennas in the absence of a specific ordinance regulating them. There were two options open to him if he wanted to engage in amateur communications. He could request a variance to the ordinance by way of a hearing before the City Council, or he could obtain affidavits from his neighbors swearing that they had no objection to the proposed antenna installation. He got the building permit after obtaining the cooperation of his neighbors. His concern, however, is that he had to get permission from several people before he could effectively engage in radio communications for which he had a valid FCC amateur license.

6. In addition to height restrictions, other limits are enacted by local jurisdictions—anti-climb devices on towers or fences around them; minimum distances from high voltage power lines; minimum distances of towers from property lines; and regulations pertaining to the structural soundness of the antenna installation. By and large, amateurs do not find these safety precautions objectionable. What they do object to are the sometimes prohibitive, non-refundable application filing fees to obtain a permit to erect an antenna installation and those provisions in ordinances which regulate antennas for purely aesthetic reasons. The amateurs contend, almost universally, that "beauty is in the eye of the beholder." They assert that an antenna installation is not more aesthetically displeasing than other objects that people keep on their property, e.g. motor homes, trailers, pick-up trucks, solar collectors and gardening equipment.

Restrictive Covenants

7. Amateur operators also oppose restrictions on their amateur operations which are contained in the deeds for their homes or in their apartment leases. Since these restrictive covenants are contractual agreements between private parties, they are not generally a matter of concern to the Commission. However, since some amateurs who commented in this proceeding provided us with examples of restrictive covenants, they are included for information. Mr. Eugene O. Thomas of Hollister, California included in his comments an extract of the Declaration of Covenants and Restrictions for Ridgemark Estates, County of San Benito, State of California. It provides:

> No antenna for transmission or reception of radio signals shall be erected outdoors for use by any dwelling unit except upon approval of the Directors. No radio or television signals or any other form of electromagnetic radiation shall be permitted to originate from any lot which may unreasonably interfere with the reception of television or radio signals upon any other lot.

Marshall Wilson, Jr. provided a copy of the restrictive covenant contained in deeds for the Bell Martin Addition #2, Irving, Texas. It is binding upon all of the owners or purchasers of the lots in the said addition, his or their heirs, executors, administrators or assigns. It reads:

> No antenna or tower shall be erected upon any lot for the purposes of radio operations.

William J. Hamilton resides in an apartment building in Gladstone, Missouri. He cites a clause in his lease prohibiting the erection of an antenna. He states that he has been forced to give up operating amateur radio equipment except a hand-held 2 meter (144-148 MHz) radio transceiver. He maintains that he should not be penalized just because he lives in an apartment.

Other restrictive covenants are less global in scope than those cited above. For example, Robert Webb purchased a home in Houston, Texas. His deed restriction prohibited "transmitting or receiving antennas extending above the roof line."

8. Amateur operators generally oppose restrictive covenants for several reasons. They maintain that such restrictions limit the places that they can reside if they want to pursue their hobby of amateur radio. Some state that they impinge on First Amendment rights of free speech. Others believe that a constitutional right is being abridged because, in their view, everyone has a right to access the airwaves regardless of where they live.

9. The contrary belief held by housing subdivision communities and condominium or homeowner's associations is that amateur radio installations constitute safety hazards, cause interference to other electronic equipment which may be operated in the home (television, radio, stereos) or are eyesores that detract from the aesthetic and tasteful appearance of the housing development or apartment complex. To counteract these negative consequences, the subdivisions and associations include in their deeds, leases or by-laws, restrictions and limitations on the location and height of antennas or, in some cases, prohibit them altogether. The restrictive covenants are contained in the contractual agreement entered into at the time of the sale or lease of the property. Purchasers or lessees are free to choose whether they wish to reside where such restrictions on amateur antennas are in effect or settle elsewhere.

Supporting Comments

10. The Department of Defense (DOD) supported the ARRL and emphasized in its comments that continued success of existing national security and emergency preparedness telecommunications plans involving amateur stations would be severely diminished if state and local ordinances were allowed to prohibit the construction and usage of effective amateur transmission facilities. DOD utilizes volunteers in the Military Affiliate Radio Service (MARS),[4] Civil Air Patrol (CAP) and the Radio Amateur Civil Emergency Service (RACES). It points out that these volunteer communicators are operating radio equipment installed in their homes and that undue restrictions on antennas by local authorities adversely affect their efforts. DOD states that the responsiveness of these volunteer systems would be impaired if local ordinances interfere with the effectiveness of these important national telecommunication resources. DOD favors the issuance of a ruling that would set limits for local and state regulatory bodies when they are dealing with amateur stations.

11. Various chapters of the American Red Cross also came forward to support the ARRL's request for a preemptive ruling. The Red Cross works closely with amateur radio volunteers. It believes that without amateurs' dedicated support, disaster relief operations would significantly suffer and that its ability to serve disaster victims would be hampered. It feels that antenna height limitations that might be imposed by local bodies will negatively affect the service now rendered by the volunteers.

12. Cities and counties from various parts of the United States filed comments in support of the ARRL's request for a Federal preemption ruling. The comments from the Director of Civil Defense, Port Arthur, Texas are representative:

> The Amateur Radio Service plays a vital role with our Civil Defense program here in Port Arthur and the design of these antennas and towers lends greatly to our ability to communicate during times of disaster.

> We do not believe there should be any restrictions on the antennas and towers except for reasonable safety precautions. Tropical storms, hurricanes and tornadoes are a way of life here on the Texas Gulf Coast and good communications are absolutely essential when preparing for a hurricane and even more so during recovery operations after the hurricane has past.

13. The Quarter Century Wireless Association took a strong stand in favor of the Issuance of a declaratory ruling. It believes that Federal preemption is necessary so that there will be uniformity for all Amateur Radio installations on private property throughout the United States.

14. In its comments, the ARRL argued that the Commission has the jurisdiction to preempt certain local land use regulations which frustrate or prohibit amateur radio communications. It said that the appropriate standard in preemption cases is not the extent of state and local interest in a given regulation, but rather the impact of that regulation on Federal goals. Its position is that Federal preemption is warranted whenever local governmental regulations relate adversely to the operational aspects of amateur communication. The ARRL maintains that localities routinely employ a variety of land use devices to preclude the installation of effective amateur antennas, including height restrictions, conditional use permits, building setbacks and dimensional limitations on antennas. It sees a declaratory ruling of Federal preemption as necessary to cause municipalities to accommodate amateur operator needs in land use planning efforts.

15. James C. O'Connell, an attorney who has represented several amateurs before local zoning authorities, said that requiring amateurs to seek variances or special use approval to erect reasonable antennas unduly restricts the operation of amateur stations. He suggested that the Commission preempt zoning ordinances which impose antenna height limits of less than 65 feet. He said that this height would represent a reasonable accommodation of the communication needs of most amateurs and the legitimate concerns of local zoning authorities.

Opposing Comments

16. The City of La Mesa, California has a zoning regulation which controls amateur antennas. Its comments reflected an attempt to reach a balanced view.

> This regulation has neither the intent, nor the effect, of precluding or inhibiting effective and reliable communications. Such antennas may be built as long as their construction does not unreasonably block views or constitute eyesores. The reasonable assumption is that there are always alternatives at a given site for different placement, and/or methods for aesthetic treatment. Thus, both public objectives of controlling land use for the public health, safety, and convenience, and providing an effective communications network, can be satisfied.
>
> A blanket ruling to completely set aside local control, or a ruling which recognizes control only for the purpose of safety of antenna construction, would be contrary to...legitimate local control.

17. Comments from the County of San Diego state:

> While we are aware of the benefits provided by amateur operators, we oppose the issuance of a preemption ruling which would elevate 'antenna effectiveness' to a position above all other considerations. We must, however, argue that the local government must have the ability to place reasonable limitations upon the placement and configuration of amateur radio transmitting and receiving antennas. Such ability is necessary to assure that the local decision-makers have the authority to protect the public health, safety and welfare of all citizens.
>
> In conclusion, I would like to emphasize an important difference between your regulatory powers and that of local governments. Your Commission's approval of the

preemptive requests would establish a "national policy." However, any regulation adopted by a local jurisdiction could be overturned by your Commission or a court if such regulation was determined to be unreasonable.

18. The City of Anderson, Indiana, summarized some of the problems that face local communities:

> I am sympathetic to the concerns of these antenna owners and I understand that to gain the maximum reception from their devices, optimal location is necessary. However, the preservation of residential zoning districts as "liveable" neighborhoods is jeopardized by placing these antennas in front yards of homes. Major problems of public safety have been encountered, particularly vision blockage for auto and pedestrian access. In addition, all communities are faced with various building lot sizes. Many building lots are so small that established setback requirements (in order to preserve adequate air and light) are vulnerable to the unregulated placement of antennas.
>
> . . . the exercise of preemptive authority by the FCC in granting this request would not be in the best interest of the general public.

19. The National Association of Counties (NACO), the American Planning Association (APA) and the National League of Cities (NCL) all opposed the issuance of an antenna preemption ruling. NACO emphasized that federal and state power must be viewed in harmony and warns that Federal intrusion into local concerns of health, safety and welfare could weaken the traditional police power exercised by the state and unduly interfere with the legitimate activities of the states. NLC believed that both Federal and local interests can be accommodated without preempting local authority to regulate the installation of amateur radio antennas. The APA said that the FCC should continue to leave the issue of regulating amateur antennas with the local government and with the state and Federal courts.

Discussion

20. When considering preemption, we must begin with two constitutional provisions. The tenth amendment provides that any powers which the constitution either does not delegate to the United States or does not prohibit the states from exercising are reserved to the states. These are the police powers of the states. The Supremacy Clause, however, provides that the constitution and the laws of the United States shall supersede any state law to the contrary. Article III, Section 2. Given these basic premises, state laws may be preempted in three ways: First, Congress may expressly preempt the state law. See *Jones v. Rath Packing Co.,* 430 U.S. 519, 525 (1977). Or, Congress may indicate its intent to completely occupy a given field so that any state law encompassed within that field would implicitly be preempted. Such intent to preempt could be found in a congressional regulatory scheme that was so pervasive that it would be reasonable to assume that Congress did not intend to permit the states to supplement it. See *Fidelity Federal Savings & Loan Ass'n v. de la Cuesta,* 458 U.S. 141, 153 (1982). Finally, preemption may be warranted when state law conflicts with federal law. Such conflicts may occur when "compliance with both Federal and state regulations is a physical impossibility," *Florida Lime & Avocado Growers, Inc. v. Paul,* 373 U.S. 132, 142, 143 (1963), or when state law "stands as an obstacle to the accomplishment and execution of the full purposes and objectives of Congress," *Hines v. Davidowitz,* 312 U.S. 52, 67 (1941). Furthermore, federal regulations have the same preemptive effect as federal statutes, *Fidelity Federal Savings & Loan Association v. de la Cuesta,* supra.

21. The situation before us requires us to determine the extent to which state and local zoning regulations may conflict with federal policies concerning amateur radio operators.

22. Few matters coming before us present such a clear dichotomy of view point as does the instant issue. The cities, countries, local communities and housing associations see an obligation to all of their citizens and try to address their concerns. This is accomplished through regulations, ordinances or covenants oriented toward the health, safety and general welfare of those they regulate. At the opposite pole are the individual amateur operators and their support groups who are troubled by local regulations which may inhibit the use of amateur stations or, in some instances, totally preclude amateur communications. Aligned with the operators are such entities as the Department of Defense, the American Red Cross and local civil defense and emergency organizations who have found in Amateur Radio a pool of skilled radio operators and a readily available backup network. In this situation, we believe it is appropriate to strike a balance between the federal interest in promoting amateur operations and the legitimate interests of local governments in regulating local zoning matters. The cornerstone on which we will predicate our decision is that a reasonable accommodation may be made between the two sides.

23. Preemption is primarily a function of the extent of the conflict between federal and state and local regulation. Thus, in considering whether our regulations or policies can tolerate a state regulation, we may consider such factors as the severity of the conflict and the reasons underlying the state's regulations. In this regard, we have previously recognized the legitimate and important state interests reflected in local zoning regulations. For example, in *Earth Satellite Communications, Inc.*, 95 FCC 2d 1223 (1983), we recognized that

> ...countervailing state interests inhere in the present situation... For example, we do not wish to preclude a state or locality from exercising jurisdiction over certain elements of an SMATV operation that properly may fall within its authority, such as zoning or public safety and health, provided the regulation in question is not undertaken as a pretext for the actual purpose of frustrating achievement of the preeminent federal objective and so long as the non-federal regulation is applied in a nondiscriminatory manner.

24. Similarly, we recognize here that there are certain general state and local interests which may, in their even-handed application, legitimately affect amateur radio facilities. Nonetheless, there is also a strong federal interest in promoting amateur communications. Evidence of this interest may be found in the comprehensive set of rules that the Commission has adopted to regulate the amateur service.[5] Those rules set forth procedures for the licensing of stations and operators, frequency allocations, technical standards which amateur radio equipment must meet and operating practices which amateur operators must follow. We recognize the amateur radio service as a voluntary, noncommercial communication service, particularly with respect to providing emergency communications. Moreover, the amateur radio service provides a reservoir of trained operators, technicians and electronic experts who can be called on in times of national or local emergencies. By its nature, the Amateur Radio Service also provides the opportunity for individual operators to further international goodwill. Upon weighing these interests, we believe a limited preemption policy is warranted. State and local regulations that operate to preclude amateur communications in their communities are in direct conflict with federal objectives and must be preempted.

25. Because amateur station communications are only as effective as the antennas employed, antenna height restrictions directly affect the effectiveness of amateur communications. Some amateur antenna configurations require more substantial installations than others if they are to provide the amateur operator with the communications that he/she desires to engage in. For example, an antenna array for international amateur communications will differ from an antenna used to contact

other amateur operators at shorter distances. We will not, however, specify any particular height limitation below which a local government may not regulate, nor will we suggest the precise language that must be contained in local ordinances, such as mechanisms for special exceptions, variances, or conditional use permits. Nevertheless, local regulations which involve placement, screening, or height of antennas based on health, safety, or aesthetic considerations must be crafted to accommodate reasonably amateur communications, and to represent the minimum practicable regulation to accomplish the local authority's legitimate purpose.[6]

26. Obviously, we do not have the staff or financial resources to review all state and local laws that affect amateur operations. We are confident, however, that state and local governments will endeavor to legislate in a manner that affords appropriate recognition to the important federal interest at stake here and thereby avoid unnecessary conflicts with federal policy, as well as time-consuming and expensive litigation in this area. Amateur operators who believe that local or state governments have been overreaching and thereby have precluded accomplishment of their legitimate communications goals, may, in addition, use this document to bring our policies to the attention of local tribunals and forums.

27. Accordingly, the Request for Declaratory Ruling filed July 16, 1984, by the American Radio Relay League, Inc., IS GRANTED to the extent indicated herein and, in all other respects, IS DENIED.

FEDERAL COMMUNICATIONS COMMISSION
William J. Tricarico
Secretary

FOOTNOTES

[1]Public Notice, August 30, 1984, Mimeo. No. 6299, 49 F.R. 36113, September 14, 1984.
[2]Public Notice, December 19, 1984, Mimeo No. 1498.
[3]Order, November 8, 1984, Mimeo. No. 770.
[4]MARS is solely under the auspices of the military which recruits volunteer amateur operators to render assistance to it. The Commission is not involved in the MARS program.
[5]47 CFR Part 97.
[6]We reiterate that our ruling herein does not reach restrictive covenants in private contractual agreements. Such agreements are voluntarily entered into by the buyer or tenant when the agreement is executed and do not usually concern this Commission.

FCC Field Offices

Boston MA office, NFPA Building, Battery March Park, Quincy, MA 02169, the states of *Connecticut, Maine, Massachusetts, New Hampshire, Rhode Island* and *Vermont.*

New York City office, 201 Varick St., corner of Houston St., New York, NY 10014. In the state of *New York,* the counties of Albany, Bronx, Columbia, Delaware, Dutchess, Greene, Kings, Nassau, New York, Orange, Putnam, Queens, Rensselaer, Richmond, Rockland, Schenectady, Suffolk, Sullivan, Ulster and Westchester; in the state of *New Jersey,* the counties of Bergen, Essex, Hudson, Hunterdon, Mercer, Middlesex, Monmouth, Morris, Passaic, Somerset, Sussex, Union and Warren.

Philadelphia, PA office, One Oxford Valley Office Building, Room 404, 2300 E. Lincoln Hwy., Langhorne, PA 19047. In the state of *Pennsylvania,* all counties; in the state of *New Jersey,* the counties of Atlantic, Burlington, Camden, Cape May, Cumberland, Gloucester, Ocean and Salem; and the county of Newcastle in the state of *Delaware.*

Baltimore, MD office, 1017 Federal Building, 31 Hopkins Plaza, Baltimore, MD 21201. The state of *Maryland*; the counties of Kent and Sussex in the state of *Delaware;*

the state of *West Virginia*; in *Virginia,* the counties of Arlington, Fairfax, Loudoun and Prince Williams.

Norfolk, VA office, 1200 Communications Circle, Virginia Beach, VA 23455. The state of *Virginia* (except the part lying in District 4); and the state of *North Carolina,* all counties.

Atlanta, GA office, Koger Center-Gwinett, Suite 320, 3575 Koger Boulevard, Duluth, GA 30136. The states of *Georgia, South Carolina* and *Tennessee,* and the state of *Alabama* except Baldwin and Mobile Counties.

Miami, FL office, 8390 NW 53rd St., Miami, FL 33166. The state of *Florida* and in the state of *Alabama,* Baldwin and Mobile Counties.

New Orleans, LA office, 800 West Commerce, Room 505, New Orleans LA 70123. The states of *Arkansas, Louisiana* and *Mississippi.*

Houston, TX office, Suite 900, 1225 North Loop West, Houston, TX 77008. In the state of *Texas,* the counties of Angelina, Aransas, Atascosa, Austin, Bandera, Bastrop, Bee, Bexar, Blanco, Brazoria, Brazos, Brooks, Burleson, Caldwell, Calhoun, Cameron, Chambers, Colorado, Comal, DeWitt, Dimmit, Duval, Edwards, Fayette, Fort Bend, Frio, Galveston, Gillespie, Goliad, Gonzales, Grimes, Guadalupe, Hardon, Harris, Hays, Hidalgo, Jackson, Jasper, Jefferson, Jim Hogg, Jim Wells, Karnes, Kendall, Kenedy, Kerr, Kinney, Kleberg, LaSalle, Lavaca, Lee, Liberty, Live Oak, Madison, Matagorda, Maverick, McMullen, Medina, Montgomery, Nacagdoches, Newton, Nueces, Orange, Polk, Real, Refugio, Sabine, San Augustine, San Jacinto, San Patricio, Starr, Travis, Trinity, Tyler, Uvalde, Val Verde, Victoria, Walker, Waller, Washington, Webb, Wharton, Willacy, Williamson, Wilson, Zapata and Zavala.

Dallas, TX office, 9330 LBJ Freeway, Suite 1170, Dallas, TX 75243. The state of *Texas* except that part which is covered by the Houston, TX office, and the state of *Oklahoma.*

Los Angeles, CA office, Cerritos Corp Tower, 18000 Studebaker Rd, RM 660, Cerritos, CA 90701. The state of *Arizona;* in the state of *Nevada,* the county of Clark; in the state of *California,* the counties of Imperial, Inyo, Kern, Los Angeles, Orange, Riverside, San Bernardino, San Diego, San Luis Obispo, Santa Barbara and Ventura.

San Francisco, CA office, 424 Customhouse, 555 Battery St., San Francisco, CA 94111. The state of *California* except that part covered by the Los Angeles, CA office, the state of *Nevada* except the county of Clark, and the state of *Utah.*

Portland, OR office, 1782 Federal Office Bldg., 1220 S.W. 3d Ave., Portland, OR 97204. The state of *Oregon;* the state of *Idaho* except that part covered by the Seattle, WA office; in the state of *Washington,* the counties of Clark, Cowlitz, Klickitat, Skamania and Wahkiakum.

Seattle, WA office, 11410 NE 122nd Way, Suite 312, Kirkland, WA 98034. The state of *Montana;* the state of *Washington* except that part which is covered by the Portland, OR office; in the state of *Idaho,* the counties of Benewah, Bonner, Boundary, Clearwater, Idaho, Kootenai, Latah, Lewis, Nez Perce and Shosshone.

Denver, CO office, 12477 W. Cedar Dr., Denver, CO 80228. The states of *Colorado, New Mexico, North Dakota, South Dakota* and *Wyoming.*

St. Paul, MN office, 691 Federal Bldg and Courthouse, 316 North Robert St., St. Paul, MN 55101. The state of *Minnesota,* the state of *Michigan,* the counties of Alger, Baraga, Chippewa, Delta, Dickinson, Gogebic, Houghton, Iron, Keweenaw, Luce, Mackinac, Marquette, Menominee, Ontonagon and Schoolcraft and the state of *Wisconsin*, except for the part covered by the Chicago, IL office.

Kansas City, MO office, Room 320 Brywood Office Tower, 8800 E. 63rd Street, Kansas City, MO 64133. The states of *Iowa, Kansas, Missouri* and *Nebraska.*

Chicago, IL office, Park Ridge Office Park, Room 306, 1550 Northwest Hwy., Park Ridge, IL 60068. The states of *Illinois* and *Indiana;* in the state of *Wisconsin,* the counties of Brown, Calumet, Columbia, Crawford, Dane, Dodge, Door, Fond du Lac, Grant, Green, Iowa, Jefferson, Kenosha, Keewanee, Lafayette, Manitowoc, Marinette, Milwaukee, Oconto, Outagamie, Ozaukee, Racine, Richland, Rock, Sauk, Sheboygan, Walworth, Washington, Waukehsa and Winnebago; the state of *Kentucky* except the part which is covered by the Detroit, MI office.

Detroit, MI office, 24897 Hathaway St., Farmington Hills, MI 48335-1552. The state of *Ohio;* the state of *Michigan* except that part which is covered by the St. Paul, MN office; in the state of *Kentucky,* the counties of Bath, Bell, Boone, Bourbon, Boyd, Bracken, Breathitt, Campbell, Carter, Clare, Clay, Elliott, Estill, Fayette, Fleming, Floyd, Franklin, Gallatin, Garrad, Grant, Greenup, Harlan, Harrison, Jackson, Jessamine, Johnson, Kenton, Knott, Knox, Laurel, Lawrence, Lee, Leslie, Letcher, Lewis, Lincoln, Madison, Magoffin, Martin, Mason, McCreary, Menifee, Montgomery, Morgan, Nicholas, Owen, Owsley, Pendleton, Perry, Pike, Powell, Pulaski, Robertson, Rockcastle, Rowan, Scott, Wayne, Whitley, Wolfe and Woodford.

Buffalo, NY office, 1307 Fed. Bldg., 111 W. Huron St., Buffalo, NY 14202. The state of *New York* except that part covered by the New York City office.

Honolulu, HI office, Waipio Access Road, Next to the Ted Makalena Golf Course, P.O. Box 1030, Waipahu HI 96797. The state of *Hawaii* and outlying Pacific possessions.

San Juan, PR office, 747 Federal Bldg., Hato Rey, PR 00918, *Puerto Rico* and the *Virgin Islands.*

Anchorage, AK office, 6721 West Raspberry Rd., Anchorage AK 99502. The state of *Alaska.*

INDEX

S

T

U

V

W

Z

FCC
RULE BOOK

PROOF OF
PURCHASE

FEED BACK

Please use this form to give us your comments on this book. Tell us what you liked best about the book, and what improvements you would like to see us make in future editions.

Name ______________________________ Call sign ______________

Daytime Phone (   ) ______________________ Age ________

Address ____

City, State, Zip ____

How long have you been licensed? ______________________

Edition 8 9 10 11 12

Printing 5 6 7 8 9 10 11 12

From ______________________________

____

____

Please affix postage. Post Office will not deliver without sufficient postage.

Editor, FCC Rule Book
American Radio Relay League
225 Main Street
Newington, CT USA 06111

please fold and tape